Michel Foucault

DISCIPLINE AND PUNISH

Michel Foucault was born in Poitiers, France, in 1926. He
lectured in universities throughout the world; served as the
director at the Institut Français in Hamburg, Germany, and
at the Institute de Philosophie at the Faculté des Lettres in
the University of Clermont-Ferrand, France; and wrote
frequently for French newspapers and reviews. At the
time of his death in 1984, he held a chair at France's most
prestigious institution, the Collège de France.

Michel Foucault

DISCIPLINE AND PUNISH

The Birth of the Prison

*Translated from the French
by* Alan Sheridan

VINTAGE BOOKS

A DIVISION OF RANDOM HOUSE, INC.   NEW YORK

SECOND VINTAGE BOOKS EDITION, MAY 1995

Library of Congress Cataloging-in-Publication Data
Foucault, Michel. Translation of Surveiller
et punir. Bibliography : p.
1. Prisons. 2. Prison discipline.
3. Punishment. I. Title.
HV8666.F6813 1979 365 78-11257
ISBN 0-679-75255-2

Manufactured in the United States of America
89 C

Contents

List of Plates

Translator's Note

Any closer translation of the French title of this book, *Surveiller et punir*, has proved unsatisfactory on various counts. To begin with, Foucault uses the infinitive, which, as here, may have the effect of an 'impersonal imperative'. Such a nuance is denied us in English. More seriously the verb *'surveiller'* has no adequate English equivalent. Our noun 'surveillance' has an altogether too restricted and technical use. Jeremy Bentham used the term 'inspect' – which Foucault translates as *'surveiller'* – but the range of connotations does not correspond. 'Supervise' is perhaps closest of all, but again the word has different associations. 'Observe' is rather too neutral, though Foucault is aware of the aggression involved in any one-sided observation. In the end Foucault himself suggested *Discipline and Punish*, which relates closely to the book's structure.

Another problem was posed by the French word *'supplice'*, which heads the first part of the book. For the sake of brevity I have entitled this first part 'Torture', but no single English word will cover the full range of the French. Here *'supplice'* refers specifically to the public torture and execution of criminals that provided one of the most popular spectacles of eighteenth-century France. By extension the word can also refer to any prolonged torture, mental as well as physical. Depending on the context, I have translated the word by 'torture', 'public execution' or 'scaffold'. The author also refers to another form of torture, *'la question'*, the extraction of confessions by interrogation and the systematic application of pain. Here I have followed the accepted translation, 'judicial torture'.

References to other works are usually given not in footnotes but in an abbreviated form in the text itself. These references, in brackets, consist of the author's name and a page number; dates of publication are used to distinguish more than one work by an author, and roman numerals refer to volume numbers. Full references are to be found in the Bibliography.

PART ONE
Torture

1. The body of the condemned

On 2 March 1757 Damiens the regicide was condemned 'to make the *amende honorable* before the main door of the Church of Paris', where he was to be 'taken and conveyed in a cart, wearing nothing but a shirt, holding a torch of burning wax weighing two pounds'; then, 'in the said cart, to the Place de Grève, where, on a scaffold that will be erected there, the flesh will be torn from his breasts, arms, thighs and calves with red-hot pincers, his right hand, holding the knife with which he committed the said parricide, burnt with sulphur, and, on those places where the flesh will be torn away, poured molten lead, boiling oil, burning resin, wax and sulphur melted together and then his body drawn and quartered by four horses and his limbs and body consumed by fire, reduced to ashes and his ashes thrown to the winds' (*Pièces originales* . . ., 372–4).

'Finally, he was quartered,' recounts the *Gazette d'Amsterdam* of 1 April 1757. 'This last operation was very long, because the horses used were not accustomed to drawing; consequently, instead of four, six were needed; and when that did not suffice, they were forced, in order to cut off the wretch's thighs, to sever the sinews and hack at the joints. . .

'It is said that, though he was always a great swearer, no blasphemy escaped his lips; but the excessive pain made him utter horrible cries, and he often repeated: "My God, have pity on me! Jesus, help me!" The spectators were all edified by the solicitude of the parish priest of St Paul's who despite his great age did not spare himself in offering consolation to the patient.'

Bouton, an officer of the watch, left us his account: 'The sulphur was lit, but the flame was so poor that only the top skin of the hand was burnt, and that only slightly. Then the executioner, his sleeves rolled up, took the steel pincers, which had been especially made

3

for the occasion, and which were about a foot and a half long, and pulled first at the calf of the right leg, then at the thigh, and from there at the two fleshy parts of the right arm; then at the breasts. Though a strong, sturdy fellow, this executioner found it so difficult to tear away the pieces of flesh that he set about the same spot two or three times, twisting the pincers as he did so, and what he took away formed at each part a wound about the size of a six-pound crown piece.

'After these tearings with the pincers, Damiens, who cried out profusely, though without swearing, raised his head and looked at himself; the same executioner dipped an iron spoon in the pot containing the boiling potion, which he poured liberally over each wound. Then the ropes that were to be harnessed to the horses were attached with cords to the patient's body; the horses were then harnessed and placed alongside the arms and legs, one at each limb.

'Monsieur Le Breton, the clerk of the court, went up to the patient several times and asked him if he had anything to say. He said he had not; at each torment, he cried out, as the damned in hell are supposed to cry out, "Pardon, my God! Pardon, Lord." Despite all this pain, he raised his head from time to time and looked at himself boldly. The cords had been tied so tightly by the men who pulled the ends that they caused him indescribable pain. Monsieur le Breton went up to him again and asked him if he had anything to say; he said no. Several confessors went up to him and spoke to him at length; he willingly kissed the crucifix that was held out to him; he opened his lips and repeated: "Pardon, Lord."

'The horses tugged hard, each pulling straight on a limb, each horse held by an executioner. After a quarter of an hour, the same ceremony was repeated and finally, after several attempts, the direction of the horses had to be changed, thus: those at the arms were made to pull towards the head, those at the thighs towards the arms, which broke the arms at the joints. This was repeated several times without success. He raised his head and looked at himself. Two more horses had to be added to those harnessed to the thighs, which made six horses in all. Without success.

'Finally, the executioner, Samson, said to Monsieur Le Breton that there was no way or hope of succeeding, and told him to ask their Lordships if they wished him to have the prisoner cut into pieces. Monsieur Le Breton, who had come down from the town, ordered that renewed efforts be made, and this was done; but the horses gave up and one of those harnessed to the thighs fell to the ground. The confessors returned and spoke to him again. He said to them (I heard him): "Kiss me, gentlemen." The parish priest of St Paul's did not dare to, so Monsieur de Marsilly slipped under the rope holding the left arm and kissed him on the forehead. The executioners gathered round and Damiens told them not to swear, to carry out their task and that he did not think ill of them; he begged them to pray to God for him, and asked the parish priest of St Paul's to pray for him at the first mass.

'After two or three attempts, the executioner Samson and he who had used the pincers each drew out a knife from his pocket and cut the body at the thighs instead of severing the legs at the joints; the four horses gave a tug and carried off the two thighs after them, namely, that of the right side first, the other following; then the same was done to the arms, the shoulders, the arm-pits and the four limbs; the flesh had to be cut almost to the bone, the horses pulling hard carried off the right arm first and the other afterwards.

'When the four limbs had been pulled away, the confessors came to speak to him; but his executioner told them that he was dead, though the truth was that I saw the man move, his lower jaw moving from side to side as if he were talking. One of the executioners even said shortly afterwards that when they had lifted the trunk to throw it on the stake, he was still alive. The four limbs were untied from the ropes and thrown on the stake set up in the enclosure in line with the scaffold, then the trunk and the rest were covered with logs and faggots, and fire was put to the straw mixed with this wood.

'. . . In accordance with the decree, the whole was reduced to ashes. The last piece to be found in the embers was still burning at half-past ten in the evening. The pieces of flesh and the trunk had taken about four hours to burn. The officers of whom I was one, as also was my son, and a detachment of archers remained in the square until nearly eleven o'clock.

'There were those who made something of the fact that a dog had lain the day before on the grass where the fire had been, had been chased away several times, and had always returned. But it is not difficult to understand that an animal found this place warmer than elsewhere' (quoted in Zevaes, 201–14).

Eighty years later, Léon Faucher drew up his rules 'for the House of young prisoners in Paris':

'Art. 17. The prisoners' day will begin at six in the morning in winter and at five in summer. They will work for nine hours a day throughout the year. Two hours a day will be devoted to instruction. Work and the day will end at nine o'clock in winter and at eight in summer.

Art. 18. *Rising*. At the first drum-roll, the prisoners must rise and dress in silence, as the supervisor opens the cell doors. At the second drum-roll, they must be dressed and make their beds. At the third, they must line up and proceed to the chapel for morning prayer. There is a five-minute interval between each drum-roll.

Art. 19. The prayers are conducted by the chaplain and followed by a moral or religious reading. This exercise must not last more than half an hour.

Art. 20. *Work*. At a quarter to six in the summer, a quarter to seven in winter, the prisoners go down into the courtyard where they must wash their hands and faces, and receive their first ration of bread. Immediately afterwards, they form into work-teams and go off to work, which must begin at six in summer and seven in winter.

Art. 21. *Meal*. At ten o'clock the prisoners leave their work and go to the refectory; they wash their hands in their courtyards and assemble in divisions. After the dinner, there is recreation until twenty minutes to eleven.

Art. 22. *School*. At twenty minutes to eleven, at the drum-roll, the prisoners form into ranks, and proceed in divisions to the school. The class lasts two hours and consists alternately of reading, writing, drawing and arithmetic.

Art. 23. At twenty minutes to one, the prisoners leave the school, in divisions, and return to their courtyards for recreation. At five minutes to one, at the drum-roll, they form into work-teams.

Art. 24. At one o'clock they must be back in the workshops: they work until four o'clock.

Art. 25. At four o'clock the prisoners leave their workshops and go into the courtyards where they wash their hands and form into divisions for the refectory.

Art. 26. Supper and the recreation that follows it last until five o'clock: the prisoners then return to the workshops.

Art. 27. At seven o'clock in the summer, at eight in winter, work stops; bread is distributed for the last time in the workshops. For a quarter of an hour one of the prisoners or supervisors reads a passage from some instructive or uplifting work. This is followed by evening prayer.

Art. 28. At half-past seven in summer, half-past eight in winter, the prisoners must be back in their cells after the washing of hands and the inspection of clothes in the courtyard; at the first drum-roll, they must undress, and at the second get into bed. The cell doors are closed and the supervisors go the rounds in the corridors, to ensure order and silence' (Faucher, 274–82).

We have, then, a public execution and a time-table. They do not punish the same crimes or the same type of delinquent. But they each define a certain penal style. Less than a century separates them. It was a time when, in Europe and in the United States, the entire economy of punishment was redistributed. It was a time of great 'scandals' for traditional justice, a time of innumerable projects for reform. It saw a new theory of law and crime, a new moral or political justification of the right to punish; old laws were abolished, old customs died out. 'Modern' codes were planned or drawn up: Russia, 1769; Prussia, 1780; Pennsylvania and Tuscany, 1786; Austria, 1788; France, 1791, Year IV, 1808 and 1810. It was a new age for penal justice.

Among so many changes, I shall consider one: the disappearance of torture as a public spectacle. Today we are rather inclined to ignore it; perhaps, in its time, it gave rise to too much inflated rhetoric; perhaps it has been attributed too readily and too emphatically to a process of 'humanization', thus dispensing with the need for further analysis. And, in any case, how important is such a change, when compared with the great institutional transformations, the formulation of explicit, general codes and unified rules of procedure; with the almost universal adoption of the jury system, the definition of the essentially corrective character of the penalty and the tendency, which has become increasingly marked since the nineteenth century, to adapt punishment to the individual offender? Punishment of a less immediately physical kind, a certain discretion in the art of inflicting pain, a combination of more subtle, more subdued sufferings, deprived of their visible display, should not all this be treated as a special case, an incidental effect of deeper changes? And yet the fact remains that a few decades saw the disappearance of the tortured, dismembered, amputated body, symbolically branded on face or shoulder, exposed alive or dead to public view. The body as the major target of penal repression disappeared.

By the end of the eighteenth and the beginning of the nineteenth century, the gloomy festival of punishment was dying out, though here and there it flickered momentarily into life. In this transformation, two processes were at work. They did not have quite the same chronology or the same *raison d'être*. The first was the disappearance of punishment as a spectacle. The ceremonial of punishment tended to decline; it survived only as a new legal or administrative practice. The *amende honorable* was first abolished in France in 1791, then again in 1830 after a brief revival; the pillory was abolished in France in 1789 and in England in 1837. The use of prisoners in public works, cleaning city streets or repairing the highways, was practised in Austria, Switzerland and certain of the United States, such as Pennsylvania. These convicts, distinguished by their 'infamous dress' and shaven heads, 'were brought before the public. The sport of the idle and the vicious, they often become incensed, and naturally took violent revenge upon the aggressors. To prevent them from returning injuries which might be inflicted on them, they were encumbered with iron collars and chains to which bombshells were attached, to be dragged along while they performed their degrading service, under the eyes of keepers armed with swords, blunderbusses and other weapons of destruction.' (Roberts Vaux, *Notices*, 21, quoted in Teeters, 1937, 24). This practice was abolished practically everywhere at the end of the eighteenth or the beginning of the nineteenth century. The public exhibition of prisoners was maintained in France in 1831, despite violent criticism – 'a disgusting scene', said Réal (cf. Bibliography); it was finally abolished in April 1848. While the chain-gang, which had dragged convicts across the whole of France, as far as Brest and Toulon, was replaced in 1837 by inconspicuous black-painted cell-carts. Punishment had gradually ceased to be a spectacle. And whatever theatrical elements it still retained were now downgraded, as if the functions of the penal ceremony were gradually ceasing to be understood, as if this rite that 'concluded the crime' was suspected of being in some undesirable way linked with it. It was as if the punishment was thought to equal, if not to exceed, in savagery the crime itself, to accustom the spectators to a ferocity from which one wished to divert them, to show them the frequency of crime, to make the executioner resemble a criminal, judges murderers, to reverse roles at the last moment, to make the tortured criminal an object of pity or admiration. As early as 1764, Beccaria remarked: 'The murder that is depicted as a horrible crime is repeated in cold blood, remorselessly' (Beccaria, 101). The public execution is now seen as a hearth in which violence bursts again into flame.

Punishment, then, will tend to become the most hidden part of the penal process. This has several consequences: it leaves the domain of more or less everyday perception and enters that of abstract consciousness; its effectiveness is seen as resulting from its inevitability, not from its visible intensity; it is the certainty of being punished and not the horrifying spectacle of public punishment that must discourage crime; the exemplary mechanics of punishment changes its mechanisms. As a result, justice no longer takes public responsibility for the violence that is bound up with its practice. If it too strikes, if it too kills, it is not as a glorification of its strength, but as an element of itself that it is obliged to tolerate, that it finds difficult to account for. The apportioning of blame is redistributed: in punishment-as-spectacle a confused horror spread from the scaffold; it enveloped both executioner and condemned; and, although it was always ready to invert the shame inflicted on the victim into pity or glory, it often turned the legal violence of the executioner into shame. Now the scandal and the light are to be distributed differently; it is the conviction itself that marks the offender with the unequivocally negative sign: the publicity has shifted to the trial, and to the sentence; the execution itself is like an additional shame that justice is ashamed to impose on the condemned man; so it keeps its distance from the act, tending always to entrust it to others, under the seal of secrecy. It is ugly to be punishable, but there is no glory in punishing. Hence that double system of protection that justice has set up between itself and the punishment it imposes. Those who carry out the penalty tend to become an autonomous sector; justice is relieved of responsibility for it by a bureaucratic concealment of the penalty itself. It is typical that in France the administration of the prisons should for so long have been the responsibility of the Ministry of the Interior, while responsibility for the *bagnes*, for penal servitude in the convict ships and penal settlements, lay with the Ministry of the Navy or the Ministry of the Colonies. And beyond this distribution of roles operates a theoretical disavowal: do not imagine that the sentences that we judges pass are activated by a desire to punish; they are intended to correct, reclaim, 'cure'; a technique of improvement represses, in the penalty, the strict expiation of evil-doing, and relieves the magistrates of the demeaning task of punishing. In modern justice and on the part of those who dispense it there is a shame in punishing, which does not always preclude zeal. This sense of shame is constantly growing: the psychologists and the minor civil servants of moral orthopaedics proliferate on the wound it leaves.

The disappearance of public executions marks therefore the decline of the spectacle; but it also marks a slackening of the hold on the body. In 1787, in an address to the Society for Promoting Political Enquiries, Benjamin Rush remarked: 'I can only hope that the time is not far away when gallows, pillory, scaffold, flogging and wheel will, in the history of punishment, be regarded as the marks of the barbarity of centuries and of countries and as proofs of the feeble influence of reason and religion over the human mind' (Teeters, 1935, 30). Indeed, sixty years later, Van Meenen, opening the second penitentiary congress, in Brussels, recalled the time of his childhood as of a past age: 'I have seen the ground strewn with wheels, gibbets, gallows, pillories; I have seen hideously stretched skeletons on wheels' (*Annales de la Charité*, 529–30). Branding had been abolished in England (1834) and in France (1832); in 1820, England no longer dared to apply the full punishment reserved for traitors (Thistlewood was not quartered). Only flogging still remained in a number of penal systems (Russia, England, Prussia). But, generally speaking, punitive practices had become more reticent. One no longer touched the body, or at least as little as possible, and then only to reach something other than the body itself. It might be objected that imprisonment, confinement, forced labour, penal servitude, prohibition from entering certain areas, deportation – which have occupied so important a place in modern penal systems – are 'physical' penalties: unlike fines, for example, they directly affect the body. But the punishment–body relation is not the same as it was in the torture during public executions. The body now serves as an instrument or intermediary: if one intervenes upon it to imprison it, or to make it work, it is in order to deprive the individual of a liberty that is regarded both as a right and as property. The body, according to this penality, is caught up in a system of constraints and privations, obligations and prohibitions. Physical pain, the pain of the body itself, is no longer the constituent element of the penalty. From being an art of unbearable sensations punishment has become an economy of suspended rights. If it is still necessary for the law to reach and manipulate the body of the convict, it will be at a distance, in the proper way, according to strict rules, and with a much 'higher' aim. As a result of this new restraint, a whole army of technicians took over from the executioner, the immediate anatomist of pain: warders, doctors, chaplains, psychiatrists, psychologists, educationalists; by their very presence near the prisoner, they sing the praises that the law needs: they reassure it that the body and pain are not the ultimate objects of its punitive action. Today a doctor must watch over those condemned to death, right up to the last moment – thus juxtaposing himself as the agent of welfare, as the alleviator of pain, with the official whose task it is to end life. This is worth thinking about. When the moment of execution approaches, the patients are injected with tranquillizers. A utopia of judicial reticence: take away life, but prevent the patient from feeling it; deprive the prisoner of all rights, but do not inflict pain; impose penalties free of all pain. Recourse to psycho-pharmacology and to various physiological 'disconnectors', even if it is temporary, is a logical consequence of this 'non-corporal' penality.

The modern rituals of execution attest to this double process: the disappearance of the spectacle and the elimination of pain. The same movement has affected the various European legal systems, each at its own rate: the same death for all – the execution no longer bears the specific mark of the crime or the social status of the criminal; a death that lasts only a moment – no torture must be added to it in advance, no further actions performed upon the corpse; an execution that affects life rather than the body. There are no longer any of those long processes in which death was both retarded by calculated interruptions and multiplied by a series of successive attacks. There are no longer any of those combinations of tortures that were organized for the killing of regicides, or of the kind advocated, at the beginning of the eighteenth century, by the anonymous author of *Hanging not Punishment Enough* (1701), by which the condemned man would be broken on the wheel, then flogged until he fainted, then hung up with chains, then finally left to die slowly of hunger. There are no longer any of those executions in which the condemned man was dragged along on a hurdle (to prevent his head smashing against the cobble-stones), in which his belly was opened up, his entrails quickly ripped out, so that he had time to see them, with his own eyes, being thrown on the fire; in which he was finally decapitated and his body quartered.[1] The reduction of these 'thousand deaths' to strict capital punishment defines a whole new morality concerning the act of punishing.

As early as 1760, a hanging machine had been tried out in England (for the execution of Lord Ferrer). It made use of a support, which opened under the feet of the condemned man, thus avoiding slow deaths and the altercations that occurred between victim and executioner. It was improved and finally adopted in 1783, the same year in which the traditional procession from Newgate to Tyburn was abolished, and in which the opportunity offered by the rebuilding of the prison, after the Gordon Riots, was used to set up the scaffolds in Newgate itself (see Hibbert, 85–6). The celebrated article 3 of the French Code of 1791 – 'Every man condemned to death will have his head cut off' – bears this triple signification: an equal death for all ('Crimes of the same kind will be punished by the same kind of punishment, whatever the rank and state of the guilty man may be,' in the words of the motion proposed by Guillotin and passed on 1 December 1789); one death per condemned man, obtained by a single blow, without recourse to those 'long and consequently cruel' methods of execution, such as the gallows, denounced by Le Peletier; lastly, punishment for the condemned man alone, since decapitation, the capital punishment of the nobility, was the least shaming for the criminal's family (Le Peletier, 720). The guillotine, first used in March 1792, was the perfect vehicle for these principles. Death was reduced to a visible, but instantaneous event. Contact between the law, or those who carry it out, and the body of the criminal, is reduced to a split second. There is no physical confrontation; the executioner need be no more than a meticulous watchmaker. 'Experience and reason demonstrate that the method used in the past to cut off the head of a criminal exposed him to a torture more frightful than the loss of life alone, which is the express intention of the law; the execution should therefore be carried out in a single moment and with a single blow; examples show how difficult it is to achieve this. For the method to work perfectly, it must necessarily depend on invariable mechanical means whose force and effect may also be determined. . . It is an easy enough matter to have such an unfailing machine built; decapitation will be performed in a moment according to the intention of the new law. If this apparatus seems necessary, it will cause no sensation and will be scarcely noticed' (Saint-Edme, 161). The guillotine takes life almost without touching the body, just as prison deprives of liberty or a fine reduces wealth. It is intended to apply the law not so much to a real body capable of feeling pain as to a juridical subject, the possessor, among other rights, of the right to exist. It had to have the abstraction of the law itself.

No doubt something of the old public execution was, for a time, superimposed in France on the sobriety of the new method. Parricides – and the regicides who were regarded as such – were led to the scaffold wearing a black veil; there, until 1832, one of their hands was cut off. Thereafter, nothing remained but the ornamental crêpe. Thus it was in the case of Fieschi, the would-be assassin of Louis-Philippe, in November 1836: 'He will be taken to the place of execution wearing a shirt, barefoot, his head covered with a black veil; he will be exhibited upon a scaffold while an usher reads the sentence to the people, and he will be immediately executed.' We should remember Damiens – and note that the last addition to penal death was a mourning veil. The condemned man was no longer to be seen. Only the reading of the sentence on the scaffold announced the crime – and that crime must be faceless. (The more monstrous a criminal was, the more he must be deprived of light: he must not see, or be seen. This was a common enough notion at the time. For the parricide one should 'construct an iron cage or dig an impenetrable dungeon that would serve him as an eternal retreat' – De Molène, 275–7.) The last vestige of the great public execution was its annulment: a drapery to hide a body. Benoît, triply infamous (his mother's murderer, a homosexual, an assassin), was the first of the parricides not to have a hand cut off: 'As the sentence was being read, he stood on the scaffold supported by the executioners. It was a horrible sight; wrapped in a large white shroud, his face covered with black crêpe, the parricide escaped the gaze of the silent crowd, and beneath these mysterious and gloomy clothes, life was manifested only by frightful cries, which soon expired under the knife' (*Gazette des tribunaux*, 30 August 1832).

At the beginning of the nineteenth century, then, the great spectacle of physical punishment disappeared; the tortured body was avoided; the theatrical representation of pain was excluded from punishment. The age of sobriety in punishment had begun. By 1830–48, public executions, preceded by torture, had almost entirely disappeared. Of course, this generalization requires some qualification. To begin with, the changes did not come about at once or as part of a single process. There were delays. Paradoxically, England was one of the countries most loath to see the disappearance of the public execution: perhaps because of the role of model that the institution of the jury, public hearings and respect of habeas corpus had given to her criminal law; above all, no doubt, because she did not wish to diminish the rigour of her penal laws during the great social disturbances of the years 1780–1820. For a long time Romilly, Mackintosh and Fowell Buxton failed in their attempts to attenuate the multiplicity and severity of the penalties laid down by English law – that 'horrible butchery', as Rossi described it. Its severity (in fact, the juries regarded the penalties laid down as excessive and were consequently more lenient in their application) had even increased: in 1760, Blackstone had listed 160 capital crimes in English legislation, while by 1819 there were 223. One should also take into account the advances and retreats that the process as a whole underwent between 1760 and 1840; the rapidity of reform in certain countries such as Austria, Russia, the United States, France under the Constituent Assembly, then the retreat at the time of the counter-revolutions in Europe and the great social fear of the years 1820–48; more or less temporary changes introduced by emergency courts or laws; the gap between the laws and the real practice of the courts (which was by no means a faithful reflection of the state of legislation). All these factors account for the irregularity of the transformation that occurred at the turn of the century.

It should be added that, although most of the changes had been achieved by 1840, although the mechanisms of punishment had by then assumed their new way of functioning, the process was far from complete. The reduction in the use of torture was a tendency that was rooted in the great transformation of the years 1760–1840, but it did not end there; it can be said that the practice of the public execution haunted our penal system for a long time and still haunts it today. In France, the guillotine, that machine for the production of rapid and discreet deaths, represented a new ethic of legal death. But the Revolution had immediately endowed it with a great theatrical ritual. For years it provided a spectacle. It had to be removed to the Barrière Saint-Jacques; the open cart was replaced by a closed carriage; the condemned man was hustled from the vehicle straight to the scaffold; hasty executions were organized at unexpected times. In the end, the guillotine had to be placed inside prison walls and made inaccessible to the public (after the execution of Weidmann in 1939), by blocking the streets leading to the prison in which the scaffold was hidden, and in which the execution would take place in secret (the execution of Buffet and Bontemps at the Santé in 1972). Witnesses who described the scene could even be prosecuted, thereby ensuring that the execution should cease to be a spectacle and remain a strange secret between the law and those it condemns. One has only to point out so many precautions to realize that capital punishment remains fundamentally, even today, a spectacle that must actually be forbidden.

Similarly, the hold on the body did not entirely disappear in the mid-nineteenth century. Punishment had no doubt ceased to be centred on torture as a technique of pain; it assumed as its principal object loss of wealth or rights. But a punishment like forced labour or even imprisonment – mere loss of liberty – has never functioned without a certain additional element of punishment that certainly concerns the body itself: rationing of food, sexual deprivation, corporal punishment, solitary confinement. Are these the unintentional, but inevitable, consequence of imprisonment? In fact, in its most explicit practices, imprisonment has always involved a certain degree of physical pain. The criticism that was often levelled at the penitentiary system in the early nineteenth century (imprisonment is not a sufficient punishment: prisoners are less hungry, less cold, less deprived in general than many poor people or even workers) suggests a postulate that was never explicitly denied: it is just that a condemned man should suffer physically more than other men. It is difficult to dissociate punishment from additional physical pain. What would a non-corporal punishment be?

There remains, therefore, a trace of 'torture' in the modern mechanisms of criminal justice – a trace that has not been entirely overcome, but which is enveloped, increasingly, by the non-corporal nature of the penal system.

The reduction in penal severity in the last 200 years is a phenomenon with which legal historians are well acquainted. But, for a long time, it has been regarded in an overall way as a quantitative phenomenon: less cruelty, less pain, more kindness, more respect, more 'humanity'. In fact, these changes are accompanied by a displacement in the very object of the punitive operation. Is there a diminution of intensity? Perhaps. There is certainly a change of objective.

If the penality in its most severe forms no longer addresses itself to the body, on what does it lay hold? The answer of the theoreticians – those who, about 1760, opened up a new period that is not yet at an end – is simple, almost obvious. It seems to be contained in the question itself: since it is no longer the body, it must be the soul. The expiation that once rained down upon the body must be replaced by a punishment that acts in depth on the heart, the thoughts, the will, the inclinations. Mably formulated the principle once and for all: 'Punishment, if I may so put it, should strike the soul rather than the body' (Mably, 326).

It was an important moment. The old partners of the spectacle of punishment, the body and the blood, gave way. A new character came on the scene, masked. It was the end of a certain kind of tragedy; comedy began, with shadow play, faceless voices, impalpable entities. The apparatus of punitive justice must now bite into this bodiless reality.

Is this any more than a mere theoretical assertion, contradicted by penal practice? Such a conclusion would be over-hasty. It is true that, today, to punish is not simply a matter of converting a soul; but Mably's principle has not remained a pious wish. Its effects can be felt throughout modern penality.

To begin with, there is a substitution of objects. By this I do not mean that one has suddenly set about punishing other crimes. No doubt the definition of offences, the hierarchy of their seriousness, the margins of indulgence, what was tolerated in fact and what was legally permitted – all this has considerably changed over the last 200 years; many crimes have ceased to be so because they were bound up with a certain exercise of religious authority or a particular type of economic activity; blasphemy has lost its status as a crime; smuggling and domestic larceny some of their seriousness. But these displacements are perhaps not the most important fact: the division between the permitted and the forbidden has preserved a certain constancy from one century to another. On the other hand, 'crime', the object with which penal practice is concerned, has profoundly altered: the quality, the nature, in a sense the substance of which the punishable element is made, rather than its formal definition. Undercover of the relative stability of the law, a mass of subtle and rapid changes has occurred. Certainly the 'crimes' and 'offences' on which judgement is passed are juridical objects defined by the code, but judgement is also passed on the passions, instincts, anomalies, infirmities, maladjustments, effects of environment or heredity; acts of aggression are punished, so also, through them, is aggressivity; rape, but at the same time perversions; murders, but also drives and desires. But, it will be objected, judgement is not actually being passed on them; if they are referred to at all it is to explain the actions in question, and to determine to what extent the the subject's will was involved in the crime. This is no answer. For it *is* these shadows lurking behind the case itself that are judged and punished. They are judged indirectly as 'attenuating circumstances' that introduce into the verdict not only 'circumstantial' evidence, but something quite different, which is not juridically codifiable: the knowledge of the criminal, one's estimation of him, what is known about the relations between him, his past and his crime, and what might be expected of him in the future. They are also judged by the interplay of all those notions that have circulated between medicine and jurisprudence since the nineteenth century (the 'monsters' of Georget's times, Chaumié's 'psychical anomalies', the 'perverts' and 'maladjusted' of our own experts) and which, behind the pretext of explaining an action, are ways of defining an individual. They are punished by means of a punishment that has the function of making the offender 'not only desirous, but also capable, of living within the law and of providing for his own needs'; they are punished by the internal economy of a penalty which, while intended to punish the crime, may be altered (shortened or, in certain cases, extended) according to changes in the prisoner's behaviour; and they are punished by the 'security measures' that accompany the penalty (prohibition of entering certain areas, probation, obligatory medical treatment), and which are intended not to punish the offence, but to supervise the individual, to neutralize his dangerous state of mind, to alter his criminal tendencies, and to continue even when this change has been achieved. The criminal's soul is not referred to in the trial merely to explain his crime and as a factor in the juridical apportioning of responsibility; if it is brought before the court, with such pomp and circumstance, such concern to understand and such 'scientific' application, it is because it too, as well as the crime itself, is to be judged and to share in the punishment. Throughout the penal ritual, from the preliminary investigation to the sentence and the final effects of the penalty, a domain has been penetrated by objects that not only duplicate, but also dissociate the juridically defined and coded objects. Psychiatric expertise, but also in a more general way criminal anthropology and the repetitive discourse of criminology, find one of their precise functions here: by solemnly inscribing offences in the field of objects susceptible of scientific knowledge, they provide the mechanisms of legal punishment with a justifiable hold not only on offences, but on individuals; not only on what they do, but also on what they are, will be, may be. The additional factor of the offender's soul, which the legal system has laid hold of, is only apparently explanatory and limitative, and is in fact expansionist. During the 150 or 200 years that Europe has been setting up its new penal systems, the judges have gradually, by means of a process that goes back very far indeed, taken to judging something other than crimes, namely, the 'soul' of the criminal.

And, by that very fact, they have begun to do something other than pass judgement. Or, to be more precise, within the very judicial modality of judgement, other types of assessment have slipped in, profoundly altering its rules of elaboration. Ever since the Middle Ages slowly and painfully built up the great procedure of investigation, to judge was to establish the truth of a crime, it was to determine its author and to apply a legal punishment. Knowledge of the offence, knowledge of the offender, knowledge of the law: these three conditions made it possible to ground a judgement in truth. But now a quite different question of truth is inscribed in the course of the penal judgement. The question is no longer simply: 'Has the act been established and is it punishable?' But also: 'What *is* this act, what *is* this act of violence or this murder? To what level or to what field of reality does it belong? Is it a phantasy, a psychotic reaction, a delusional episode, a perverse action?' It is no longer simply: 'Who committed it?' But: 'How can we assign the causal process that produced it? Where did it originate in the author himself? Instinct, unconscious, environment, heredity?' It is no longer simply: 'What law punishes this offence?' But: 'What would be the most appropriate measures to take? How do we see the future development of the offender? What would be the best way of rehabilitating him?' A whole set of assessing, diagnostic, prognostic, normative judgements concerning the criminal have become lodged in the framework of penal judgement. Another truth has penetrated the truth that was required by the legal machinery; a truth which, entangled with the first, has turned the assertion of guilt into a strange scientifico-juridical complex. A significant fact is the way in which the question of madness has evolved in penal practice. According to the 1810 code, madness was dealt with only in terms of article 64. Now this article states that there is neither crime nor offence if the offender was of unsound mind at the time of the act. The possibility of ascertaining madness was, therefore, a quite separate matter from the definition of an act as a crime; the gravity of the act was not altered by the fact that its author was insane, nor the punishment reduced as a consequence; the crime itself disappeared. It was impossible, therefore, to declare that someone was both guilty and mad; once the diagnosis of madness had been accepted, it could not be included in the judgement; it interrupted the procedure and loosened the hold of the law on the author of the act. Not only the examination of the criminal suspected of insanity, but the very effects of this examination had to be external and anterior to the sentence. But, very soon, the courts of the nineteenth century began to misunderstand the meaning of article 64. Despite several decisions of the supreme court of appeal confirming that insanity could not result either in a light penalty, or even in an acquittal, but required that the case be dismissed, the ordinary courts continued to bring the question of insanity to bear on their verdicts. They accepted that one could be both guilty and mad; less guilty the madder one was; guilty certainly, but someone to be put away and treated rather than punished; not only a guilty man, but also dangerous, since quite obviously sick, etc. From the point of view of the penal code, the result was a mass of juridical absurdities. But this was the starting point of an evolution that jurisprudence and legislation itself was to precipitate in the course of the next 150 years: already the reform of 1832, introducing attenuating circumstances, made it possible to modify the sentence according to the supposed degrees of an illness or the forms of a semi-insanity. And the practice of calling on psychiatric expertise, which is widespread in the assize courts and sometimes extended to courts of summary jurisdiction, means that the sentence, even if it is always formulated in terms of legal punishment, implies, more or less obscurely, judgements of normality, attributions of causality, assessments of possible changes, anticipations as to the offender's future. It would be wrong to say that all these operations give substance to a judgement from the outside; they are directly integrated in the process of forming the sentence. Instead of insanity eliminating the crime according to the original meaning of article 64, every crime and even every offence now carries within it, as a legitimate suspicion, but also as a right that may be claimed, the hypothesis of insanity, in any case of anomaly. And the sentence that condemns or acquits is not simply a judgement of guilt, a legal decision that lays down punishment; it bears within it an assessment of normality and a technical prescription for a possible normalization. Today the judge – magistrate or juror – certainly does more than 'judge'.

And he is not alone in judging. Throughout the penal procedure and the implementation of the sentence there swarms a whole series of subsidiary authorities. Small-scale legal systems and parallel judges have multiplied around the principal judgement: psychiatric or psychological experts, magistrates concerned with the implementation of sentences, educationalists, members of the prison service, all fragment the legal power to punish; it might be objected that none of them really shares the right to judge; that some, after sentence is passed, have no other right than to implement the punishment laid down by the court and, above all, that others – the experts – intervene before the sentence not to pass judgement, but to assist the judges in their decision. But as soon as the penalties and the security measures defined by the court are not absolutely determined, from the moment they may be modified along the way, from the moment one leaves to others than the judges of the offence the task of deciding whether the condemned man 'deserves' to be placed in semi-liberty or conditional liberty, whether they may bring his penal tutelage to an end, one is handing over to them mechanisms of legal punishment to be used at their discretion: subsidiary judges they may be, but they are judges all the same. The whole machinery that has been developing for years around the implementation of sentences, and their adjustment to individuals, creates a proliferation of the authorities of judicial decision-making and extends its powers of decision well beyond the sentence. The psychiatric experts, for their part, may well refrain from judging. Let us examine the three questions to which, since the 1958 ruling, they have to address themselves: Does the convicted person represent a danger to society? Is he susceptible to penal punishment? Is he curable or readjustable? These questions have nothing to do with article 64, nor with the possible insanity of the convicted person at the moment of the act. They do not concern 'responsibility'. They concern nothing but the administration of the penalty, its necessity, its usefulness, its possible effectiveness; they make it possible to show, in an almost transparent vocabulary, whether the mental hospital would be a more suitable place of confinement than the prison, whether this confinement should be short or long, whether medical treatment or security measures are called for. What, then, is the role of the psychiatrist in penal matters? He is not an expert in responsibility, but an adviser on punishment; it is up to him to say whether the subject is 'dangerous', in what way one should be protected from him, how one should intervene to alter him, whether it would be better to try to force him into submission or to treat him. At the very beginning of its history, psychiatric expertise was called upon to formulate 'true' propositions as to the part that the liberty of the offender had played in the act he had committed; it is now called upon to suggest a prescription for what might be called his 'medico-judicial treatment'.

To sum up, ever since the new penal system – that defined by the great codes of the eighteenth and nineteenth centuries – has been in operation, a general process has led judges to judge something other than crimes; they have been led in their sentences to do something other than judge; and the power of judging has been transferred, in part, to other authorities than the judges of the offence. The whole penal operation has taken on extra-juridical elements and personnel. It will be said that there is nothing extraordinary in this, that it is part of the destiny of the law to absorb little by little elements that are alien to it. But what is odd about modern criminal justice is that, although it has taken on so many extra-juridical elements, it has done so not in order to be able to define them juridically and gradually to integrate them into the actual power to punish: on the contrary, it has done so in order to make them function within the penal operation as non-juridical elements; in order to stop this operation being simply a legal punishment; in order to exculpate the judge from being purely and simply he who punishes. 'Of course, we pass sentence, but this sentence is not in direct relation to the crime. It is quite clear that for us it functions as a way of treating a criminal. We punish, but this is a way of saying that we wish to obtain a cure.' Today, criminal justice functions and justifies itself only by this perpetual reference to something other than itself, by this unceasing reinscription in non-juridical systems. Its fate is to be redefined by knowledge.

Beneath the increasing leniency of punishment, then, one may map a displacement of its point of application; and through this displacement, a whole field of recent objects, a whole new system of truth and a mass of roles hitherto unknown in the exercise of criminal justice. A corpus of knowledge, techniques, 'scientific' discourses is formed and becomes entangled with the practice of the power to punish.

This book is intended as a correlative history of the modern soul and of a new power to judge; a genealogy of the present scientifico-legal complex from which the power to punish derives its bases, justifications and rules, from which it extends its effects and by which it masks its exorbitant singularity.

But from what point can such a history of the modern soul on trial be written? If one confined oneself to the evolution of legislation or of penal procedures, one would run the risk of allowing a change in the collective sensibility, an increase in humanization or the development of the human sciences to emerge as a massive, external, inert and primary fact. By studying only the general social forms, as Durkheim did (cf. Bibliography), one runs the risk of positing as the principle of greater leniency in punishment processes of individualization that are rather one of the effects of the new tactics of power, among which are to be included the new penal mechanisms. This study obeys four general rules:

1. Do not concentrate the study of the punitive mechanisms on their 'repressive' effects alone, on their 'punishment' aspects alone, but situate them in a whole series of their possible positive effects, even if these seem marginal at first sight. As a consequence, regard punishment as a complex social function.

2. Analyse punitive methods not simply as consequences of legislation or as indicators of social structures, but as techniques possessing their own specificity in the more general field of other ways of exercising power. Regard punishment as a political tactic.

3. Instead of treating the history of penal law and the history of the human sciences as two separate series whose overlapping appears to have had on one or the other, or perhaps on both, a disturbing or useful effect, according to one's point of view, see whether there is not some common matrix or whether they do not both derive from a single process of 'epistemologico-juridical' formation; in short, make the technology of power the very principle both of the humanization of the penal system and of the knowledge of man.

4. Try to discover whether this entry of the soul on to the scene of penal justice, and with it the insertion in legal practice of a whole corpus of 'scientific' knowledge, is not the effect of a transformation of the way in which the body itself is invested by power relations.

In short, try to study the metamorphosis of punitive methods on the basis of a political technology of the body in which might be read a common history of power relations and object relations. Thus, by an analysis of penal leniency as a technique of power, one might understand both how man, the soul, the normal or abnormal individual have come to duplicate crime as objects of penal intervention; and in what way a specific mode of subjection was able to give birth to man as an object of knowledge for a discourse with a 'scientific' status.

But I am not claiming to be the first to have worked in this direction.[2]

Rusche and Kirchheimer's great work, *Punishment and Social Structures*, provides a number of essential reference points. We must first rid ourselves of the illusion that penality is above all (if not exclusively) a means of reducing crime and that, in this role, according to the social forms, the political systems or beliefs, it may be severe or lenient, tend towards expiation of obtaining redress, towards the pursuit of individuals or the attribution of collective responsibility. We must analyse rather the 'concrete systems of punishment', study them as social phenomena that cannot be accounted for by the juridical structure of society alone, nor by its fundamental ethical choices; we must situate them in their field of operation, in which the punishment of crime is not the sole element; we must show that punitive measures are not simply 'negative' mechanisms that make it possible to repress, to prevent, to exclude, to eliminate; but that they are linked to a whole series of positive and useful effects which it is their task to support (and, in this sense, although legal punishment is carried out in order to punish offences, one might say that the definition of offences and their prosecution are carried out in turn in order to maintain the punitive mechanisms and their functions). From this point of view, Rusche and Kirchheimer relate the different systems of punishment with the systems of production within which they operate: thus, in a slave economy, punitive mechanisms serve to provide an additional labour force – and to constitute a body of 'civil' slaves in addition to those provided by war or trading; with feudalism, at a time when money and production were still at an early stage of development, we find a sudden increase in corporal punishments – the body being in most cases the only property accessible; the penitentiary (the Hôpital Général, the Spinhuis or the Rasphuis), forced labour and the prison factory appear with the development of the mercantile economy. But the industrial system requires a free market in labour and, in the nineteenth century, the role of forced labour in the mechanisms of punishment diminishes accordingly and 'corrective' detention takes its place. There are no doubt a number of observations to be made about such a strict correlation.

But we can surely accept the general proposition that, in our societies, the systems of punishment are to be situated in a certain 'political economy' of the body: even if they do not make use of violent or bloody punishment, even when they use 'lenient' methods involving confinement or correction, it is always the body that is at issue – the body and its forces, their utility and their docility, their distribution and their submission. It is certainly legitimate to write a history of punishment against the background of moral ideas or legal structures. But can one write such a history against the background of a history of bodies, when such systems of punishment claim to have only the secret souls of criminals as their objective?

Historians long ago began to write the history of the body. They have studied the body in the field of historical demography or pathology; they have considered it as the seat of needs and appetites, as the locus of physiological processes and metabolisms, as a target for the attacks of germs or viruses; they have shown to what extent historical processes were involved in what might seem to be the purely biological base of existence; and what place should be given in the history of society to biological 'events' such as the circulation of bacilli, or the extension of the life-span (cf. Le Roy-Ladurie). But the body is also directly involved in a political field; power relations have an immediate hold upon it; they invest it, mark it, train it, torture it, force it to carry out tasks, to perform ceremonies, to emit signs. This political investment of the body is bound up, in accordance with complex reciprocal relations, with its economic use; it is largely as a force of production that the body is invested with relations of power and domination; but, on the other hand, its constitution as labour power is possible only if it is caught up in a system of subjection (in which need is also a political instrument meticulously prepared, calculated and used); the body becomes a useful force only if it is both a productive body and a subjected body. This subjection is not only obtained by the instruments of violence or ideology; it can also be direct, physical, pitting force against force, bearing on material elements, and yet without involving violence; it may be calculated, organized, technically thought out; it may be subtle, make use neither of weapons nor of terror and yet remain of a physical order. That is to say, there may be a 'knowledge' of the body that is not exactly the science of its functioning, and a mastery of its forces that is more than the ability to conquer them: this knowledge and this mastery constitute what might be called the political technology of the body. Of course, this technology is diffuse, rarely formulated in continuous, systematic discourse; it is often made up of bits and pieces; it implements a disparate set of tools or methods. In spite of the coherence of its results, it is generally no more than a multiform instrumentation. Moreover, it cannot be localized in a particular type of institution or state apparatus. For they have recourse to it; they use, select or impose certain of its methods. But, in its mechanisms and its effects, it is situated at a quite different level. What the apparatuses and institutions operate is, in a sense, a micro-physics of power, whose field of validity is situated in a sense between these great functionings and the bodies themselves with their materiality and their forces.

Now, the study of this micro-physics presupposes that the power exercised on the body is conceived not as a property, but as a strategy, that its effects of domination are attributed not to 'appropriation', but to dispositions, manoeuvres, tactics, techniques, functionings; that one should decipher in it a network of relations, constantly in tension, in activity, rather than a privilege that one might possess; that one should take as its model a perpetual battle rather than a contract regulating a transaction or the conquest of a territory. In short this power is exercised rather than possessed; it is not the 'privilege', acquired or preserved, of the dominant class, but the overall effect of its strategic positions – an effect that is manifested and sometimes extended by the position of those who are dominated. Furthermore, this power is not exercised simply as an obligation or a prohibition on those who 'do not have it'; it invests them, is transmitted by them and through them; it exerts pressure upon them, just as they themselves, in their struggle against it, resist the grip it has on them. This means that these relations go right down into the depths of society, that they are not localized in the relations between the state and its citizens or on the frontier between classes and that they do not merely reproduce, at the level of individuals, bodies, gestures and behaviour, the general form of the law or government; that, although there is continuity (they are indeed articulated on this form through a whole series of complex mechanisms), there is neither analogy nor homology, but a specificity of mechanism and modality. Lastly, they are not univocal; they define innumerable points of confrontation, focuses of instability, each of which has its own risks of conflict, of struggles, and of an at least temporary inversion of the power relations. The overthrow of these 'micro-powers' does not, then, obey the law of all or nothing; it is not acquired once and for all by a new control of the apparatuses nor by a new functioning or a destruction of the institutions; on the other hand, none of its localized episodes may be inscribed in history except by the effects that it induces on the entire network in which it is caught up.

Perhaps, too, we should abandon a whole tradition that allows us to imagine that knowledge can exist only where the power relations are suspended and that knowledge can develop only outside its injunctions, its demands and its interests. Perhaps we should abandon the belief that power makes mad and that, by the same token, the renunciation of power is one of the conditions of knowledge. We should admit rather that power produces knowledge (and not simply by encouraging it because it serves power or by applying it because it is useful); that power and knowledge directly imply one another; that there is no power relation without the correlative constitution of a field of knowledge, nor any knowledge that does not presuppose and constitute at the same time power relations. These 'power-knowledge relations' are to be analysed, therefore, not on the basis of a subject of knowledge who is or is not free in relation to the power system, but, on the contrary, the subject who knows, the objects to be known and the modalities of knowledge must be regarded as so many effects of these fundamental implications of power-knowledge and their historical transformations. In short, it is not the activity of the subject of knowledge that produces a corpus of knowledge, useful or resistant to power, but power-knowledge, the processes and struggles that traverse it and of which it is made up, that determines the forms and possible domains of knowledge.

To analyse the political investment of the body and the microphysics of power presupposes, therefore, that one abandons – where power is concerned – the violence–ideology opposition, the metaphor of property, the model of the contract or of conquest; that – where knowledge is concerned – one abandons the opposition between what is 'interested' and what is 'disinterested', the model of knowledge and the primacy of the subject. Borrowing a word from Petty and his contemporaries, but giving it a different meaning from the one current in the seventeenth century, one might imagine a political 'anatomy'. This would not be the study of a state in terms of a 'body' (with its elements, its resources and its forces), nor would it be the study of the body and its surroundings in terms of a small state. One would be concerned with the 'body politic', as a set of material elements and techniques that serve as weapons, relays, communication routes and supports for the power and knowledge relations that invest human bodies and subjugate them by turning them into objects of knowledge.

It is a question of situating the techniques of punishment – whether they seize the body in the ritual of public torture and execution or whether they are addressed to the soul – in the history of this body politic; of considering penal practices less as a consequence of legal theories than as a chapter of political anatomy.

Kantorowitz gives a remarkable analysis of 'The King's Body': a double body according to the juridical theology of the Middle Ages, since it involves not only the transitory element that is born and dies, but another that remains unchanged by time and is maintained as the physical yet intangible support of the kingdom; around this duality, which was originally close to the Christological model, are organized an iconography, a political theory of monarchy, legal mechanisms that distinguish between as well as link the person of the king and the demands of the Crown, and a whole ritual that reaches its height in the coronation, the funeral and the ceremonies of submission. At the opposite pole one might imagine placing the body of the condemned man; he, too, has his legal status; he gives rise to his own ceremonial and he calls forth a whole theoretical discourse, not in order to ground the 'surplus power' possessed by the person of the sovereign, but in order to code the 'lack of power' with which those subjected to punishment are marked. In the darkest region of the political field the condemned man represents the symmetrical, inverted figure of the king. We should analyse what might be called, in homage to Kantorowitz, 'the least body of the condemned man'.

If the surplus power possessed by the king gives rise to the duplication of his body, has not the surplus power exercised on the subjected body of the condemned man given rise to another type of duplication? That of a 'non-corporal', a 'soul', as Mably called it. The history of this 'micro-physics' of the punitive power would then be a genealogy or an element in a genealogy of the modern 'soul'. Rather than seeing this soul as the reactivated remnants of an ideology, one would see it as the present correlative of a certain technology of power over the body. It would be wrong to say that the soul is an illusion, or an ideological effect. On the contrary, it exists, it has a reality, it is produced permanently around, on, within the body by the functioning of a power that is exercised on those punished – and, in a more general way, on those one supervises, trains and corrects, over madmen, children at home and at school, the colonized, over those who are stuck at a machine and supervised for the rest of their lives. This is the historical reality of this soul, which, unlike the soul represented by Christian theology, is not born in sin and subject to punishment, but is born rather out of methods of punishment, supervision and constraint. This real, non-corporal soul is not a substance; it is the element in which are articulated the effects of a certain type of power and the reference of a certain type of knowledge, the machinery by which the power relations give rise to a possible corpus of knowledge, and knowledge extends and reinforces the effects of this power. On this reality-reference, various concepts have been constructed and domains of analysis carved out: psyche, subjectivity, personality, consciousness, etc.; on it have been built scientific techniques and discourses, and the moral claims of humanism. But let there be no misunderstanding: it is not that a real man, the object of knowledge, philosophical reflection or technical intervention, has been substituted for the soul, the illusion of the theologians. The man described for us, whom we are invited to free, is already in himself the effect of a subjection much more profound than himself. A 'soul' inhabits him and brings him to existence, which is itself a factor in the mastery that power exercises over the body. The soul is the effect and instrument of a political anatomy; the soul is the prison of the body.

That punishment in general and the prison in particular belong to a political technology of the body is a lesson that I have learnt not so much from history as from the present. In recent years, prison revolts have occurred throughout the world. There was certainly something paradoxical about their aims, their slogans and the way they took place. They were revolts against an entire state of physical misery that is over a century old: against cold, suffocation and overcrowding, against decrepit walls, hunger, physical maltreatment. But they were also revolts against model prisons, tranquillizers, isolation, the medical or educational services. Were they revolts whose aims were merely material? Or contradictory revolts: against the obsolete, but also against comfort; against the warders, but also against the psychiatrists? In fact, all these movements – and the innumerable discourses that the prison has given rise to since the early nineteenth century – have been about the body and material things. What has sustained these discourses, these memories and invectives are indeed those minute material details. One may, if one is so disposed, see them as no more than blind demands or suspect the existence behind them of alien strategies. In fact, they were revolts, at the level of the body, against the very body of the prison. What was at issue was not whether the prison environment was too harsh or too aseptic, too primitive or too efficient, but its very materiality as an instrument and vector of power; it is this whole technology of power over the body that the technology of the 'soul' – that of the educationalists, psychologists and psychiatrists – fails either to conceal or to compensate, for the simple reason that it is one of its tools. I would like to write the history of this prison, with all the political investments of the body that it gathers together in its closed architecture. Why? Simply because I am interested in the past? No, if one means by that writing a history of the past in terms of the present. Yes, if one means writing the history of the present.[3]

2. The spectacle of the scaffold

The ordinance of 1670 regulated the general forms of penal practice up to the Revolution. It laid down the following hierarchy of penalties: 'Death, judicial torture pending proof, penal servitude, flogging, *amende honorable*, banishment.' A high proportion of physical punishment. Customs, the nature of the crimes, the status of the condemned accounted for still more variations. 'Capital punishment comprises many kinds of death: some prisoners may be condemned to be hanged, others to having their hands cut off or their tongues cut out or pierced and then to be hanged; others, for more serious crimes, to be broken alive and to die on the wheel, after having their limbs broken; others to be broken until they die a natural death, others to be strangled and then broken, others to be burnt alive, others to be burnt after first being strangled; others to be drawn by four horses, others to have their heads cut off, and others to have their heads broken' (Soulatges, 169–71). And Soulatges adds, almost in passing, that there are also lighter penalties not mentioned by the ordinance: satisfaction to the injured party, warning, reprimand, a short period of imprisonment, prohibition from entering a certain area and, lastly, pecuniary punishments – fines or confiscation.

But we must not be misled. There was a considerable gap between this arsenal of horrors and everyday penal practice. Public torture and execution was by no means the most frequent form of punishment. To us today the proportion of death sentences in the penal practice of the classical age may seem high: at the Châtelet[1] during the period 1755–85 under 10 per cent of the sentences passed involved capital punishment: the wheel, the gallows or the stake (Petrovitch, 226ff); the Parlement of Flanders passed thirty-nine death sentences, out of a total of 260 sentences, between 1721 and

1730 (and twenty-six out of 500 between 1781 and 1790 – cf. Dautricourt). But it must not be forgotten that the courts found many ways of relaxing the rigours of the penal system, either by refusing to prosecute offences that were too heavily punished or by modifying the definition of the crime; sometimes too the royal power indicated that some particularly severe ordinance was not to be applied too strictly (which was how Choiseul dealt with the declaration of 3 August 1744 on vagabonds – Choiseul, 128–9). In any case, the majority of the sentences involved banishment or fines: in a court such as that of the Châtelet (which dealt only with relatively serious offences), banishment represented over half the sentences passed between 1755 and 1785. But many of these non-corporal penalties were accompanied by additional penalties that involved a degree of torture: public exhibition, pillory, carcan, flogging, branding; this was the case for all sentences to the 'galleys' or to what was the equivalent for women – reclusion in the hospital; banishment was often preceded by public exhibition and branding; fines were sometimes accompanied by flogging. It was not only in the great solemn executions, but also in this additional form of punishment, that torture revealed the significant part it played in penality: every penalty of a certain seriousness had to involve an element of torture, of *supplice*.

What is a *supplice*? 'Corporal punishment, painful to a more or less horrible degree,' said Jaucourt in his *Encyclopédie* article and added: 'It is an inexplicable phenomenon that the extension of man's imagination creates out of the barbarous and the cruel.' Inexplicable, perhaps, but certainly neither irregular nor primitive. Torture is a technique; it is not an extreme expression of lawless rage. To be torture, punishment must obey three principal criteria: first, it must produce a certain degree of pain, which may be measured exactly, or at least calculated, compared and hierarchized; death is a torture in so far as it is not simply a withdrawal of the right to live, but is the occasion and the culmination of a calculated gradation of pain: from decapitation (which reduces all pain to a single gesture, performed in a single moment – the zero degree of torture), through hanging, the stake and the wheel (all of which prolong the agony), to quartering, which carries pain almost to infinity; death-torture is the art of maintaining life in pain, by subdividing it into a 'thousand deaths', by achieving before life ceases 'the most exquisite agonies' (cf. Ollyffe). Torture rests on a whole quantitative art of pain. But there is more to it: this production of pain is regulated. Torture correlates the type of corporal effect, the quality, intensity, duration of pain, with the gravity of the crime, the person of the criminal, the rank of his victims. There is a legal code of pain; when it involves torture, punishment does not fall upon the body indiscriminately or equally; it is calculated according to detailed rules: the number of lashes of the whip, the positioning of the branding iron, the duration of the death agony on the stake or the wheel (the court decides whether the criminal is to be strangled at once or allowed to die slowly, and the points at which this gesture of pity must occur), the type of mutilation to be used (hand cut off, lips or tongue pierced). All these various elements multiply the punishments and are combined according to the court and the crime. 'The poetry of Dante put into laws,' was how Rossi described it; a long course in physico-penal knowledge, in any case. Furthermore, torture forms part of a ritual. It is an element in the liturgy of punishment and meets two demands. It must mark the victim: it is intended, either by the scar it leaves on the body, or by the spectacle that accompanies it, to brand the victim with infamy; even if its function is to 'purge' the crime, torture does not reconcile; it traces around or, rather, on the very body of the condemned man signs that must not be effaced; in any case, men will remember public exhibition, the pillory, torture and pain duly observed. And, from the point of view of the law that imposes it, public torture and execution must be spectacular, it must be seen by all almost as its triumph. The very excess of the violence employed is one of the elements of its glory: the fact that the guilty man should moan and cry out under the blows is not a shameful side-effect, it is the very ceremonial of justice being expressed in all its force. Hence no doubt those tortures that take place even after death: corpses burnt, ashes thrown to the winds, bodies dragged on hurdles and exhibited at the roadside. Justice pursues the body beyond all possible pain.

The term 'penal torture' does not cover any corporal punishment: it is a differentiated production of pain, an organized ritual for the marking of victims and the expression of the power that punishes; not the expression of a legal system driven to exasperation and, forgetting its principles, losing all restraint. In the 'excesses' of torture, a whole economy of power is invested.

The tortured body is first inscribed in the legal ceremonial that must produce, open for all to see, the truth of the crime.

In France, as in most European countries, with the notable exception of England, the entire criminal procedure, right up to the sentence, remained secret: that is to say, opaque, not only to the public but also to the accused himself. It took place without him, or at least without his having any knowledge either of the charges or of the evidence. In the order of criminal justice, knowledge was the absolute privilege of the prosecution. The preliminary investigation was carried out 'as diligently and secretly as may be', as the edict of 1498 put it. According to the ordinance of 1670, which confirmed and, on certain points, reinforced the severity of the preceding period, it was impossible for the accused to have access to the documents of the case, impossible to know the identity of his accusers, impossible to know the nature of the evidence before objecting to witnesses, impossible to make use, until the last moments of the trial, of the documents in proof, impossible to have a lawyer, either to ensure the proper conduct of the case, or to take part, on the main issue, in the defence. The magistrate, for his part, had the right to accept anonymous denunciations, to conceal from the accused the nature of the action, to question him with a view to catching him out, to use insinuations. (Up to the eighteenth century, lengthy arguments took place as to whether, in the course of 'captious' questioning, it was lawful for the judge to use false promises, lies, words with double meaning – a whole casuistry of legal bad faith.) The magistrate constituted, in solitary omnipotence, a truth by which he invested the accused; and the judges received this truth ready made, in the form of documents and written statements; for them, these factors alone were proof; they met the accused only once in order to question him before passing sentence. The secret and written form of the procedure reflects the principle that in criminal matters the establishment of truth was the absolute right and the exclusive power of the sovereign and his judges. Ayrault supposed that this procedure (which was more or less established by the sixteenth century) originated in 'the fear of the uproar, shouting and cheering that the people usually indulge in, the fear that there would be disorder, violence, and outbursts against the parties, or even against the judges'; the king wished to show in this that the 'sovereign power' from which the right to punish derived could in no case belong to the 'multitude' (cf. Ayrault, LIII, chapters LXXII and LXIX). Before the justice of the sovereign, all voices must be still.

Yet, despite the use of secrecy, certain rules had to be obeyed in establishing the truth. Secrecy itself required that a rigorous model of penal truth be defined. A whole tradition dating from the Middle Ages and considerably developed by the great lawyers of the Renaissance laid down what the nature and the use of evidence might be. Even in the eighteenth century, it was still common to meet distinctions like the following: true, direct, or legitimate proof (that provided by witnesses, for example) and indirect, conjectural, artificial proof (obtained by argument); or, again, manifest proof, considerable proof, imperfect or slight (Jousse, 660); or, again, 'urgent or necessary' proof that did not allow one to doubt the truth of the deed (this was 'full' proof: thus two irreproachable witnesses affirming that they saw the accused, carrying an unsheathed and bloody sword, leave the place where, some time later, the body of the dead man was found with stab wounds); approximate or semi-full proof, which may be regarded as true as long as the accused does not destroy it with evidence to the contrary (the evidence of a single eye-witness or death threats preceding a murder); lastly, distant or 'adminicule' clues, which consisted only of opinion (rumour, the flight of the suspect, his manner when questioned, etc. – Muyart de Vouglans, 1757, 345–7). Now, these distinctions are not simply theoretical subtleties. They have an operational function. First, because each of these kinds of evidence, taken in isolation, may have a particular type of judicial effect: 'full' proof may lead to any sentence; 'semi-full' proof may lead to any of the *peines afflictives*, or heavy penalties, except death; imperfect and slight clues are enough for the suspect to have a writ issued against him, to have the case deferred for further inquiry or to have a fine imposed on him. Secondly, because they are combined according to precise arithmetical rules: two 'semi-full' proofs may make a complete proof; *'adminicules'*, providing there are several of them and they concur, may be combined to form a semi-proof; but, however many there may be of them, they can never, of themselves, constitute a complete proof. We have, then, a penal arithmetic that is meticulous on many points, but which still leaves a margin for a good deal of argument: in order for a capital sentence to be passed, is a single full proof enough or must it be accompanied by other slighter clues? Are two approximate proofs always equivalent to a full proof? Should not three be required or two plus distant clues? Are there elements that may be regarded as clues only for certain crimes, in certain circumstances and in relation to certain persons (thus evidence is disregarded if it comes from a vagabond; it is reinforced, on the contrary, if it is provided by 'a considerable person' or by a master in the case of a domestic offence). It is an arithmetic modulated by casuistry, whose function is to define how a legal proof is to be constructed. On the one hand, this system of 'legal proofs' makes truth in the penal domain the result of a complex art; it obeys rules known only to specialists, and, consequently, it reinforces the principle of secrecy. 'It is not enough that the judge should have the conviction that any reasonable man may have. . . Nothing is more incorrect than this way of judging, which, in truth, is no other than a more or less well-founded opinion.' But, on the other hand, it is a severe constraint for the magistrate; in the absence of this regularity, 'every sentence would be reckless, and in a sense it may be said that it is unjust even when, in truth, the accused is guilty' (Poullain du Parc, 112–13 – see also Esmein, 260–83 and Mittermaier, 15–19). The day will come when the singularity of this judicial truth will appear scandalous: as if the law did not have to obey the rules of common truth. 'What would be said of a semi-proof in the sciences capable of demonstration? What would a geometrical or algebraic semi-proof amount to?' (Seigneux de Correvon, 63). But it should not be forgotten that these formal constraints on legal proof were a mode of regulation internal to absolute power and exclusive of knowledge.

Written, secret, subjected, in order to construct its proofs, to rigorous rules, the penal investigation was a machine that might produce the truth in the absence of the accused. And by this very fact, though the law strictly speaking did not require it, this procedure was to tend necessarily to the confession. And for two reasons: first, because the confession constituted so strong a proof

that there was scarcely any need to add others, or to enter the difficult and dubious combinatory of clues; the confession, provided it
was obtained in the correct manner, almost discharged the prosecution of the obligation to provide further evidence (in any case, the
most difficult evidence). Secondly, the only way that this procedure
might use all its unequivocal authority, and become a real victory
over the accused, the only way in which the truth might exert all its
power, was for the criminal to accept responsibility for his own
crime and himself sign what had been skilfully and obscurely
constructed by the preliminary investigation. 'It is not enough', as
Ayrault, who did not care for these secret procedures, remarked,
'that wrong-doers be justly punished. They must if possible judge
and condemn themselves' (Ayrault, 1. I, chapter 14). Within the
crime reconstituted by writing, the criminal who confessed came to
play the role of living truth. The confession, an act of the criminal,
responsible and speaking subject, was the complement to the written,
secret preliminary investigation. Hence the importance that all this
procedure of an inquisitorial type accorded to the confession.

Hence, too, the ambiguities of its role. On the one hand, an
attempt was made to introduce it into the general arithmetic of
evidence; it was stressed that it was no more than one proof among
many. It was not the *evidentia rei*; nor was it the strongest of the
proofs, it was not in itself enough to bring conviction, it had to be
accompanied by additional, circumstantial evidence; for it is a well-
known fact that the accused sometimes declare themselves to be
guilty of crimes that they have not committed; the examining magistrate had therefore to carry out additional investigations if he
possessed no more than the confession of the accused. But, on the
other hand, the confession had priority over any other kind of
evidence. To a certain extent, it transcended all other evidence; an
element in the calculation of the truth, it was also the act by which
the accused accepted the charge and recognized its truth; it transformed an investigation carried out without him into a voluntary
affirmation. Through the confession, the accused himself took part
in the ritual of producing penal truth. As medieval law put it, the
confession 'renders the thing notorious and manifest'. To this first
ambiguity was added a second: as a particularly strong proof,
requiring for a conviction only a few additional clues, thus reducing

to the minimum the work of investigation and the mechanics of demonstration, the confession was therefore highly valued; every possible coercion would be used to obtain it. But, although it had to be, in the procedure, the living and oral counterpart of the written preliminary investigation, although it had to be its reply, its authentication, as it were, on the part of the accused, it had to be surrounded by guarantees and formalities. It preserved something of a transaction: that is why it had to be 'spontaneous', why it had to be formulated before the competent court, why it had to be made in full consciousness, why it should not concern impossible things, etc.[2] Through the confession, the accused committed himself to the procedure; he signed the truth of the preliminary investigation.

This double ambiguity of the confession (an element of proof and the counterpart of preliminary investigation; the effect of constraint and a semi-voluntary transaction) explains the two great means used by classical criminal law to obtain it: the oath that the accused was asked to make before his interrogatory (and therefore under threat of perjury before both human and divine justice; and, at the same time, a ritual act of commitment); judicial torture (physical violence to obtain truth, which, in any case, had then to be repeated before the judges, as a 'spontaneous' confession, if it were to constitute proof). At the end of the eighteenth century, torture was to be denounced as a survival of the barbarities of another age: the mark of a savagery that was denounced as 'Gothic'. It is true that the practice of torture is of ancient origin: it goes back at least as far as the Inquisition, of course, and probably to the torture of slaves. But it did not figure in classical law as a survival or defect. It occupied a strict place in a complex penal mechanism, in which the procedure of an inquisitorial type was reinforced with elements of the accusatory system; in which the written demonstration required an oral correlative; in which the techniques of proof administered by the magistrates were mingled with the methods of the ordeal to which the accused was challenged; in which he was called upon – if necessary by the most violent persuasion – to play the role of voluntary partner in the procedure; in which it was a question, in short, of producing truth by a mechanism consisting of two elements – that of the investigation carried out in secret by the judicial authority and that of the act ritually performed by the accused. The body of the accused, the speaking and, if necessary, suffering body, assured the interlocking of these two mechanisms; that is why, until the classical system of punishment was re-examined from top to bottom, there were so few radical criticisms of torture (the most famous being Nicolas's *Si la torture est un moyen à vérifier les crimes* of 1682). Much more frequent were simple recommendations of prudence: 'Judicial torture is a dangerous means of arriving at knowledge of the truth; that is why judges must not resort to it without due consideration. Nothing is more equivocal. There are guilty men who have enough firmness to hide a true crime . . . and innocent victims who are made to confess crimes of which they were not guilty' (Ferrière, 612).

On this basis one may see the functioning of judicial torture, or interrogation under torture, as a torture of the truth. To begin with, judicial torture was not a way of obtaining the truth at all costs; it was not the unrestrained torture of modern interrogations; it was certainly cruel, but it was not savage. It was a regulated practice, obeying a well-defined procedure; the various stages, their duration, the instruments used, the length of ropes and the heaviness of the weights used, the number of interventions made by the interrogating magistrate, all this was, according to the different local practices, carefully codified (In 1729, Aguesseau ordered an investigation into the means and rules of torture used in France. For a summary of the findings, cf. Joly de Fleury, 322–8.) Torture was a strict judicial game. And, as such, it was linked to the old tests or trials – ordeals, judicial duels, judgements of God – that were practised in accusatory procedures long before the techniques of the Inquisition. Something of the joust survived, between the judge who ordered the judicial torture and the suspect who was tortured; the 'patient' – this is the term used to designate the victim – was subjected to a series of trials, graduated in severity, in which he succeeded if he 'held out', or failed if he confessed. (The first degree of torture was the sight of the instruments. In the case of children or of persons over the age of seventy, one did not go beyond this stage.) But the examining magistrate did not employ torture without himself taking certain risks (apart, that is, from the danger of causing the suspect's death); he had a stake in the game, namely, the evidence that he had already collected; for the rule was that if the accused 'held out' and did not confess, the magistrate was forced to drop the charges. The tortured man had then won. Hence the custom, which had been introduced for the most serious cases, of imposing judicial torture 'pending proof': in this case the magistrate could continue with his investigation after the torture had failed; the suspect was not declared innocent by his resistance; but at least his victory saved him from being condemned to death. The judge kept all his cards, except the principal one. *Omnia citra mortem*. Hence the recommendation often made to magistrates, in the case of the most serious crimes, not to subject to judicial torture a suspect against whom the evidence was sufficiently convincing for, if he managed to resist the torture, the magistrate would no longer have the right to pass the death sentence, which he nevertheless deserved; in such a joust, justice would be the loser: if the evidence was sufficient 'to condemn such a guilty person to death', one should not 'leave the conviction to chance and to the outcome of a provisional interrogation that often leads to nothing; for it is in the interest of public safety to make examples of grave, horrible and capital crimes' (Rousseaud de la Combe, 503).

Beneath an apparently determined, impatient search for truth, one finds in classical torture the regulated mechanism of an ordeal: a physical challenge that must define the truth; if the patient is guilty, the pains that it imposes are not unjust; but it is also a mark of exculpation if he is innocent. In the practice of torture, pain, confrontation and truth were bound together: they worked together on the patient's body. The search for truth through judicial torture was certainly a way of obtaining evidence, the most serious of all – the confession of the guilty person; but it was also the battle, and this victory of one adversary over the other, that 'produced' truth according to a ritual. In torture employed to extract a confession, there was an element of the investigation; there also was an element of the duel.

It is as if investigation and punishment had become mixed. And this is not the least paradoxical thing about it. Judicial torture was indeed defined as a way of complementing the demonstration when 'there are not sufficient penalties in the trial'. For it was included among the penalties; it was a penalty so grave that, in the hierarchy of punishments, the ordinance of 1760 placed it immediately after death. How can a penalty be used as a means? one was later to ask. How can one treat as a punishment what ought to be a method of demonstration? The reason is to be found in the way in which criminal justice, in the classical period, operated the production of truth. The different pieces of evidence did not constitute so many neutral elements, until such time as they could be gathered together into a single body of evidence that would bring the final certainty of guilt. Each piece of evidence aroused a particular degree of abomination. Guilt did not begin when all the evidence was gathered together; piece by piece, it was constituted by each of the elements that made it possible to recognize a guilty person. Thus a semi-proof did not leave the suspect innocent until such time as it was completed; it made him semi-guilty; slight evidence of a serious crime marked someone as slightly criminal. In short, penal demonstration did not obey a dualistic system: true or false; but a principle of continuous gradation; a degree reached in the demonstration already formed a degree of guilt and consequently involved a degree of punishment. The suspect, as such, always deserved a certain punishment; one could not be the object of suspicion and be completely innocent. Suspicion implied an element of demonstration as regards the judge, the mark of a certain degree of guilt as regards the suspect and a limited form of penalty as regards punishment. A suspect, who remained a suspect, was not for all that declared innocent, but was partially punished. When one reached a certain degree of presumption, one could then legitimately bring into play a practice that had a dual role: to begin the punishment in pursuance of the information already collected and to make use of this first stage of punishment in order to extort the truth that was still missing. In the eighteenth century, judicial torture functioned in that strange economy in which the ritual that produced the truth went side by side with the ritual that imposed the punishment. The body interrogated in torture constituted the point of application of the punishment and the locus of extortion of the truth. And just as presumption was inseparably an element in the investigation and a fragment of guilt, the regulated pain involved in judicial torture was a means both of punishment and of investigation.

Now, curiously enough, this interlocking of the two rituals

through the body continued, evidence having been confirmed and sentence passed, in the actual carrying out of the penalty; and the body of the condemned man was once again an essential element in the ceremonial of public punishment. It was the task of the guilty man to bear openly his condemnation and the truth of the crime that he had committed. His body, displayed, exhibited in procession, tortured, served as the public support of a procedure that had hitherto remained in the shade; in him, on him, the sentence had to be legible for all. This immediate, striking manifestation of the truth in the public implementation of penalties assumed, in the eighteenth century, several aspects.

1. It made the guilty man the herald of his own condemnation. He was given the task, in a sense, of proclaiming it and thus attesting to the truth of what he had been charged with: the procession through the streets, the placard attached to his back, chest or head as a reminder of the sentence; the halts at various crossroads, the reading of the sentence, the *amende honorable* performed at the doors of churches, in which the condemned man solemnly acknowledged his crime: 'Barefoot, wearing a shirt, carrying a torch, kneeling, to say and to declare that wickedly, horribly, treacherously, he has committed the most detestable crime, etc.'; exhibition at a stake where his deeds and the sentence were read out; yet another reading of the sentence at the foot of the scaffold; whether he was to go simply to the pillory or to the stake and the wheel, the condemned man published his crime and the justice that had been meted out to him by bearing them physically on his body.

2. It took up once again the scene of the confession. It duplicated the forced proclamation of the *amende honorable* with a spontaneous, public acknowledgement. It established the public execution as the moment of truth. These last moments, when the guilty man no longer has anything to lose, are won for the full light of truth. After the passing of the sentence, the court could decide on some new torture to obtain the names of possible accomplices. It was also recognized that at the very moment he mounted the scaffold the condemned man could ask for a respite in order to make new revelations. The public expected this new turn in the course of truth. Many made use of it in order to gain time, as did Michel Barbier, found guilty of armed assault: 'He stared impudently at the

scaffold and said that it had certainly not been set up for him, since he was innocent; he first asked to return to the chamber, where he beat about the bush for half an hour, still trying to justify himself; then, when he was sent back to execution, he ascended the scaffold with a purposeful air, but, when he saw himself undressed and tied to the cross before being stretched, he asked to go back to the chamber a second time and there made a full confession of his crimes and even declared that he was guilty of another murder' (Hardy, IV, 80). The function of the public torture and execution was to reveal the truth; and in this respect it continued, in the public eye, the work of the judicial torture conducted in private. It added to the conviction the signature of the convicted man. A successful public execution justified justice, in that it published the truth of the crime in the very body of the man to be executed. An example of the good condemned man was François Billiard, a senior postal official, who murdered his wife in 1772. The executioner wanted to hide his face to spare him the insults of the crowd: ' "This punishment, which I have merited, has not been inflicted upon me," he said, "so that I should not be seen by the public. . ." He was still wearing mourning dress in honour of his wife. . . He was wearing new shoes, his hair had been recently curled and powdered, and he had a countenance so modest and so dignified that those present who found themselves observing him more closely said that he must be the most perfect Christian or the greatest of all hypocrites. The placard that he was wearing on his chest had gone askew, and it was noticed that he had straightened it himself, no doubt so that people could read it the more easily' (Hardy, I, 327). If each of the participants played his role well, the penal ceremony had the effectiveness of a long public confession.

3. It pinned the public torture on to the crime itself; it established from one to the other a series of decipherable relations. It was an exhibition of the corpse of the condemned man at the scene of his crime, or at one of the near-by crossroads. The execution was often carried out at the very place where the crime had been committed – as in the case of the student who, in 1723, had killed several persons and for whom the presidial court of Nantes decided to set up a scaffold in front of the inn where he had committed his murders (Nantes, F.F. 124; cf. Parfouru, XXV). There was the use of

'symbolic' torture in which the forms of the execution referred to the nature of the crime: the tongues of blasphemers were pierced, the impure were burnt, the right hand of murderers was cut off; sometimes the condemned man was made to carry the instrument of his crime – thus Damiens was made to hold in his guilty right hand the famous dagger with which he had committed the crime, hand and dagger being smeared with sulphur and burnt together. As Vico remarked, this old jurisprudence was 'an entire poetics'.

There were even some cases of an almost theatrical reproduction of the crime in the execution of the guilty man – with the same instruments, the same gestures. Thus justice had the crime re-enacted before the eyes of all, publishing it in its truth and at the same time annulling it in the death of the guilty man. Even as late in the eighteenth century as 1772, one finds sentences like the following: a servant girl at Cambrai, having killed her mistress, was condemned to be taken to the place of her execution in a cart 'used to collect rubbish at the crossroads'; there a gibbet was to be set up 'at the foot of which will be placed the same chair in which the said Laleu, her mistress, was sitting at the time of the murder; and having seated the criminal there, the executioner of the High Court of Justice will cut off her right hand, throw it in her presence into the fire, and, immediately afterwards, will strike her four blows with the cleaver with which she murdered the said Laleu, the first and second being on the head, the third on the left forearm and the fourth on the chest; this done, she will be hung and strangled on the said gibbet until she be dead; and when two hours have elapsed her dead body will be removed and the head separated from it at the foot of the said gibbet on the said scaffold, with the same cleaver she used to murder her mistress, and the same head exhibited on a pole twenty feet high outside the gates of the said Cambrai, within reach of the road that leads to Douai, and the rest of the body put in a sack, and buried near the said pole at a depth of ten feet' (quoted in Dautricourt, 269–70).

4. Lastly, the slowness of the process of torture and execution, its sudden dramatic moments, the cries and sufferings of the condemned man serve as an ultimate proof at the end of the judicial ritual. Every death agony expresses a certain truth: but, when it takes place on the scaffold, it does so with more intensity, in that it

is hastened by pain; with more rigour, because it occurs exactly at the juncture between the judgement of men and the judgement of God; with more ostentation, because it takes place in public. The sufferings of the condemned man are an extension of those of the judicial torture that precedes them; in the judicial torture, however, the game was not yet over and one could still save one's life; now one will die, without any doubt, and it is one's soul that one must save. The eternal game has already begun: the torture of the execution anticipates the punishments of the beyond; it shows what they are; it is the theatre of hell; the cries of the condemned man, his struggles, his blasphemies, already signify his irremediable destiny. But the pains here below may also be counted as penitence and so alleviate the punishments of the beyond: God will not fail to take such a martyrdom into account, providing it is borne with resignation. The cruelty of the earthly punishment will be deducted from the punishment to come: in it is glimpsed the promise of forgiveness. But, it might be said, are not such terrible sufferings a sign that God has abandoned the guilty man to the mercy of his fellow creatures? And, far from securing future absolution, do they not prefigure imminent damnation; so that, if the condemned man dies quickly, without a prolonged agony, is it not proof that God wishes to protect him and to prevent him from falling into despair? There is, therefore, an ambiguity in this suffering that may signify equally well the truth of the crime or the error of the judges, the goodness or the evil of the criminal, the coincidence or the divergence between the judgement of men and that of God. Hence the insatiable curiosity that drove the spectators to the scaffold to witness the spectacle of sufferings truly endured; there one could decipher crime and innocence, the past and the future, the here below and the eternal. It was a moment of truth that all the spectators questioned: each word, each cry, the duration of the agony, the resisting body, the life that clung desperately to it, all this constituted a sign. There was the man who survived 'six hours on the wheel, and did not want the executioner, who consoled and heartened him no doubt as best he could, to leave him for a moment'; there was the man who died 'with true Christian feeling, and who manifested the most sincere repentance'; the man who 'expired on the wheel an hour after being put there; it is said that the spectators of his torture were moved by the outward signs of religion and repentance that he gave'; the man who had shown the most marked signs of contrition throughout the journey to the scaffold, but who, when placed alive on the wheel, 'did not cease to let forth the most horrible cries'; or again the woman who 'had preserved her calm up to the moment when the sentence was read, but whose wits then began to turn; she was quite mad by the time she was hanged' (Hardy, I, 13; IV, 42; V, 134).

We have come full circle: from the judicial torture to the execution, the body has produced and reproduced the truth of the crime —or rather it constitutes the element which, through a whole set of rituals and trials, confesses that the crime took place, admits that the accused did indeed commit it, shows that he bore it inscribed in himself and on himself, supports the operation of punishment and manifests its effects in the most striking way. The body, several times tortured, provides the synthesis of the reality of the deeds and the truth of the investigation, of the documents of the case and the statements of the criminal, of the crime and the punishment. It is an essential element, therefore, in a penal liturgy, in which it must serve as the partner of a procedure ordered around the formidable rights of the sovereign, the prosecution and secrecy.

The public execution is to be understood not only as a judicial, but also as a political ritual. It belongs, even in minor cases, to the ceremonies by which power is manifested.

An offence, according to the law of the classical age, quite apart from the damage it may produce, apart even from the rule that it breaks, offends the rectitude of those who abide by the law: 'If one commits something that the law forbids, even if there is neither harm nor injury to the individual, it is an offence that demands reparation, because the right of the superior man is violated and because it offends the dignity of his character' (Risi, 9). Besides its immediate victim, the crime attacks the sovereign: it attacks him personally, since the law represents the will of the sovereign; it attacks him physically, since the force of the law is the force of the prince. 'For a law to be in force in this kingdom, it must necessarily have emanated directly from the sovereign, or at least been confirmed by the seal of his authority' (Muyart de Vouglans, xxxiv). The intervention of the sovereign is not, therefore, an arbitration between two adversaries; it is much more, even, than an action to enforce respect for the rights of the individual; it is a direct reply to the person who has offended him. There can be no doubt that 'the exercise of the sovereign power in the punishment of crime is one of the essential parts of the administration of justice' (Jousse, vii). Punishment, therefore, cannot be identified with or even measured by the redress of the injury; in punishment, there must always be a portion that belongs to the prince, and, even when it is combined with the redress laid down, it constitutes the most important element in the penal liquidation of the crime. Now, this portion belonging to the prince is not in itself simple: on the one hand, it requires redress for the injury that has been done to his kingdom (as an element of disorder and as an example given to others, this considerable injury is out of all proportion to that which has been committed upon a private individual); but it also requires that the king take revenge for an affront to his very person.

The right to punish, therefore, is an aspect of the sovereign's right to make war on his enemies: to punish belongs to 'that absolute power of life and death which Roman law calls *merum imperium*, a right by virtue of which the prince sees that his law is respected by ordering the punishment of crime' (Muyart de Vouglans, xxxiv). But punishment is also a way of exacting retribution that is both personal and public, since the physico-political force of the sovereign is in a sense present in the law: 'One sees by the very definition of the law that it tends not only to prohibit, but also to avenge contempt for its authority by the punishment of those who violate its prohibitions' (Muyart de Vouglans, xxxiv). In the execution of the most ordinary penalty, in the most punctilious respect of legal forms, reign the active forces of revenge.

The public execution, then, has a juridico-political function. It is a ceremonial by which a momentarily injured sovereignty is reconstituted. It restores that sovereignty by manifesting it at its most spectacular. The public execution, however hasty and everyday, belongs to a whole series of great rituals in which power is eclipsed and restored (coronation, entry of the king into a conquered city, the submission of rebellious subjects); over and above the crime that has placed the sovereign in contempt, it deploys before all eyes an invincible force. Its aim is not so much to re-establish a balance as to bring into play, as its extreme point, the dissymmetry between the subject who has dared to violate the law and the all-powerful sovereign who displays his strength. Although redress of the private injury occasioned by the offence must be proportionate, although the sentence must be equitable, the punishment is carried out in such a way as to give a spectacle not of measure, but of imbalance and excess; in this liturgy of punishment, there must be an emphatic affirmation of power and of its intrinsic superiority. And this superiority is not simply that of right, but that of the physical strength of the sovereign beating down upon the body of his adversary and mastering it: by breaking the law, the offender has touched the very person of the prince; and it is the prince – or at least those to whom he has delegated his force – who seizes upon the body of the condemned man and displays it marked, beaten, broken. The ceremony of punishment, then, is an exercise of 'terror'. When the jurists of the eighteenth century began their polemic with the reformers, they offered a restrictive, 'modernist' interpretation of the physical cruelty of the penalties imposed by the law: if severe penalties are required, it is because their example must be deeply inscribed in the hearts of men. Yet, in fact, what had hitherto maintained this practice of torture was not an economy of example, in the sense in which it was to be understood at the time of the *idéologues* (that the representation of the penalty should be greater than the interest of the crime), but a policy of terror: to make everyone aware, through the body of the criminal, of the unrestrained presence of the sovereign. The public execution did not re-establish justice; it reactivated power. In the seventeenth century, and even in the early eighteenth century, it was not, therefore, with all its theatre of terror, a lingering hang-over from an earlier age. Its ruthlessness, its spectacle, its physical violence, its unbalanced play of forces, its meticulous ceremonial, its entire apparatus were inscribed in the political functioning of the penal system.

This enables us to understand some of the characteristics of the liturgy of torture and execution – above all, the importance of a ritual that was to deploy its pomp in public. Nothing was to be hidden of this triumph of the law. Its episodes were traditionally the same and yet the sentences never failed to list them, so important were they in the penal mechanism: processions, halts at crossroads and church doors, the public reading of the sentence, kneeling, declarations of repentance for the offence to God and to the king. Sometimes questions of precedence and ceremonial were settled by the court itself: 'The officers will ride according to the following order: namely, at the head two police sergeants; then the patient; after the patient, Bonfort and Le Corre on his left will walk together, followed by the clerk of the court and in this manner shall go to the market square at which place the judgement shall be carried out' (quoted in Corre, 7). Now, this meticulous ceremonial was not only legal, but quite explicitly military. The justice of the king was shown to be an armed justice. The sword that punished the guilty was also the sword that destroyed enemies. A whole military machine surrounded the scaffold: cavalry of the watch, archers, guardsmen, soldiers. This was intended, of course, to prevent any escape or show of force; it was also to prevent any outburst of sympathy or anger on the part of the people, any attempt to save the condemned or to have them immediately put to death; but it was also a reminder that every crime constituted as it were a rebellion against the law and that the criminal was an enemy of the prince. All these reasons – whether a matter of precaution in particular circumstances or a functional element in the performance of the ritual – made the public execution more than an act of justice; it was a manifestation of force; or rather, it was justice as the physical, material and awesome force of the sovereign deployed there. The ceremony of the public torture and execution displayed for all to see the power relation that gave his force to the law.

As a ritual of armed law, in which the prince showed himself, indissociably, both as head of justice and head of war, the public execution had two aspects: one of victory, the other of struggle. It brought to a solemn end a war, the outcome of which was decided in advance, between the criminal and the sovereign; it had to manifest the disproportion of power of the sovereign over those whom he had reduced to impotence. The dissymmetry, the irreversible imbalance of forces were an essential element in the public execution. A body effaced, reduced to dust and thrown to the winds, a body destroyed piece by piece by the infinite power of the sovereign constituted not only the ideal, but the real limit of punishment. Take the celebrated torture and execution of Massola, which took place at Avignon and which was one of the first to arouse the indignation of contemporaries. This was an apparently paradoxical ceremony, since it took place almost entirely after death, and since justice did little more than deploy its magnificent theatre, the ritual praise of its force, on a corpse. The condemned man was blind-folded and tied to a stake; all around, on the scaffold, were stakes with iron hooks. 'The confessor whispered in the patient's ear and, after he had given him the blessing, the executioner, who had an iron bludgeon of the kind used in slaughter houses, delivered a blow with all his might on the temple of the wretch, who fell dead: the *mortis exactor*, who had a large knife, then cut his throat, which spattered him with blood; it was a horrible sight to see; he severed the sinews near the two heels, and then opened up the belly from which he drew the heart, liver, spleen and lungs, which he stuck on an iron hook, and cut and dissected into pieces, which he then stuck on the other hooks as he cut them, as one does with an animal. Look who can at such a sight' (Bruneau, 259). In the explicit reference to the butcher's trade, the infinitesimal destruction of the body is linked here with spectacle: each piece is placed on display.

The execution was accompanied by a whole ceremonial of triumph; but it also included, as a dramatic nucleus in its monotonous progress, a scene of confrontation: this was the immediate, direct action of the executioner on the body of the 'patient'. It was a coded action, of course, since custom and, often quite explicitly, the sentence prescribed its principal episodes. Nevertheless, it did preserve something of the battle. The executioner not only implemented the law, he also deployed the force; he was the agent of a violence applied, in order to master it, to the violence of the crime. Materially, physic-ally, he was the adversary of this crime: an adversary who could show pity or ruthlessness. Damhoudère complained, with many of his contemporaries, that the executioners exercised 'every cruelty with regard to the evil-doing patients, treating them, buffeting and killing them as if they had a beast in their hands' (Damhoudère, 219). And for a long time the habit did not die out.[3] There was still an element of challenge and of jousting in the ceremony of public execution. If the executioner triumphed, if he managed to cut off the head with a single blow, he 'showed it to the people, put it down on the ground and then waved to the public who greatly applauded his skill by clapping'. (A scene observed by T. S. Gueulette, at the execution of Montigny in 1737 – cf. Anchel, 62–9.) Conversely, if he failed, if he did not succeed in killing the 'patient' as required, he was liable to punishment. This was the case of Damiens's executioner who, being unable to quarter his patient according to the rules, had to cut him up with a knife; as a result, Damiens's hair, which had been promised to him, was confiscated and the money obtained from the sale given to the poor. Some years later, an executioner at Avignon caused excessive pain to three bandits, who were nevertheless formidable characters, whom he had to hang; the spectators became angry; they denounced him; in order to punish him and also to protect him from mob violence, he was put into prison (Duhamel, 25). And, behind this punishment of the unskilful executioner, stands a tradition, which is still close to us, according to which the condemned man should be pardoned if the execution happened to fail. It was a custom clearly established in certain countries: in Burgundy, for instance (cf. Chassanée, 55). The people often expected it to be applied, and would sometimes protect a condemned man who had escaped death in this way. In order to abolish both custom and expectation, they had to revive the adage, 'the gibbet does not lose its prey', to introduce explicit instructions in capital sentences, such as 'hanged by the neck until he be dead'. And jurists like Serpillon or Blackstone were insisting in the middle of the eighteenth century that a failure on the part of the executioner did not mean that the condemned man's life was spared (Serpillon, III, 1100). In his *Commentaries on the Laws of England*, Blackstone remarks: 'It is clear, that if, upon judgement to be hanged by the neck till he is dead, the criminal be not thoroughly killed, but revives, the sheriff must hang him again. For the former hanging was no execution of the sentence; and, if a false tenderness were to be indulged in such cases, a multitude of collusions might ensue' (Blackstone, 199). There was something of the ordeal and something of God's judgement that was still indecipherable in the ceremony of execution. In his confrontation with the condemned man, the executioner was a little like the king's champion. Yet he was an unacknowledgeable and unacknowledged champion: the tradition was, it seems, that when the executioner's letters were sealed, they were not placed on the table, but thrown on the ground. The various prohibitions surrounding this 'very necessary' yet 'unnatural' office are well known (Loyseau, 80–81). The executioner may have been, in a sense, the king's sword, but he shared the infamy of his adversary. The sovereign power that enjoined him to kill, and which through him did kill, was not present in him; it was not identified with his own ruthlessness. And it never appeared with more spectacular effect than when it interrupted the executioner's gesture with a letter of pardon. The short time that usually elapsed between sentence and execution (often a few hours) meant that the pardon usually arrived at the very last moment. But the ceremony, by the very slowness of its progress, was no doubt arranged to leave room for this eventuality. (Cf. Hardy, 30 January 1769, I, 125 and 14 December 1779, IV, 229; Anchel, 162–3, tells the story of Antoine Boulleteix, who was already at the foot of the scaffold when a horseman arrived carrying the celebrated parchment. Shouts of 'God save the King' arose and Boulleteix was taken to the tavern, while the clerk of the court made a collection on his behalf.) The condemned always hoped for a pardon and, in order to drag things out, they would pretend, even at the foot of the scaffold, that they had further revelations to make. When the people wanted a pardon they called for it aloud and tried to postpone the last moment, looking out for the arrival of the messenger bearing the letter with the green wax seal and if necessary claiming that he was on his way (this happened during the execution of those condemned for the uprising against child abduction on 3 August 1750). The sovereign was present at the execution not only as the power exacting the vengeance of the law, but as the power that could suspend both law and vengeance. He alone must remain master, he alone could wash away the offences committed on his person; although it is true that he delegated to the courts the task of exercising his power to dispense justice, he had not transferred it; he retained it in its entirety and he could suspend the sentence or increase it at will.

We must regard the public execution, as it was still ritualized in the eighteenth century, as a political operation. It was logically inscribed in a system of punishment, in which the sovereign, directly or indirectly, demanded, decided and carried out punishments, in so far as it was he who, through the law, had been injured by the crime. In every offence there was a *crimen majestatis* and in the least criminal a potential regicide. And the regicide, in turn, was neither more nor less, than the total, absolute criminal since, instead of attacking, like any offender, a particular decision or wish of the sovereign power, he attacked the very principle and physical person of the prince. The ideal punishment of the regicide had to constitute the *summum* of all possible tortures. It would be an expression of infinite vengeance: French law, in any case, made provisions for no fixed penalties for this sort of monstrosity. For the execution of Ravaillac the form of the ceremony had to be invented, by combining all the cruellest tortures then practised in France. For Damiens, an attempt was made to think up still more atrocious tortures. Suggestions were made, but they were considered to be less perfect. So the form of Ravaillac's execution was repeated. And it must be admitted that it was relatively modest if one thinks how in 1584 the assassin of William of Orange was abandoned to what seems like an infinity of vengeance. 'On the first day, he was taken to the square where he found a cauldron of boiling water, in which was submerged the arm with which he had committed the crime. The next day the arm was cut off, and, since it fell at his feet, he was constantly kicking it up and down the scaffold; on the third day, red-hot pincers were applied to his breasts and the front of his arm; on the fourth day, the pincers were applied similarly on the back of his arm and on his buttocks; and thus, consecutively, this man was tortured for eighteen days.' On the last day, he was put to the wheel and '*mailloté*' [beaten with a wooden club]. After six hours, he was still asking for water, which was not given him. 'Finally the police magistrate was begged to put an end to him by strangling, so that his soul should not despair and be lost' (Brantôme, II, 191–2).

There can be no doubt that the existence of public tortures and executions were connected with something quite other than this internal organization. Rusche and Kirchheimer are right to see it as the effect of a system of production in which labour power, and therefore the human body, has neither the utility nor the commercial value that are conferred on them in an economy of an industrial type. Moreover, this 'contempt' for the body is certainly related to a general attitude to death; and, in such an attitude, one can detect not only the values proper to Christianity, but a demographical, in a sense biological, situation: the ravages of disease and hunger, the periodic massacres of the epidemics, the formidable child mortality rate, the precariousness of the bio-economic balances – all this made death familiar and gave rise to rituals intended to integrate it, to make it acceptable and to give a meaning to its permanent aggression. But in analysing why the public executions survived for so long, one must also refer to the historical conjuncture; it must not be forgotten that the ordinance of 1670 that regulated criminal justice almost up to the Revolution had even increased in certain respects the rigour of the old edicts; Pussort, who, among the commissioners entrusted with the task of drawing up the documents, represented the intentions of the king, was responsible for this, despite the views of such magistrates as Lamoignon; the number of uprisings at the very height of the classical age, the rumbling close at hand of civil war, the king's desire to assert his power at the expense of the parlements go a long way to explain the survival of so severe a penal system.

In accounting for a penal system involving so much torture, these are general and in a sense external reasons; they explain not only the possibility and the long survival of physical punishments, but also the weakness and the rather sporadic nature of the opposition to them. Against this general background we must bring out their precise function. If torture was so strongly embedded in legal practice, it was because it revealed truth and showed the operation of power. It assured the articulation of the written on the oral, the secret on the public, the procedure of investigation on the operation of the confession; it made it possible to reproduce the crime on the visible body of the criminal; in the same horror, the crime had to be manifested and annulled. It also made the body of the condemned man the place where the vengeance of the sovereign was applied, the anchoring point for a manifestation of power, an opportunity of affirming the dissymmetry of forces. We shall see later that the truth–power relation remains at the heart of all mechanisms of punishment and that it is still to be found in contemporary penal practice – but in a quite different form and with very different effects. The Enlightenment was soon to condemn public torture and execution as an 'atrocity' – a term that was often used to describe it, but without any critical intention, by jurists themselves. Perhaps the notion of 'atrocity' is one of those that best designates the economy of the public execution in the old penal practice. To begin with, atrocity is a characteristic of some of the great crimes: it refers to the number of natural or positive, divine or human laws that they attack, to the scandalous openness or, on the contrary, to the secret cunning with which they have been committed, to the rank and status of those who are their authors and victims, to the disorder that they presuppose or bring with them, to the horror they arouse. In so far as it must bring the crime before everyone's eyes, in all its severity, the punishment must take responsibility for this atrocity: it must bring it to light by confessions, statements, inscriptions that make it public; it must reproduce it in ceremonies that apply it to the body of the guilty person in the form of humiliation and pain. Atrocity is that part of the crime that the punishment turns back as torture in order to display it in the full light of day: it is a figure inherent in the mechanism that produces the visible truth of the crime at the very heart of the punishment itself. The public execution formed part of the procedure that established the reality of what one punished. Furthermore, the atrocity of a crime was also the violence of the challenge flung at the sovereign; it was that which would move him to make a reply whose function was to go further than this atrocity, to master it, to overcome it by an excess that annulled it. The atrocity that haunted the public execution played, therefore, a double role: it was the principle of the communication between the crime and the punishment, it was also the exacerbation of the punishment in relation to the crime. It provided the spectacle with both truth and power; it was the culmination of the ritual of the investigation and the ceremony in which the sovereign triumphed. And it joined both together in the tortured body. The punitive practice of the nineteenth century was to strive to put as much distance as possible between the 'serene' search for truth and the violence that cannot be entirely effaced from punishment. It set out to mark the heterogeneity that separates the crime that is to be punished and the punishment imposed by the public power. Between truth and punishment, there should no longer be any other relation than one of legitimate consequence. The punishing power should not soil its hands with a crime greater than the one it wished to punish. It should remain innocent of the penalty that it inflicts. 'Let us hasten to proscribe such tortures. They were worthy only of the crowned monsters who governed the Romans' (Pastoret, on the subject of the punishment of regicides, II, 61). But, according to the penal practice of the preceding period, the proximity in the public execution of the sovereign and the crime, the mixture that was produced in it of 'demonstration' and punishment, were not the result of a barbarous confusion; what joined them together was the mechanism of atrocity and its necessary concatenations. The atrocity of the expiation organized the ritual destruction of infamy by omnipotence.

The fact that the crime and the punishment were related and bound up in the form of atrocity was not the result of some obscurely accepted law of retaliation. It was the effect, in the rites of punishment, of a certain mechanism of power: of a power that not only did not hesitate to exert itself directly on bodies, but was exalted and strengthened by its visible manifestations; of a power that asserted itself as an armed power whose functions of maintaining order were not entirely unconnected with the functions of war; of a power that presented rules and obligations as personal bonds, a breach of which constituted an offence and called for vengeance; of a power for which disobedience was an act of hostility, the first sign of rebellion, which is not in principle different from civil war; of a power that had to demonstrate not why it enforced its laws, but who were its enemies, and what unleashing of force threatened them; of a power which, in the absence of continual supervision, sought a renewal of its effect in the spectacle of its individual manifestations; of a power that was recharged in the ritual display of its reality as 'super-power'.

Of all the reasons why punishment that was not in the least ashamed of being 'atrocious' was replaced by punishment that was to claim the honour of being 'humane' there is one that must be analysed at once, for it is internal to the public execution itself: at once an element of its functioning and the principle of its perpetual disorder.

In the ceremonies of the public execution, the main character was the people, whose real and immediate presence was required for the performance. An execution that was known to be taking place, but which did so in secret, would scarcely have had any meaning. The aim was to make an example, not only by making people aware that the slightest offence was likely to be punished, but by arousing feelings of terror by the spectacle of power letting its anger fall upon the guilty person: 'In criminal matters, the most difficult point is the imposition of the penalty: it is the aim and the end of the procedure, and its only fruit, by example and terror, when it is well applied to the guilty person' (Bruneau, unnumbered preface to the first part).

But, in this scene of terror, the role of the people was an ambiguous one. People were summoned as spectators: they were assembled to observe public exhibitions and *amendes honorables*; pillories, gallows and scaffolds were erected in public squares or by the roadside; sometimes the corpses of the executed persons were displayed for several days near the scenes of their crimes. Not only must people know, they must see with their own eyes. Because they must be made to be afraid; but also because they must be the witnesses, the guarantors, of the punishment, and because they must to a certain extent take part in it. The right to be witnesses was one that they possessed and claimed; a hidden execution was a privileged execution, and in such cases it was often suspected that it had not taken place with all its customary severity. There were protests when at the last moment the victim was taken away out of sight. The senior postal official who had been put on public exhibition for killing his wife was later taken away from the crowd. 'He was put into a hired coach; it was thought that if he had not been well escorted, it would have been difficult to protect him from being ill-treated by the populace, who yelled and jeered at him' (Hardy, I, 328). When the woman Lescombat was hanged, care was taken to hide her face; she had 'a kerchief over her neck and head, which made the public murmur and say that it was not Lescombat' (Anchel, 70–71). The people claimed the right to observe the execution and to see who was being executed. The first time the guillotine was used the *Chronique de Paris* reported that people complained that they could not see anything and chanted, 'Give us back our gallows' (Lawrence, 71ff). The people also had a right to take part. The condemned man, carried in procession, exhibited, humiliated, with the horror of his crime recalled in innumerable ways, was offered to the insults, sometimes to the attacks of the spectators. The vengeance of the people was called upon to become an unobtrusive part of the vengeance of the sovereign. Not that it was in any way fundamental, or that the king had to express in his own way the people's revenge; it was rather that the people had to bring its assistance to the king when the king undertook 'to be avenged on his enemies', especially when those enemies were to be found among the people. It was rather like a 'scaffold service' that the people owed the king's vengeance. This 'service' had been specified in the old ordinances; the edict of 1347 concerning blasphemers stipulated that they would be exhibited at the pillory 'from the hour of prime, to that of their deaths. And mud and other refuse, though no stone or anything injurious, could be thrown at their faces. . . The second time, in case of relapse, it is our will that he be put in the pillory on a solemn market day, and that his upper lip be split so that the teeth appear.' No doubt, at the classical period, this form of participation in the torture was no more than tolerated and attempts were made to limit it: because of the barbarities that it gave rise to and the usurpation it involved of the power to punish. But it belonged too closely to the general economy of the public execution for it to be eliminated altogether. Even in the eighteenth century, there were scenes like the one that accompanied the execution of Montigny in 1737; as the executioner was carrying out the execution, the local fish-wives walked in procession, holding aloft an effigy of the condemned man, and then cut off its head (Anchel, 63). And very often, as they moved slowly in procession through it, criminals had to be 'protected' from the crowd – both as an example and as a target, a possible threat and a 'prey', promised but also forbidden. In calling on the crowd to manifest its power, the sovereign tolerated for a moment acts of violence, which he accepted as a sign of allegiance, but which were strictly limited by the sovereign's own privileges.

Now it was on this point that the people, drawn to the spectacle intended to terrorize it, could express its rejection of the punitive power and sometimes revolt. Preventing an execution that was regarded as unjust, snatching a condemned man from the hands of the executioner, obtaining his pardon by force, possibly pursuing and assaulting the executioners, in any case abusing the judges and causing an uproar against the sentence – all this formed part of the popular practices that invested, traversed and often overturned the ritual of the public execution. This often happened, of course, in the case of those condemned for rioting: there were the disturbances that followed a famous case of child abduction, when the crowd wanted to prevent the execution of three supposed rioters, who were to be hanged at the cemetery of Saint-Jean, 'because there were fewer entrances and processions to guard';[4] the terrified executioner cut down one of the condemned men; the archers let fly their arrows. It occurred again after the corn riots of 1775; and again in 1786, when the day-labourers marched on Versailles and set about freeing their arrested comrades. But apart from these cases, when the process of agitation had been triggered off previously and for reasons that did not concern some measure of penal justice, one finds many examples when the agitation was provoked directly by a verdict and an execution: small, but innumerable 'disturbances around the scaffold'.

In their most elementary forms, these disturbances began with the shouts of encouragement, sometimes the cheering, that accompanied the condemned man to his execution. Throughout the long procession, he was sustained by 'the compassion of the meek and tender-hearted, and with the applause, admiration and envy of all the bold and hardened' (Fielding, 449). If the crowd gathered round the scaffold, it was not simply to witness the sufferings of the condemned man or to excite the anger of the executioner: it was also to hear an individual who had nothing more to lose curse the judges, the laws, the government and religion. The public execution allowed the luxury of these momentary saturnalia, when nothing remained to prohibit or to punish. Under the protection of imminent death, the criminal could say everything and the crowd cheered. 'If there were annals in which the last words of the tortured and executed were scrupulously recorded, and if one had the courage to read through them, even if one did no more than question the vile populace that gathers around the scaffolds out of cruel curiosity, one would be told that no one who had died on the wheel did not accuse heaven for the misery that brought him to the crime, reproach his judges for their barbarity, curse the minister of the altars who accompanies them and blaspheme against the God whose organ he is' (Boucher d'Argis, 128–9). In these executions, which ought to show only the terrorizing power of the prince, there was a whole aspect of the carnival, in which rules were inverted, authority mocked and criminals transformed into heroes. The shame was turned round; the courage, like the tears and the cries of the condemned, caused offence only to the law. Fielding notes with regret: 'To unite the ideas of death and shame is not so easy as may be imagined ... I will appeal to any man who hath seen an execution, or a procession to an execution; let him tell me. When he hath beheld a poor wretch, bound in a cart, just on the verge of eternity, all pale and trembling with his approaching fate, whether the idea of shame hath ever intruded on his mind? much less will the bold daring rogue, who glories in his present condition, inspire the beholder with any such sensation' (Fielding, 450). For the people who are there and observe, there is always, even in the most extreme vengeance of the sovereign a pretext for revenge.

This was especially the case if the conviction was regarded as unjust – or if one saw a man of the people put to death, for a crime that would have merited, for someone better born or richer, a comparatively light penalty. It would seem that certain practices of penal justice were no longer supported in the eighteenth century – and perhaps for longer – by the lower strata of the population. This would explain why executions could easily lead to the beginnings of social disturbances. Since the poorest – it was a magistrate who made the observation (Dupaty, 1786, 247) – could not be heard in the courts of law, it was where the law was manifested publicly, where they were called upon to act as witnesses and almost as co-adjutors of this law, that they could intervene, physically: enter by force into the punitive mechanism and redistribute its effects; take up in another sense the violence of the punitive rituals. There was agitation against the difference in penalties according to social class: in 1781, the parish priest of Champré had been killed by the lord of the manor, and an attempt was made to declare the murderer insane; 'the peasants, who were extremely attached to their pastor, were furious and had at first seemed ready to lay violent hands upon their lord and to set fire to the castle. . . Everyone protested, and rightly, against the indulgence of the minister who deprived justice of the means of punishing so abominable a crime' (Hardy, IV, 394).

There was agitation, too, against the excessive sentences passed on certain common offences that were not regarded as serious (such as house-breaking); or against punishments for certain offences connected with social conditions such as petty larceny; the death penalty for this crime aroused a great deal of discontent, because there were many domestic servants in a single household and it was difficult for them, in such a case, to prove their innocence, and also because they could easily be victims of their employers' spite and because the indulgence of certain masters who shut their eyes to such behaviour made the fate of servants accused, condemned and hanged even more iniquitous. The execution of such servants often gave rise to protests (cf. Hardy, I, 319, 367; III, 227–8; IV, 180). There was a small riot in Paris in 1761 in favour of a servant woman who had stolen a piece of cloth from her master. Despite the fact that the woman admitted her guilt, handed back the material and begged for mercy, the master refused to withdraw his complaint; on the day of the execution, the local people prevented the hanging, invaded the merchant's shop and looted it; in the end, the servant was pardoned, but a woman, who attempted, unsuccessfully, to stick a needle into the wicked master, was banished for three years (Anchel, 226).

One remembers the great legal affairs of the eighteenth century, when enlightened opinion intervened in the persons of the *philosophes* and certain magistrates: Calas, Sirven and the Chevalier de La Barre, for instance. But less attention is given to the popular agitations caused by punitive practice. Indeed, they seldom spread beyond a town, or even a district. Yet they did have a real importance. Sometimes these movements, which originated from below, spread and attracted the attention of more highly placed persons who, taking them up, gave them a new dimension (in the years preceding the Revolution, the affair of Catherine Espinas, falsely convicted of parricide in 1785, or the case of the three men of Chaumont, condemned to the wheel, for whom Dupaty, in 1786, wrote his celebrated memoir, or that of Marie Françoise Salmon, whom the parlement of Rouen in 1782 had condemned to the stake, for poisoning, but who in 1786 had still not been executed). More usually, those disturbances had maintained around penal justice and its manifestations, which ought to have been exemplary, a state of permanent unrest. How often had it proved necessary, in order to ensure order around the scaffolds, to take steps that were 'distressing to the people' and 'humiliating for the authorities' (Argenson, 241)? It was evident that the great spectacle of punishment ran the risk of being rejected by the very people to whom it was addressed. In fact, the terror of the public execution created centres of illegality: on execution days, work stopped, the taverns were full, the authorities were abused, insults or stones were thrown at the executioner, the guards and the soldiers; attempts were made to seize the condemned man, either to save him or to kill him more surely; fights broke out, and there was no better prey for thieves than the curious throng around the scaffold. (Hardy recounts a number of cases like the important theft that was committed in the very house in which the police magistrate was lodging – IV, 56.) But above all – and this was why these disadvantages became a political danger – the people never felt closer to those who paid the penalty than in those rituals intended to show the horror of the crime and the invincibility of power; never did the people feel more threatened, like them, by a legal violence exercised without moderation or restraint. The solidarity of a whole section of the population with those we would call petty offenders – vagrants, false beggars, the indigent poor, pickpockets, receivers and dealers in stolen goods – was constantly expressed: resistance to police searches, the pursuit of informers, attacks on the watch or inspectors provide abundant evidence of this (cf. Richet, 118–19). And it was the breaking up of this solidarity that was becoming the aim of penal and police repression. Yet out of the ceremony of the public execution, out of that uncertain festival in which violence was instantaneously reversible, it was this solidarity much more than the sovereign power that was likely to emerge with redoubled strength. The reformers of the eighteenth and nineteenth centuries were not to forget that, in the last resort, the executions did not, in fact, frighten the people. One of their first cries was to demand their abolition.

To clarify the political problem posed by the intervention of the people in the spectacle of the executions, one need only cite two events. The first took place at Avignon at the end of the seventeenth century. It contained all the principal elements of the theatre of horror: the physical confrontation between the executioner and the condemned man, the reversal of the duel, the executioner pursued by the people, the condemned man saved by the ensuing riot and the violent inversion of the penal machinery. A murderer by the name of Pierre du Fort was to be hanged; several times he 'had caught his feet in the steps' and had not been able to swing freely. 'Seeing this, the executioner had pulled his jerkin up over his face and struck him below the knees, on the stomach and on the belly. When the people saw that the executioner was causing him too much pain, and even believing that he was killing him down there with a bayonet ... moved by compassion for the patient and fury at the executioner, they threw stones at the scaffold just as the executioner knocked away the two ladders and threw the patient down and leaped on to his shoulders and kicked him, while the wife of the said executioner pulled at his feet from under the gallows. In doing so, they made blood come from his mouth. But the hail of stones came thicker – one stone even struck the hanged man on the head – which forced the executioner to dash to the ladder, which he descended so rapidly that half-way down he fell from it, and struck his head on the ground. Then a crowd of people fell upon him. He got to his feet, bayonet in hand, threatening to kill anyone who came near him; after falling several times, he finally got to his feet, only to be beaten by the crowd, rolled in the mud and nearly drowned in the stream, then dragged by the excited and enraged crowd to the University and to the Cordeliers Cemetery. His servant was also beaten and, with bruises on his head and body, was taken to the hospital where he died some days later. However, some strangers and unknown people mounted the ladder and cut the rope while others caught the hanged man from below after he had been hanging there longer than it took to say a full Miserere. The crowd then smashed the gallows and broke the executioner's ladder into pieces. . . Children carried off the gallows and threw it into the Rhône.' The condemned man was then taken to a cemetery 'so that he should not be recaptured by the law and from there to the church of Sainte-Antoine'. The archbishop gave him his pardon, had him taken to the hospital and asked that particular care be taken of him. Lastly, adds the writer of the account, 'we had a new suit, two pairs of stockings and shoes made for him. We dressed him in new clothes from head to toe. Our colleagues gave him shirts, breeches and a wig' (Duhamel, 5–6; scenes of this kind were still taking place in the nineteenth century – cf. Lawrence, 56 and 195–8).

The other event took place in Paris, a century later. It was in 1775, shortly after the corn riot. Because of the state of extreme tension among the people, the authorities wanted the execution to take place without interruption. Between the scaffold and the public, kept at a safe distance, two ranks of soldiers stood on guard, one facing the execution that was about to take place, the other facing the people in case of riot. Contact was broken: it was a public execution, but one in which the element of spectacle was neutralized, or rather reduced to abstract intimidation. Protected by force of arms, on an empty square, justice quietly did its work. If it showed the death that it had dealt, it was from high and far: 'The two gallows, which were eighteen feet high, no doubt by way of an example, were not set up until three o'clock in the afternoon. From two o'clock, the Place de Grève and all the surrounding streets had been filled with detachments of different troops, some on foot, some on horse; the Swiss and the French guards continued to patrol the adjacent streets. No one was allowed on to the Grève during the execution, and all around one could see a double row of soldiers, bayonets at the ready, standing back to back, so that some looked outwards and some into the square; the two wretches . . . cried out all the way that they were innocent and continued to protest in like manner as they mounted the ladder' (Hardy, III, 67). Whatever the part played by feelings of humanity for the condemned in the abandonment of the liturgy of the public executions, there was, in any case, on the part of the state power, a political fear of the effects of these ambiguous rituals.

Such an equivocal attitude appeared clearly in what might be called the 'gallows speeches'. The rite of execution was so arranged that the condemned man would himself proclaim his guilt by the *amende honorable* that he spoke, by the placard that he displayed and also by the statements that he was no doubt forced to make. Furthermore, at the moment of the execution, it seems that he was given another opportunity to speak, not to proclaim his innocence, but to acknowledge his crime and the justice of his conviction. The chronicles relate a good many speeches of this kind. Were they actually delivered? In a number of cases, certainly. Or were they fictional speeches that were later circulated by way of example and exhortation? This, no doubt, was more often the case. What credit are we to accord, for example, to the account of the death of Marion Le Goff, who had been a famous bandit leader in Brittany in the mid-eighteenth century? She is supposed to have cried out from the scaffold: 'Fathers and mothers who hear me now, watch over your children and teach them well; in my childhood I was a liar and good-for-nothing; I began by stealing a small six-liard knife. . . Then I robbed pedlars and cattle dealers; finally, I led a robber band and that is why I am here. Tell all this to your children and let it be an example to them' (Corre, 257). Such a speech is too close, even in its turn of phrase, to the morality traditionally to be found in the broadsheets and pamphlets for it not to be apocryphal. But the existence of the 'last words of a condemned man' genre is in itself significant. The law required that its victim should authenticate in some sense the tortures that he had undergone. The criminal was asked to consecrate his own punishment by proclaiming the black-ness of his crimes; he was made to say, as was Jean-Dominique Langlade, three times a murderer: 'Listen to my horrible, infamous and lamentable deed, committed in the city of Avignon, where the memory of me is execrable, for having inhumanly violated the sacred rites of friendship' (Duhamel, 32). In one sense, the broad-sheet and the death song were the sequel to the trial; or rather they pursued that mechanism by which the public execution transferred the secret, written truth of the procedure to the body, gesture and speech of the criminal. Justice required these apocrypha in order to be grounded in truth. Its decisions were thus surrounded by all these posthumous 'proofs'. Sometimes, too, accounts of crimes and infamous lives were published, simply as propaganda, before any trial had taken place, in order to force the hand of a court that was suspected of being too tolerant. In order to discredit smugglers, the Compagnie des Fermes published 'bulletins' recounting their crimes: in 1768, it distributed broadsheets against a certain Mon-tagne, the leader of a gang, of whom the writer himself says: 'Some thefts have been ascribed to him the truth of which is somewhat uncertain . . .; Montagne has been depicted as a wild beast, a second hyena to be hunted down; given the hotheads of the Auvergne, this idea has caught on' (cf. Juillard, 24).

But the effect, like the use, of this literature was equivocal. The condemned man found himself transformed into a hero by the sheer extent of his widely advertised crimes, and sometimes the affirmation of his belated repentance. Against the law, against the rich, the powerful, the magistrates, the constabulary or the watch, against taxes and their collectors, he appeared to have waged a struggle with which one all too easily identified. The proclamation of these crimes blew up to epic proportions the tiny struggle that passed unperceived in everyday life. If the condemned man was shown to be repentant, accepting the verdict, asking both God and man for forgiveness for his crimes, it was as if he had come through some process of purification: he died, in his own way, like a saint. But indomitability was an alternative claim to greatness: by not giving in under torture, he gave proof of a strength that no power had succeeded in bending: 'On the day of the execution – this will seem scarcely credible – I showed no trace of emotion, as I performed my *amende honorable*, and when I finally lay down on the cross I showed no fear' (the *Complainte* of J.-D. Langlade, executed at Avignon 12 April 1768). Black hero or reconciled criminal, defender of the true right or an indomitable force, the criminal of the broadsheets, pamphlets, almanacs and adventure stories brought with him, beneath the apparent morality of the example not to be followed, a whole memory of struggles and confrontations. A convicted criminal could become after his death a sort of saint, his memory honoured and his grave respected. (This was the case of Tanguy, executed in Brittany about 1740. Before being convicted, it is true, he had begun a long penitence ordered by his confessor. Was this a conflict between civil justice and religious penitence? Cf. Corre, 21.) The criminal has been almost entirely transformed into a positive hero. There were those for whom glory and abomination were not dissociated, but coexisted in a reversible figure. Perhaps we should see this literature of crime, which proliferated around a few exemplary figures,[5] neither as a spontaneous form of 'popular expression', nor as a concerted programme of propaganda and moralization from above; it was a locus in which two investments of penal practice met – a sort of battleground around the crime, its punishment and its memory. If these accounts were allowed to be printed and circulated, it was because they were expected to have the effect of an ideological control – the printing and the distribution of these almanacs, broadsheets, etc. was in principle subject to strict control. But if these true stories of everyday history were received so avidly, if they formed part of the basic reading of the lower classes, it was because people found in them not only memories, but also precedents; the interest of 'curiosity' is also a political interest. Thus these texts may be read as two-sided discourses, in the facts that they relate, in the effects they give to these facts and in the glory they confer on those 'illustrious' criminals, and no doubt in the very words they use (one should study the use of such categories as 'misfortune' or 'abomination' or such epithets as 'famous' or 'lamentable' in accounts such as *The History of the Life, Great Robberies and Tricks of Guilleri and his Companions and of their Lamentable and Unhappy End.*[6]

Perhaps we should compare this literature with the 'disturbances around the scaffold' in which, through the tortured body of the criminal, the power that condemned confronted the people that was the witness, the participant, the possible and indirect victim of this execution. In the wake of a ceremony that inadequately channelled the power relations it sought to ritualize, a whole mass of discourses appeared pursuing the same confrontation; the posthumous proclamation of the crimes justified justice, but also glorified the criminal. That was why the reformers of the penal system were soon demanding suppression of these broadsheets.[7] That was why the people showed so lively an interest in what served more or less as the minor, everyday epic of illegalities. That was why the broadsheets lost their importance as the political function of popular illegality altered.

And they disappeared as a whole new literature of crime developed: a literature in which crime is glorified, because it is one of the fine arts, because it can be the work only of exceptional natures, because it reveals the monstrousness of the strong and powerful, because villainy is yet another mode of privilege: from the adventure story to de Quincey, or from the *Castle of Otranto* to Baudelaire, there is a whole aesthetic rewriting of crime, which is also the appropriation of criminality in acceptable forms. In appearance, it is the discovery of the beauty and greatness of crime; in fact, it is the affirmation that greatness too has a right to crime and that it even becomes the exclusive privilege of those who are really great. The great murders are not for the pedlars of petty crime. While, from Gaboriau onwards, the literature of crime follows this first shift: by his cunning, his tricks, his sharp-wittedness, the criminal represented in this literature has made himself impervious to suspicion; and the struggle between two pure minds – the murderer and the detective – will constitute the essential form of the confrontation. We are far removed indeed from those accounts of the life and misdeeds of the criminal in which he admitted his crimes, and which recounted in detail the tortures of his execution: we have moved from the exposition of the facts or the confession to the slow process of discovery; from the execution to the investigation; from the physical confrontation to the intellectual struggle between criminal and investigator. It was not only the broadsheets that disappeared with the birth of a literature of crime; the glory of the rustic malefactor and his sombre transformation into a hero by the process of torture and execution went with them. The man of the people was now too simple to be the protagonist of subtle truths. In this new genre, there were no more popular heroes or great executions; the criminal was wicked, of course, but he was also intelligent; and although he was punished, he did not have to suffer. The literature of crime transposes to another social class the spectacle that had surrounded the criminal. Meanwhile the newspapers took over the task of recounting the grey, unheroic details of everyday crime and punishment. The split was complete; the people was robbed of its old pride in its crimes; the great murders had become the quiet game of the well behaved.

PART TWO
Punishment

1. Generalized punishment

'Let penalties be regulated and proportioned to the offences, let the death sentence be passed only on those convicted of murder, and let the tortures that revolt humanity be abolished.' Thus, in 1789, the chancellery summed up the general position of the petitions addressed to the authorities concerning tortures and executions (cf. Seligman, and Desjardin, 13–20). Protests against the public executions proliferated in the second half of the eighteenth century: among the philosophers and theoreticians of the law; among lawyers and *parlementaires*; in popular petitions and among the legislators of the assemblies. Another form of punishment was needed: the physical confrontation between the sovereign and the condemned man must end; this hand-to-hand fight between the vengeance of the prince and the contained anger of the people, through the mediation of the victim and the executioner, must be concluded. Very soon the public execution became intolerable. On the side of power, where it betrayed tyranny, excess, the thirst for revenge, and 'the cruel pleasure taken in punishing' (Petion de Villeneuve, 641), it was revolting. On the side of the victim who, though reduced to despair, was still expected to bless 'heaven and its judges who appeared to have abandoned him' (Boucher d'Argis, 1781, 125), it was shameful. It was, in any case, dangerous, in that it provided a support for a confrontation between the violence of the king and the violence of the people. It was as if the sovereign power did not see, in this emulation of atrocity, a challenge that it itself threw down and which might one day be taken up: accustomed as it was to 'seeing blood flow', the people soon learnt that 'it could be revenged only with blood' (Lachère). In these ceremonies, which were the object of so much adverse investment, one sees the intersection of the excess of armed justice and the anger of the threatened people. Joseph de Maistre was to recognize in this relation one of the fundamental mechanisms of absolute power: the executioner acts as a cog between the prince and the people; the death he deals is like that of the serfs who built St Petersburg over swamp and pestilence: it is a principle of universality; of the individual will of the despot, it makes a law for all, and of each of those destroyed bodies, a stone for the State; it hardly matters that innocents, too, are struck down! In this same dangerous and ritual violence, the eighteenth-century reformers denounced, on the contrary, that which exceeded, on both sides, the legitimate exercise of power: in this violence, according to them, tyranny confronts rebellion; each calls forth the other. It is a double danger. Instead of taking revenge, criminal justice should simply punish.

This need for punishment without torture was first formulated as a cry from the heart or from an outraged nature. In the worst of murderers, there is one thing, at least, to be respected when one punishes: his 'humanity'. The day was to come, in the nineteenth century, when this 'man', discovered in the criminal, would become the target of penal intervention, the object that it claimed to correct and transform, the domain of a whole series of 'criminological' sciences and strange 'penitentiary' practices. But, at the time of the Enlightenment, it was not as a theme of positive knowledge that man was opposed to the barbarity of the public executions, but as a legal limit: the legitimate frontier of the power to punish. Not that which must be reached in order to alter him, but that which must be left intact in order to respect him. *Noli me tangere*. It marks the end of the sovereign's vengeance. The 'man' that the reformers set up against the despotism of the scaffold has also become a 'man-measure': not of things, but of power.

There is, therefore, a problem here: how was this man-measure opposed to the traditional practice of punishment? How did he become the great moral justification of the reform movement? Why this universal horror of torture and such lyrical insistence that punishment be 'humane'? Or, which amounts to the same thing, how are the two elements, which are everywhere present in demands for a more lenient penal system, 'measure' and 'humanity', to be articulated upon one another, in a single strategy? These elements are so necessary and yet so uncertain that it is they, as disturbing as ever and still associated in the same dubious relation, that one finds today whenever the problem of an economy of punishment is posed. It is as if the eighteenth century had opened up the crisis of this economy and, in order to resolve it, proposed the fundamental law that punishment must have 'humanity' as its 'measure', without any definitive meaning being given to this principle, which nevertheless is regarded as insuperable. We must, therefore, recount the birth and early days of this enigmatic 'leniency'.

Homage is paid to the 'great reformers' – Beccaria, Servan, Dupaty, Lacretelle, Duport, Pastoret, Target, Bergasse, the compilers of the *Cahiers*, or petitions, and the Constituent Assembly – for having imposed this leniency on a legal machinery and on 'classical' theoreticians who, at the end of the eighteenth century, were still rejecting it with well-formulated arguments. (Cf., in particular, Muyart de Vouglans's polemic against Beccaria – Muyart, 1766.)

Yet this reform must be situated in a process that historians have recently uncovered through the study of legal archives: the relaxation of penality in the eighteenth century or, to be more precise, the double movement by which, during this period, crimes seemed to lose their violence, while punishments, reciprocally, lost some of their intensity, but at the cost of greater intervention. From the end of the seventeenth century, in fact, one observes a considerable diminution in murders and, generally speaking, in physical acts of aggression; offences against property seem to take over from crimes of violence; theft and swindling, from murder and assault; the diffuse, occasional, but frequent delinquency of the poorest classes was superseded by a limited, but 'skilled' delinquency; the criminals of the seventeenth century were 'harassed men, ill-fed, quick to act, quick to anger, seasonal criminals'; those of the eighteenth, 'crafty, cunning, sly, calculating' criminals on the fringes of society (Chaunu, 1962, 236 and 1966, 107–8). Lastly, the internal organizations of delinquency altered; the great gangs of malefactors (looters working in small, armed units, groups of smugglers firing on the agents of the tax authorities, disbanded soldiers or deserters who roamed the countryside together) tended to break up; tracked down more efficiently and forced to work in smaller groups – often no more than half-a-dozen men – in order to pass undetected, they contented themselves with more furtive operations, with a more modest deployment of forces and less risk of bloodshed: 'The physical destruction or institutional dislocation of large gangs ... left the field free for an anti-property form of delinquency practised by individuals or very small groups of robbers and pickpockets, seldom more than four in number' (Le Roy-Ladurie). A general movement shifted criminality from the attack of bodies to the more or less direct seizure of goods; and from a 'mass criminality' to a 'marginal criminality', partly the preserve of professionals. It was as if there had been a gradual lowering of level – 'a defusion of the tensions that dominate human relations, ... a better control of violent impulses'[1] – and as if the illegal practices had themselves slackened their hold on the body and turned to other targets. Crime became less violent long before punishment became less severe. But this transformation cannot be separated from several underlying processes. The first of these, as P. Chaunu observes, was a change in the operation of economic pressures, a general rise in the standard of living, a large demographic expansion, an increase in wealth and property and 'a consequent need for security' (Chaunu, 1971, 56). Furthermore, throughout the eighteenth century, one can observe a certain increased severity in the law: in England, out of the 223 capital crimes in force at the beginning of the nineteenth century, 156 had been introduced during the preceding hundred years (Buxton, XXXIX); in France, the legislation on vagabondage had been revised in the direction of greater severity on several occasions since the seventeenth century; a tighter, more meticulous implementation of the law tended to take account of a mass of minor offences that it once allowed to escape more easily: 'in the eighteenth century, the law became slower, heavier, harder on theft, whose relative frequency had increased, and towards which it now assumed the bourgeois appearances of a class justice';[2] the growth in France above all, and especially in Paris, of a police apparatus that prevented the development of organized, open criminality, shifted it towards more discreet forms; to this set of precautions, one should add the very widespread belief in a constant and dangerous rise in crime. Whereas the historians of today observe a diminution in the great gangs of malefactors, Le Trosne saw them roaming the French countryside like swarms of locusts: 'It is these voracious insects who daily lay waste the subsistence of the cultivators. They are, quite literally, enemy troops spreading over the surface of the territory, living as they wish, as in a conquered country, exacting levies under the name of alms.' They cost the poorest peasants more than taxes: the richer peasants had to pay anything up to a third of their incomes (Le Trosne, 1764, 4). Most observers maintained that crime was increasing – they included, of course, those who advocated sterner measures; they also included those who thought that a law that was more restrained in its use of violence would be more effective, less liable to retreat before its own consequences (cf., for example, Dupaty, 247); and they included the magistrates who claimed to be swamped by the number of trials: 'the misery of the people and the corruption of morals have increased the number of crimes and convicted criminals' (one of the judges of the Chambre de la Tournelle in an address to the king, 2 August 1768, quoted in Farge, 66); in any case, that crime was on the increase was shown by the real practice of the courts. 'The revolutionary and imperial era could already be sensed in the last years of the Ancien Régime. One is struck, in the trials of 1782–9, by the increase in tension. There is a new severity towards the poor, a concerted rejection of evidence, a rise in mutual mistrust, hatred and fear' (Chaunu, 1966, 108).

In fact, the shift from a criminality of blood to a criminality of fraud forms part of a whole complex mechanism, embracing the development of production, the increase of wealth, a higher juridical and moral value placed on property relations, stricter methods of surveillance, a tighter partitioning of the population, more efficient techniques of locating and obtaining information: the shift in illegal practices is correlative with an extension and a refinement of punitive practices.

Was this a general change of attitude, a 'change that belongs to the domain of the spirit and the subconscious' (the expression is Mogensen's)? Perhaps, but more certainly and more immediately it was an effort to adjust the mechanisms of power that frame the everyday lives of individuals; an adaptation and a refinement of the machinery that assumes responsibility for and places under surveillance their everyday behaviour, their identity, their activity, their apparently unimportant gestures; another policy for that multiplicity of bodies and forces that constitutes a population. What was emerging no doubt was not so much a new respect for the humanity of the condemned – torture was still frequent in the execution of even minor criminals – as a tendency towards a more finely tuned justice, towards a closer penal mapping of the social body. Following a circular process, the threshold of the passage to violent crimes rises, intolerance to economic offences increases, controls become more thorough, penal interventions at once more premature and more numerous.

If one compares this process with the critical discourse of the reformers, a remarkable strategic coincidence emerges. What they were attacking in traditional justice, before they set out the principles of a new penality, was certainly the excessive nature of the punishments; but an excess that was bound up with an irregularity even more than with an abuse of the power to punish. On 24 March 1790, Thouret opened the debate in the Constituent Assembly on the new organization of the judicial power. In his view, this power had become 'denatured' in France in three ways. By private appropriation: the offices of judge were sold; they were hereditary; they had a commercial value and, for that reason, the justice that was handed out was onerous. By a confusion between two types of power: that which dispenses justice and formulates a sentence by applying the law and that which creates the law itself. Lastly, by the existence of a whole series of privileges that made the implementation of the law inconsistent: there were courts, procedures, litigants, even offences that were 'privileged' and fell outside common law (*Archives parlementaires*, XII, 344). This was only one of the many criticisms that had been levied at the legal system for the past fifty years at least, all of which denounced in this denaturation the principle of an irregular justice. Penal justice was irregular first of all by virtue of the multiplicity of courts responsible for assuring it, without ever forming a single and continuous pyramid (cf. Linguet or Boucher d'Argis, 1789). Quite apart from the ecclesiastical jurisdictions, we must take into account the discontinuities, overlappings and conflicts between the different legal systems: those of the nobility, which still played an important role in judging petty offences; those of the king, which were themselves numerous and badly coordinated (the sovereign courts were often in conflict with the bailiffs' courts and above all with the presidial courts, which had recently been created as intermediary instances); those which, *de jure* or *de facto*, were administered by governmental authorities (such as the *intendants*, or provincial administrators) or police authorities (such as the provosts and police magistrates); to these should also be added the right possessed by the king or his representatives to take decisions on internment or exile quite outside any regular procedure. By their very plethora these innumerable authorities cancelled each other out and were incapable of covering the social body in its entirety. Paradoxically, their overlapping left penal justice with innumerable loopholes. This incompleteness was a result of differences of custom and procedure, despite the Ordonnance Générale of 1670; of internal conflicts of responsibility; of private interests – political or economic – which each authority found itself defending; and, lastly, of the interventions of the royal power, which could prevent, by means of pardons, commuted sentences, the evocation of a case before the royal council or direct pressure exerted on magistrates, the regular, austere course of justice.

The criticism of the reformers was directed not so much at the weakness or cruelty of those in authority, as at a bad economy of power. There was too much power in the lower jurisdictions, which could – aided by the ignorance and poverty of those convicted – ignore appeal procedure and carry out arbitrary sentences without adequate supervision; there was too much power on the side of the prosecution, which possessed almost unlimited means of pursuing its investigations, while the accused opposed it virtually unarmed – this led judges to be sometimes over-severe and sometimes, by way of reaction, too lenient; there was too much power in the hands of the judges who were able to content themselves with futile evidence, providing it was 'legal' evidence, and who were allowed too great a freedom in the choice of penalty; there was too much power in the hands of the '*gens du roi*', or royal magistrates, in relation to the accused, but also in relation to other magistrates; lastly, there was too much power exercised by the king, who could suspend courts of justice, alter their decisions, remove magistrates from office, or exile them, and replace them by judges acting under royal commission. The paralysis of justice was due not so much to a weakening as to a badly regulated distribution of power, to its concentration at a certain number of points and to the conflicts and discontinuities that resulted.

This dysfunction of power was related to a central excess: what might be called the monarchical 'super-power', which identified the right to punish with the personal power of the sovereign. This theoretical identification made the king the *fons justitiae*; but the practical consequences of this were to be found even in that which appeared to oppose him and to limit his absolutism. It was because the king, in order to raise money, had appropriated the right to sell legal offices, which 'belonged' to him, that he was confronted by magistrates who owned their offices and who were not only intractable, but ignorant, self-interested and frequently compromised. It was because he was constantly creating new offices that he multiplied the conflicts of power and authority. It was because he exercised too close a power over his *'gens'* and conferred on them almost discretionary powers that he intensified the conflicts within the magistrature. It was because he had brought the law into conflict with too many summary acts of justice (the jurisdictions of the provosts or police magistrates) or with administrative measures, that he paralysed normal justice, rendered it sometimes lenient and inconsistent, but sometimes over-hasty and severe.[3]

It was not so much, or not only, the privileges of justice, its arbitrariness, its archaic arrogance, its uncontrolled rights that were criticized; but rather the mixture of its weaknesses and excesses, its exaggerations and its loopholes, and above all the very principle of this mixture, the 'super-power' of the monarch. The true objective of the reform movement, even in its most general formulations, was not so much to establish a new right to punish based on more equitable principles, as to set up a new 'economy' of the power to punish, to assure its better distribution, so that it should be neither too concentrated at certain privileged points, nor too divided between opposing authorities; so that it should be distributed in homogeneous circuits capable of operating everywhere, in a continuous way, down to the finest grain of the social body.[4] The reform of criminal law must be read as a strategy for the rearrangement of the power to punish, according to modalities that render it more regular, more effective, more constant and more detailed in its effects; in short, which increase its effects while diminishing its economic cost (that is to say, by dissociating it from the system of property, of buying and selling, of corruption in obtaining not only offices, but the decisions themselves) and its political cost (by dissociating it from the arbitrariness of monarchical power). The new juridical theory of penality corresponds in fact to a new 'political economy' of the power to punish. This explains why the 'reform' did not have a single origin. It was not the more enlightened members of the public, nor the *philosophes*, who regarded themselves as enemies of despotism and friends of mankind; it was not even the social groups opposed to the *parlementaires* who instigated the reform. Or rather it was not they alone; in this same overall project of a new distribution of the power to punish, and of a new distribution of its effects, many different interests came together. The reform was not prepared outside the legal machinery and against all its representatives; it was prepared, for the most part, from within, by a large number of magistrates and on the basis of shared objectives and the power conflicts that divided them. Certainly the reformers did not form a majority of the magistrates; but it was a body of lawyers who outlined its general principles: a power to judge that would not be affected by the immediate exercise of the prince's sovereignty; that would be relieved of any claim to legislate; that would be detached from property relations; and which, having no other functions but to judge, would exercise that power to the full. In short, the power to judge should no longer depend on the innumerable, discontinuous, sometimes contradictory privileges of sovereignty, but on the continuously distributed effects of public power. This general principle defined an overall strategy that covered many different struggles. Those of philosophers like Voltaire and of publicists like Brissot or Marat; but also those of magistrates whose interests were nevertheless very diverse: Le Trosne, a judge at the presidial court of Orléans, and Lacretelle, the advocate-general at the parlement; Target, who with the parlements was opposed to Maupeou's reform; but also J. N. Moreau, who supported the royal power against the *parlementaires*; Servan and Dupaty, both magistrates, but in conflict with their colleagues, etc.

Throughout the eighteenth century, inside and outside the legal apparatus, in both everyday penal practice and the criticism of institutions, one sees the emergence of a new strategy for the exercise of the power to punish. And 'reform', in the strict sense, as it was formulated in the theories of law or as it was outlined in the various projects, was the political or philosophical resumption of this strategy, with its primary objectives: to make of the punishment and repression of illegalities a regular function, coextensive with society; not to punish less, but to punish better; to punish with an attenuated severity perhaps, but in order to punish with more universality and necessity; to insert the power to punish more deeply into the social body.

The conjuncture that saw the birth of reform is not, therefore, that of a new sensibility, but that of another policy with regard to illegalities.

Roughly speaking, one might say that, under the Ancien Régime each of the different social strata had its margin of tolerated illegality: the non-application of the rule, the non-observance of the innumerable edicts or ordinances were a condition of the political and economic functioning of society. This feature may not have been peculiar to the Ancien Régime. But illegality was so deeply rooted and so necessary to the life of each social stratum, that it had in a sense its own coherence and economy. Sometimes it took on an absolutely statutory form – as with the privileges accorded certain individuals and groups – which made it not so much an illegality as a regular exemption. Sometimes it took the form of a massive general non-observance, which meant that for decades, sometimes for centuries, ordinances could be published and constantly renewed without ever being implemented. Sometimes it was a matter of laws gradually falling into abeyance, then suddenly being reactivated; sometimes of silent consent on the part of the authorities, neglect, or quite simply the actual impossibility of imposing the law and apprehending offenders. The least-favoured strata of the population did not have, in principle, any privileges: but they benefited, within the margins of what was imposed on them by law and custom, from a space of tolerance, gained by force or obstinacy; and this space was for them so indispensable a condition of existence that they were often ready to rise up to defend it; the attempts that were made periodically to reduce it, by reviving old laws or by improving the methods of apprehending, provoked popular disturbances, just as attempts to reduce certain privileges disturbed the nobility, the clergy and the bourgeoisie.

This necessary illegality, of which every social stratum bore within itself specific forms, was caught up in a series of paradoxes. In its lower regions, it was identified with criminality, from which it was difficult to distinguish it juridically, if not morally: from fiscal illegality to customs illegality, to smuggling, to looting, to the armed struggle against the government's taxation agents, then against the soldiers themselves and, finally, to rebellion, there was a continuity, in which it was difficult to mark the frontiers; or, again, vagabondage (severely punished according to the terms of ordinances that were never implemented) with the pillage, aggravated theft, even murder that went with it, provided a welcome environment to the unemployed, to workers who had left their employers in irregular circumstances, to domestic servants who had some reason to flee their masters, to ill-treated apprentices, to deserting soldiers, to all those who wished to escape the press-gang. So criminality merged into a wider illegality, to which the lower strata were attached as to conditions of existence; and, conversely, this illegality was a perpetual factor in the increase of crime. Hence an ambiguity in popular attitudes: on the one hand, the criminal – especially when he happened to be a smuggler or a peasant who had fled from the exactions of a master – benefited from a spontaneous wave of sympathy: his acts of violence were seen as descending directly from old struggles. On the other hand, a man who, under cover of an illegality accepted by the population, committed crimes at the expense of this population, the vagrant beggar, for example, who robbed and murdered, easily became the object of a special hate: he had redirected upon the least favoured illegality that was integral to their conditions of existence. Thus there grew up around crimes a network of glorification and blame; effective help and fear alternated with regard to this shifting population, which one knew was very near, but from which one felt that crime could emerge. Popular illegality enveloped a whole nucleus of criminality that was both its extreme form and its internal danger.

Between this illegality of the depths and those of the other social castes, there was neither an exact convergence nor a profound opposition. Generally speaking, the different illegalities proper to each group maintained relations with one another that involved not only rivalry, competition and conflicts of interest, but also mutual help and complicity: the peasants' refusal to pay certain state or ecclesiastical rents was not necessarily disapproved of by the landowners; the non-application by artisans of manufacturing regulations was often encouraged by the new entrepreneurs; smuggling – the story of Mandrin, welcomed by the entire population, received in castles and protected by *parlementaires* proves this – was very widely supported. At most, one had seen in the seventeenth century the different fiscal refusals coalesce in serious revolts among widely separated social strata. In short, the reciprocal interplay of illegalities formed part of the political and economic life of society. Or rather, a number of transformations (the abeyance into which Colbert's regulations had fallen, for example, the non-observance of customs barriers within the kingdom, the breakdown of guild practices) had operated in the breach that was being widened every day by popular illegality; the bourgeoisie had needed these transformations; and economic growth was due, in part, to them. Tolerance then became encouragement.

In the second half of the eighteenth century, the process tended to be reversed. First, with the general increase in wealth, but also with the sudden demographic expansion, the principal target of popular illegality tended to be not so much rights, as goods: pilfering and theft tended to replace smuggling and the armed struggle against the tax agents. And, in this respect, the peasants, farmers and artisans were often its principal victims. Le Trosne was no doubt exaggerating a real tendency when he described the peasants' suffering under the exactions of vagabonds, even more than they had suffered under feudal demands: thieves now attacked them like a cloud of maleficent insects, devouring crops and depleting the granaries (Le Trosne, 1764, 4). It might be said that gradually in the eighteenth century a crisis of popular illegality had occurred; and neither the movements at the beginning of the Revolution (around the refusal of seigniorial rights), nor those later movements, in which the struggle against property rights, political and religious protests and the refusal of conscription came together, recombined illegality in its old, welcoming form. Furthermore, although a large part of the bourgeoisie had accepted, without too much trouble, the illegality of rights, it found it difficult to support illegality when it was a question of its own property rights. Nothing could be more typical of this than the problem of peasant delinquency at the end of the eighteenth century and especially after the Revolution (Bercé, 161). The transition to an intensive agriculture exercised, over the rights to use common lands, over various tolerated practices, over small accepted illegalities, a more and more restrictive pressure. Furthermore, as it was acquired in part by the bourgeoisie, now free of the feudal burdens that once weighed upon it, landed property became absolute property: all the tolerated 'rights' that the peasantry had acquired or preserved (the abandonment of old obligations or the consolidation of irregular practices: the right of free pasture, wood-collecting, etc.) were now rejected by the new owners who regarded them quite simply as theft (thus leading, among the people, to a series of chain reactions of an increasingly illegal, or, if one prefers the term, criminal kind: breaches of close, the theft or killing of cattle, fires, assaults, murders (cf. Festy and Agulhon). The illegality of rights, which often meant the survival of the most deprived, tended, with the new status of property, to become an illegality of property. It then had to be punished.

And this illegality, while resented by the bourgeoisie where the ownership of land was concerned, was intolerable in commercial and industrial ownership: the development of the ports, the appearance of great warehouses in which merchandise was stored, the organization of huge workshops (with considerable quantities of raw materials, tools and manufactured articles, which belonged to the entrepreneurs and which were difficult to supervise) also necessitated a severe repression of illegality. The way in which wealth tended to be invested, on a much larger scale than ever before, in commodities and machines presupposed a systematic, armed intolerance of illegality. The phenomenon was obviously very evident where economic development was most intense. Colquhoun set out to give proof, supported by figures, of the urgent need to check the innumerable illegal practices that had grown up: according to the estimates of the entrepreneurs and insurance companies, the theft of produce imported from America and warehoused along the banks of the Thames had risen, on average, to £250,000 per annum; in all, approximately £500,000 worth of goods was stolen each year in the Port of London itself (and this did not include the arsenals and warehouses outside the port proper); to this should be added £700,000 for the town itself. In this situation of permanent pilfering, three phenomena, says Colquhoun, should be taken into consideration: first, the complicity and often the active participation of the clerks, overseers, foremen and workers: 'Whenever a large number of workers are gathered together in one place, there are bound to be a lot of bad characters among them'; second, the existence of a whole organization of illicit commerce, which began in the workshops or docks, then passed on to the receivers – wholesale receivers, specializing in certain kinds of commodity, and retail receivers whose stalls offered a 'wretched display of old iron, rags and worn clothes, whereas at the back of the shop were hidden naval munitions of great value, copper bolts and nails, pieces of cast iron and precious metals, produce from the West Indies, furniture and all kinds of goods bought from the labourers' – then on to dealers and pedlars who distributed the stolen goods far into the countryside (Colquhoun, 1797; in chapters VII, VIII and XV, he gives a very detailed account of this process); third, counterfeiting (it seems that there were between forty and fifty mints producing counterfeit money throughout England, in permanent operation). But what facilitated the work of this huge undertaking, involving both depredation and competition, was a whole set of tolerances: some amounted almost to acquired right (the right, for example, to collect bits of iron or rope around ships or to resell the sugar sweepings); others were of the nature of a moral acceptance; the pilferers themselves regarded their work as a kind of smuggling, which 'they did not regard as a serious offence'.

It proved necessary, therefore, to control these illicit practices and introduce new legislation to cover them. The offences had to be properly defined and more surely punished; out of this mass of irregularities, sometimes tolerated and sometimes punished with a severity out of all proportion to the offence, one had to determine what was an intolerable offence, and the offenders had to be apprehended and punished. With the new forms of capital accumulation, new relations of production and the new legal status of property, all the popular practices that belonged, either in a silent, everyday, tolerated form, or in a violent form, to the illegality of rights were reduced by force to an illegality of property. In that movement which transformed a society of juridico-political levies into a society of the appropriation of the means and products of labour, theft tended to become the first of the great loopholes in legality. Or, to put it another way, the economy of illegalities was restructured with the development of capitalist society. The illegality of property was separated from the illegality of rights. This distinction represents a class opposition because, on the one hand, the illegality that was to be most accessible to the lower classes was that of property – the violent transfer of ownership – and because, on the other, the bourgeoisie was to reserve to itself the illegality of rights: the possibility of getting round its own regulations and its own laws, of ensuring for itself an immense sector of economic circulation by a skilful manipulation of gaps in the law – gaps that were foreseen by its silences, or opened up by *de facto* tolerance. And this great redistribution of illegalities was even to be expressed through a specialization of the legal circuits: for illegalities of property – for theft – there were the ordinary courts and punishments; for the illegalities of rights – fraud, tax evasion, irregular commercial operations – special legal institutions applied with transactions, accommodations, reduced fines, etc. The bourgeoisie reserved to itself the fruitful domain of the illegality of rights. And at the same time as this split was taking place, there emerged the need for a constant policing concerned essentially with this illegality of property. It became necessary to get rid of the old economy of the power to punish, based on the principles of the confused and inadequate multiplicity of authorities, the distribution and concentration of the power correlative with actual inertia and inevitable tolerance, punishments that were spectacular in their manifestations and haphazard in their application. It became necessary to define a strategy and techniques of punishment in which an economy of continuity and permanence would replace that of expenditure and excess. In short, penal reform was born at the point of junction between the struggle against the super-power of the sovereign and that against the infra-power of acquired and tolerated illegalities. And if penal reform was anything more than the temporary result of a purely circumstantial encounter, it was because, between this super-power and this infra-power, a whole network of relations was being formed. By placing on the side of the sovereign the additional burden of a spectacular, unlimited, personal, irregular and discontinuous power, the form of monarchical sovereignty left the subjects free to practise a constant illegality; this illegality was like the correlative of this type of power. So much so that in attacking the various prerogatives of the sovereign one was also attacking the functioning of the illegalities. The two objectives were in continuity. And, according to particular circumstances or tactics, the reformers laid more stress on one or the other. Le Trosne, the physiocrat who was a judge at the presidial court of Orléans, may serve as an example. In 1764, he published a memorandum on vagabondage: that hot-bed of thieves and murderers 'who live in the midst of society without being members of it', who wage 'a veritable war on all citizens', and who are in the midst of us 'in that state that one supposes existed before the establishment of civil society'. Against them, he demanded the most severe penalties (characteristically, he expressed surprise that one should be more indulgent towards them than to smugglers); he wanted the police to be reinforced, the mounted constabulary to hunt them down with the help of the population that suffered from their depredations; he demanded that these useless and dangerous people should be 'acquired by the state and that they should belong to it as slaves to their masters'; and if necessary one should organize collective round-ups in the woods to drive them out, and anyone making a capture should be paid: 'A reward of ten pounds is given for anyone who kills a wolf. A vagabond is infinitely more dangerous for society' (Le Trosne, 1764, 8, 50, 54, 61–2). In 1777 in *Vues sur la justice criminelle*, the same Le Trosne demanded that the prerogatives of the Crown be reduced, that the accused be regarded as innocent until proved guilty, that the judge be a just arbiter between them and society, that laws be 'fixed, constant, determined in the most precise way', so that subjects know 'to what they are exposed' and that magistrates be nothing more than the 'organ of the law' (Le Trosne, 1777, 31, 37, 103–6). For Le Trosne, as for so many others at that time, the struggle for the delimitation of the power to punish was articulated directly on the need to subject popular illegality to a stricter and more constant control. It is understandable that the criticism of the public execution should have assumed such importance in penal reform: for it was the form in which, in the most visible way, the unlimited power of the sovereign and the ever-active illegality of the people came together. Humanity in the sentences was the rule given to a system of punishment that must fix their limits on both. The 'man' that must be respected in the sentence was the juridical and moral form given to this double delimitation.

But, although it is true that reform, as a penal theory and as a strategy of the power to punish, took shape at the point of coincidence of these two objectives, its stability in the future was due to the fact that, for a long time, priority was given to the second. It was because the pressure on popular illegalities had become, at the period of the Revolution, then under the Empire, and finally throughout the nineteenth century, an essential imperative, that reform was able to pass from the project stage to that of an institution and set of practices. That is to say, although the new criminal legislation appears to be characterized by less severe penalties, a clearer codification, a marked diminution of the arbitrary, a more generally accepted consensus concerning the power to punish (in the absence of a more real division in its exercise), it is sustained in reality by an upheaval in the traditional economy of illegalities and a rigorous application of force to maintain their new adjustment. A penal system must be conceived as a mechanism intended to administer illegalities differentially, not to eliminate them all.

Shift the object and change the scale. Define new tactics in order to reach a target that is now more subtle but also more widely spread in the social body. Find new techniques for adjusting punishment to it and for adapting its effects. Lay down new principles for regularizing, refining, universalizing the art of punishing. Homogenize its application. Reduce its economic and political cost by increasing its effectiveness and by multiplying its circuits. In short, constitute a new economy and a new technology of the power to punish: these are no doubt the essential *raisons d'être* of penal reform in the eighteenth century.

At the level of principles, this new strategy falls easily into the general theory of the contract. The citizen is presumed to have accepted once and for all, with the laws of society, the very law by which he may be punished. Thus the criminal appears as a juridically paradoxical being. He has broken the pact, he is therefore the enemy of society as a whole, but he participates in the punishment that is practised upon him. The least crime attacks the whole of society; and the whole of society – including the criminal – is present in the least punishment. Penal punishment is therefore a generalized function, coextensive with the function of the social body and with each of its elements. This gives rise to the problem of the degree of punishment, the economy of the power to punish.

In effect the offence opposes an individual to the entire social body; in order to punish him, society has the right to oppose him in its entirety. It is an unequal struggle: on one side are all the forces, all the power, all the rights. And this is how it should be, since the defence of each individual is involved. Thus a formidable right to punish is established, since the offender becomes the common enemy. Indeed, he is worse than an enemy, for it is from within society that he delivers his blows – he is nothing less than a traitor, a 'monster'. How could society not have an absolute right over him? How could it not demand, quite simply, his elimination? And, although it is true that the principle of punishment must be subscribed to in the pact, must not each citizen, logically, accept the extreme penalty for those of them who attack them as a body. 'Every malefactor, by attacking the social rights, becomes, by his crimes, a rebel and a traitor to his country; by violating its laws he ceases to be a member of it; he even makes war upon it. In such a case the preservation of the state is inconsistent with his own, and one or the other must perish; in putting the guilty to death we slay not so much the citizen as the enemy.'[5] The right to punish has been shifted from the vengeance of the sovereign to the defence of society. But it now finds itself recombined with elements so strong that it becomes almost more to be feared. The malefactor has been saved from a threat that is by its very nature excessive, but he is exposed to a penalty that seems to be without bounds. It is a return to a terrible 'super-power'. It brings with it the need to establish a principle of moderation for the power of punishment.

'Who does not shudder with horror when reading in history of so many terrible and useless torments, invented and coldly applied by monsters who took upon themselves the name of sage?' (Beccaria,

87). Or again: 'The laws summon me to the greatest punishment of crimes. I go with all the fury that it has inspired in me. But what is this? They even go beyond it. . . God, who has imprinted in our hearts an aversion to pain for ourselves and for our fellow men, are they then those same beings, whom thou hast created so weak and so sensible, who have invented such barbarous, such refined tortures?' (Lacretelle, 129). The principle of moderation in punishment, even when it is a question of punishing the enemy of the social body, is articulated first as a discourse of the heart. Or rather, it leaps forth like a cry from the body, which is revolted at the sight or at the imagination of too much cruelty. The formulation of the principle that penality must remain 'humane' is expressed by the reformers in the first person. It is as if the sensibility of the speaker were being expressed directly; as if the body of the philosopher or theoretician had come, between executioner and victim, to affirm his own law and to impose it finally on the entire economy of punishment. Does this lyricism express an inability to find a rational foundation for a penal arithmetic? Between the contractual principle that expels the criminal from society and the image of the monster 'vomited' by nature, where is one to find a limit, if not in a human nature that is manifested – not in the rigour of the law, not in the ferocity of the delinquent – but in the sensibility of the reasonable man who makes the law and does not commit crime?

But this recourse to 'sensibility' does not exactly express a theoretical impossibility. In fact, it bears within it a principle of calculation. The body, the imagination, pain, the heart to be respected are not, in effect, those of the criminal that is to be punished, but those of the men who, having subscribed to the pact, have the right of exercising against him the power of assembly. The pain that must exclude any reduction in punishment is that felt by the judges or spectators with all the hardness of heart that it may bring with it, all the ferocity induced by familiarity, or on the contrary, ill-founded feelings of pity and indulgence: 'Thank God for those gentle, sensitive souls on whom those horrible executions exert a kind of torture' (Lacretelle, 131). What has to be arranged and calculated are the return effects of punishment on the punishing authority and the power that it claims to exercise.

Here the principle takes root that one should never apply 'in-humane' punishments to a criminal, who, nevertheless, may well be a traitor and a monster. If the law must now treat in a 'humane' way an individual who is 'outside nature' (whereas the old justice treated the 'outlaw' inhumanely), it is not on account of some profound humanity that the criminal conceals within him, but because of a necessary regulation of the effects of power. It is this 'economic' rationality that must calculate the penalty and prescribe the appro-priate techniques. 'Humanity' is the respectable name given to this economy and to its meticulous calculations. 'Where punishment is concerned, the minimum is ordered by humanity and counselled by policy.'[6]

So, in order to understand this techno-politics of punishment, let us take the extreme case, the ultimate crime: a deed of such enormity that it violates all the most respected laws. It is produced in circum-stances so extraordinary, in such profound secrecy, with such lack of restraint, as if at the very limit of possibility, that it could not be other than unique, in any case the last of its kind: no one could ever imitate it; no one could take it as an example, or even feel scandalized that it should have been committed. It is doomed to disappear without trace. This fable[7] of the 'ultimate crime' is, to the new penality, what original sin was to the old: the pure form in which the reason for punishment appears.

Ought such a crime to be punished? According to what calcula-tion? Of what use could its punishment be in the economy of the power to punish? It would be useful to the extent that it could make reparation for 'the harm done to society' (Pastoret, II, 21). Now, if one sets aside the strictly material damage – which even when it is irreparable as in the case of a murder is of little account in relation to society as a whole – the injury that a crime inflicts upon the social body is the disorder that it introduces into it: the scandal that it gives rise to, the example that it gives, the incitement to repeat it if it is not punished, the possibility of becoming widespread that it bears within it. In order to be useful, punishment must have as its objective the consequences of the crime, that is to say, the series of disorders that it is capable of initiating: 'The proportion between the penalty and the quality of the offence is determined by the influence that the violation of the pact has on the social order'

(Filangieri, 214). But this influence of a crime is not necessarily in direct proportion to its horror; a crime that horrifies the conscience is often of less effect than an offence that everyone tolerates and feels quite ready to imitate. There is a scarcity of great crimes; on the other hand, there is the danger that everyday offences may multiply. So one must not seek a qualitative relation between the crime and its punishment, an equivalence of horror: 'Can the cries of a wretch in torment bring back from the depths of a past that cannot return an action that has already been committed?' (Beccaria, 87). One must calculate a penalty in terms not of the crime, but of its possible repetition. One must take into account not the past offence, but the future disorder. Things must be so arranged that the malefactor can have neither any desire to repeat his offence, nor any possibility of having imitators.[8] Punishment, then, will be an art of effects; rather than opposing the enormity of the penalty to the enormity of the crime, one must adjust to one another the two series that follow from the crime: its own effects and those of the penalty. A crime without a dynasty does not call for punishment; any more than, according to another version of the same fable, a society on the verge of dissolution and disappearance would have the right to erect scaffolds. The last crime cannot but remain unpunished.

This was an old view. The function of punishment as example was to be found long before the eighteenth-century reform. That punishment looks towards the future, and that at least one of its major functions is to prevent crime had, for centuries, been one of the current justifications of the right to punish. But the difference was that the prevention that was expected as an effect of the punishment and its spectacle – and therefore of its excess – tended now to become the principle of its economy and the measure of its just proportions. One must punish exactly enough to prevent repetition. There is, then, a shift in the mechanics of example: in a penalty employing public torture and execution, example was the answer to the crime; it had, by a sort of twin manifestation, to show the crime and at the same time to show the sovereign power that mastered it; in a penalty calculated according to its own effects, example must refer back to the crime, but in the most discreet way possible and with the greatest possible economy indicate the intervention of power; ideally, too, it should prevent any subsequent reappearance of either. The example is no longer a ritual that manifests; it is a sign that serves as an obstacle. Through this technique of punitive signs, which tends to reverse the whole temporal field of penal action, the reformers thought they were giving to the power to punish an economic, effective instrument that could be made general throughout the entire social body, capable of coding all its behaviour and consequently of reducing the whole diffuse domain of illegalities. The semio-technique with which one tried to arm the power to punish rested on five or six major rules.

The rule of minimum quantity. A crime is committed because it procures certain advantages. If one linked, to the idea of crime, the idea of a slightly greater disadvantage, it would cease to be desirable. 'For punishment to produce the effect that must be expected of it, it is enough that the harm that it causes exceed the good that the criminal has derived from the crime' (Beccaria, 89). A proximity between penalty and crime can, indeed must, be accepted; but no longer in its old form, where the public execution had to be equivalent in intensity to the crime, with an additional factor that marked the 'surplus power' of the sovereign carrying out his legitimate vengeance; it is a quasi-equivalence at the level of interests: a little more interest in avoiding the penalty than in risking the crime.

The rule of sufficient ideality. If the motive of a crime is the advantage expected of it, the effectiveness of the penalty is the disadvantage expected of it. This means that the 'pain' at the heart of punishment is not the actual sensation of pain, but the idea of pain, displeasure, inconvenience – the 'pain' of the idea of 'pain'. Punishment has to make use not of the body, but of representation. Or rather, if it does make use of the body, it is not so much as the subject of a pain as the object of a representation: the memory of pain must prevent a repetition of the crime, just as the spectacle, however artificial it may be, of a physical punishment may prevent the contagion of a crime. But it is not pain in itself that will be the instrument of the technique of punishment. Therefore, as long as possible, and except in cases requiring an effective representation, one should avoid recourse to the great panoply of the scaffold. There is an elision of the body as the subject of the punishment, but not necessarily as an element in a spectacle. The rejection of the public execution which, at the threshold of the theory, had found no more than a lyrical expression, was now offered the possibility of a rational articulation: what must be maximized is the representation of the penalty, not its corporal reality.

The rule of lateral effects. The penalty must have its most intense effects on those who have not committed the crime; to carry the argument to its limit, if one could be sure that the criminal could not repeat the crime, it would be enough to make others believe that he had been punished. There is a centrifugal intensification of effects, which leads to the paradox that in the calculation of penalties the least important element is still the criminal (unless he is likely to repeat the offence). Beccaria illustrated this paradox in the punishment that he proposed to replace the death sentence – perpetual slavery. Is this not a physically more cruel punishment than death? Not at all, he says: because the pain of slavery, for the condemned man, is divided into as many portions as he has moments left to live; it is an infinitely divisible penalty, an Eleatic penalty, much less severe than capital punishment, which is only one step away from the public execution. On the other hand, for those who see these slaves, or represent them to themselves, the pains they bear are concentrated into a single idea; all the moments of slavery are contracted into a representation that then becomes more terrifying than the idea of death. It is the economically ideal punishment: it is minimal for him who undergoes it (and who, reduced to slavery, cannot repeat his crime) and it is maximal for him who represents it to himself. 'Among the penalties, and in the way of applying them in proportion to the offences, one must choose the means that will leave the most lasting impression on the minds of the people, and the least cruel on the body of the criminal' (Beccaria, 87).

The rule of perfect certainty. With the idea of each crime and the advantages to be expected of it must be associated the idea of a particular punishment with the precise inconveniences that result from it; the link from one to the other must be regarded as necessary and unbreakable. This general element of certainty that must give the system of punishment its effectiveness involves a number of precise measures. The laws that define the crime and lay down the penalties must be perfectly clear, 'so that each member of society may distinguish criminal actions from virtuous actions' (Brissot, 24). These laws must be published, so that everyone has access to them; what is needed is not oral traditions and customs, but a written legislation which can be 'the stable monument of the social pact', printed texts available to all: 'Only printing can make the public as a whole and not just a few persons depositories of the sacred code of the laws' (Beccaria, 26). The monarch must renounce his right of pardon so that the force that is present in the idea of punishment is not attenuated by the hope of intervention: 'If one allows men to see that the crime may be pardoned and that punishment is not a necessary consequence of it, one nourishes in them the hope of going unpunished. . . The laws must be inexorable, those who execute them inflexible.'[9] Above all, no crime committed must escape the gaze of those whose task it is to dispense justice. Nothing so weakens the machinery of the law than the hope of going unpunished; how could one establish in the minds of the public a strict link between the offence and a penalty if it were affected by a certain coefficient of improbability? Would it not be necessary to make the penalty the more to be feared in its violence as it is less to be feared in its uncertainty? Rather than imitate the old system in this way and be 'more severe, one must be more vigilant'.[10] Hence the idea that the machinery of justice must be duplicated by an organ of surveillance that would work side by side with it, and which would make it possible either to prevent crimes, or, if committed, to arrest their authors; police and justice must work together as two complementary actions of the same process – the police assuring 'the action of society on each individual', justice 'the rights of individuals against society' (Duport, *Archives parlementaires*, XXI, 45). Thus every crime will come to the light of day and be punished in all certainty. But it is also necessary that the legal procedures should not remain secret, that the reasons why a defendant is condemned or acquitted should be known to all, and each individual must be able to recognize the reasons for a penalty: 'Let the magistrate speak his opinion aloud, let him be obliged to read in his judgement the text of the law that condemns the defendant. . . Let the procedures that are buried mysteriously in the obscurity of the records office be opened to all citizens who are concerned at the fate of the condemned' (Mably, 348).

The rule of common truth. Beneath this ordinary-seeming principle is hidden an important transformation. The old system of legal proofs, the use of torture, the extraction of confessions, the use of the public execution, the body and spectacle for the reproduction of truth had long isolated penal practice from the common forms of demonstration: semi-proofs produced semi-truths and semi-guilty persons, words extracted by pain had greater authenticity, presumption involved a degree of punishment. The heterogeneity of this system with the ordinary system of proof really constituted a scandal only when the power to punish needed, for its own economy, a climate of irrefutable certainty. How can one link absolutely in the minds of men the idea of crime and the idea of punishment, if the reality of the punishment does not follow, in all cases, the reality of the offence? To establish the offence, in all evidence, and according to the means valid for all, becomes a task of first importance. The verification of the crime must obey the general criteria for all truth. In the arguments it employs, in the proofs it provides, legal judgement must be homogeneous with judgement in general. There is, therefore, an abandonment of legal proof, a rejection of torture, the need for a complete demonstration of the truth, an effacement of all correlation between degrees of suspicion and degrees of punishment. Like a mathematical truth, the truth of the crime will be accepted only when it is completely proven. It follows that, up to the final demonstration of his crime, the defendant must be regarded as innocent; and that, in order to carry out this demonstration, the judge must use not ritual forms, but common instruments, that reason possessed by everyone, which is also that of philosophers and scientists: 'In theory, I regard the magistrate as a philosopher who sets out to discover an interesting truth. . . His sagacity will enable him to grasp all the circumstances and all the relations, bring together or separate whatever needs to be brought together or separated in order to arrive at a sane judgement' (Seigneux de Correvon, 49). The investigation, the exercise of common reason, lays aside the old inquisitorial model and adopts the much more subtle model (doubly validated by science and common sense) of empirical research. The judge will be like a 'pilot steering between the rocks': 'What proofs or what clues will be considered to be sufficient neither I nor anyone else has dared to determine in general; since circumstances are subject to infinite variations, since proofs and clues must be deduced from these circumstances, the clearest clues and proofs must necessarily vary in proportion' (Risi, 53). Henceforth, penal practice was to be subject to a common rule of truth, or rather to a complex rule in which heterogeneous elements of scientific demonstration, the evidence of the senses and common sense come together to form the judge's 'deep-seated conviction'. Although penal justice preserves the forms that guarantee its equity, it may now be opened up to all manner of truths, providing they are evident, well founded, acceptable to all. The legal ritual in itself no longer generates a divided truth. It is resituated in the field of reference of common proofs. With the multiplicity of scientific discourses, a difficult, infinite relation was then forged that penal justice is still unable to control. The master of justice is no longer the master of its truth.

The rule of optimal specification. For penal semiotics to cover the whole field of illegalities that one wishes to eliminate, all offences must be defined; they must be classified and collected into species from which none of them can escape. A code is therefore necessary and this code must be sufficiently precise for each type of offence to be clearly present in it. The silence of the law must not harbour the hope of impunity. An exhaustive, explicit code is required, defining crimes and fixing penalties. (On this theme, cf., among others, Linguet, 8.) But the same imperative need for a total coincidence between all possible offences and the effects-signs of punishment forces one to go further. The idea of the same punishment does not have the same effect on everyone: the rich do not fear fines nor the notorious infamy. The injury caused by an offence and its value as example differ according to the status of the offender; a crime committed by a noble is more injurious to society than one committed by a man of the people (Lacretelle, 144). Lastly, since punishment must prevent a repetition of the offence, it must take into account the profound nature of the criminal himself, the presumable degree of his wickedness, the intrinsic quality of his will: 'Of two men who have committed the same theft, how much less guilty is he who scarcely had the necessities of life than he who overflowed with excess? Of two perjurers, how much more criminal is he on whom one has striven from his childhood to impress feelings of honour than he who, abandoned to nature, never received the benefit of education' (Marat, 34). One sees the emergence at the same time of the need for a parallel classification of crimes and punishments, the need for an individualization of sentences, in accordance with the particular characteristics of each criminal. This individualization was to weigh very heavily throughout the history of modern penal law; it is rooted precisely here: in terms of the theory of law and according to the requirements of everyday practice, it is no doubt in radical opposition to the principle of codification; but from the standpoint of the economy of the power to punish, and of the techniques by which one wishes to circulate throughout the social body precisely calibrated signs of punishment, with neither excesses nor loopholes, with neither a useless 'expenditure' of power nor with timidity, it becomes evident that the codification of the offences–punishments system and the modulation of the criminal–punishment dyad go side by side, each requiring the other. Individualization appears as the ultimate aim of a precisely adapted code.

But this individualization is very different in its nature from the modulations of punishment to be found in the old jurisprudence. The old system – and on this point it followed Christian penitentiary practice – used two series of variables to adjust the punishment, those of 'circumstances' and those of 'intention'; elements, that is to say, that made it possible to qualify the act itself. The modulation of the penalty belonged to 'casuistry' in the broad sense. (On the non-individualizing character of casuistry, cf. Cariou.) But what was now beginning to emerge was a modulation that referred to the defendant himself, to his nature, to his way of life and his attitude of mind, to his past, to the 'quality' and not to the intention of his will. One perceives, but as a place as yet unfilled, the locus in which, in penal practice, psychological knowledge will take over the role of casuistic jurisprudence. Of course, at the end of the eighteenth century, that moment was still far off. The code–individualization link was sought in the scientific models of the period. Natural history no doubt offered the most adequate schema: the taxonomy of species according to an uninterrupted gradation. One sought to constitute a Linnaeus of crimes and punishments, so that each particular offence and each punishable individual might come, without the slightest risk of any arbitrary action, within the provisions of a general law. 'A table must be drawn up of all the genera of crimes to be observed in different countries. According to the enumeration of crimes, a division into species must be carried out. The best rule of this division is, it seems to me, to separate the crimes according to their objects. This division must be such that each species is quite distinct from another, and that each particular crime, considered in all its relations may be placed between that which must precede it and that which must follow it, in the strictest gradation; lastly, this table must be such that it may be compared with another table that will be drawn up for penalties, in such a way that they may correspond exactly to one another' (Lacretelle, 351–352). In theory, or rather in dream, the double taxonomy of punishments and crimes will solve the problem: but how is one to apply fixed laws to particular individuals?

Far removed from this speculative model, forms of anthropological individualization were being constituted at the same period in what was still a very rough and ready way. Let us take first the notion of the repetition of crime. Not that this was unknown to the old criminal laws.[11] But it was tending to become a description of the defendant himself capable of altering the sentence passed: according to the legislation of 1791, recidivists were liable in almost all cases to a doubling of the penalty; according to the law of Floréal Year X, they had to be branded with the letter R; and the penal code of 1810 inflicted on them either the maximum possible of the normal penalty, or the penalty immediately above it. Now, through the repetition of the crime, what one was aiming at was not the author of an act defined by law, but the delinquent subject himself, a certain will that manifested his intrinsically criminal character. Gradually, as criminality, rather than crime, became the object of penal intervention, the opposition between first offender and recidivist tended to become more important. And on the basis of this opposition, reinforcing it on several points, one sees at the same period the formation of the notion of the 'crime passionel' – an involuntary, unpremeditated crime, bound up with extraordinary circumstances, which, while not offering the same excuse as madness, nevertheless prevented it from being regarded as an ordinary crime. As early as 1791, Le Peletier remarked that the subtle gradation of penalties that he had presented to the Constituent Assembly might dissuade from crime 'the evil-doer who plans a wicked action in cold blood', and who may be restrained by thoughts of the penalty; but, on the other hand, it was powerless against crimes due to 'violent passions that have no regard to consequences'; this, however, was unimportant, since such crimes revealed in their authors 'no reasoned wickedness.'[12]

Beneath the humanization of the penalties, what one finds are all those rules that authorize, or rather demand, 'leniency', as a calculated economy of the power to punish. But they also provoke a shift in the point of application of this power: it is no longer the body, with the ritual play of excessive pains, spectacular brandings in the ritual of the public execution; it is the mind or rather a play of representations and signs circulating discreetly but necessarily and evidently in the minds of all. It is no longer the body, but the soul, said Mably. And we see very clearly what he meant by this term: the correlative of a technique of power. Old 'anatomies' of punishment are abandoned. But have we really entered the age of non-corporal punishment?

At the point of departure, then, one may place the political project of rooting out illegalities, generalizing the punitive function and delimiting, in order to control it, the power to punish. From this there emerge two lines of objectification of crime and of the criminal. On the one hand, the criminal designated as the enemy of all, whom it is in the interest of all to track down, falls outside the pact, disqualifies himself as a citizen and emerges, bearing within him as it were, a wild fragment of nature; he appears as a villain, a monster, a madman, perhaps, a sick and, before long, 'abnormal' individual. It is as such that, one day, he will belong to a scientific objectification and to the 'treatment' that is correlative to it. On the other hand, the need to measure, from within, the effects of the punitive power prescribes tactics of intervention over all criminals, actual or potential: the organization of a field of prevention, the calculation of interests, the circulation of representations and signs, the constitution of a horizon of certainty and proof, the adjustment of penalties to ever more subtle variables; all this also leads to an objectification of criminals and crimes. In either case, one sees that the power relation that underlies the exercise of punishment begins to be duplicated by an object relation in which are caught up not only the crime as a fact to be established according to common norms, but the criminal as an individual to be known according to specific criteria. One also sees that this object relation is not superimposed, from the outside, on the punitive practice, as would be a prohibition laid on the fury of the public execution by the limits of the sensibility, or as would be a rational or 'scientific' interrogation as to what this man that one is punishing really is. The processes of objectification originate in the very tactics of power and of the arrangement of its exercise.

However, the two types of objectification that emerge with the project of penal reform are very different from one another: both in their chronology and in their effects. The objectification of the criminal as outside the law, as natural man, is still only a potentiality, a vanishing trace, in which are entangled the themes of political criticism and the figures of the imagination. One will have to wait a long time before *homo criminalis* becomes a definite object in the field of knowledge. The other, on the contrary, has had much more rapid and decisive effects in so far as it was linked more directly to the reorganization of the power to punish: codification, definition of offences, the fixing of a scale of penalties, rules of procedure, definition of the role of magistrates. And also because it made use of the discourse already constituted by the *Idéologues*. This discourse provided, in effect, by means of the theory of interests, representations and signs, by the series and geneses that it reconstituted, a sort of general recipe for the exercise of power over men: the 'mind' as a surface of inscription for power, with semiology as its tool; the submission of bodies through the control of ideas; the analysis of representations as a principle in a politics of bodies that was much more effective than the ritual anatomy of torture and execution. The thought of the *Idéologues* was not only a theory of the individual and society; it developed as a technology of subtle, effective, economic powers, in opposition to the sumptuous expenditure of the power of the sovereign. Let us hear once more what Servan has to say: the ideas of crime and punishment must be strongly linked and 'follow one another without interruption. . . When you have thus formed the chain of ideas in the heads of your citizens, you will then be able to pride yourselves on guiding them and being their masters. A stupid despot may constrain his slaves with iron chains; but a true politician binds them even more strongly by the chain of their own ideas; it is at the stable point of reason that he secures the end of the chain; this link is all the stronger in that we do not know of what it is made and we believe it to be our own work; despair and time eat away the bonds of iron and steel, but they are powerless against the habitual union of ideas, they can only tighten it still more; and on the soft fibres of the brain is founded the unshakable base of the soundest of Empires' (Servan, 35).

It is this semio-technique of punishments, this 'ideological power' which, partly at least, will remain in suspense and will be superseded by a new political anatomy, in which the body, once again, but in a new form, will be the principal character. And this new political anatomy will permit the intersection of the two divergent lines of objectification that are to be seen emerging in the eighteenth century: that which rejects the criminal 'from the other side' – from the side of a nature against nature; and that which seeks to control delinquency by a calculated economy of punishments. A glance at the new art of punishing clearly reveals the supersession of the punitive semio-technique by a new politics of the body.

2. The gentle way in punishment

The art of punishing, then, must rest on a whole technology of representation. The undertaking can succeed only if it forms part of a natural mechanics. 'Like the gravitation of bodies, a secret force compels us ever towards our well-being. This impulsion is affected only by the obstacles that laws oppose to it. All the diverse actions of man are the effects of this interior tendency.' To find the suitable punishment for a crime is to find the disadvantage whose idea is such that it robs for ever the idea of a crime of any attraction. It is an art of conflicting energies, an art of images linked by association, the forging of stable connections that defy time: it is a matter of establishing the representation of pairs of opposing values, of establishing quantitative differences between the opposing forces, of setting up a complex of obstacle-signs that may subject the movement of the forces to a power relation. 'Let the idea of torture and execution be ever present in the heart of the weak man and dominate the feeling that drives him to crime' (Beccaria, 119). These obstacle-signs must constitute the new arsenal of penalties, just as the old public executions were organized around a system of retaliatory marks. But in order to function, they must obey several conditions.

1. They must be as unarbitrary as possible. It is true that it is society that defines, in terms of its own interests, what must be regarded as a crime: it is not therefore natural. But, if punishment is to present itself to the mind as soon as one thinks of committing a crime, as immediate a link as possible must be made between the two: a link of resemblance, analogy, proximity. 'The penalty must be made to conform as closely as possible to the nature of the offence, so that fear of punishment diverts the mind from the road along which the prospect of an advantageous crime was leading it' (Beccaria, 119). The ideal punishment would be transparent to the

crime that it punishes; thus, for him who contemplates it, it will be infallibly the sign of the crime that it punishes; and for him who dreams of the crime, the idea of the offence will be enough to arouse the sign of the punishment. This is an advantage for the stability of the link, an advantage for the calculation of the proportions between crime and punishment and the quantitative reading of interests; it also has the advantage that, by assuming the form of a natural sequence, punishment does not appear as the arbitrary effect of a human power: 'To derive the offence from the punishment is the best means of proportioning punishment to crime. If this is the triumph of justice, it is also the triumph of liberty, for then penalties no longer proceed from the will of the legislator, but from the nature of things; one no longer sees man committing violence on man' (Marat, 33). In analogical punishment, the power that punishes is hidden.

The reformers proposed a whole panoply of penalties that were natural by institution and which represented in their form the content of the crime. Take Vermeil, for example: those who abuse public liberty will be deprived of their own; those who abuse the benefits of law and the privileges of public office will be deprived of their civil rights; speculation and usury will be punished by fines; theft will be punished by confiscation; 'vainglory' by humiliation; murder by death; fire-raising by the stake. In the case of the poisoner, 'the executioner will present him with a goblet the contents of which will be thrown into his face; thus he will be made to feel the horror of his crime by being offered an image of it; he will then be thrown into a cauldron of boiling water' (Vermeil, 68–145; cf. also Dufriche de Valazé, 349) Mere day-dreaming? Perhaps. But the principle of a symbolic communication was clearly formulated by Le Peletier, when in 1791 he presented the new criminal legislation: 'Exact relations are required between the nature of the offence and the nature of the punishment'; he who has used violence in his crime must be subjected to physical pain; he who has been lazy must be sentenced to hard labour; he who has acted despicably will be subjected to infamy (Le Peletier, 321–2).

Despite cruelties that are strongly reminiscent of the tortures of the Ancien Régime, a quite different mechanism is at work in these analogical penalties. Horror is not opposed to horror in a joust of power; it is no longer the symmetry of vengeance, but the transparency of the sign to that which it signifies; what is required is to establish, in the theatre of punishments, a relation that is immediately intelligible to the senses and on which a simple calculation may be based: a sort of reasonable aesthetic of punishment. 'It is not only in the fine arts that one must follow nature faithfully; political institutions, at least those that display wisdom and permanence, are founded on nature' (Beccaria, 114). The punishment must proceed from the crime; the law must appear to be a necessity of things, and power must act while concealing itself beneath the gentle force of nature.

2. This complex of signs must engage with the mechanics of forces: reduce the desire that makes the crime attractive; increase the interest that makes the penalty be feared; reverse the relation of intensities, so that the representation of the penalty and its disadvantages is more lively than that of the crime and its pleasures. There is a whole mechanics, therefore, of interest, of its movement, of the way that one represents it to oneself and of the liveliness of this representation. 'The legislator must be a skilful architect who knows how to employ all the forces that may contribute to the solidity of the building and reduce all those that might ruin it' (Beccaria, 135).

There are several ways of achieving this. 'Go straight to the source of evil' (Mably, 246). Smash the mainspring that animates the representation of the crime. Weaken the interest that brought it to birth. Behind the offences of the vagabond, there is laziness; that is what one must fight against. 'One will not succeed by locking beggars up in filthy prisons that are more like cesspools'; they will have to be forced to work. 'The best way of punishing them is to employ them' (Brissot, 258). Against a bad passion, a good habit; against a force, another force, but it must be the force of sensibility and passion, not that of armed power. 'Must one not deduce all penalties from this principle, which is so simple, so appropriate and already well known, namely, to choose them in that which is most subduing for the passion that led to the crime committed?' (Lacretelle, 361).

Set the force that drove the criminal to the crime against itself. Divide interest, use it to make the penalty something to be feared.

Let the punishment irritate it and stimulate it more than the crime was able to flatter it. If pride led to the committing of a crime, let it be hurt, let the punishment disgust it. Shameful punishments are effective because they are based on the vanity that was at the root of the crime. Fanatics glory both in their opinions and in the tortures that they endure for them. Let us, therefore, set against fanaticism the proud obstinacy that sustains it: 'Reduce it with ridicule and shame; if one humiliates the proud vanity of fanatics before a great crowd of spectators, one may expect happy effects from this punishment.' It would be quite useless, on the other hand, to impose physical pain on them. (Beccaria, 113).

Reanimate the useful, virtuous interest that has been so weakened by the crime. The feeling of respect for property – for wealth, but also for honour, liberty, life – this the criminal loses when he robs, calumniates, abducts or kills. So he must be taught this feeling once again. And one will begin by teaching it to him for his own benefit; one will show him what it is to lose the freedom to dispose as one wishes of one's own wealth, honour, time and body, so that he may respect it in others (Pastoret, I, 49). The penalty that forms stable and easily legible signs must also recompose the economy of interests and the dynamics of passions.

3. Consequently, one must use a temporal modulation. The penalty transforms, modifies, establishes signs, arranges obstacles. What use would it be if it had to be permanent? A penalty that had no end would be contradictory: all the constraints that it imposes on the convict and of which, having become virtuous once more, he would never be able to take advantage, would be little better than torture; and the effort made to reform him would be so much trouble and expense lost by society. If incorrigibles there be, one must be determined to eliminate them. But, for all the others, punishment can function only if it comes to an end. This analysis was accepted by the Constituent Assembly: the code of 1791 lays down the death penalty for traitors and murderers; all other penalties must have an end (the maximum is twenty years).

But above all the role of duration must be integrated into the economy of the penalty. In its very violence, the public execution tended to have the following result: the more serious the crime, the shorter the punishment. Duration certainly intervened in the old system of penalties; days at the pillory, years of banishment, hours spent dying on the wheel. But it was a time of ordeal, not of concerted transformation. Duration must now facilitate the proper action of the punishment: 'A prolonged succession of painful privations, sparing mankind the horror of torture, has much more effect on the guilty party than a passing moment of pain. . . It constantly renews in the eyes of the people that witness it the memory of vengeful laws and revives in all the moments of a salutary terror.'[1] Time, operator of punishment.

But the delicate mechanism of the passions must not be constrained in the same way or with the same insistence when they begin to improve; the punishment should diminish as it produces its effects. It may well be fixed, in the sense that it is determined for all, in the same way, by law, but its internal mechanism must be variable. In the bill put before the Constituent Assembly, Le Peletier proposed a system of diminishing penalties: a convict condemned to the most serious penalty would be subjected to the '*cachot*' (manacles on hands and feet, darkness, solitude, bread and water) only during the first stage of his imprisonment; he would be allowed to work first two then three days a week. After two thirds of his sentence had been served, he could pass to the '*gêne*' (a cell with light, chain around the waist, solitary work for five hours a day, but with other prisoners on the other two days; this work would be paid and would enable him to improve his daily fare). Lastly, when he approached the end of his sentence, he could pass to the normal prison régime: 'He will be allowed every day to meet other prisoners for work in common. If he prefers, he will be able to work alone. He will pay for his food from what he earns from his work' (Le Peletier, 329–30).

4. For the convict, the penalty is a mechanics of signs, interests and duration. But the guilty person is only one of the targets of punishment. For punishment is directed above all at others, at all the potentially guilty. So these obstacle-signs that are gradually engraved in the representation of the condemned man must therefore circulate rapidly and widely; they must be accepted and redistributed by all; they must shape the discourse that each individual has with others and by which crime is forbidden to all by all – the true coin that is substituted in people's minds for the false profits of crime.

For this, everyone must see punishment not only as natural, but in his own interest; everyone must be able to read in it his own advantage. There must be no more spectacular, but useless penalties. There must be no secret penalties either; but punishment must be regarded as a retribution that the guilty man makes to each of his fellow citizens, for the crime that has wronged them all – penalties that are constantly placed before citizens' eyes, and which 'bring out the public utility of common and particular *movements*' (Dufriche de Valazé, 346). The ideal would be for the convict to appear as a sort of rentable property: a slave at the service of all. Why would society eliminate a life and a body that it could appropriate? It would be more useful to make him 'serve the state in a slavery that would be more or less extended according to the nature of his crime'; France has all too many impracticable roads that impede trade; thieves who also obstruct the free circulation of goods could be put to rebuilding the highways. Far more telling than death would be 'the example of a man who is ever before one's eyes, whom one has deprived of liberty and who is forced to spend the rest of his days repairing the loss that he has caused society' (Boucher d'Argis, 1781, 139).

In the old system, the body of the condemned man became the king's property, on which the sovereign left his mark and brought down the effects of his power. Now he will be rather the property of society, the object of a collective and useful appropriation. This explains why the reformers almost always proposed public works as one of the best possible penalties; in this, they were supported by the *Cahiers de doléances*: 'Let those condemned to penalties short of death be put to the public works of the country for a time proportionate to their crime.'[2] Public works meant two things: the collective interest in the punishment of the condemend man and the visible, verifiable character of the punishment. Thus the convict pays twice; by the labour he provides and by the signs that he produces. At the heart of society, on the public squares or highways, the convict is a focus of profit and signification. Visibly, he is serving everyone; but, at the same time, he lets slip into the minds of all the crime-punishment sign: a secondary, purely moral, but much more real utility.

5. Hence a whole learned economy of publicity. In physical

torture, the example was based on terror: physical fear, collective horror, images that must be engraved on the memories of the spectators, like the brand on the cheek or shoulder of the condemned man. The example is now based on the lesson, the discourse, the decipherable sign, the representation of public morality. It is no longer the terrifying restoration of sovereignty that will sustain the ceremony of punishment, but the reactivation of the code, the collective reinforcements of the link between the idea of crime and the idea of punishment. In the penalty, rather than seeing the presence of the sovereign, one will read the laws themselves. The laws associated a particular crime with a particular punishment. As soon as the crime is committed, the punishment will follow at once, enacting the discourse of the law and showing that the code, which links ideas, also links realities. The junction, immediate in the text, must be immediate in acts. 'Consider those first movements in which the news of some horrible act spreads through our towns and countryside; the citizens are like men who see lightning falling about them; everyone is moved by indignation and horror. . . That is the moment to punish the crime: do not let it slip by; hasten to prove it and judge it. Set up scaffolds, stakes, drag out the guilty man to the public squares, summon the people with great cries; you will then hear them applaud the proclamation of your judgements, as the proclamation of peace and liberty; you will see them run to these terrible spectacles as to the triumph of the laws' (Servan, 35–6). Public punishment is the ceremony of immediate recoding.

The law is re-formed: it takes up its place on the side of the crime that violated it. The criminal, on the other hand, is detached from society, he leaves it. But not in those ambiguous festivals of the Ancien Régime in which the people inevitably took part, either in the crime or in the execution, but in a ceremony of mourning. The society that has rediscovered its laws has lost the citizen who violated them. Public punishment must manifest this double affliction: that a citizen should have been capable of ignoring the law and that one should have been obliged to separate oneself from a citizen. 'Associate the scaffold with the most lugubrious and most moving ceremonies; let this terrible day be a day of mourning for the nation; let the general sorrow be painted everywhere in bold letters. . . Let the magistrate, wearing black, funereal crêpe, announce the crime and the sad necessity of a legal vengeance to the people. Let the different scenes of this tragedy strike all the senses, stir all gentle, honest affections' (Dufau, 688).

The meaning of this mourning must be clear to all; each element of its ritual must speak, repeat the crime, recall the law, show the need for punishment and justify its degree. Posters, placards, signs, symbols must be distributed, so that everyone may learn their significations. The publicity of punishment must not have the physical effect of terror; it must open up a book to be read. Le Peletier suggested that, once a month, the people should be allowed to visit convicts, 'in their mournful cells: they will read, written in bold letters above the door, the name of the convict, his crime and his sentence' (Le Peletier, 329–30). And in the simple, military style of the imperial ceremonies, Bexon was to imagine some years later a whole tableau of penal heraldry: 'The prisoner condemned to death will be taken to the scaffold in a cart "hung or painted in black and red"; if he is a traitor, he will wear a red coat on which will be inscribed, in front and behind, the word "traitor"; if he is a parricide, his head will be covered with a black veil and on his shirt will be embroidered daggers or whatever instruments of death he used; if he is a poisoner, his red shirt will be decorated with snakes and other venomous animals' (Bexon, 24–5 – this project was presented to the King of Bavaria).

This legible lesson, this ritual recoding, must be repeated as often as possible; the punishments must be a school rather than a festival; an ever-open book rather than a ceremony. The duration that makes the punishment effective for the guilty is also useful for the spectators. They must be able to consult at each moment the permanent lexicon of crime and punishment. A secret punishment is a punishment half wasted. Children should be allowed to come to the places where the penalty is being carried out; there they will attend their classes in civics. And grown men will periodically relearn the laws. Let us conceive of places of punishment as a Garden of the Laws that families would visit on Sundays. 'I propose that, from time to time, after preparing people's minds with a reasoned discourse on the preservation of the social order, on the utility of punishment, men as well as boys should be taken to the mines and to the work camps and contemplate the frightful fate of these outlaws. Such pilgrimages would be more useful than the pilgrimages made by the Turks to Mecca' (Brissot). And Le Peletier considered that this visibility of punishment was one of the fundamental principles of the new penal code: 'Often, at certain special times, the presence of the people must bring down shame upon the heads of the guilty; and the presence of the guilty person in the pitiful state to which his crime has reduced him must bring useful instruction to the souls of the people' (Le Peletier, 322). Long before he was regarded as an object of science, the criminal was imagined as a source of instruction. Once one made charitable visits to prisoners to share in their sufferings (the seventeenth century had invented or revived this practice); now it was being suggested that children should come and learn how the benefits of the law are applied to crime – a living lesson in the museum of order.

6. This will make possible in society an inversion of the traditional discourse of crime. How can one extinguish the dubious glory of the criminal? This was a matter of grave concern to the lawmakers of the eighteenth century. How can one silence the adventures of the great criminals celebrated in the almanacs, broadsheets and popular tales? If the recoding of punishment is well done, if the ceremony of mourning takes place as it should, the crime can no longer appear as anything but a misfortune and the criminal as an enemy who must be re-educated into social life. Instead of those songs of praise that turn the criminal into a hero, only those obstacle-signs that arrest the desire to commit the crime by the calculated fear of punishment will circulate in men's discourse. The positive mechanics will operate to the full in the language of every day, which will constantly reinforce it with new accounts. Discourse will become the vehicle of the law: the constant principle of universal recoding. The poets of the people will at last join those who call themselves the 'missionaries of eternal reason'; they will become moralists. 'Filled with these terrible images and salutary ideas, each citizen will spread them through his family and there, by long accounts delivered with as much fervour as they are avidly listened to, his children gathered around him, will open up their young memories to receive, in imperishable lineaments, the notion of crime and punishment, the love of law and country, the respect and trust of the magistrature. Country people, too, will be witnesses of

these examples and will sow them around their huts, the taste of virtue will take root in these coarse souls, while the evil-doer, dismayed at the public joy, fearful at the sight of so many enemies, may abandon plans whose outcome will be as prompt as it is gloomy' (Servan, 37).

This, then, is how one must imagine the punitive city. At the crossroads, in the gardens, at the side of roads being repaired or bridges built, in workshops open to all, in the depths of mines that may be visited, will be hundreds of tiny theatres of punishment. Each crime will have its law; each criminal his punishment. It will be a visible punishment, a punishment that tells all, that explains, justifies itself, convicts: placards, different-coloured caps bearing inscriptions, posters, symbols, texts read or printed, tirelessly repeat the code. Scenery, perspectives, optical effects, *trompe-l'œil* sometimes magnify the scene, making it more fearful than it is, but also clearer. From where the public is sitting, it is possible to believe in the existence of certain cruelties which, in fact, do not take place. But the essential point, in all these real or magnified severities, is that they should all, according to a strict economy, teach a lesson: that each punishment should be a fable. And that, in counterpoint with all the direct examples of virtue, one may at each moment encounter, as a living spectacle, the misfortunes of vice. Around each of these moral 'representations', schoolchildren will gather with their masters and adults will learn what lessons to teach their offspring. The great terrifying ritual of the public execution gives way, day after day, street after street, to this serious theatre, with its multifarious and persuasive scenes. And popular memory will reproduce in rumour the austere discourse of the law. But perhaps it will be necessary, above these innumerable spectacles and narratives, to place the major sign of punishment for the most terrible of crimes: the keystone of the penal edifice. In any case, Vermeil had imagined the scene of absolute punishment that should dominate all the theatres of everyday punishment: the only case in which one had to seek to reach an infinity of punishment, something equivalent in the new penal system to what regicide had been in the old. The man found guilty of this crime would have his eyes put out; he would be put into an iron cage, suspended in the air, above a public square; he would be completely naked; he would be attached to the bars of the cage by an iron belt around his waist; to the end of his days, he would be fed on bread and water. 'Thus he would be exposed to all the rigours of the seasons, sometimes his head would be covered with snow, sometimes burnt by a scorching sun. It is in this energetic torture, presenting rather the extension of a painful death than that of a painful life, that one would truly recognize a villain deserving of the horror of nature in its entirety, condemned to see no longer the heaven that he has outraged and to live no longer on the earth that he has sullied' (Vermeil, 148–9). Above the punitive city hangs this iron spider; and the criminal who is to be thus crucified by the new law is the parricide.

There is a whole new arsenal of picturesque punishments. 'Avoid inflicting the same punishments,' said Mably. The idea of a uniform penalty, modulated only according to the gravity of the crime is banished. To be more precise: the use of imprisonment as a general form of punishment is never presented in these projects for specific, visible and 'telling' penalties. Imprisonment is envisaged, but as one among other penalties; it is the specific punishment for certain offences, those that infringe the liberty of individuals (such as abduction) or those that result from an abuse of liberty (disorder, violence). It is also envisaged as a condition to enable certain punishments to be carried out (forced labour, for example). But it does not cover the whole field of penality with its duration as the sole principle of variation. Or rather, the idea of penal imprisonment is explicitly criticized by many reformers. Because it is incapable of corresponding to the specificity of crimes. Because it has no effect on the public. Because it is useless, even harmful, to society: it is costly, it maintains convicts in idleness, it multiplies their vices (cf. *Archives parlementaires*, XXVI, 712). Because the execution of such a penalty is difficult to supervise and because there is a risk of exposing prisoners to the arbitrary will of their guards. Because the job of depriving a man of his liberty and of supervising him is an exercise of tyranny. 'You are demanding that there should be monsters among you; and if these odious men existed, the legislator ought perhaps to treat them as murderers' (Mably, 338). Prison as the universal penalty is incompatible with this whole technique of penalty-effect, penalty-representation, penalty-general function, penalty-sign and discourse. It is obscurity, violence and suspicion. 'It is a place of darkness in which the citizen's eye cannot count the victims, in which consequently their number is lost as an example. . . . Whereas if, without multiplying crimes, one could multiply the example of punishments, one would succeed at last in rendering them less necessary; indeed, the obscurity of the prisons becomes a subject of defiance for the citizens; they easily suppose that great injustices are committed there. . . There is certainly something wrong when the law, which is made for the good of the multitude, instead of arousing its gratitude, continually arouses its discontent' (Dufriche de Valazé, 344–5).

The idea that imprisonment might as it does today cover the whole middle ground of punishment, between death and light penalties, was one that the reformers could not arrive at immediately.

The problem is the following: within a short space of time, detention became the essential form of punishment. In the penal code of 1810, between death and fines, it occupies, in a number of forms, almost the whole field of possible punishments. 'What is the system of penality accepted by the new law? It is incarceration in all its forms. Indeed, compare the four principal penalties that remain in the penal code. Forced labour is a form of incarceration. The convict-ship is an open-air prison. Detention, reclusion, imprisonment for a minor offence are in a sense merely different names for one and the same punishment' (Rémusat, 185). And the Empire decided at once to translate this imprisonment, envisaged by the law, into reality, according to a whole penal, administrative, geographical hierarchy; at the lowest degree, associated with each justice of the peace, municipal *maisons de police*; in each arrondissement, *maisons d'arrêt*; in each département, a *maison de correction*; at the summit, several *maisons centrales* for convicted criminals or *correctionels* serving sentences of over one year; lastly, in a few ports, convict-ships. A great prison structure was planned, whose different levels would correspond exactly to the levels of the centralized administration. The scaffold, where the body of the tortured criminal had been exposed to the ritually manifested force of the sovereign, the punitive theatre in which the representation of punishment was permanently available to the social body, was replaced by a great enclosed, complex and hierarchized structure that was integrated into the very body of the state apparatus. A quite different materiality, a quite different physics of power, a quite different way of investing men's bodies had emerged. During the Restoration and the July monarchy, there were, apart from a few exceptional moments, between 40,000 and 43,000 prisoners in French gaols (approximately one prisoner per 600 inhabitants). The high wall, no longer the wall that surrounds and protects, no longer the wall that stands for power and wealth, but the meticulously sealed wall, uncrossable in either direction, closed in upon the now mysterious work of punishment, will become, near at hand, sometimes even at the very centre of the cities of the nineteenth century, the monotonous figure, at once material and symbolic, of the power to punish. Already under the Consulate, the Minister of the Interior had been appointed to investigate the different 'places of safety' that were already functioning and which could be used in different towns. A few years later, sums had been allocated for the construction, in keeping with the power that they were to represent and serve, of these new castles of the new civil order. The empire used them in fact, for another war (cf. Decazes). A less extravagant, but more obstinate economy continued to build them throughout the nineteenth century.

In under twenty years, in any case, the principle so clearly formulated in the Constituent Assembly, of specific, appropriate, effective penalties, constituting, in each case, a lesson for all, became the law of detention for every offence of any importance, except those requiring the death penalty. The theatre of punishment of which the eighteenth century dreamed and which would have acted essentially on the minds of the general public was replaced by the great uniform machinery of the prisons, whose network of immense buildings was to extend across France and Europe. But twenty years is perhaps too long a chronology for this conjuring trick. It may be argued that it occurred almost instantaneously. One has only to look at the bill for the criminal code presented in the Constituent Assembly by Le Peletier. The principle stated at the outset is the need for 'exact relations between the nature of the offence and the nature of the punishment': physical pain should be inflicted on those who commit crimes of violence, hard labour on the idle, shame on those with degraded souls. But the severe penalties actually proposed are three forms of detention: the '*cachot*', in which the penalty of imprisonment is augmented by various measures (solitude, a deprivation of light, restrictions on food); the'*gêne*', in which these ancillary measures are attenuated, and lastly imprisonment proper, which is reduced to simple confinement. The diversity, so solemnly promised, is reduced in the end to this grey, uniform penalty. Indeed, at the time, there were deputies who expressed surprise that, instead of establishing a natural relation between offences and penalties, a quite different plan had been adopted: 'So that if I have betrayed my country, I go to prison; if I have killed my father, I go to prison; every imaginable offence is punished in the same uniform way. One might as well see a physician who has the same remedy for all ills' (Chabroud, 618).

This prompt substitution was not confined to France. It was to be found, to a greater or lesser degree, in other countries. When Catherine II, in the years immediately following the treatise *Des délits et des peines*, gave instructions to the commission entrusted with the task of drawing up a 'new code of laws', Beccaria's lesson on the specificity and variety of penalties was not forgotten; it was repeated almost word for word: 'It is a triumph of civil liberty when the criminal laws derive each penalty from the particular nature of each crime. In this way all arbitrariness ceases; the penalty does not depend on the caprice of the legislator, but on the nature of the thing; it is not man who does violence to man, but the man's own action' (article 67). A few years later, Beccaria's general principle served as a foundation for the new Tuscan Code and for the new code given by Joseph II to Austria; and yet both legislations made imprisonment – modulated according to its duration and augmented in certain cases by branding or the use of irons – an almost uniform penalty: at least thirty years' detention for an attempt on the sovereign's life, for counterfeiting and for murder with robbery; fifteen to thirty years for voluntary homicide or armed robbery; one month to five years for simple theft, etc.[3]

But if this colonization of the penalty by the prison is surprising, it is because imprisonment was not, as one might imagine, a punishment that was already securely established in the penal system, just below the death penalty, and which naturally occupied the place left vacant by the disappearance of public torture. In fact, imprisonment

– and on this point many countries were in the same situation as France – had only a limited and marginal position in the system of penalties. This is shown by the texts themselves. The ordinance of 1670 does not include detention among the *peines afflictives*, or serious penalties. Perpetual or temporary imprisonment was no doubt included among certain local customs and practices (cf., for example, Coquille). But contemporary writers maintained that it was falling into disuse together with other forms of torture: 'There were formerly penalties that are no longer practised in France, such as writing a condemned man's penalty on his face or forehead and perpetual imprisonment, just as one no longer condemns a criminal to be exposed to wild beasts or sent down the mines' (Rousseaud de la Combe, 3). In fact, it is certain that imprisonment had survived tenaciously as a punishment for less serious offences, according to local customs and practices. In this sense, Soulatges spoke of the 'light penalties' that the ordinance of 1670 had not mentioned: reprimand, admonition, banishment from a certain place, satisfaction to the injured party and a term of imprisonment. In certain regions, especially those that had most preserved their legal peculiarities, the penalty of imprisonment was still widespread, but this had its difficulties, as in the recently annexed province of Roussillon.

Yet, despite these divergencies, jurists held firmly to the principle that 'imprisonment is not to be regarded as a penalty in our civil law' (Serpillon, 1095 – however, one does find in Serpillon the idea that the rigour of imprisonment is the beginning of a penalty). Its role is rather that of holding the person and his body as security: *ad continendos homines, non ad puniendos*, as the tag has it; in this sense, the imprisonment of a suspect has a role similar to that of a debtor. Through imprisonment, one has security for someone, one does not punish him.[4] This was the general principle. And although imprisonment sometimes served as a penalty, even in important cases, it did so essentially as a substitute: it replaced the galleys for those – women, children, invalids – who could not serve there: 'The sentence of imprisonment for a term or for life is equivalent to being sent to the galleys.'[5] In this equivalence, one can see clearly enough the emergence of a possible connection. But, for this to take place, the prison had to change its juridical status.

It was also necessary to overcome a second obstacle, which, for

France at least, was a considerable one. Imprisonment was especially disqualified for this role by the fact that it was, in practice, directly bound up with arbitrary royal decision and the excesses of the sovereign power. The '*maisons de force*', the general hospitals, the 'king's orders' or the orders of the police magistrates, letters under the king's private seal obtained by notables or by families, constituted a whole repressive practice, juxtaposed with 'regular justice' and more usually opposed to it. And this extra-judicial imprisonment came to be rejected by both classical jurists and reformers. Prisons are made by princes, said a traditionalist like Serpillon, who sheltered behind the authority of Judge Bouhier: 'Although, for reasons of state, princes are sometimes inclined to inflict this penalty, ordinary justice makes no use of this kind of sentence' (Serpillon, 1095). Detention was described by the reformers in innumerable statements as a figure and privileged instrument of despotism: 'What is one to say of those secret prisons conjured up by the fatal spirit of monarchism, reserved in the main either for philosophers, in whose hands nature has placed her torch and who dared to enlighten their century, or for those proud independent souls who lack the cowardice to keep silent on the ills of their country; prisons whose gloomy doors are opened by mysterious letters and swallow up forever its unfortunate victims? What is to be said even of those letters, those masterpieces of ingenious tyranny, which overthrow the privilege of every citizen to be heard before he is judged, and which are a thousand times more dangerous for men than the invention of Phalaris . . .'[6] (Brissot, 173).

No doubt these protests, coming from such diverse sources, are directed not at imprisonment as a legal penalty, but at the 'illegal' use of arbitrary, indeterminate detention. Nevertheless, imprisonment was seen, generally speaking, as branded by the abuses of power. And many *cahiers de doléances* rejected it as incompatible with good justice. Sometimes in the name of classical juridical principles: 'Prisons were intended by the law not to punish but to secure the persons of the offenders . . .' (Desjardin, 477). Sometimes in the name of the effects of imprisonment, which punishes those who have not yet been convicted, which communicates and generalizes the evil that it ought to prevent, and which runs counter to the principle of the individuality of penalties by punishing a whole family; it was said that 'imprisonment is not a penalty. Humanity rises up against the frightful thought that it is not a punishment to deprive a citizen of his most precious possession, to plunge him ignominiously into the den of crime, to snatch him from everything that is dear to him, to bring him perhaps to ruin and to deprive not only him but his unfortunate family of all means of subsistence' (Desjardin, 483). And, on several occasions, the *cahiers* demanded the abolition of those 'houses of internment': 'We believe that the *maisons de force* must be razed to the ground. . .'[7] And the decree of 13 March 1790 ordered the freeing of 'all persons detained in castles, religious houses, *maisons de force*, *maisons de police* or any other prisons, by orders under the king's private seal or by orders of the agents of the executive power'.

How then could detention, so evidently bound up with an illegality that was denounced even in the power of the prince, become in so short a time one of the most general forms of legal punishment?

The explanation most usually given is the formation, during the classical age, of a number of great models of punitive imprisonment. Their prestige, which was all the greater in that the most recent examples came from England and above all from America, appears to have made it possible to overcome the double obstacle constituted by the age-old rules of law and the despotic functioning of imprisonment. Very soon, it seems, these obstacles were swept away by the punitive marvels thought up by the reformers, and detention became a serious reality. There can be no doubt about the importance of these models. But it is precisely these models that, before providing a solution, themselves pose problems: the problem of their existence and the problem of their diffusion. How were they able to come into being and, above all, how did they become so generally accepted? For it is easy to show that, although they correspond on a number of points with the general principles of penal reform, they fail to do so on an even greater number; sometimes they are even quite incompatible.

The oldest of these models, the one that is generally regarded as having more or less inspired all the others, was the Rasphuis of Amsterdam, opened in 1596.[8] Originally, it was intended for beggars or young malefactors. Its functioning obeyed three great principles: the duration of the penalties could, at least within certain limits, be determined by the administration itself, according to the prisoner's conduct (indeed this latitude could be given in the sentence itself: in 1597 a prisoner was condemned to twelve years' imprisonment, which could be reduced to eight, if his behaviour proved satisfactory). Work was obligatory; it was performed in common (indeed the individual cell was used only as an additional punishment; prisoners slept two or three to a bed, in cells containing between four and twelve persons); and, for the work done, the prisoners received wages. A strict time-table, a system of prohibitions and obligations, continual supervision, exhortations, religious readings, a whole complex of methods 'to draw towards good' and 'to turn away from evil' held the prisoners in its grip from day to day. One may take the Rasphuis of Amsterdam as a basic figure. Historically, it forms the link between the theory, so characteristic of the sixteenth century, of a pedagogical and spiritual transformation of individuals brought about by continuous exercise, and the penitentiary techniques conceived in the second half of the eighteenth century. And it provided the three institutions that were then set up with the fundamental principles that each was to develop in its own particular direction.

The *maison de force* at Ghent organized penal labour above all around economic imperatives. The reason given was that idleness was the general cause of most crimes. An investigation – no doubt one of the first – carried out among those sentenced under the jurisdiction of Alost, in 1749, showed that malefactors were not 'artisans or labourers' (workers think only of the work that feeds them), but 'idlers given up to begging'.[9] Hence the idea of a house that would in a sense provide a universal pedagogy of work for those who had proved to be resistant to it. This had four advantages: it reduced the number of criminal prosecutions, which were costly to the state (it was estimated that this would save over 100,000 pounds in Flanders); this would make it unnecessary to return money paid in taxes to the owners of woods ruined by vagabonds; it would create a mass of new workers, which would help 'by competition to bring down the cost of labour'; lastly, it would enable the true poor to benefit, to the full, from necessary charity (Vilan, 68).

This useful pedagogy would revive for the lazy individual a liking for work, force him back into a system of interests in which labour would be more advantageous than laziness, form around him a small, miniature, simplified, coercive society in which the maxim, 'he who wants to live must work', would be clearly revealed. Work would be compulsory, but so too would be remuneration, which enables the prisoner to improve his lot during and after detention. 'The man who does not find his subsistence must be made to desire to procure it for himself by work; he is offered it by supervision and discipline; in a sense, he is forced to acquire it; he is then tempted by the bait of gain; corrected in his morals, accustomed to work, his anxiety aroused by the little money he has kept for his release,' he has learned a trade 'that will guarantee a subsistence without danger' (Vilan, 107). This reconstruction of *homo oeconomicus* excluded the use of penalties that were too short – this would prevent the acquisition of habits and skills of work – or too long – which would make any apprenticeship useless. 'The term of six months is too short to correct criminals, and to bring them to the spirit of work'; on the other hand, 'a life sentence throws them into despair; they become indifferent to the correction of their morals and to the spirit of work; they become concerned only with plans to escape and to rebel; and since the judgements that were passed on them did not deprive them of life, why should one seek to render it unbearable for them?' (Vilan, 102–3). The duration of the penalty has meaning only in relation to possible correction, and to an economic use of the corrected criminal.

To the principle of work, the English models added, as an essential addition to correction, isolation. The outlines had been provided in 1775, by Hanway, who justified it first with negative reasons: promiscuity in the prison provided bad examples and possibilities of escape in the short term and of blackmail or complicity in the long term. The prison would be too much like a factory if one left the prisoners to work together. The positive reasons followed: isolation provides a 'terrible shock' which, while protecting the prisoner from bad influences, enables him to go into himself and rediscover in the depths of his conscience the voice of good; solitary work would then become not only an apprenticeship, but also an exercise in spiritual conversion; it would rearrange not only the complex of interests proper to *homo oeconomicus*, but also the imperatives of the moral subject. The cell, that technique of Christian monachism, which had survived only in Catholic countries, becomes in this protestant society the instrument by which one may reconstitute both *homo oeconomicus* and the religious conscience. Between the crime and the return to right and virtue, the prison would constitute the 'space between two worlds' the place for the individual transformation that would restore to the state the subject it had lost. Hanway called this apparatus for modifying individuals a 'reformatory' (cf. Hanway). These were the general principles that Howard and Blackstone put into operation in 1779 when the independence of the United States put an end to deportation and when a law was being drawn up to modify the system of penalties. Imprisonment, with the purpose of transforming the soul and conduct, made its entry into the system of civil laws. The preamble of the bill, written by Blackstone and Howard, describes individual imprisonment in terms of its triple function as example to be feared, instrument of conversion and condition for an apprenticeship: subjected 'to isolated detention, regular work and the influence of religious instruction', certain criminals might not only inspire terror in those who would be tempted to imitate them, 'but also to correct themselves and to acquire the habit of work' (Preamble of the bill of 1779). Hence the decision to build two penitentiaries, one for men, one for women, in which the isolated prisoners would be put 'to the most servile labours, most compatible with the ignorance, negligence and obstinacy of the criminals': walking in a wheel to move a machine, fixing a winch, polishing marble, beating hemp, rasping logwood, cutting up rags, rope-making and sewing sacks. In fact, only one penitentiary was built, at Gloucester, and it corresponded only partially to the initial plan: total confinement for the most dangerous criminals; for the others, day work in common and separation at night.

Then came the Philadelphia model. This was no doubt the most famous because it was associated in people's minds with the political innovations of the American system and also because it was not, like the others, doomed to immediate failure and abandonment; it was continuously re-examined and transformed right up to the great debates of the 1830s on penitentiary reform. In many respects the Walnut Street Prison, opened in 1790, under the direct influence of the Quakers, was modelled on those of Ghent and Gloucester.[10] There was compulsory work in workshops; the prisoners were kept constantly occupied; the prison was financed by this work, but the prisoners were also rewarded individually as a way of reinserting them morally and materially into the strict world of the economy; by keeping the prisoners 'constantly employed on productive works, they were able to defray the expenses of the prison, they were not left idle and they were able to save a little money for the time when their captivity would cease' (La Rochefoucauld-Liancourt, 9). Life was partitioned, therefore, according to an absolutely strict time-table, under constant supervision; each moment of the day was devoted to a particular type of activity, and brought with it its own obligations and prohibitions: 'All prisoners rise at daybreak, so that, after making their beds, cleaning and washing themselves and attending to other needs, they generally begin their work at sunrise. From that moment, no one may go into the rooms or other places except to the workshops and places assigned for their work. . . . At nightfall, a bell rings to mark the end of their work. . . They are given half an hour to arrange their beds, after which they are not allowed to converse aloud or to make the least noise' (Turnbull, 15–16). As at Gloucester, solitary confinement was not total; it was used for certain prisoners who would in former times have incurred the death penalty, and for those inside the prison who deserved special punishment: 'There, without occupation, without anything to distract him, waiting in uncertainty for the moment when he would be delivered', the prisoner spent 'long anxious hours, with nothing but the reflections that are present to the minds of all guilty persons' (Teeters, 1935, 49). Lastly, as at Ghent, the length of the imprisonment could vary with the behaviour of the prisoner: after consulting the files, the prison inspectors obtained from the authorities – without much difficulty up to the 1820s – pardons for prisoners who had shown good behaviour.

Furthermore, Walnut Street had a number of characteristics that were specific to it, or which at least developed what was potentially present in the other models. First, the principle of not publicizing the penalty. Though the sentence and the reasons for it should be known to all, the penalty should be carried out in secret; the public was to intervene neither as a witness, nor as a guarantor of punishment; the certainty that, behind the walls, the prisoner was serving his sentence must suffice as an example: there were to be no more of those street spectacles which the law of 1786 has given rise to by imposing on certain prisoners public works to be carried out in towns and on the highways.[11] The punishment and correction that it must operate are processes that unfold between the prisoner and those who supervise him. They are processes that effect a transformation of the individual as a whole – of his body and of his habits by the daily work that he is forced to perform, of his mind and his will by the spiritual attentions that are paid to him: 'Bibles and other books of religious practice are provided; the clergy of the different obediences to be found in the town and suburbs perform the services once a week and any other edifying person may have access to the prisoners at any time' (Teeters, 1935, 53–4). But this transformation is entrusted to the administration itself. Solitude and self-examination are not enough; nor are purely religious exhortations. Work on the prisoner's soul must be carried out as often as possible. The prison, though an administrative apparatus, will at the same time be a machine for altering minds. On first entering the prison, the prisoner will be read the regulations; 'at the same time, the inspectors seek to strengthen in him the moral obligations that he now has; they represent to him the offence that he has committed with regard to them, the evil that has consequently resulted for the society that protected him and the need to make compensation by his example and his amendment. They then make him promise to do his duty gladly, to behave decently, promising him or allowing him to hope that, before the expiration of the term of the sentence, he will be able to obtain his discharge if he behaves well. . . From time to time the inspectors make it their duty to converse with the criminals one after the other, concerning their duties as men and as members of society' (Turnbull, 27).

But no doubt the most important thing was that this control and transformation of behaviour were accompanied – both as a condition and as a consequence – by the development of a knowledge of the individuals. When the new prisoner arrived, the Walnut Street administration received a report concerning his crime, the circumstances in which it was committed, a summary of the examinations of the defendant, notes on his behaviour before and after sentence: indispensable elements if one wished to 'decide what steps will have to be taken to destroy his old habits'.[12] And throughout his detention he would be observed; his conduct would be noted daily and the inspectors – twelve local worthies appointed in 1795 – who, two by two, visited the prison each week, would be kept informed of events, follow the conduct of each prisoner and decide which of them deserved a shortening of his term. This ever-growing knowledge of the individuals made it possible to divide them up in the prison not so much according to their crimes as according to the dispositions that they revealed. The prison became a sort of permanent observatory that made it possible to distribute the varieties of vice or weakness. From 1797, the prisoners were divided into four classes: the first for those who were explicitly condemned to solitary confinement or who had committed serious offences in the prison; the second for those who were 'well known as old offenders . . . whose depraved morality, dangerous character, irregular dispositions, or disorderly conduct' became apparent during the time they were in prison; the third for those 'whose character and circumstances, before and after conviction, led one to believe that they were not habitual offenders'; the fourth and last was a special section, a probationary class for those whose character was still not known, or who, if they were better known, did not deserve to be put in the preceding category (Teeters, 1935, 59). A whole corpus of individualizing knowledge was being organized that took as its field of reference not so much the crime committed (at least in isolation), but the potentiality of danger that lies hidden in an individual and which is manifested in his observed everyday conduct. The prison functions in this as an apparatus of knowledge.

Between this apparatus of punishment proposed by the Flemish, English and American models, between these 'reformatories' and all the punishments imagined by the reformers, one may establish the points of convergence and the disparities.

Points of convergence. In the first instance, there is a difference in the temporal direction of punishment. The 'reformatories' were mechanisms directed towards the future; they too were intended not to efface a crime, but to prevent its repetition. 'As to the *end*, or final cause of human punishments. This is not by way of atonement or expiation for the crime committed; for that must be left to the just determination of the supreme being . . .' (Blackstone, 11). And in Pennsylvania, Buxton declared, the principles of Montesquieu and Beccaria should now have the 'force of axioms', that 'the prevention of crimes is the sole end of punishment' (Bradford, 3). So one punishes not to efface the crime, but to transform a criminal (actual or potential); punishment must bring with it a certain corrective technique. Here, too, Rush is close to the reforming jurists – were it not, perhaps, for the metaphor he uses when he says: we have invented machines that facilitate labour; how much more one should praise the inventor of 'the most speedy and effectual methods of restoring the vicious part of mankind to virtue and happiness, and of extirpating a portion of vice from the world'.[13] Lastly, the English and the American models, like the projects of the legislators and theoreticians, require methods to individualize the penalty: in its duration, its nature, its intensity, the way in which it is carried out, the punishment must be adjusted to the individual character and to the danger that he bears within him for others. The system of penalties must be open to individual variables. In their general outline, the models more or less inspired by the Rasphuis of Amsterdam were not in contradiction with the proposals of the reformers. It might even be thought at first glance that they were merely a development of them – or a sketch – at the level of concrete institutions.

Yet the disparity emerges clearly enough when one defines the techniques of this individualizing correction. The difference is to be found in the procedure of access to the individual, the way in which the punishing power gets control over him, the instruments that it uses in order to achieve this transformation; it is in the technology of the penalty, not in its theoretical foundation; in the relation that it establishes with the body and with the soul, and not in the way that it is inserted within the legal system.

That was the method of the reformers. Where exactly did the penalty apply its pressure, gain control of the individual? Representations: the representations of his interests, the representation of his advantages and disadvantages, pleasure and displeasure; and, if the punishment happens to seize the body, to apply techniques to it that are little short of torture, it is because it is – for the condemned man and for the spectators – an object of representation. By what instrument did one act on the representations? Other representations, or rather couplings of ideas (crime-punishment, the imagined advantage of crime-disadvantage perceived in the punishments); these pairings could function only in the element of publicity: punitive scenes that established them or reinforced them in the eyes of all, a discourse that circulated, brought back into currency at each moment the complex of signs. The role of the criminal in punishment was to reintroduce, in the face of crime and the criminal code, the real presence of the signified – that is to say, of the penalty which, according to the terms of the code, must be infallibly associated with the offence. By producing this signified abundantly and visibly, and therefore reactivating the signifying system of the code, the idea of crime functioning as a sign of punishment, it is with this coin that the offender pays his debt to society. Individual correction must, therefore, assure the process of redefining the individual as subject of law, through the reinforcement of the systems of signs and representations that they circulate.

The apparatus of corrective penality acts in a quite different way. The point of application of the penalty is not the representation, but the body, time, everyday gestures and activities; the soul, too, but in so far as it is the seat of habits. The body and the soul, as principles of behaviour, form the element that is now proposed for punitive intervention. Rather than on an art of representations, this punitive intervention must rest on a studied manipulation of the individual: 'I have no more doubt of every crime having its cure in moral and physical influence . . .'; so, in order to decide on punishments, one 'will require some knowledge of the principles of sensation, and of the sympathies which occur in the nervous system' (Rush, 13). As for the instruments used, these are no longer complexes of representation, reinforced and circulated, but forms of coercion, schemata of constraint, applied and repeated. Exercises, not signs: time-tables, compulsory movements, regular activities, solitary meditation, work in common, silence, application, respect, good habits. And, ultimately, what one is trying to restore in this technique of correction is not so much the juridical subject, who is caught up in the fundamental interests of the social pact, but the obedient subject, the individual subjected to habits, rules, orders, an authority that is exercised continually around him and upon him, and which he must allow to function automatically in him. There are two quite distinct ways, therefore, of reacting to the offence: one may restore the juridical subject of the social pact, or shape an obedient subject, according to the general and detailed form of some power.

All this would no doubt amount to little more than a speculative difference – for in each case it is a question of forming obedient individuals – if the penality of 'coercion' did not bring with it certain crucial consequences. The training of behaviour by a full time-table, the acquisition of habits, the constraints of the body imply a very special relation between the individual who is punished and the individual who punishes him. It is a relation that not only renders the dimension of the spectacle useless: it excludes it.[14] The agent of punishment must exercise a total power, which no third party can disturb; the individual to be corrected must be entirely enveloped in the power that is being exercised over him. Secrecy is imperative, and so too is autonomy, at least in relation to this technique of punishment: it must have its own functioning, its own rules, its own techniques, its own knowledge; it must fix its own norms, decide its own results. There is a discontinuity, or in any case a specificity, in relation to the legal power that declares guilt and fixes the general limits of punishment. These two consequences – secrecy and autonomy in the exercise of the power to punish – are unacceptable for a theory and a policy of penality that has two aims in view: to get all citizens to participate in the punishment of the social enemy and to render the exercise of the power to punish entirely adequate and transparent to the laws that publicly define it. Secret punishments and punishments not specified in the legal code, a power to punish exercised in the shadows according to criteria and with instruments that elude control – this was enough to compromise the whole strategy of the reform. After the sentence, a power was constituted that was reminiscent of the power exercised in the old system. The power that applied the penalties now threatened to be as arbitrary, as despotic, as the power that once decided them.

In short, the divergence is the following: punitive city or coercive institution? On the one hand, a functioning of penal power, distributed throughout the social space; present everywhere as scene, spectacle, sign, discourse; legible like an open book; operating by a permanent recodification of the mind of the citizens; eliminating crime by those obstacles placed before the idea of crime; acting invisibly and uselessly on the 'soft fibres of the brain', as Servan put it. A power to punish that ran the whole length of the social network would act at each of its points, and in the end would no longer be perceived as a power of certain individuals over others, but as an immediate reaction of all in relation to the individual. On the other hand, a compact functioning of the power to punish: a meticulous assumption of responsibility for the body and the time of the convict, a regulation of his movements and behaviour by a system of authority and knowledge; a concerted orthopaedy applied to convicts in order to reclaim them individually; an autonomous administration of this power that is isolated both from the social body and from the judicial power in the strict sense. The emergence of the prison marks the institutionalization of the power to punish, or, to be more precise: will the power to punish (with the strategic aim adopted in the late eighteenth century, the reduction of popular illegality) be better served by concealing itself beneath a general social function, in the 'punitive city', or by investing itself in a coercive institution, in the enclosed space of the 'reformatory'?

In any case, it can be said that, in the late eighteenth century, one is confronted by three ways of organizing the power to punish. The first is the one that was still functioning and which was based on the old monarchical law. The other two both refer to a preventive, utilitarian, corrective conception of a right to punish that belongs to society as a whole; but they are very different from one another at the level of the mechanisms they envisage. Broadly speaking, one might say that, in monarchical law, punishment is a ceremonial of sovereignty; it uses the ritual marks of the vengeance that it applies to the body of the condemned man; and it deploys before the eyes of the spectators an effect of terror as intense as it is discontinuous, irregular and always above its own laws, the physical presence of the sovereign and of his power. The reforming jurists, on the other hand, saw punishment as a procedure for requalifying individuals as subjects, as juridical subjects; it uses not marks, but signs, coded sets of representations, which would be given the most rapid circulation and the most general acceptance possible by citizens witnessing the scene of punishment. Lastly, in the project for a prison institution that was then developing, punishment was seen as a technique for the coercion of individuals; it operated methods of training the body – not signs – by the traces it leaves, in the form of habits, in behaviour; and it presupposed the setting up of a specific power for the administration of the penalty. We have, then, the sovereign and his force, the social body and the administrative apparatus; mark, sign, trace; ceremony, representation, exercise; the vanquished enemy, the juridical subject in the process of re-qualification, the individual subjected to immediate coercion; the tortured body, the soul with its manipulated representations, the body subjected to training. We have here the three series of elements that characterize the three mechanisms that face one another in the second half of the eighteenth century. They cannot be reduced to theories of law (though they overlap with such theories), nor can they be identified with apparatuses or institutions (though they are based on them), nor can they be derived from moral choices (though they find their justification in morality). They are modalities according to which the power to punish is exercised: three technologies of power.

The problem, then, is the following: how is it that, in the end, it was the third that was adopted? How did the coercive, corporal, solitary, secret model of the power to punish replace the representative, scenic, signifying, public, collective model? Why did the physical exercise of punishment (which is not torture) replace, with the prison that is its institutional support, the social play of the signs of punishment and the prolix festival that circulated them?

PART THREE
Discipline

1. Docile bodies

Let us take the ideal figure of the soldier as it was still seen in the early seventeenth century. To begin with, the soldier was someone who could be recognized from afar; he bore certain signs: the natural signs of his strength and his courage, the marks, too, of his pride; his body was the blazon of his strength and valour; and although it is true that he had to learn the profession of arms little by little – generally in actual fighting – movements like marching and attitudes like the bearing of the head belonged for the most part to a bodily rhetoric of honour; 'The signs for recognizing those most suited to this profession are a lively, alert manner, an erect head, a taut stomach, broad shoulders, long arms, strong fingers, a small belly, thick thighs, slender legs and dry feet, because a man of such a figure could not fail to be agile and strong'; when he becomes a pike-bearer, the soldier 'will have to march in step in order to have as much grace and gravity as possible, for the pike is an honourable weapon, worthy to be borne with gravity and boldness' (Montgommery, 6 and 7). By the late eighteenth century, the soldier has become something that can be made; out of a formless clay, an inapt body, the machine required can be constructed; posture is gradually corrected; a calculated constraint runs slowly through each part of the body, mastering it, making it pliable, ready at all times, turning silently into the automatism of habit; in short, one has 'got rid of the peasant' and given him 'the air of a soldier' (ordinance of 20 March 1764). Recruits become accustomed to 'holding their heads high and erect; to standing upright, without bending the back, to sticking out the belly, throwing out the chest and throwing back the shoulders; and, to help them acquire the habit, they are given this position while standing against a wall in such a way that the heels, the thighs, the waist and the shoulders touch it, as also do the backs of the hands, as one turns the arms outwards, without moving them away from the body. . . . Likewise, they will be taught never to fix their eyes on the ground, but to look straight at those they pass . . . to remain motionless until the order is given, without moving the head, the hands or the feet . . . lastly to march with a bold step, with knee and ham taut, on the points of the feet, which should face outwards' (ordinance of 20 March 1764).

The classical age discovered the body as object and target of power. It is easy enough to find signs of the attention then paid to the body – to the body that is manipulated, shaped, trained, which obeys, responds, becomes skilful and increases its forces. The great book of Man-the-Machine was written simultaneously on two registers: the anatomico-metaphysical register, of which Descartes wrote the first pages and which the physicians and philosophers continued, and the technico-political register, which was constituted by a whole set of regulations and by empirical and calculated methods relating to the army, the school and the hospital, for controlling or correcting the operations of the body. These two registers are quite distinct, since it was a question, on the one hand, of submission and use and, on the other, of functioning and explanation: there was a useful body and an intelligible body. And yet there are points of overlap from one to the other. La Mettrie's *L'Homme-machine* is both a materialist reduction of the soul and a general theory of *dressage*, at the centre of which reigns the notion of 'docility', which joins the analysable body to the manipulable body. A body is docile that may be subjected, used, transformed and improved. The celebrated automata, on the other hand, were not only a way of illustrating an organism, they were also political puppets, small-scale models of power: Frederick II, the meticulous king of small machines, well-trained regiments and long exercises, was obsessed with them.

What was so new in these projects of docility that interested the eighteenth century so much? It was certainly not the first time that the body had become the object of such imperious and pressing investments; in every society, the body was in the grip of very strict powers, which imposed on it constraints, prohibitions or obligations. However, there were several new things in these techniques. To begin with, there was the scale of the control: it was a question not of treating the body, *en masse*, 'wholesale', as if it were an indissociable unity, but of working it 'retail', individually; of exercising upon it a subtle coercion, of obtaining holds upon it at the level of the mechanism itself – movements, gestures, attitudes, rapidity: an infinitesimal power over the active body. Then there was the object of the control: it was not or was no longer the signifying elements of behaviour or the language of the body, but the economy, the efficiency of movements, their internal organization; constraint bears upon the forces rather than upon the signs; the only truly important ceremony is that of exercise. Lastly, there is the modality: it implies an uninterrupted, constant coercion, supervising the processes of the activity rather than its result and it is exercised according to a codification that partitions as closely as possible time, space, movement. These methods, which made possible the meticulous control of the operations of the body, which assured the constant subjection of its forces and imposed upon them a relation of docility-utility, might be called 'disciplines'. Many disciplinary methods had long been in existence – in monasteries, armies, workshops. But in the course of the seventeenth and eighteenth centuries the disciplines became general formulas of domination. They were different from slavery because they were not based on a relation of appropriation of bodies; indeed, the elegance of the discipline lay in the fact that it could dispense with this costly and violent relation by obtaining effects of utility at least as great. They were different, too, from 'service', which was a constant, total, massive, non-analytical, unlimited relation of domination, established in the form of the individual will of the master, his 'caprice'. They were different from vassalage, which was a highly coded, but distant relation of submission, which bore less on the operations of the body than on the products of labour and the ritual marks of allegiance. Again, they were different from asceticism and from 'disciplines' of a monastic type, whose function was to obtain renunciations rather than increases of utility and which, although they involved obedience to others, had as their principal aim an increase of the mastery of each individual over his own body. The historical moment of the disciplines was the moment when an art of the human body was born, which was directed not only at the growth of its skills, nor at the intensification of its subjection, but at the formation of a relation that in the mechanism itself makes it more obedient as it becomes more useful, and conversely. What was then being formed was a policy of coercions that act upon the body, a calculated manipulation of its elements, its gestures, its behaviour. The human body was entering a machinery of power that explores it, breaks it down and rearranges it. A 'political anatomy', which was also a 'mechanics of power', was being born; it defined how one may have a hold over others' bodies, not only so that they may do what one wishes, but so that they may operate as one wishes, with the techniques, the speed and the efficiency that one determines. Thus discipline produces subjected and practised bodies, 'docile' bodies. Discipline increases the forces of the body (in economic terms of utility) and diminishes these same forces (in political terms of obedience). In short, it dissociates power from the body; on the one hand, it turns it into an 'aptitude', a 'capacity', which it seeks to increase; on the other hand, it reverses the course of the energy, the power that might result from it, and turns it into a relation of strict subjection. If economic exploitation separates the force and the product of labour, let us say that disciplinary coercion establishes in the body the constricting link between an increased aptitude and an increased domination.

The 'invention' of this new political anatomy must not be seen as a sudden discovery. It is rather a multiplicity of often minor processes, of different origin and scattered location, which overlap, repeat, or imitate one another, support one another, distinguish themselves from one another according to their domain of application, converge and gradually produce the blueprint of a general method. They were at work in secondary education at a very early date, later in primary schools; they slowly invested the space of the hospital; and, in a few decades, they restructured the military organization. They sometimes circulated very rapidly from one point to another (between the army and the technical schools or secondary schools), sometimes slowly and discreetly (the insidious militarization of the large workshops). On almost every occasion, they were adopted in response to particular needs: an industrial innovation, a renewed outbreak of certain epidemic diseases, the invention of the rifle or the victories of Prussia. This did not prevent them being totally inscribed in general and essential transformations, which we must now try to delineate.

There can be no question here of writing the history of the different disciplinary institutions, with all their individual differences. I simply intend to map on a series of examples some of the essential techniques that most easily spread from one to another. These were always meticulous, often minute, techniques, but they had their importance: because they defined a certain mode of detailed political investment of the body, a 'new micro-physics' of power; and because, since the seventeenth century, they had constantly reached out to ever broader domains, as if they tended to cover the entire social body. Small acts of cunning endowed with a great power of diffusion, subtle arrangements, apparently innocent, but profoundly suspicious, mechanisms that obeyed economies too shameful to be acknowledged, or pursued petty forms of coercion – it was nevertheless they that brought about the mutation of the punitive system, at the threshold of the contemporary period. Describing them will require great attention to detail: beneath every set of figures, we must seek not a meaning, but a precaution; we must situate them not only in the inextricability of a functioning, but in the coherence of a tactic. They are the acts of cunning, not so much of the greater reason that works even in its sleep and gives meaning to the insignificant, as of the attentive 'malevolence' that turns everything to account. Discipline is a political anatomy of detail.

Before we lose patience we would do well to recall the words of Marshal de Saxe: 'Although those who concern themselves with details are regarded as folk of limited intelligence, it seems to me that this part is essential, because it is the foundation, and it is impossible to erect any building or establish any method without understanding its principles. It is not enough to have a liking for architecture. One must also know stone-cutting' (Saxe, 5). There is a whole history to be written about such 'stone-cutting' – a history of the utilitarian rationalization of detail in moral accountability and political control. The classical age did not initiate it; rather it accelerated it, changed its scale, gave it precise instruments, and perhaps found some echoes for it in the calculation of the infinitely small or in the description of the most detailed characteristics of natural beings. In any case, 'detail' had long been a category of

theology and asceticism: every detail is important since, in the sight
of God, no immensity is greater than a detail, nor is anything so
small that it was not willed by one of his individual wishes. In this
great tradition of the eminence of detail, all the minutiae of Christian education, of scholastic or military pedagogy, all forms of
'training' found their place easily enough. For the disciplined man,
as for the true believer, no detail is unimportant, but not so much
for the meaning that it conceals within it as for the hold it provides
for the power that wishes to seize it. Characteristic is the great hymn
to the 'little things' and to their eternal importance, sung by Jean-
Baptiste de La Salle, in his *Traité sur les obligations des frères des
Écoles chrétiennes*. The mystique of the everyday is joined here with
the discipline of the minute. 'How dangerous it is to neglect little
things. It is a very consoling reflection for a soul like mine, little
disposed to great actions, to think that fidelity to little things may,
by an imperceptible progress, raise us to the most eminent sanctity:
because little things lead to greater . . . Little things; it will be said,
alas, my God, what can we do that is great for you, weak and mortal
creatures that we are. Little things; if great things presented themselves would we perform them? Would we not think them beyond
our strength? Little things; and if God accepts them and wishes to
receive them as great things? Little things; has one ever felt this?
Does one judge according to experience? Little things; one is certainly guilty, therefore, if seeing them as such, one refuses them?
Little things; yet it is they that in the end have made great saints!
Yes, little things; but great motives, great feelings, great fervour,
great ardour, and consequently great merits, great treasures, great
rewards' (La Salle, *Traité . . .*, 238–9). The meticulousness of
the regulations, the fussiness of the inspections, the supervision of
the smallest fragment of life and of the body will soon provide, in the
context of the school, the barracks, the hospital or the workshop,
a laicized content, an economic or technical rationality for this
mystical calculus of the infinitesimal and the infinite. And a History
of Detail in the eighteenth century, presided over by Jean-Baptiste
de La Salle, touching on Leibniz and Buffon, via Frederick II,
covering pedagogy, medicine, military tactics and economics,
should bring us, at the end of the century, to the man who dreamt
of being another Newton, not the Newton of the immensities of

the heavens and the planetary masses, but a Newton of 'small bodies', small movements, small actions; to the man who replied to Monge's remark, 'there was only one world to discover': 'What do I hear? But the world of details, who has never dreamt of that other world, what of that world? I have believed in it ever since I was fifteen. I was concerned with it then, and this memory lives within me, as an obsession never to be abandoned. . . That other world is the most important of all that I flatter myself I have discovered: when I think of it, my heart aches' (these words are attributed to Bonaparte in the Introduction to Saint-Hilaire's *Notions synthétiques et historiques de philosophie naturelle*). Napoleon did not discover this world; but we know that he set out to organize it; and he wished to arrange around him a mechanism of power that would enable him to see the smallest event that occurred in the state he governed; he intended, by means of the rigorous discipline that he imposed, 'to embrace the whole of this vast machine without the slightest detail escaping his attention' (Treilhard, 14).

A meticulous observation of detail, and at the same time a political awareness of these small things, for the control and use of men, emerge through the classical age bearing with them a whole set of techniques, a whole corpus of methods and knowledge, descriptions, plans and data. And from such trifles, no doubt, the man of modern humanism was born.[1]

The art of distributions

In the first instance, discipline proceeds from the distribution of individuals in space. To achieve this end, it employs several techniques.

1. Discipline sometimes requires *enclosure*, the specification of a place heterogeneous to all others and closed in upon itself. It is the protected place of disciplinary monotony. There was the great 'confinement' of vagabonds and paupers; there were other more discreet, but insidious and effective ones. There were the *collèges*, or secondary schools: the monastic model was gradually imposed; boarding appeared as the most perfect, if not the most frequent, educational régime; it became obligatory at Louis-le-Grand when, after the departure of the Jesuits, it was turned into a model school (cf. Ariès, 308–13 and Snyders, 35–41). There were the military

barracks: the army, that vagabond mass, has to be held in place; looting and violence must be prevented; the fears of local inhabitants, who do not care for troops passing through their towns, must be calmed; conflicts with the civil authorities must be avoided; desertion must be stopped, expenditure controlled. The ordinance of 1719 envisaged the construction of several hundred barracks, on the model of those already set up in the south of the country; there would be strict confinements: 'The whole will be enclosed by an outer wall ten feet high, which will surround the said houses, at a distance of thirty feet from all the sides'; this will have the effect of maintaining the troops in 'order and discipline, so that an officer will be in a position to answer for them' (*L'Ordonnance militaire*, IXL, 25 September 1719). In 1745, there were barracks in about 320 towns; and it was estimated that the total capacity of the barracks in 1775 was approximately 200,000 men (Daisy, 201–9; an anonymous memoir of 1775, in Dépôt de la guerre, 3689, f. 156; Navereau, 132–5). Side by side with the spread of workshops, there also developed great manufacturing spaces, both homogeneous and well defined: first, the combined manufactories, then, in the second half of the eighteenth century, the works or factories proper (the Chaussade ironworks occupied almost the whole of the Médine peninsula, between Nièvre and Loire; in order to set up the Indret factory in 1777, Wilkinson, by means of embankments and dikes, constructed an island on the Loire; Toufait built Le Creusot in the valley of the Charbonnière, which he transformed, and he had workers' accommodation built in the factory itself); it was a change of scale, but it was also a new type of control. The factory was explicitly compared with the monastery, the fortress, a walled town; the guardian 'will open the gates only on the return of the workers, and after the bell that announces the resumption of work has been rung'; a quarter of an hour later no one will be admitted; at the end of the day, the workshops' heads will hand back the keys to the Swiss guard of the factory, who will then open the gates (*Amboise*, f. 12,1301). The aim is to derive the maximum advantages and to neutralize the inconveniences (thefts, interruptions of work, disturbances and 'cabals'), as the forces of production become more concentrated; to protect materials and tools and to master the labour force: 'The order and inspection that must be maintained require that all workers be assembled under the same roof, so that the partner who is entrusted with the management of the manufactory may prevent and remedy abuses that may arise among the workers and arrest their progress at the outset' (Dauphin, 199).

2. But the principle of 'enclosure' is neither constant, nor indispensable, nor sufficient in disciplinary machinery. This machinery works space in a much more flexible and detailed way. It does this first of all on the principle of elementary location or *partitioning*. Each individual has his own place; and each place its individual. Avoid distributions in groups; break up collective dispositions; analyse confused, massive or transient pluralities. Disciplinary space tends to be divided into as many sections as there are bodies or elements to be distributed. One must eliminate the effects of imprecise distributions, the uncontrolled disappearance of individuals, their diffuse circulation, their unusable and dangerous coagulation; it was a tactic of anti-desertion, anti-vagabondage, anti-concentration. Its aim was to establish presences and absences, to know where and how to locate individuals, to set up useful communications, to interrupt others, to be able at each moment to supervise the conduct of each individual, to assess it, to judge it, to calculate its qualities or merits. It was a procedure, therefore, aimed at knowing, mastering and using. Discipline organizes an analytical space.

And there, too, it encountered an old architectural and religious method: the monastic cell. Even if the compartments it assigns become purely ideal, the disciplinary space is always, basically, cellular. Solitude was necessary to both body and soul, according to a certain asceticism: they must, at certain moments at least, confront temptation and perhaps the severity of God alone. 'Sleep is the image of death, the dormitory is the image of the sepulchre ... although the dormitories are shared, the beds are nevertheless arranged in such a way and closed so exactly by means of curtains that the girls may rise and retire without being seen' (*Règlement pour la communauté des filles du Bon Pasteur*, in Delamare, 507). But this is still a very crude form.

3. The rule of *functional sites* would gradually, in the disciplinary institutions, code a space that architecture generally left at the disposal of several different uses. Particular places were defined to correspond not only to the need to supervise, to break dangerous

communications, but also to create a useful space. The process appeared clearly in the hospitals, especially in the military and naval hospitals. In France, it seems that Rochefort served both as experiment and model. A port, and a military port is – with its circulation of goods, men signed up willingly or by force, sailors embarking and disembarking, diseases and epidemics – a place of desertion, smuggling, contagion: it is a crossroads for dangerous mixtures, a meeting-place for forbidden circulations. The naval hospital must therefore treat, but in order to do this it must be a filter, a mechanism that pins down and partitions; it must provide a hold over this whole mobile, swarming mass, by dissipating the confusion of illegality and evil. The medical supervision of diseases and contagions is inseparable from a whole series of other controls: the military control over deserters, fiscal control over commodities, administrative control over remedies, rations, disappearances, cures, deaths, simulations. Hence the need to distribute and partition off space in a rigorous manner. The first steps taken at Rochefort concerned things rather than men, precious commodities, rather than patients. The arrangements of fiscal and economic supervision preceded the techniques of medical observation: placing of medicines under lock and key, recording their use; a little later, a system was worked out to verify the real number of patients, their identity, the units to which they belonged; then one began to regulate their comings and goings; they were forced to remain in their wards; to each bed was attached the name of its occupant; each individual treated was entered in a register that the doctor had to consult during the visit; later came the isolation of contagious patients and separate beds. Gradually, an administrative and political space was articulated upon a therapeutic space; it tended to individualize bodies, diseases, symptoms, lives and deaths; it constituted a real table of juxtaposed and carefully distinct singularities. Out of discipline, a medically useful space was born.

In the factories that appeared at the end of the eighteenth century, the principle of individualizing partitioning became more complicated. It was a question of distributing individuals in a space in which one might isolate them and map them; but also of articulating this distribution on a production machinery that had its own requirements. The distribution of bodies, the spatial arrangement of production machinery and the different forms of activity in the distribution of 'posts' had to be linked together. The Oberkampf manufactory at Jouy obeyed this principle. It was made up of a series of workshops specified according to each broad type of operation: for the printers, the handlers, the colourists, the women who touched up the design, the engravers, the dyers. The largest of the buildings, built in 1791, by Toussaint Barré, was 110 metres long and had three storeys. The ground floor was devoted mainly to block printing; it contained 132 tables arranged in two rows, the length of the workshop, which had eighty-eight windows; each printer worked at a table with his 'puller', who prepared and spread the colours. There were 264 persons in all. At the end of each table was a sort of rack on which the material that had just been printed was left to dry (Saint-Maur). By walking up and down the central aisle of the workshop, it was possible to carry out a supervision that was both general and individual: to observe the worker's presence and application, and the quality of his work; to compare workers with one another, to classify them according to skill and speed; to follow the successive stages of the production process. All these serializations formed a permanent grid: confusion was eliminated[2]: that is to say, production was divided up and the labour process was articulated, on the one hand, according to its stages or elementary operations, and, on the other hand, according to the individuals, the particular bodies, that carried it out: each variable of this force – strength, promptness, skill, constancy – would be observed, and therefore characterized, assessed, computed and related to the individual who was its particular agent. Thus, spread out in a perfectly legible way over the whole series of individual bodies, the work force may be analysed in individual units. At the emergence of large-scale industry, one finds, beneath the division of the production process, the individualizing fragmentation of labour power; the distributions of the disciplinary space often assured both.

4. In discipline, the elements are interchangeable, since each is defined by the place it occupies in a series, and by the gap that separates it from the others. The unit is, therefore, neither the territory (unit of domination), nor the place (unit of residence), but the *rank*: the place one occupies in a classification, the point at which a line and a column intersect, the interval in a series of intervals that

one may traverse one after the other. Discipline is an art of rank, a technique for the transformation of arrangements. It individualizes bodies by a location that does not give them a fixed position, but distributes them and circulates them in a network of relations.

Take the example of the 'class'. In the Jesuit colleges, one still found an organization that was at once binary and unified; the classes, which might comprise up to two or three hundred pupils, were subdivided into groups of ten; each of these groups, with its 'decurion', was placed in a camp, Roman or Carthaginian; each 'decury' had its counterpart in the opposing camp. The general form was that of war and rivalry; work, apprenticeship and classification were carried out in the form of the joust, through the confrontation of two armies; the contribution of each pupil was inscribed in this general duel; it contributed to the victory or the defeat of a whole camp; and the pupils were assigned a place that corresponded to the function of each individual and to his value as a combatant in the unitary group of his 'decury' (Rochemonteix, 51ff). It should be observed moreover that this Roman comedy made it possible to link, to the binary exercises of rivalry, a spatial disposition inspired by the legion, with rank, hierarchy, pyramidal supervision. One should not forget that, generally speaking, the Roman model, at the Enlightenment, played a dual role: in its republican aspect, it was the very embodiment of liberty; in its military aspect, it was the ideal schema of discipline. The Rome of the eighteenth century and of the Revolution was the Rome of the Senate, but it was also that of the legion; it was the Rome of the Forum, but it was also that of the camps. Up to the empire, the Roman reference transmitted, somewhat ambiguously, the juridical ideal of citizenship and the technique of disciplinary methods. In any case, the strictly disciplinary element in the ancient fable used by the Jesuit colleges came to dominate the element of joust and mock warfare. Gradually – but especially after 1762 – the educational space unfolds; the class becomes homogeneous, it is no longer made up of individual elements arranged side by side under the master's eye. In the eighteenth century, 'rank' begins to define the great form of distribution of individuals in the educational order: rows or ranks of pupils in the class, corridors, courtyards; rank attributed to each pupil at the end of each task and each examination; the rank he obtains from week to week, month to month, year to year; an alignment of age groups, one after another; a succession of subjects taught and questions treated, according to an order of increasing difficulty. And, in this ensemble of compulsory alignments, each pupil, according to his age, his performance, his behaviour, occupies sometimes one rank, sometimes another; he moves constantly over a series of compartments – some of these are 'ideal' compartments, marking a hierarchy of knowledge or ability, others express the distribution of values or merits in material terms in the space of the college or classroom. It is a perpetual movement in which individuals replace one another in a space marked off by aligned intervals.

The organization of a serial space was one of the great technical mutations of elementary education. It made it possible to supersede the traditional system (a pupil working for a few minutes with the master, while the rest of the heterogeneous group remained idle and unattended). By assigning individual places it made possible the supervision of each individual and the simultaneous work of all. It organized a new economy of the time of apprenticeship. It made the educational space function like a learning machine, but also as a machine for supervising, hierarchizing, rewarding. Jean-Baptiste de La Salle dreamt of a classroom in which the spatial distribution might provide a whole series of distinctions at once: according to the pupils' progress, worth, character, application, cleanliness and parents' fortune. Thus, the classroom would form a single great table, with many different entries, under the scrupulously 'classificatory' eye of the master: 'In every class there will be places assigned for all the pupils of all the lessons, so that all those attending the same lesson will always occupy the same place. Pupils attending the highest lessons will be placed in the benches closest to the wall, followed by the others according to the order of the lessons moving towards the middle of the classroom. . . Each of the pupils will have his place assigned to him and none of them will leave it or change it except on the order or with the consent of the school inspector.' Things must be so arranged that 'those whose parents are neglectful and verminous must be separated from those who are careful and clean; that an unruly and frivolous pupil should be placed between two who are well behaved and serious, a libertine either alone or between two pious pupils'.[3]

In organizing 'cells', 'places' and 'ranks', the disciplines create complex spaces that are at once architectural, functional and hierarchical. It is spaces that provide fixed positions and permit circulation; they carve out individual segments and establish operational links; they mark places and indicate values; they guarantee the obedience of individuals, but also a better economy of time and gesture. They are mixed spaces: real because they govern the disposition of buildings, rooms, furniture, but also ideal, because they are projected over this arrangement of characterizations, assessments, hierarchies. The first of the great operations of discipline is, therefore, the constitution of '*tableaux vivants*', which transform the confused, useless or dangerous multitudes into ordered multiplicities. The drawing up of 'tables' was one of the great problems of the scientific, political and economic technology of the eighteenth century: how one was to arrange botanical and zoological gardens, and construct at the same time rational classifications of living beings; how one was to observe, supervise, regularize the circulation of commodities and money and thus build up an economic table that might serve as the principle of the increase of wealth; how one was to inspect men, observe their presence and absence and constitute a general and permanent register of the armed forces; how one was to distribute patients, separate them from one another, divide up the hospital space and make a systematic classification of diseases: these were all twin operations in which the two elements – distribution and analysis, supervision and intelligibility – are inextricably bound up. In the eighteenth century, the table was both a technique of power and a procedure of knowledge. It was a question of organizing the multiple, of providing oneself with an instrument to cover it and to master it; it was a question of imposing upon it an 'order'. Like the army general of whom Guibert spoke, the naturalist, the physician, the economist was 'blinded by the immensity, dazed by the multitude . . . the innumerable combinations that result from the multiplicity of objects, so many concerns together form a burden above his strength. In perfecting itself, in approaching true principles, the science of modern warfare might become simpler and less difficult'; armies 'with simple, similar tactics, capable of being adapted to every movement . . . would be easier to move and lead' (Guibert, xxxvi). Tactics, the spatial ordering of men; taxonomy, the disciplinary space of natural beings; the economic table, the regulated movement of wealth.

But the table does not have the same function in these different registers. In the order of the economy, it makes possible the measurement of quantities and the analysis of movements. In the form of taxonomy, it has the function of characterizing (and consequently reducing individual singularities) and constituting classes (and therefore of excluding considerations of number). But in the form of the disciplinary distribution, on the other hand, the table has the function of treating multiplicity itself, distributing it and deriving from it as many effects as possible. Whereas natural taxonomy is situated on the axis that links character and category, disciplinary tactics is situated on the axis that links the singular and the multiple. It allows both the characterization of the individual as individual and the ordering of a given multiplicity. It is the first condition for the control and use of an ensemble of distinct elements: the base for a micro-physics of what might be called a 'cellular' power.

The control of activity

1. The *time-table* is an old inheritance. The strict model was no doubt suggested by the monastic communities. It soon spread. Its three great methods – establish rhythms, impose particular occupations, regulate the cycles of repetition – were soon to be found in schools, workshops and hospitals. The new disciplines had no difficulty in taking up their place in the old forms; the schools and poorhouses extended the life and the regularity of the monastic communities to which they were often attached. The rigours of the industrial period long retained a religious air; in the seventeenth century, the regulations of the great manufactories laid down the exercises that would divide up the working day: 'On arrival in the morning, before beginning their work, all persons shall wash their hands, offer up their work to God and make the sign of the cross' (Saint-Maur, article 1); but even in the nineteenth century, when the rural populations were needed in industry, they were sometimes formed into 'congregations', in an attempt to inure them to work in the workshops; the framework of the 'factory–monastery' was

imposed upon the workers. In the Protestant armies of Maurice of Orange and Gustavus Adolphus, military discipline was achieved through a rhythmics of time punctuated by pious exercises; army life, Boussanelle was later to say, should have some of the 'perfections of the cloister itself' (Boussanelle, 2; on the religious character of discipline in the Swedish army, cf. *The Swedish Discipline*, London, 1632). For centuries, the religious orders had been masters of discipline: they were the specialists of time, the great technicians of rhythm and regular activities. But the disciplines altered these methods of temporal regulation from which they derived. They altered them first by refining them. One began to count in quarter hours, in minutes, in seconds. This happened in the army, of course: Guibert systematically implemented the chronometric measurement of shooting that had been suggested earlier by Vauban. In the elementary schools, the division of time became increasingly minute; activities were governed in detail by orders that had to be obeyed immediately: 'At the last stroke of the hour, a pupil will ring the bell, and at the first sound of the bell all the pupils will kneel, with their arms crossed and their eyes lowered. When the prayer has been said, the teacher will strike the signal once to indicate that the pupils should get up, a second time as a sign that they should salute Christ, and a third that they should sit down' (La Salle, *Conduite* . . ., 27–8). In the early nineteenth century, the following time-table was suggested for the *Écoles mutuelles*, or 'mutual improvement schools': 8.45 entrance of the monitor, 8.52 the monitor's summons, 8.56 entrance of the children and prayer, 9.00 the children go to their benches, 9.04 first slate, 9.08 end of dictation, 9.12 second slate, etc. (Tronchot, 221). The gradual extension of the wage-earning class brought with it a more detailed partitioning of time: 'If workers arrive later than a quarter of an hour after the ringing of the bell . . .' (Amboise, article 2); 'if any one of the companions is asked for during work and loses more than five minutes . . .', 'anyone who is not at his work at the correct time . . .' (Oppenheim, article 7–8). But an attempt is also made to assure the quality of the time used: constant supervision, the pressure of supervisors, the elimination of anything that might disturb or distract; it is a question of constituting a totally useful time: 'It is expressly forbidden during work to amuse one's companions by gestures or in any other way, to play at any game whatsoever, to eat, to sleep, to tell stories and comedies' (Oppenheim, article 16); and even during the meal-break, 'there will be no telling of stories, adventures or other such talk that distracts the workers from their work'; 'it is expressly forbidden for any worker, under any pretext, to bring wine into the manufactory and to drink in the workshops' (*Amboise*, article 4). Time measured and paid must also be a time without impurities or defects; a time of good quality, throughout which the body is constantly applied to its exercise. Precision and application are, with regularity, the fundamental virtues of disciplinary time. But this is not the newest thing about it. Other methods are more characteristic of the disciplines.

2. *The temporal elaboration of the act.* There are, for example, two ways of controlling marching troops. In the early seventeenth century, we have: 'Accustomed soldiers marching in file or in battalion to march to the rhythm of the drum. And to do this, one must begin with the right foot so that the whole troop raises the same foot at the same time' (Montgommery, 86). In the mid-eighteenth century, there are four sorts of steps: 'The length of the the short step will be a foot, that of the ordinary step, the double step and the marching step will be two feet, the whole measured from one heel to the next; as for the duration, that of the small step and the ordinary step will last one second, during which two double steps would be performed; the duration of the marching step will be a little longer than one second. The oblique step will take one second; it will be at most eighteen inches from one heel to the next. ... The ordinary step will be executed forwards, holding the head up high and the body erect, holding oneself in balance successively on a single leg, and bringing the other forwards, the ham taut, the point of the foot a little turned outwards and low, so that one may without affectation brush the ground on which one must walk and place one's foot, in such a way that each part may come to rest there at the same time without striking the ground' ('Ordonnance du 1er janvier 1766, pour régler l'exercise de l'infanterie'). Between these two instructions, a new set of restraints had been brought into play, another degree of precision in the breakdown of gestures and movements, another way of adjusting the body to temporal imperatives.

What the ordinance of 1766 defines is not a time-table – the general framework for an activity; it is rather a collective and obligatory rhythm, imposed from the outside; it is a 'programme'; it assures the elaboration of the act itself; it controls its development and its stages from the inside. We have passed from a form of injunction that measured or punctuated gestures to a web that constrains them or sustains them throughout their entire succession. A sort of anatomo-chronological schema of behaviour is defined. The act is broken down into its elements; the position of the body, limbs, articulations is defined; to each movement are assigned a direction, an aptitude, a duration; their order of succession is prescribed. Time penetrates the body and with it all the meticulous controls of power.

3. Hence *the correlation of the body and the gesture*. Disciplinary control does not consist simply in teaching or imposing a series of particular gestures; it imposes the best relation between a gesture and the overall position of the body, which is its condition of efficiency and speed. In the correct use of the body, which makes possible a correct use of time, nothing must remain idle or useless: everything must be called upon to form the support of the act required. A well-disciplined body forms the operational context of the slightest gesture. Good handwriting, for example, presupposes a gymnastics – a whole routine whose rigorous code invests the body in its entirety, from the points of the feet to the tip of the index finger. The pupils must always 'hold their bodies erect, somewhat turned and free on the left side, slightly inclined, so that, with the elbow placed on the table, the chin can be rested upon the hand, unless this were to interfere with the view; the left leg must be somewhat more forward under the table than the right. A distance of two fingers must be left between the body and the table; for not only does one write with more alertness, but nothing is more harmful to the health than to acquire the habit of pressing one's stomach against the table; the part of the left arm from the elbow to the hand must be placed on the table. The right arm must be at a distance from the body of about three fingers and be about five fingers from the table, on which it must rest lightly. The teacher will place the pupils in the posture that they should maintain when writing, and will correct it either by sign or otherwise, when they change this position' (La Salle, *Conduite . . .*, 63–4). A disciplined body is the prerequisite of an efficient gesture.

4. *The body–object articulation*. Discipline defines each of the

relations that the body must have with the object that it manipulates. Between them, it outlines a meticulous meshing. 'Bring the weapon forward. In three stages. Raise the rifle with the right hand, bringing it close to the body so as to hold it perpendicular with the right knee, the end of the barrel at eye level, grasping it by striking it with the right hand, the arm held close to the body at waist height. At the second stage, bring the rifle in front of you with the left hand, the barrel in the middle between the two eyes, vertical, the right hand grasping it at the small of the butt, the arm outstretched, the trigger-guard resting on the first finger, the left hand at the height of the notch, the thumb lying along the barrel against the moulding. At the third stage, let go of the rifle with the left hand, which falls along the thigh, raising the rifle with the right hand, the lock outwards and opposite the chest, the right arm half flexed, the elbow close to the body, the thumb lying against the lock, resting against the first screw, the hammer resting on the first finger, the barrel perpendicular' ('Ordonnance du 1er janvier 1766 . . ., titre XI, article 2'). This is an example of what might be called the instrumental coding of the body. It consists of a breakdown of the total gesture into two parallel series: that of the parts of the body to be used (right hand, left hand, different fingers of the hand, knee, eye, elbow, etc.) and that of the parts of the object manipulated (barrel, notch, hammer, screw, etc.); then the two sets of parts are correlated together according to a number of simple gestures (rest, bend); lastly, it fixes the canonical succession in which each of these correlations occupies a particular place. This obligatory syntax is what the military theoreticians of the eighteenth century called '*manoeuvre*'. The traditional recipe gives place to explicit and obligatory prescriptions. Over the whole surface of contact between the body and the object it handles, power is introduced, fastening them to one another. It constitutes a body-weapon, body-tool, body-machine complex. One is as far as possible from those forms of subjection that demanded of the body only signs or products, forms of expression or the result of labour. The regulation imposed by power is at the same time the law of construction of the operation. Thus disciplinary power appears to have the function not so much of deduction as of synthesis, not so much of exploitation of the product as of coercive link with the apparatus of production.

5. *Exhaustive use*. The principle that underlay the time-table in its traditional form was essentially negative; it was the principle of non-idleness: it was forbidden to waste time, which was counted by God and paid for by men; the time-table was to eliminate the danger of wasting it – a moral offence and economic dishonesty. Discipline, on the other hand, arranges a positive economy; it poses the principle of a theoretically ever-growing use of time: exhaustion rather than use; it is a question of extracting, from time, ever more available moments and, from each moment, ever more useful forces. This means that one must seek to intensify the use of the slightest moment, as if time, in its very fragmentation, were inexhaustible or as if, at least by an ever more detailed internal arrangement, one could tend towards an ideal point at which one maintained maximum speed and maximum efficiency. It was precisely this that was implemented in the celebrated regulations of the Prussian infantry that the whole of Europe imitated after the victories of Frederick II:[4] the more time is broken down, the more its subdivisions multiply, the better one disarticulates it by deploying its internal elements under a gaze that supervises them, the more one can accelerate an operation, or at least regulate it according to an optimum speed; hence this regulation of the time of an action that was so important in the army and which was to be so throughout the entire technology of human activity: the Prussian regulations of 1743 laid down six stages to bring the weapon to one's foot, four to extend it, thirteen to raise it to the shoulder, etc. By other means, the 'mutual improvement school' was also arranged as a machine to intensify the use of time; its organization made it possible to obviate the linear, successive character of the master's teaching: it regulated the counterpoint of operations performed, at the same moment, by different groups of pupils under the direction of monitors and assistants, so that each passing moment was filled with many different, but ordered activities; and, on the other hand, the rhythm imposed by signals, whistles, orders imposed on everyone temporal norms that were intended both to accelerate the process of learning and to teach speed as a virtue;[5] 'the sole aim of these commands . . . is to accustom the children to executing well and quickly the same operations, to diminish as far as possible by speed the loss of time caused by moving from one operation to another' (Bernard).

Through this technique of subjection a new object was being formed; slowly, it superseded the mechanical body – the body composed of solids and assigned movements, the image of which had for so long haunted those who dreamt of disciplinary perfection. This new object is the natural body, the bearer of forces and the seat of duration; it is the body susceptible to specified operations, which have their order, their stages, their internal conditions, their constituent elements. In becoming the target for new mechanisms of power, the body is offered up to new forms of knowledge. It is the body of exercise, rather than of speculative physics; a body manipulated by authority, rather than imbued with animal spirits; a body of useful training and not of rational mechanics, but one in which, by virtue of that very fact, a number of natural requirements and functional constraints are beginning to emerge. This is the body that Guibert discovered in his critique of excessively artificial movements. In the exercise that is imposed upon it and which it resists, the body brings out its essential correlations and spontaneously rejects the incompatible: 'On entering most of our training schools, one sees all those unfortunate soldiers in constricting and forced attitudes, one sees all their muscles contracted, the circulation of their blood interrupted. . . If we studied the intention of nature and the construction of the human body, we would find the position and the bearing that nature clearly prescribes for the soldier. The head must be erect, standing out from the shoulders, sitting perpendicularly between them. It must be turned neither to left nor to right, because, in view of the correspondence between the vertebrae of the neck and the shoulder-blade to which they are attached, none of them may move in a circular manner without slightly bringing with it from the same side that it moves one of the shoulders and because, the body no longer being placed squarely, the soldier can no longer walk straight in front of him or serve as a point of alignment. . . Since the hip-bone, which the ordinance indicates as the point against which the butt end should rest, is not situated the same in all men, the rifle must be placed more to the right for some, and more to the left for others. For the same reason of inequality of structure, the trigger-guard is more or less pressed against the body, depending on whether the outer parts of a man's shoulder is more or less fleshy' (Guibert, 21–2).

We have seen how the procedures of disciplinary distribution had their place among the contemporary techniques of classification and tabulation; but also how they introduced into them the specific problem of individuals and multiplicity. Similarly, the disciplinary controls of activity belonged to a whole series of researches, theoretical or practical, into the natural machinery of bodies; but they began to discover in them specific processes; behaviour and its organized requirements gradually replaced the simple physics of movement. The body, required to be docile in its minutest operations, opposes and shows the conditions of functioning proper to an organism. Disciplinary power has as its correlative an individuality that is not only analytical and 'cellular', but also natural and 'organic'.

The organization of geneses

In 1667, the edict that set up the manufactory of the Gobelins envisaged the organization of a school. Sixty scholarship children were to be chosen by the superintendent of royal buildings, entrusted for a time to a master whose task it would be to provide them with 'upbringing and instruction', then apprenticed to the various master tapestry makers of the manufactory (who by virtue of this fact received compensation deducted from the pupils' scholarships); after six years' apprenticeship, four years of service and a qualifying examination, they were given the right to 'set up and run a shop' in any town of the kingdom. We find here the characteristics of guild apprenticeship: the relation of dependence on the master that is both individual and total; the statutory duration of the training, which is concluded by a qualifying examination, but which is not broken down according to a precise programme; an overall exchange between the master who must give his knowledge and the apprentice who must offer his services, his assistance and often some payment. The form of domestic service is mixed with a transference of knowledge.[6] In 1737, an edict organized a school of drawing for the apprentices of the Gobelins; it was not intended to replace the training given by the master workers, but to complement it. It involved a quite different arrangement of time. Two hours a day, except on Sundays and feast days, the pupils met in the school. A roll-call was taken, from a list on the wall; the absentees were noted down in a register. The school was divided into three classes. The first for those who had no notion of drawing; they were made to copy models, which were more or less difficult according to the abilities of each pupil. The second 'for those who already have some principles', or who had passed through the first class; they had to reproduce pictures 'at sight, without tracing', but considering only the drawing. In the third class, they learnt colouring and pastel drawing, and were introduced to the theory and practice of dyeing. The pupils performed individual tasks at regular intervals; each of these exercises, signed with the name of its author and date of execution, was handed in to the teacher; the best were rewarded; assembled together at the end of the year and compared, they made it possible to establish the progress, the present ability and the relative place of each pupil; it was then decided which of them could pass into the next class. A general book, kept by the teachers and their assistants, recorded from day to day the behaviour of the pupils and everything that happened in the school; it was periodically shown to an inspector (Gerspach, 1892).

The Gobelins school is only one example of an important phenomenon: the development, in the classical period, of a new technique for taking charge of the time of individual existences; for regulating the relations of time, bodies and forces; for assuring an accumulation of duration; and for turning to ever-increased profit or use the movement of passing time. How can one capitalize the time of individuals, accumulate it in each of them, in their bodies, in their forces or in their abilities, in a way that is susceptible of use and control? How can one organize profitable durations? The disciplines, which analyse space, break up and rearrange activities, must also be understood as machinery for adding up and capitalizing time. This was done in four ways, which emerge most clearly in military organization.

1. Divide duration into successive or parallel segments, each of which must end at a specific time. For example, isolate the period of training and the period of practice; do not mix the instruction of recruits and the exercise of veterans; open separate military schools for the armed service (in 1764, the creation of the École Militaire in Paris, in 1776 the creation of twelve schools in the provinces);

recruit professional soldiers at the youngest possible age, take children, 'have them adopted by the nation, and brought up in special schools' (Servan, J., 456); teach in turn posture, marching, the handling of weapons, shooting, and do not pass to another activity until the first has been completely mastered: 'One of the principal mistakes is to show a soldier every exercise at once' ('Règlement de 1743 . . .'); in short, break down time into separate and adjusted threads. 2. Organize these threads according to an analytical plan – successions of elements as simple as possible, combining according to increasing complexity. This presupposes that instruction should abandon the principle of analogical repetition. In the sixteenth century, military exercise consisted above all in copying all or part of the action, and of generally increasing the soldier's skill or strength;[7] in the eighteenth century, the instruction of the 'manual' followed the principle of the 'elementary' and not of the 'exemplary': simple gestures – the position of the fingers, the bend of the leg, the movement of the arms – basic elements for useful actions that also provide a general training in strength, skill, docility. 3. Finalize these temporal segments, decide on how long each will last and conclude it with an examination, which will have the triple function of showing whether the subject has reached the level required, of guaranteeing that each subject undergoes the same apprenticeship and of differentiating the abilities of each individual. When the sergeants, corporals, etc. 'entrusted with the task of instructing the others, are of the opinion that a particular soldier is ready to pass into the first class, they will present him first to the officers of their company, who will carefully examine him; if they do not find him sufficiently practised, they will refuse to admit him; if, on the other hand, the man presented seems to them to be ready, the said officers will themselves propose him to the commanding officer of the regiment, who will see him if he thinks it necessary, and will have him examined by the senior officers. The slightest mistakes will be enough to have him rejected, and no one will be able to pass from the second class to the first until he has undergone this first examination' (*Instruction par l'exercise de l'infanterie*, 14 mai 1754). 4. Draw up series of series; lay down for each individual, according to his level, his seniority, his rank, the exercises that are suited to him; common exercises have a differing role and each difference involves specific exercises. At the end of each series, others begin, branch off and subdivide in turn. Thus each individual is caught up in a temporal series which specifically defines his level or his rank. It is a disciplinary polyphony of exercises: 'Soldiers of the second class will be exercised every morning by sergeants, corporals, *anspessades*, lance-corporals. . . The lance-corporals will be exercised every Sunday by the head of the section . . .; the corporals and *anspessades* will be exercised every Tuesday afternoon by the sergeants and their company and these in turn on the afternoons of every second, twelfth and twenty-second day of each month by senior officers' (*Instruction . . .*).

It is this disciplinary time that was gradually imposed on pedagogical practice – specializing the time of training and detaching it from the adult time, from the time of mastery; arranging different stages, separated from one another by graded examinations; drawing up programmes, each of which must take place during a particular stage and which involves exercises of increasing difficulty; qualifying individuals according to the way in which they progress through these series. For the 'initiatory' time of traditional training (an overall time, supervised by the master alone, authorized by a single examination), disciplinary time had substituted its multiple and progressive series. A whole analytical pedagogy was being formed, meticulous in its detail (it broke down the subject being taught into its simplest elements, it hierarchized each stage of development into small steps) and also very precocious in its history (it largely anticipated the genetic analyses of the *idéologues*, whose technical model it appears to have been). At the beginning of the eighteenth century, Demia suggested a division of the process of learning to read into seven levels: the first for those who are beginning to learn the letters, the second for those who are learning to spell, the third for those who are learning to join syllables together to make words, the fourth for those who are reading Latin in sentences or from punctuation to punctuation, the fifth for those who are beginning to read French, the sixth for the best readers, the seventh for those who can read manuscripts. But, where there are a great many pupils, further subdivisions would have to be introduced; the first class would comprise four streams: one for those who are learning the 'simple letters'; a second for those who are learning the 'mixed' letters; a third for those who are learning the abbreviated letters ($\hat{a}$, $\hat{e}$ . . .); a fourth for those who are learning the double letters (ff, ss, tt, st). The second class would be divided into three streams: for those who 'count each letter aloud before spelling the syllable, *D.O.*, *DO*'; for those 'who spell the most difficult syllables, such as *bant*, *brand*, *spinx*', etc. (Demia, 19–20). Each stage in the combinatory of elements must be inscribed within a great temporal series, which is both a natural progress of the mind and a code for educative procedures.

The 'seriation' of successive activities makes possible a whole investment of duration by power: the possibility of a detailed control and a regular intervention (of differentiation, correction, punishment, elimination) in each moment of time; the possibility of characterizing, and therefore of using individuals according to the level in the series that they are moving through; the possibility of accumulating time and activity, of rediscovering them, totalized and usable in a final result, which is the ultimate capacity of an individual. Temporal dispersal is brought together to produce a profit, thus mastering a duration that would otherwise elude one's grasp. Power is articulated directly onto time; it assures its control and guarantees its use.

The disciplinary methods reveal a linear time whose moments are integrated, one upon another, and which is orientated towards a terminal, stable point; in short, an 'evolutive' time. But it must be recalled that, at the same moment, the administrative and economic techniques of control reveal a social time of a serial, orientated, cumulative type: the discovery of an evolution in terms of 'progress'. The disciplinary techniques reveal individual series: the discovery of an evolution in terms of 'genesis'. These two great 'discoveries' of the eighteenth century – the progress of societies and the geneses of individuals – were perhaps correlative with the new techniques of power, and more specifically, with a new way of administering time and making it useful, by segmentation, seriation, synthesis and totalization. A macro- and a micro-physics of power made possible, not the invention of history (it had long had no need of that), but the integration of a temporal, unitary, continuous, cumulative dimension in the exercise of controls and the practice of dominations. 'Evolutive' historicity, as it was then constituted – and so profoundly that it is still self-evident for many today – is bound up with a mode of functioning of power. No doubt it is as if the 'history-remember-ing' of the chronicles, genealogies, exploits, reigns and deeds had long been linked to a modality of power. With the new techniques of subjection, the 'dynamics' of continuous evolutions tends to re-place the 'dynastics' of solemn events.

In any case, the small temporal continuum of individuality-genesis certainly seems to be, like the individuality-cell or the individuality-organism, an effect and an object of discipline. And, at the centre of this seriation of time, one finds a procedure that is, for it, what the drawing up of 'tables' was for the distribution of individuals and cellular segmentation, or, again, what *'manoeuvre'* was for the economy of activities and organic control. This proce-dure is 'exercise'. Exercise is that technique by which one imposes on the body tasks that are both repetitive and different, but always graduated. By bending behaviour towards a terminal state, exercise makes possible a perpetual characterization of the individual either in relation to this term, in relation to other individuals, or in relation to a type of itinerary. It thus assures, in the form of continuity and constraint, a growth, an observation, a qualification. Before adopt-ing this strictly disciplinary form, exercise had a long history: it is to be found in military, religious and university practices either as initiation ritual, preparatory ceremony, theatrical rehearsal or examination. Its linear, continuously progressive organization, its genetic development in time were, at least in the army and the school, introduced at a later date – and were no doubt of religious origin. In any case, the idea of an educational 'programme' that would follow the child to the end of his schooling and which would involve from year to year, month to month, exercises of increasing complexity, first appeared, it seems, in a religious group, the Brothers of the Common Life (cf. Meir, 160 ff). Strongly inspired by Ruysbroek and Rhenish mysticism, they transposed certain of the spiritual techniques to education – and to the education not only of clerks, but also of magistrates and merchants: the theme of a per-fection towards which the exemplary master guides the pupil became with them that of an authoritarian perfection of the pupils by the teacher; the ever-increasing rigorous exercises that the ascetic life proposed became tasks of increasing complexity that marked the gradual acquisition of knowledge and good behaviour; the striving of the whole community towards salvation became the collective, permanent competition of individuals being classified in relation to one another. Perhaps it was these procedures of community life and salvation that were the first nucleus of methods intended to produce individually characterized, but collectively useful aptitudes.[8] In its mystical or ascetic form, exercise was a way of ordering earthly time for the conquest of salvation. It was gradually, in the history of the West, to change direction while preserving certain of its characteristics; it served to economize the time of life, to accumulate it in a useful form and to exercise power over men through the mediation of time arranged in this way. Exercise, having become an element in the political technology of the body and of duration, does not culminate in a beyond, but tends towards a subjection that has never reached its limit.

The composition of forces

'Let us begin by destroying the old prejudice, according to which one believed one was increasing the strength of a troop by increasing its depth. All the physical laws of movement become chimeras when one wishes to adapt them to tactics.'[9] From the end of the seventeenth century, the technical problem of infantry had been freed from the physical model of mass. In an army of pikes and muskets – slow, imprecise, practically incapable of selecting a target and taking aim – troops were used as a projectile, a wall or a fortress: 'the formidable infantry of the army of Spain'; the distribution of soldiers in this mass was carried out above all according to their seniority and their bravery; at the centre, with the task of providing weight and volume, of giving density to the body, were the least experienced; in front, at the angles and on the flanks, were the bravest or reputedly most skilful soldiers. In the course of the classical period, one passed over to a whole set of delicate articulations. The unit – regiment, battalion, section and, later, 'division'[10] – became a sort of machine with many parts, moving in relation to one another, in order to arrive at a configuration and to obtain a specific result. What were the reasons for this mutation? Some were economic: to make each individual useful and the training, maintenance, and arming of troops profitable; to give to each soldier, a precious unit, maximum efficiency. But these economic reasons could become determinant only with a technical transformation: the invention of the rifle:[11] more accurate, more rapid than the musket, it gave greater value to the soldier's skill; more capable of reaching a particular target, it made it possible to exploit fire-power at an individual level; and, conversely, it turned every soldier into a possible target, requiring by the same token greater mobility; it involved therefore the disappearance of a technique of masses in favour of an art that distributed units and men along extended, relatively flexible, mobile lines. Hence the need to find a whole calculated practice of individual and collective dispositions, movements of groups or isolated elements, changes of position, of movement from one disposition to another; in short, the need to invent a machinery whose principle would no longer be the mobile or immobile mass, but a geometry of divisible segments whose basic unity was the mobile soldier with his rifle;[12] and, no doubt, below the soldier himself, the minimal gestures, the elementary stages of actions, the fragments of spaces occupied or traversed.

The same problems arose when it was a question of constituting a productive force whose effect had to be superior to the sum of elementary forces that composed it: 'The combined working-day produces, relatively to an equal sum of working-days, a greater quantity of use-values, and, consequently, diminishes the labour-time necessary for the production of a given useful effect. Whether the combined working-day, in a given case, acquires this increased productive power, because it heightens the mechanical force of labour, or extends its sphere of action over a greater space, or contracts the field of production relatively to the scale of production, or at the critical moment sets large masses of labour to work ... the special productive power of the combined working-day is, under all circumstances, the social productive power of labour, or the productive power of social labour. This power is due to cooperation itself' (Marx, *Capital*, vol. 1, 311–12). On several occasions, Marx stresses the analogy between the problems of the division of labour and those of military tactics. For example: 'Just as the offensive power of a squadron of cavalry, or the defensive power of a regiment of infantry, is essentially different from the sum of the offensive or defensive powers of the individual cavalry or infantry soldiers taken separately, so the sum total of the mechanical forces exerted by isolated workmen differs from the social force that is developed, when many hands take part simultaneously in one and the same undivided operation' (Marx, *Capital*, vol. 1, 308).

Thus a new demand appears to which discipline must respond: to construct a machine whose effect will be maximized by the concerted articulation of the elementary parts of which it is composed. Discipline is no longer simply an art of distributing bodies, of extracting time from them and accumulating it, but of composing forces in order to obtain an efficient machine. This demand is expressed in several ways.

1. The individual body becomes an element that may be placed, moved, articulated on others. Its bravery or its strength are no longer the principal variables that define it; but the place it occupies, the interval it covers, the regularity, the good order according to which it operates its movements. The soldier is above all a fragment of mobile space, before he is courage or honour. Guibert describes the soldier in the following way: 'When he is under arms, he occupies two feet along his greatest diameter, that is to say, taking him from one end to the other, and about one foot in his greatest thickness taken from the chest to the shoulders, to which one must add an interval of a foot between him and the next man; this gives two feet in all directions per soldier and indicates that a troop of infantry in battle occupies, either in its front or in its depth, as many steps as it has ranks' (Guibert, 27). This is a functional reduction of the body. But it is also an insertion of this body-segment in a whole ensemble over which it is articulated. The soldier whose body has been trained to function part by part for particular operations must in turn form an element in a mechanism at another level. The soldiers will be instructed first 'one by one, then two by two, then in greater numbers. . . For the handling of weapons, one will ascertain that, when the soldiers have been separately instructed, they will carry it out two by two, and then change places alternately, so that the one on the left may learn to adapt himself to the one on the right' ('Ordonnance . . .'). The body is constituted as a part of a multi-segmentary machine.

2. The various chronological series that discipline must combine to form a composite time are also pieces of machinery. The time of

each must be adjusted to the time of the others in such a way that the maximum quantity of forces may be extracted from each and combined with the optimum result. Thus Servan dreamt of a military machine that would cover the whole territory of the nation and in which each individual would be occupied without interruption but in a different way according to the evolutive segment, the genetic sequence in which he finds himself. Military life would begin in childhood, when young children would be taught the profession of arms in 'military manors'; it would end in these same manors when the veterans, right up to their last day, would teach the children, exercise the recruits, preside over the soldiers' exercises, supervise them when they were carrying out works in the public interest, and finally make order reign in the country, when the troops were fighting at the frontiers. There is not a single moment of life from which one cannot extract forces, providing one knows how to differentiate it and combine it with others. Similarly, one uses the labour of children and of old people in the great workshops; this is because they have certain elementary capacities for which it is not necessary to use workers who have many other aptitudes; furthermore, they constitute a cheap labour force; lastly, if they work, they are no longer at anyone's charge: 'Labouring mankind', said a tax collector of an enterprise at Angers, 'may find in this manufactory, from the age of ten to old age, resources against idleness and the penury that follows from it' (Marchegay, 360). But it was probably in primary education that this adjustment of different chronologies was to be carried out with most subtlety. From the seventeenth century to the introduction, at the beginning of the nineteenth, of the Lancaster method, the complex clockwork of the mutual improvement school was built up cog by cog: first the oldest pupils were entrusted with tasks involving simple supervision, then of checking work, then of teaching; in the end, all the time of all the pupils was occupied either with teaching or with being taught. The school became a machine for learning, in which each pupil, each level and each moment, if correctly combined, were permanently utilized in the general process of teaching. One of the great advocates of the mutual improvement schools gives us some idea of this progress: 'In a school of 360 children, the master who would like to instruct each pupil in turn for a session of three hours would not be able to give half a minute to each. By the new method, each of the 360 pupils writes, reads or counts for two and a half hours' (cf. Bernard).

3. This carefully measured combination of forces requires a precise system of command. All the activity of the disciplined individual must be punctuated and sustained by injunctions whose efficacity rests on brevity and clarity; the order does not need to be explained or formulated; it must trigger off the required behaviour and that is enough. From the master of discipline to him who is subjected to it the relation is one of signalization: it is a question not of understanding the injunction but of perceiving the signal and reacting to it immediately, according to a more or less artificial, prearranged code. Place the bodies in a little world of signals to each of which is attached a single, obligatory response: it is a technique of training, of *dressage*, that 'despotically excludes in everything the least representation, and the smallest murmur'; the disciplined soldier 'begins to obey whatever he is ordered to do; his obedience is prompt and blind; an appearance of indocility, the least delay would be a crime' (Boussanelle, 2). The training of school-children was to be carried out in the same way: few words, no explanation, a total silence interrupted only by signals – bells, clapping of hands, gestures, a mere glance from the teacher, or that little wooden apparatus used by the Brothers of the Christian Schools; it was called *par excellence* the 'Signal' and it contained in its mechanical brevity both the technique of command and the morality of obedience. 'The first and principal use of the signal is to attract at once the attention of all the pupils to the teacher and to make them attentive to what he wishes to impart to them. Thus, whenever he wishes to attract the attention of the children, and to bring the exercise to an end, he will strike the signal once. Whenever a good pupil hears the noise of the signal, he will imagine that he is hearing the voice of the teacher or rather the voice of God himself calling him by his name. He will then partake of the feelings of the young Samuel, saying with him in the depths of his soul: "Lord, I am here." ' The pupil will have to have learnt the code of the signals and respond automatically to them. 'When prayer has been said, the teacher will strike the signal at once and, turning to the child whom he wishes to read, he will make the sign to begin. To make a sign to stop to a pupil who is reading, he will strike the signal

once. . . To make a sign to a pupil to repeat when he has read badly or mispronounced a letter, a syllable or a word, he will strike the signal twice in rapid succession. If, after the sign had been made two or three times, the pupil who is reading does not find and repeat the word that he has badly read or mispronounced – because he has read several words beyond it before being called to order – the teacher will strike three times in rapid succession, as a sign to him to begin to read farther back; and he will continue to make the sign till the pupil finds the word which he has said incorrectly' (La Salle, *Conduite* . . . 137–8; cf. also Demia, 21). The mutual improvement school was to exploit still further this control of behaviour by the system of signals to which one had to react immediately. Even verbal orders were to function as elements of signalization: 'Enter your benches. At the word *enter*, the children bring their right hands down on the table with a resounding thud and at the same time put one leg into the bench; at the words *your benches* they put the other leg in and sit down opposite their slates . . . *Take your slates.* At the word *take*, the children, with their right hands, take hold of the string by which the slate is suspended from the nail before them, and, with their left hands, they grasp the slate in the middle; at the word *slates*, they unhook it and place it on the table'.[13]

To sum up, it might be said that discipline creates out of the bodies it controls four types of individuality, or rather an individuality that is endowed with four characteristics: it is cellular (by the play of spatial distribution), it is organic (by the coding of activities), it is genetic (by the accumulation of time), it is combinatory (by the composition of forces). And, in doing so, it operates four great techniques: it draws up tables; it prescribes movements; it imposes exercises; lastly, in order to obtain the combination of forces, it arranges 'tactics'. Tactics, the art of constructing, with located bodies, coded activities and trained aptitudes, mechanisms in which the product of the various forces is increased by their calculated combination are no doubt the highest form of disciplinary practice. In this knowledge, the eighteenth-century theoreticians saw the general foundation of all military practice, from the control and exercise of individual bodies to the use of forces specific to the most complex multiplicities. The architecture, anatomy, mechanics, economy of the disciplinary body: 'In the eyes of most soldiers, tactics are only a branch of the vast science of war; for me, they are the base of this science; they are this science itself, because they teach how to constitute troops, order them, move them, get them to fight; because tactics alone may make up for numbers, and handle the multitude; lastly, it will include knowledge of men, weapons, tensions, circumstances, because it is all these kinds of knowledge brought together that must determine those movements' (Guibert, 4). Or again: 'The term tactics . . . gives some idea of the respective position of the men who make up a particular troop in relation to that of the different troops that make up an army, their movements and their actions, their relations with one another' (Joly de Maizeroy, 2).

It may be that war as strategy is a continuation of politics. But it must not be forgotten that 'politics' has been conceived as a continuation, if not exactly and directly of war, at least of the military model as a fundamental means of preventing civil disorder. Politics, as a technique of internal peace and order, sought to implement the mechanism of the perfect army, of the disciplined mass, of the docile, useful troop, of the regiment in camp and in the field, on manoeuvres and on exercises. In the great eighteenth-century states, the army guaranteed civil peace no doubt because it was a real force, an ever-threatening sword, but also because it was a technique and a body of knowledge that could project their schema over the social body. If there is a politics-war series that passes through strategy, there is an army-politics series that passes through tactics. It is strategy that makes it possible to understand warfare as a way of conducting politics between states; it is tactics that makes it possible to understand the army as a principle for maintaining the absence of warfare in civil society. The classical age saw the birth of the great political and military strategy by which nations confronted each other's economic and demographic forces; but it also saw the birth of meticulous military and political tactics by which the control of bodies and individual forces was exercised within states. The *'militaire'* – the military institution, military science, the *militaire* himself, so different from what was formerly characterized by the term *'homme de guerre'* – was specified, during this period, at the point of junction between war and the noise of battle on the one hand, and order and silence, subservient to peace, on the other.

Historians of ideas usually attribute the dream of a perfect society to the philosophers and jurists of the eighteenth century; but there was also a military dream of society; its fundamental reference was not to the state of nature, but to the meticulously subordinated cogs of a machine, not to the primal social contract, but to permanent coercions, not to fundamental rights, but to indefinitely progressive forms of training, not to the general will but to automatic docility.

'Discipline must be made national,' said Guibert. 'The state that I depict will have a simple, reliable, easily controlled administration. It will resemble those huge machines, which by quite uncomplicated means produce great effects; the strength of this state will spring from its own strength, its prosperity from its own prosperity. Time, which destroys all, will increase its power. It will disprove that vulgar prejudice by which we are made to imagine that empires are subjected to an imperious law of decline and ruin' (Guibert, xxiii–xxiv; cf. what Marx says about the army and forms of bourgeois society in his letter to Engels, 25 September 1857). The Napoleonic régime was not far off and with it the form of state that was to survive it and, we must not forget, the foundations of which were laid not only by jurists, but also by soldiers, not only councillors of state, but also junior officers, not only the men of the courts, but also the men of the camps. The Roman reference that accompanied this formation certainly bears with it this double index: citizens and legionaries, law and manoeuvres. While jurists or philosophers were seeking in the pact a primal model for the construction or reconstruction of the social body, the soldiers and with them the technicians of discipline were elaborating procedures for the individual and collective coercion of bodies.

1 Medal commemorating Louis XIV's first military
 revue in 1668 (B.N. Cabinet des médailles).
 Cf. p. 188.
2 Handwriting model (Collections historiques de
 l'I.N.R.D.P.). Cf. p. 152.

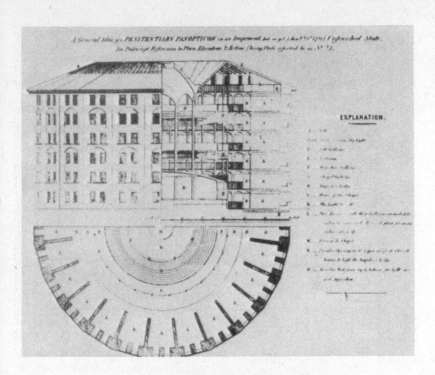

3   J. Bentham. Plan of the Panopticon (*The Works of Jeremy Bentham,* ed. Bowring, vol. IV. 1843. 172-3). Cf. p. 201.

4 N Harou-Romain. Plan for a penitentiary, 1840 A prisoner, in his cell, kneeling at prayer before the central inspection tower. Cf. p 250.

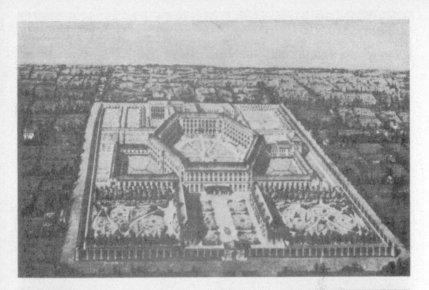

5 The Maison centrale at Rennes in 1877. Cf. p. 250.

6 Interior of the penitentiary at Stateville, United States, twentieth century. Cf. p. 250.

7   Bedtime at the reformatory of Mettray. Cf. p. 294.

8 Lecture on the evils of alcoholism in the auditorium of Fresnes prison

MACHINE A VAPEUR POUR LA CORRECTION CELERIFERE DES PETITES FILLES ET DES PETITS GARÇONS

9   Steam machine for the 'celeriferous' correction of young boys and girls 'Fathers
and Mothers. Uncles and Aunts, Guardian Masters and Mistresses of boarding
schools and all those who have lazy, greedy, disobedient, rebellious insolent.
quarrelsome, tale-bearing, chattering, irreligious children, or children having any
other defect, are hereby informed that Mr Bogeyman and Mrs Bricabrac have just set
up in every *mairie* of the city of Paris a machine similar to the one represented in this
engraving and are ready to accept all naughty children in need of correction in
their establishments each day, from midday to two o'clock Mr Werewolf, Coalman
Scarecrow, Eat-without-Hunger and Mrs Wildcat, Spiteful Slag and Drink-without-
Thirst, friends and relations of Mr Bogeyman and Mrs Bricabrac, will, for a small sum,
set up similar machines to be sent into provincial towns and will themselves supervise
their operation The cheapness of correction given by the steam machine and the
surprising effects that it produces will persuade parents to avail themselves of it as
often as the bad behaviour of their children will require it We also take incorrigible
children as boarders , they are fed on bread and water ' Engraving of the late
eighteenth century (Collections historiques de l'I.N R.D P.).

10 N Andry, *L'orthopédie ou l'art de prévenir et de corriger dans les enfants les difformités du corps* (Orthopaedics or the art of preventing and correcting deformities of the body in children). 1749.

2. The means of correct training

At the beginning of the seventeenth century, Walhausen spoke of 'strict discipline' as an art of correct training. The chief function of the disciplinary power is to 'train', rather than to select and to levy; or, no doubt, to train in order to levy and select all the more. It does not link forces together in order to reduce them; it seeks to bind them together in such a way as to multiply and use them. Instead of bending all its subjects into a single uniform mass, it separates, analyses, differentiates, carries its procedures of decomposition to the point of necessary and sufficient single units. It 'trains' the moving, confused, useless multitudes of bodies and forces into a multiplicity of individual elements -- small, separate cells, organic autonomies, genetic identities and continuities, combinatory segments. Discipline 'makes' individuals; it is the specific technique of a power that regards individuals both as objects and as instruments of its exercise. It is not a triumphant power, which because of its own excess can pride itself on its omnipotence; it is a modest, suspicious power, which functions as a calculated, but permanent economy. These are humble modalities, minor procedures, as compared with the majestic rituals of sovereignty or the great apparatuses of the state. And it is precisely they that were gradually to invade the major forms, altering their mechanisms and imposing their procedures. The legal apparatus was not to escape this scarcely secret invasion. The success of disciplinary power derives no doubt from the use of simple instruments; hierarchical observation, normalizing judgement and their combination in a procedure that is specific to it, the examination.

Hierarchical observation

The exercise of discipline presupposes a mechanism that coerces by means of observation; an apparatus in which the techniques that make it possible to see induce effects of power, and in which, conversely, the means of coercion make those on whom they are applied clearly visible. Slowly, in the course of the classical age, we see the construction of those 'observatories' of human multiplicity for which the history of the sciences has so little good to say. Side by side with the major technology of the telescope, the lens and the light beam, which were an integral part of the new physics and cosmology, there were the minor techniques of multiple and intersecting observations, of eyes that must see without being seen; using techniques of subjection and methods of exploitation, an obscure art of light and the visible was secretly preparing a new knowledge of man.

These 'observatories' had an almost ideal model: the military camp – the short-lived, artificial city, built and reshaped almost at will; the seat of a power that must be all the stronger, but also all the more discreet, all the more effective and on the alert in that it is exercised over armed men. In the perfect camp, all power would be exercised solely through exact observation; each gaze would form a part of the overall functioning of power. The old, traditional square plan was considerably refined in innumerable new projects. The geometry of the paths, the number and distribution of the tents, the orientation of their entrances, the disposition of files and ranks were exactly defined; the network of gazes that supervised one another was laid down: 'In the parade ground, five lines are drawn up, the first is sixteen feet from the second; the others are eight feet from one another; and the last is eight feet from the arms dépôts. The arms dépôts are ten feet from the tents of the junior officers, immediately opposite the first tentpole. A company street is fifty-one feet wide. . . All tents are two feet from one another. The tents of the subalterns are opposite the alleys of their companies. The rear tentpole is eight feet from the last soldiers' tent and the gate is opposite the captains' tent. . . The captains' tents are erected opposite the streets of their companies. The entrance is opposite the companies themselves.'[1] The camp is the diagram of a power that acts by means of general visibility. For a long time this model of the camp or at least its underlying principle was found in urban development, in the construction of working-class housing estates, hospitals, asylums, prisons, schools: the spatial 'nesting' of hierarchized surveillance. The principle was one of 'embedding' (*'encastrement'*). The camp was to the rather shameful art of surveillance what the dark room was to the great science of optics.

A whole problematic then develops: that of an architecture that is no longer built simply to be seen (as with the ostentation of palaces), or to observe the external space (cf. the geometry of fortresses), but to permit an internal, articulated and detailed control – to render visible those who are inside it; in more general terms, an architecture that would operate to transform individuals: to act on those it shelters, to provide a hold on their conduct, to carry the effects of power right to them, to make it possible to know them, to alter them. Stones can make people docile and knowable. The old simple schema of confinement and enclosure – thick walls, a heavy gate that prevents entering or leaving – began to be replaced by the calculation of openings, of filled and empty spaces, passages and transparencies. In this way the hospital building was gradually organized as an instrument of medical action: it was to allow a better observation of patients, and therefore a better calibration of their treatment; the form of the buildings, by the careful separation of the patients, was to prevent contagions; lastly, the ventilation and the air that circulated around each bed was to prevent the deleterious vapours from stagnating around the patient, breaking down his humours and spreading the disease by their immediate effects. The hospital – which was to be built in the second half of the century and for which so many plans were drawn up after the Hôtel-Dieu was burnt down for the second time – was no longer simply the roof under which penury and imminent death took shelter; it was, in its very materiality, a therapeutic operator.

Similarly, the school building was to be a mechanism for training. It was as a pedagogical machine that Pâris-Duverney conceived the École Militaire, right down to the minute details that he had imposed on the architect, Gabriel. Train vigorous bodies, the imperative of health; obtain competent officers, the imperative of qualification; create obedient soldiers, the imperative of politics; prevent debauchery and homosexuality, the imperative of morality. A fourfold reason for establishing sealed compartments between individuals, but also apertures for continuous surveillance. The very building of the École was to be an apparatus for observation; the rooms were distributed along a corridor like a series of small cells; at regular intervals, an officer's quarters were situated, so that 'every ten pupils had an officer on each side'; the pupils were confined to their cells throughout the night; and Pâris had insisted that 'a window be placed on the corridor wall of each room from chest-level to within one or two feet of the ceiling. Not only is it pleasant to have such windows, but one would venture to say that it is useful, in several respects, not to mention the disciplinary reasons that may determine this arrangement' (quoted in Laulan, 117–18). In the dining-rooms was 'a slightly raised platform for the tables of the inspectors of studies, so that they may see all the tables of the pupils of their divisions during meals'; latrines had been installed with half-doors, so that the supervisor on duty could see the head and legs of the pupils, and also with side walls sufficiently high 'that those inside cannot see one another'.[2] This infinitely scrupulous concern with surveillance is expressed in the architecture by innumerable petty mechanisms. These mechanisms can only be seen as unimportant if one forgets the role of this instrumentation, minor but flawless, in the progressive objectification and the ever more subtle partitioning of individual behaviour. The disciplinary institutions secreted a machinery of control that functioned like a microscope of conduct; the fine, analytical divisions that they created formed around men an apparatus of observation, recording and training. How was one to subdivide the gaze in these observation machines? How was one to establish a network of communications between them? How was one so to arrange things that a homogeneous, continuous power would result from their calculated multiplicity?

The perfect disciplinary apparatus would make it possible for a single gaze to see everything constantly. A central point would be both the source of light illuminating everything, and a locus of convergence for everything that must be known: a perfect eye that nothing would escape and a centre towards which all gazes would be turned. This is what Ledoux had imagined when he built Arc-et-Senans; all the buildings were to be arranged in a circle, opening on the inside, at the centre of which a high construction was to house the administrative functions of management, the policing functions of surveillance, the economic functions of control and checking, the religious functions of encouraging obedience and work; from here all orders would come, all activities would be recorded, all offences perceived and judged; and this would be done immediately with no other aid than an exact geometry. Among all the reasons for the prestige that was accorded in the second half of the eighteenth century, to circular architecture, one must no doubt include the fact that it expressed a certain political utopia.

But, the disciplinary gaze did, in fact, need relays. The pyramid was able to fulfil, more efficiently than the circle, two requirements: to be complete enough to form an uninterrupted network – consequently the possibility of multiplying its levels, and of distributing them over the entire surface to be supervised; and yet to be discreet enough not to weigh down with an inert mass on the activity to be disciplined, and not to act as a brake or an obstacle to it; to be integrated into the disciplinary mechanism as a function that increases its possible effects. It had to be broken down into smaller elements, but in order to increase its productive function: specify the surveillance and make it functional.

This was the problem of the great workshops and factories, in which a new type of surveillance was organized. It was different from the one practised in the régimes of the manufactories, which had been carried out from the outside by inspectors, entrusted with the task of applying the regulations; what was now needed was an intense, continuous supervision; it ran right through the labour process; it did not bear – or not only – on production (the nature and quantity of raw materials, the type of instruments used, the dimensions and quality of the products); it also took into account the activity of the men, their skill, the way they set about their tasks, their promptness, their zeal, their behaviour. But it was also different from the domestic supervision of the master present beside his workers and apprentices; for it was carried out by clerks, supervisors and foremen. As the machinery of production became larger and more complex, as the number of workers and the division of labour increased, supervision became ever more necessary and more difficult. It became a special function, which had nevertheless to form an integral part of the production process, to run parallel to it throughout its entire length. A specialized personnel became indispensable, constantly present and distinct from the workers: 'In the large factory, everything is regulated by the clock. The workers are treated strictly and harshly. The clerks, who are used to treating them with an air of superiority and command, which is really necessary with the multitude, treat them with severity or contempt; hence these workers either cost more or leave the factory soon after arrival' (*Encyclopédie*, article on 'Manufacture'). But, although the workers preferred a framework of a guild type to this new régime of surveillance, the employers saw that it was indissociable from the system of industrial production, private property and profit. At the scale of a factory, a great iron-works or a mine, 'the objects of expenditure are so multiplied, that the slightest dishonesty on each object would add up to an immense fraud, which would not only absorb the profits, but would lead to a loss of capital . . . the slightest incompetence, if left unnoticed and therefore repeated each day, may prove fatal to the enterprise to the extent of destroying it in a very short time'; hence the fact that only agents, directly dependent on the owner, and entrusted with this task alone would be able to see 'that not a sou is spent uselessly, that not a moment of the day is lost'; their role would be 'to supervise the workers, to inspect all the places of work, to inform the directors of everything that takes place' (Cournol). Surveillance thus becomes a decisive economic operator both as an internal part of the production machinery and as a specific mechanism in the disciplinary power. 'The work of directing, superintending and adjusting becomes one of the functions of capital, from the moment that the labour under the control of capital, becomes cooperative. Once a function of capital, it requires special characteristics' (Marx, *Capital*, vol. 1, 313).

The same movement was to be found in the reorganization of elementary teaching: the details of surveillance were specified and it was integrated into the teaching relationship. The development of the parish schools, the increase in the number of their pupils, the absence of methods for regulating simultaneously the activity of a whole class, and the disorder and confusion that followed from this made it necessary to work out a system of supervision. In order to help the teacher, Batencour selected from among the best pupils a whole series of 'officers' – intendants, observers, monitors, tutors, reciters of prayers, writing officers, receivers of ink, almoners and visitors. The roles thus defined were of two kinds: the first involved material tasks (distributing ink and paper, giving alms to the poor, reading spiritual texts on feast days, etc.); the second involved surveillance: the 'observers must record who left his bench, who was talking, who did not have his rosary, or Book of Hours, who did not comport himself properly at mass, who committed an impure act, who indulged in idle talk or was unruly in the street'; the 'admonitors' were placed in charge of those 'who talk or hum when studying their lessons and those who will not write and who waste their time in play'; the 'visitors' called on the families of pupils who had been absent or who had committed serious offences. The 'intendants' supervised all the other officers. Only the 'tutors' had a pedagogical role: their task was to teach the pupils reading, two by two, in low tones (M.I.D.B., 68–83). A few decades later, Demia favoured a hierarchy of the same type but almost all the functions of surveillance were duplicated by a pedagogical role: an assistant teacher taught the holding of the pen, guided the pupil's hand, corrected mistakes and at the same time 'marked down trouble-makers'; another assistant teacher had the same tasks in the reading class; the intendant who supervised the other officers and was in charge of behaviour in general also had the task of 'initiating newcomers into the customs of the school'; the decurions got the pupils to recite their lessons and 'marked down' those who did not know them.[3] We have here a sketch of an institution of the 'mutual' type in which three procedures are integrated into a single mechanism: teaching proper, the acquisition of knowledge by the very practice of the pedagogical activity and a reciprocal, hierarchized observation. A relation of surveillance, defined and regulated, is inscribed at the heart of the practice of teaching, not as an additional or adjacent part, but as a mechanism that is inherent to it and which increases its efficiency.

Hierarchized, continuous and functional surveillance may not be one of the great technical 'inventions' of the eighteenth century, but its insidious extension owed its importance to the mechanisms of power that it brought with it. By means of such surveillance, disciplinary power became an 'integrated' system, linked from the inside to the economy and to the aims of the mechanism in which it was practised. It was also organized as a multiple, automatic and anonymous power; for although surveillance rests on individuals, its functioning is that of a network of relations from top to bottom, but also to a certain extent from bottom to top and laterally; this network 'holds' the whole together and traverses it in its entirety with effects of power that derive from one another: supervisors, perpetually supervised. The power in the hierarchized surveillance of the disciplines is not possessed as a thing, or transferred as a property; it functions like a piece of machinery. And, although it is true that its pyramidal organization gives it a 'head', it is the apparatus as a whole that produces 'power' and distributes individuals in this permanent and continuous field. This enables the disciplinary power to be both absolutely indiscreet, since it is everywhere and always alert, since by its very principle it leaves no zone of shade and constantly supervises the very individuals who are entrusted with the task of supervising; and absolutely 'discreet', for it functions permanently and largely in silence. Discipline makes possible the operation of a relational power that sustains itself by its own mechanism and which, for the spectacle of public events, substitutes the uninterrupted play of calculated gazes. Thanks to the techniques of surveillance, the 'physics' of power, the hold over the body, operate according to the laws of optics and mechanics, according to a whole play of spaces, lines, screens, beams, degrees and without recourse, in principle at least, to excess, force or violence. It is a power that seems all the less 'corporal' in that it is more subtly 'physical'.

Normalizing judgement

1. At the orphanage of the Chevalier Paulet, the sessions of the tribunal that met each morning gave rise to a whole ceremonial: 'We found all the pupils drawn up as if for battle, in perfect alignment, immobility and silence. The major, a young gentleman of sixteen years, stood outside the ranks, sword in hand; at his command, the troop broke ranks at the double and formed a circle. The council met in the centre; each officer made a report of his troop for the preceding twenty-four hours. The accused were allowed to defend themselves; witnesses were heard; the council deliberated and, when agreement was reached, the major announced the number of guilty, the nature of the offences and the punishments ordered. The troop then marched off in the greatest order' (Pictet). At the heart of all disciplinary systems functions a small penal mechanism.

It enjoys a kind of judicial privilege with its own laws, its specific offences, its particular forms of judgement. The disciplines established an 'infra-penality'; they partitioned an area that the laws had left empty; they defined and repressed a mass of behaviour that the relative indifference of the great systems of punishment had allowed to escape. 'On entering, the companions will greet one another . . . on leaving, they must lock up the materials and tools that they have been using and also make sure that their lamps are extinguished'; 'it is expressly forbidden to amuse companions by gestures or in any other way'; they must 'comport themselves honestly and decently'; anyone who is absent for more than five minutes without warning M. Oppenheim will be 'marked down for a half-day'; and in order to be sure that nothing is forgotten in this meticulous criminal justice, it is forbidden to do 'anything that may harm M. Oppenheim and his companions' (Oppenheim, 29 September 1809). The workshop, the school, the army were subject to a whole micro-penality of time (latenesses, absences, interruptions of tasks), of activity (inattention, negligence, lack of zeal), of behaviour (impoliteness, disobedience), of speech (idle chatter, insolence), of the body ('incorrect' attitudes, irregular gestures, lack of cleanliness), of sexuality (impurity, indecency). At the same time, by way of punishment, a whole series of subtle procedures was used, from light physical punishment to minor deprivations and petty humiliations. It was a question both of making the slightest departures from correct behaviour subject to punishment, and of giving a punitive function to the apparently indifferent elements of the disciplinary apparatus: so that, if necessary, everything might serve to punish the slightest thing; each subject find himself caught in a punishable, punishing universality. 'By the word punishment, one must understand everything that is capable of making children feel the offence they have committed, everything that is capable of humiliating them, of confusing them: . . . a certain coldness, a certain indifference, a question, a humiliation, a removal from office' (La Salle, *Conduite* . . ., 204–5).

2. But discipline brought with it a specific way of punishing that was not only a small-scale model of the court. What is specific to the disciplinary penality is non-observance, that which does not measure up to the rule, that departs from it. The whole indefinite

domain of the non-conforming is punishable: the soldier commits an 'offence' whenever he does not reach the level required; a pupil's 'offence' is not only a minor infraction, but also an inability to carry out his tasks. The regulations for the Prussian infantry ordered that a soldier who had not correctly learnt to handle his rifle should be treated with the 'greatest severity'. Similarly, 'when a pupil has not retained the catechism from the previous day, he must be forced to learn it, without making any mistake, and repeat it the following day; either he will be forced to hear it standing or kneeling, his hands joined, or he will be given some other penance'.

The order that the disciplinary punishments must enforce is of a mixed nature: it is an 'artificial' order, explicitly laid down by a law, a programme, a set of regulations. But it is also an order defined by natural and observable processes: the duration of an apprenticeship, the time taken to perform an exercise, the level of aptitude refer to a regularity that is also a rule. The children of the Christian Schools must never be placed in a 'lesson' of which they are not yet capable, for this would expose them to the danger of being unable to learn anything; yet the duration of each stage is fixed by regulation and a pupil who at the end of three examinations has been unable to pass into the higher order must be placed, well in evidence, on the bench of the 'ignorant'. In a disciplinary régime punishment involves a double juridico-natural reference.

3. Disciplinary punishment has the function of reducing gaps. It must therefore be essentially *corrective*. In addition to punishments borrowed directly from the judicial model (fines, flogging, solitary confinement), the disciplinary systems favour punishments that are exercise – intensified, multiplied forms of training, several times repeated: the regulations of 1766 for the infantry laid down that lance-corporals 'who show some negligence or lack of willingness will be reduced to the rank of private', and they will be able to rise to their former rank only after new exercises and a new examination. As Jean-Baptiste de La Salle put it: 'Of all penances, impositions are the most honest for a teacher, the most advantageous for the parents'; they make it possible to 'derive, from the very offences of the children, means of advancing their progress by correcting their defects'; to those, for example, 'who have not written all that they were supposed to write or who have not applied

themselves to doing it well, one can give some impositions to write out or to learn by heart' (La Salle, *Conduite . . .*, 205). Disciplinary punishment is, in the main, isomorphic with obligation itself; it is not so much the vengeance of an outraged law as its repetition, its reduplicated insistence. So much so that the corrective effect expected of it involves only incidentally expiation and repentance; it is obtained directly through the mechanics of a training. To punish is to exercise.

4. In discipline, punishment is only one element of a double system: gratification-punishment. And it is this system that operates in the process of training and correction. The teacher 'must avoid, as far as possible, the use of punishment; on the contrary, he must endeavour to make rewards more frequent than penalties, the lazy being more encouraged by the desire to be rewarded in the same way as the diligent than by the fear of punishment; that is why it will be very beneficial, when the teacher is obliged to use punishment, to win the heart of the child if he can before doing so' (Demia, 17). This mechanism with two elements makes possible a number of operations characteristic of disciplinary penality. First, the definition of behaviour and performance on the basis of the two opposed values of good and evil; instead of the simple division of the prohibition, as practised in penal justice, we have a distribution between a positive pole and a negative pole; all behaviour falls in the field between good and bad marks, good and bad points. Moreover, it is possible to quantify this field and work out an arithmetical economy based on it. A penal accountancy, constantly brought up to date, makes it possible to obtain the punitive balance-sheet of each individual. School 'justice', rudiments of which are to be found in the army and the workshops, carried this system very far. The Brothers of the Christian Schools organized a whole micro-economy of privileges and impositions: 'Privileges may be used by pupils to gain exemption from penances which have been imposed on them. . . For example, a pupil may have been given four or six catechism questions to copy out as an imposition; he will be able to gain exemption from this penance by accumulating a certain number of privilege points; the teacher will assign the number for each question. . . Since privileges are worth a certain number of points, the teacher also has others of less value, which serve as small change

for the first. For example, a child has an imposition from which he can redeem himself with six points; he earns a privilege of ten; he presents it to the teacher who gives him back four points, and so on' (La Salle, *Conduite . . .*, 156ff). What we have here is a transposition of the system of indulgences. And by the play of this quantification, this circulation of awards and debits, thanks to the continuous calculation of plus and minus points, the disciplinary apparatuses hierarchized the 'good' and the 'bad' subjects in relation to one another. Through this micro-economy of a perpetual penality operates a differentiation that is not one of acts, but of individuals themselves, of their nature, their potentialities, their level or their value. By assessing acts with precision, discipline judges individuals 'in truth'; the penality that it implements is integrated into the cycle of knowledge of individuals.

5. The distribution according to ranks or grade has a double role: it marks the gaps, hierarchizes qualities, skills and aptitudes; but it also punishes and rewards. It is the penal functioning of setting in order and the ordinal character of judging. Discipline rewards simply by the play of awards, thus making it possible to attain higher ranks and places; it punishes by reversing this process. Rank in itself serves as a reward or punishment. At the École Militaire, a complex system of 'honorary' classification was developed; this classification was visible to all in the form of slight variations in uniform and more or less noble or ignoble punishments were associated, as a mark of privilege or infamy, with the ranks thus distributed. This classificatory, penal distribution was carried out at short intervals by the reports that the officers, teachers and their assistants made, without consideration of age or grade, on 'the moral qualities of the pupils' and on 'their universally recognized behaviour'. The first class, known as the 'very good', were distinguished by a silver epaulette; they enjoyed the honour of being treated as 'purely military troops'; they therefore had a right to military punishment (arrests and, in serious cases, imprisonment). The second class, 'the good', wore an epaulette of red silk and silver; they could be arrested and condemned to prison, but also to the cage and to kneeling. The class of '*médiocres*', had the right to an epaulette of red wool; to the preceding penalties was added, if necessary, the wearing of sackcloth. The last class, that of the 'bad', was marked by

an epaulette of brown wool; 'the pupils of this class will be subjected to all the punishments used in the Hôtel or all those that are thought necessary, even solitary confinement in a dark dungeon'. To this was added, for a time, the 'shameful' class, for which special regulations were drawn up 'so that those who belonged to it would always be separated from the others and would be dressed in sackcloth'. Since merit and behaviour alone must decide the place of the pupil, 'those of the last two classes would be able to flatter themselves that they would be able to rise to the first two and bear its marks, when, by universal agreement, they will be recognized as having made themselves worthy of it by the change in their conduct and by their progress; and those of the top classes will similarly descend into the others if they become slack and if the various reports taken together are to their disadvantage and show that they no longer deserve the rewards and prerogatives of the higher classes. . .' The penal classification should tend to disappear. The 'shameful' class existed only to disappear: 'In order to judge the kind of conversion undergone by pupils of the shameful class who behave well', they were reintroduced into the other classes, and given back their uniforms; but they would remain with their comrades in infamy during meals and recreation; they would remain there if they did not continue to behave well; they 'would leave it absolutely, if their conduct was considered satisfactory both in this class and in this division' (Archives nationales, MM 658, 30 March 1758 and MM 666, 15 September 1763). This hierarchizing penality had, therefore, a double effect: it distributed pupils according to their aptitudes and their conduct, that is, according to the use that could be made of them when they left the school; it exercised over them a constant pressure to conform to the same model, so that they might all be subjected to 'subordination, docility, attention in studies and exercises, and to the correct practice of duties and all the parts of discipline'. So that they might all be like one another.

In short, the art of punishing, in the régime of disciplinary power, is aimed neither at expiation, nor even precisely at repression. It brings five quite distinct operations into play: it refers individual actions to a whole that is at once a field of comparison, a space of differentiation and the principle of a rule to be followed. It differentiates individuals from one another, in terms of the following overall rule: that the rule be made to function as a minimal threshold, as an average to be respected or as an optimum towards which one must move. It measures in quantitative terms and hierarchizes in terms of value the abilities, the level, the 'nature' of individuals. It introduces, through this 'value-giving' measure, the constraint of a conformity that must be achieved. Lastly, it traces the limit that will define difference in relation to all other differences, the external frontier of the abnormal (the 'shameful' class of the École Militaire). The perpetual penalty that traverses all points and supervises every instant in the disciplinary institutions compares, differentiates, hierarchizes, homogenizes, excludes. In short, it *normalizes*.

It is opposed, therefore, term by term, to a judicial penalty whose essential function is to refer, not to a set of observable phenomena, but to a corpus of laws and texts that must be remembered; that operates not by differentiating individuals, but by specifying acts according to a number of general categories; not by hierarchizing, but quite simply by bringing into play the binary opposition of the permitted and the forbidden; not by homogenizing, but by operating the division, acquired once and for all, of condemnation. The disciplinary mechanisms secreted a 'penalty of the norm', which is irreducible in its principles and functioning to the traditional penalty of the law. The minor court that seems to sit permanently in the buildings of discipline, and which sometimes assumes the theatrical form of the great legal apparatus, must not mislead us: it does not bring, except for a few formal remnants, the mechanisms of criminal justice to the web of everyday existence; or at least that is not its essential role; the disciplines created – drawing on a whole series of very ancient procedures – a new functioning of punishment, and it was this that gradually invested the great external apparatus that it seemed to reproduce in either a modest or an ironic way. The juridico-anthropological functioning revealed in the whole history of modern penality did not originate in the super-imposition of the human sciences on criminal justice and in the requirements proper to this new rationality or to the humanism that it appeared to bring with it; it originated in the disciplinary tech-nique that operated these new mechanisms of normalizing judgement.

The power of the Norm appears through the disciplines. Is this the new law of modern society? Let us say rather that, since the eighteenth century, it has joined other powers – the Law, the Word (*Parole*) and the Text, Tradition – imposing new delimitations upon them. The Normal is established as a principle of coercion in teaching with the introduction of a standardized education and the establishment of the *écoles normales* (teachers' training colleges); it is established in the effort to organize a national medical profession and a hospital system capable of operating general norms of health; it is established in the standardization of industrial processes and products (on this topic, one should refer to the important contribution of Canguilhem, 171–91). Like surveillance and with it, normalization becomes one of the great instruments of power at the end of the classical age. For the marks that once indicated status, privilege and affiliation were increasingly replaced – or at least supplemented – by a whole range of degrees of normality indicating membership of a homogeneous social body but also playing a part in classification, hierarchization and the distribution of rank. In a sense, the power of normalization imposes homogeneity; but it individualizes by making it possible to measure gaps, to determine levels, to fix specialities and to render the differences useful by fitting them one to another. It is easy to understand how the power of the norm functions within a system of formal equality, since within a homogeneity that is the rule, the norm introduces, as a useful imperative and as a result of measurement, all the shading of individual differences.

The examination

The examination combines the techniques of an observing hierarchy and those of a normalizing judgement. It is a normalizing gaze, a surveillance that makes it possible to qualify, to classify and to punish. It establishes over individuals a visibility through which one differentiates them and judges them. That is why, in all the mechanisms of discipline, the examination is highly ritualized. In it are combined the ceremony of power and the form of the experiment, the deployment of force and the establishment of truth. At the heart of the procedures of discipline, it manifests the subjection of those who are perceived as objects and the objectification of those who are subjected. The superimposition of the power relations and knowledge relations assumes in the examination all its visible brilliance. It is yet another innovation of the classical age that the historians of science have left unexplored. People write the history of experiments on those born blind, on wolf-children or under hypnosis. But who will write the more general, more fluid, but also more determinant history of the 'examination' – its rituals, its methods, its characters and their roles, its play of questions and answers, its systems of marking and classification? For in this slender technique are to be found a whole domain of knowledge, a whole type of power. One often speaks of the ideology that the human 'sciences' bring with them, in either discreet or prolix manner. But does their very technology, this tiny operational schema that has become so widespread (from psychiatry to pedagogy, from the diagnosis of diseases to the hiring of labour), this familiar method of the examination, implement, within a single mechanism, power relations that make it possible to extract and constitute knowledge? It is not simply at the level of consciousness, of representations and in what one thinks one knows, but at the level of what makes possible the knowledge that is transformed into political investment.

One of the essential conditions for the epistemological 'thaw' of medicine at the end of the eighteenth century was the organization of the hospital as an 'examining' apparatus. The ritual of the visit was its most obvious form. In the seventeenth century, the physician, coming from the outside, added his inspection to many other controls – religious, administrative, etc.; he hardly participated in the everyday administration of the hospital. Gradually, the visit became more regular, more rigorous, above all more extended: it became an ever more important part of the functioning of the hospital. In 1661, the physician of the Hôtel-Dieu of Paris was called upon to make a daily visit; in 1687, an 'expectant' physician was to examine, in the afternoon, certain seriously sick patients. The eighteenth-century regulations laid down the hours of the visit and its duration (at least two hours); they insisted on a rotation of physicians, which would guarantee visits every day 'even on Easter Sunday'; at last, in 1771, a resident physician was appointed, charged with 'providing all the services of his state, at night as well as in the day, in the intervals between visits by an outside physician' (*Registre des déliberations du bureau de l'Hôtel-Dieu*). The old form of inspection, irregular and rapid, was transformed into a regular observation that placed the patient in a situation of almost perpetual examination. This had two consequences: in the internal hierarchy, the physician, hitherto an external element, begins to gain over the religious staff and to relegate them to a clearly specified, but subordinate role in the technique of the examination; the category of the 'nurse' then appears; while the hospital itself, which was once little more than a poorhouse, was to become a place of training and of the correlation of knowledge; it represented a reversal therefore of the power relations and the constitution of a corpus of knowledge. The 'well-disciplined' hospital became the physical counterpart of the medical 'discipline'; this discipline could now abandon its textual character and take its references not so much from the tradition of author-authorities as from a domain of objects perpetually offered for examination.

Similarly, the school became a sort of apparatus of uninterrupted examination that duplicated along its entire length the operation of teaching. It became less and less a question of jousts in which pupils pitched their forces against one another and increasingly a perpetual comparison of each and all that made it possible both to measure and to judge. The Brothers of the Christian Schools wanted their pupils to be examined every day of the week: on the first for spelling, on the second for arithmetic, on the third for catechism in the morning and for handwriting in the afternoon, etc. Moreover, there was to be an examination each month in order to pick out those who deserved to be submitted for examination by the inspector (La Salle, *Conduite* . . ., 160). From 1775, there existed at the École des Ponts et Chaussées sixteen examinations a year: three in mathematics, three in architecture, three in drawing, two in writing, one in stone-cutting, one in style, one in surveying, one in levelling, one in quantity surveying. The examination did not simply mark the end of an apprenticeship; it was one of its permanent factors; it was woven into it through a constantly repeated ritual of power. The examination enabled the teacher, while transmitting his knowledge, to transform his pupils into a whole field of knowledge. Whereas the examination with which an apprenticeship ended in the guild tradition validated an acquired aptitude – the 'master-work' authenticated a transmission of knowledge that had already been accomplished – the examination in the school was a constant exchanger of knowledge; it guaranteed the movement of knowledge from the teacher to the pupil, but it extracted from the pupil a knowledge destined and reserved for the teacher. The school became the place of elaboration for pedagogy. And just as the procedure of the hospital examination made possible the epistemological 'thaw' of medicine, the age of the 'examining' school marked the beginnings of a pedagogy that functions as a science. The age of inspections and endlessly repeated movements in the army also marked the development of an immense tactical knowledge that had its effect in the period of the Napoleonic wars.

The examination introduced a whole mechanism that linked to a certain type of the formation of knowledge a certain form of the exercise of power.

1. *The examination transformed the economy of visibility into the exercise of power.* Traditionally, power was what was seen, what was shown and what was manifested and, paradoxically, found the principle of its force in the movement by which it deployed that force. Those on whom it was exercised could remain in the shade; they received light only from that portion of power that was conceded to them, or from the reflection of it that for a moment they carried. Disciplinary power, on the other hand, is exercised through its invisibility; at the same time it imposes on those whom it subjects a principle of compulsory visibility. In discipline, it is the subjects who have to be seen. Their visibility assures the hold of the power that is exercised over them. It is the fact of being constantly seen, of being able always to be seen, that maintains the disciplined individual in his subjection. And the examination is the technique by which power, instead of emitting the signs of its potency, instead of imposing its mark on its subjects, holds them in a mechanism of objectification. In this space of domination, disciplinary power manifests its potency, essentially, by arranging objects. The examination is, as it were, the ceremony of this objectification.

Hitherto the role of the political ceremony had been to give rise to the excessive, yet regulated manifestation of power; it was a spectacular expression of potency, an 'expenditure', exaggerated and coded, in which power renewed its vigour. It was always more or less related to the triumph. The solemn appearance of the sovereign brought with it something of the consecration, the coronation, the return from victory; even the funeral ceremony took place with all the spectacle of power deployed. Discipline, however, had its own type of ceremony. It was not the triumph, but the review, the 'parade', an ostentatious form of the examination. In it the 'subjects' were presented as 'objects' to the observation of a power that was manifested only by its gaze. They did not receive directly the image of the sovereign power; they only felt its effects – in replica, as it were – on their bodies, which had become precisely legible and docile. On 15 March 1666, Louis XIV took his first military review: 18,000 men, 'one of the most spectacular actions of the reign', which was supposed to have 'kept all Europe in disquiet'. Several years later, a medal was struck to commemorate the event (cf. Jucquiot, 50–54). It bears the exergue, 'Disciplina militaris restituta' and the legend 'Prolusio ad victorias'. On the right, the king, right foot forward, commands the exercise itself with a stick. On the left, several ranks of soldiers are shown full face and aligned in depth; they have raised their right arms to shoulder height and are holding their rifles exactly vertical, their right legs are slightly forward and their left feet turned outwards. On the ground, lines intersect at right angles, to form, beneath the soldiers' feet, broad rectangles that serve as references for different phases and positions of the exercise. In the background is a piece of classical architecture. The columns of the palace extend those formed by the ranks of men and the erect rifles, just as the paving no doubt extends the lines of the exercise. But above the balustrade that crowns the building are statues representing dancing figures: sinuous lines, rounded gestures, draperies. The marble is covered with movements whose principle of unity is harmonic. The men, on the other hand, are frozen into a uniformly repeated attitude of ranks and lines: a tactical unity. The order of the architecture, which frees at its summit the figures of the dance, imposes its rules and its geometry on the disciplined men on the ground. The columns of power. 'Very good', Grand Duke Mikhail once remarked of a regiment, after having kept it for one hour presenting arms, 'only they breathe' (Kropotkin, 8; I owe this reference to G. Canguilhem).

Let us take this medal as evidence of the moment when, paradoxically but significantly, the most brilliant figure of sovereign power is joined to the emergence of the rituals proper to disciplinary power. The scarcely sustainable visibility of the monarch is turned into the unavoidable visibility of the subjects. And it is this inversion of visibility in the functioning of the disciplines that was to assure the exercise of power even in its lowest manifestations. We are entering the age of the infinite examination and of compulsory objectification.

2. *The examination also introduces individuality into the field of documentation.* The examination leaves behind it a whole meticulous archive constituted in terms of bodies and days. The examination that places individuals in a field of surveillance also situates them in a network of writing; it engages them in a whole mass of documents that capture and fix them. The procedures of examination were accompanied at the same time by a system of intense registration and of documentary accumulation. A 'power of writing' was constituted as an essential part in the mechanisms of discipline. On many points, it was modelled on the traditional methods of administrative documentation, though with particular techniques and important innovations. Some concerned methods of identification, signalling or description. This was the problem in the army, where it was necessary to track down deserters, avoid repeating enrolments, correct fictitious 'information' presented by officers, know the services and value of each individual, establish with certainty the balance-sheet of those who had disappeared or died. It was the problem of the hospitals, where it was necessary to recognize the patients, expel shammers, follow the evolution of diseases, study the effectiveness of treatments, map similar cases and the beginnings of epidemics. It was the problem of the teaching establishments, where one had to define the aptitude of each individual, situate his level and his abilities, indicate the possible use that might be made of them: 'The register enables one, by being available in time and place, to know the habits of the children, their progress in piety, in catechism, in the letters, during the time they have been at the School' (M.I.D.B., 64).

Hence the formation of a whole series of codes of disciplinary individuality that made it possible to transcribe, by means of homogenization the individual features established by the examination:

the physical code of signalling, the medical code of symptoms, the educational or military code of conduct or performance. These codes were still very crude, both in quality and quantity, but they marked a first stage in the 'formalization' of the individual within power relations.

The other innovations of disciplinary writing concerned the correlation of these elements, the accumulation of documents, their seriation, the organization of comparative fields making it possible to classify, to form categories, to determine averages, to fix norms. The hospitals of the eighteenth century, in particular, were great laboratories for scriptuary and documentary methods. The keeping of registers, their specification, the modes of transcription from one to the other, their circulation during visits, their comparison during regular meetings of doctors and administrators, the transmission of their data to centralizing bodies (either at the hospital or at the central office of the poorhouses), the accountancy of diseases, cures, deaths, at the level of a hospital, a town and even of the nation as a whole formed an integral part of the process by which hospitals were subjected to the disciplinary régime. Among the fundamental conditions of a good medical 'discipline', in both senses of the word, one must include the procedures of writing that made it possible to integrate individual data into cumulative systems in such a way that they were not lost; so to arrange things that an individual could be located in the general register and that, conversely, each datum of the individual examination might affect overall calculations.

Thanks to the whole apparatus of writing that accompanied it, the examination opened up two correlative possibilities: firstly, the constitution of the individual as a describable, analysable object, not in order to reduce him to 'specific' features, as did the naturalists in relation to living beings, but in order to maintain him in his individual features, in his particular evolution, in his own aptitudes or abilities, under the gaze of a permanent corpus of knowledge; and, secondly, the constitution of a comparative system that made possible the measurement of overall phenomena, the description of groups, the characterization of collective facts, the calculation of the gaps between individuals, their distribution in a given 'population'.

These small techniques of notation, of registration, of constituting files, of arranging facts in columns and tables that are so familiar to us now, were of decisive importance in the epistemological 'thaw' of the sciences of the individual. One is no doubt right to pose the Aristotelean problem: is a science of the individual possible and legitimate? A great problem needs great solutions perhaps. But there is the small historical problem of the emergence, towards the end of the eighteenth century, of what might generally be termed the 'clinical' sciences; the problem of the entry of the individual (and no longer the species) into the field of knowledge; the problem of the entry of the individual description, of the cross-examination, of anamnesis, of the 'file' into the general functioning of scientific discourse. To this simple question of fact, one must no doubt give an answer lacking in 'nobility': one should look into these procedures of writing and registration, one should look into the mechanisms of examination, into the formation of the mechanisms of discipline, and of a new type of power over bodies. Is this the birth of the sciences of man? It is probably to be found in these 'ignoble' archives, where the modern play of coercion over bodies, gestures and behaviour has its beginnings.

3. *The examination, surrounded by all its documentary techniques, makes each individual a 'case':* a case which at one and the same time constitutes an object for a branch of knowledge and a hold for a branch of power. The case is no longer, as in casuistry or jurisprudence, a set of circumstances defining an act and capable of modifying the application of a rule; it is the individual as he may be described, judged, measured, compared with others, in his very individuality; and it is also the individual who has to be trained or corrected, classified, normalized, excluded, etc.

For a long time ordinary individuality – the everyday individuality of everybody – remained below the threshold of description. To be looked at, observed, described in detail, followed from day to day by an uninterrupted writing was a privilege. The chronicle of a man, the account of his life, his historiography, written as he lived out his life formed part of the rituals of his power. The disciplinary methods reversed this relation, lowered the threshold of describable individuality and made of this description a means of control and a method of domination. It is no longer a monument for future memory, but a document for possible use. And this new describability is all the more marked in that the disciplinary framework is a strict one: the child, the patient, the madman, the prisoner, were to become, with increasing ease from the eighteenth century and according to a curve which is that of the mechanisms of discipline, the object of individual descriptions and biographical accounts. This turning of real lives into writing is no longer a procedure of heroization; it functions as a procedure of objectification and subjection. The carefully collated life of mental patients or delinquents belongs, as did the chronicle of kings or the adventures of the great popular bandits, to a certain political function of writing; but in a quite different technique of power.

The examination as the fixing, at once ritual and 'scientific', of individual differences, as the pinning down of each individual in his own particularity (in contrast with the ceremony in which status, birth, privilege, function are manifested with all the spectacle of their marks) clearly indicates the appearance of a new modality of power in which each individual receives as his status his own individuality, and in which he is linked by his status to the features, the measurements, the gaps, the 'marks' that characterize him and make him a 'case'.

Finally, the examination is at the centre of the procedures that constitute the individual as effect and object of power, as effect and object of knowledge. It is the examination which, by combining hierarchical surveillance and normalizing judgement, assures the great disciplinary functions of distribution and classification, maximum extraction of forces and time, continuous genetic accumulation, optimum combination of aptitudes and, thereby, the fabrication of cellular, organic, genetic and combinatory individuality. With it are ritualized those disciplines that may be characterized in a word by saying that they are a modality of power for which individual difference is relevant.

The disciplines mark the moment when the reversal of the political axis of individualization – as one might call it – takes place. In certain societies, of which the feudal régime is only one example, it may be said that individualization is greatest where sovereignty is exercised and in the higher echelons of power. The more one possesses power or privilege, the more one is marked as an individual, by rituals, written accounts or visual reproductions. The 'name' and the genealogy that situate one within a kinship group, the performance of deeds that demonstrate superior strength and which are immortalized in literary accounts, the ceremonies that mark the power relations in their very ordering, the monuments or donations that bring survival after death, the ostentation and excess of expenditure, the multiple, intersecting links of allegiance and suzerainty, all these are procedures of an 'ascending' individualization. In a disciplinary régime, on the other hand, individualization is 'descending': as power becomes more anonymous and more functional, those on whom it is exercised tend to be more strongly individualized; it is exercised by surveillance rather than ceremonies, by observation rather than commemorative accounts, by comparative measures that have the 'norm' as reference rather than genealogies giving ancestors as points of reference; by 'gaps' rather than by deeds. In a system of discipline, the child is more individualized than the adult, the patient more than the healthy man, the madman and the delinquent more than the normal and the non-delinquent. In each case, it is towards the first of these pairs that all the individualizing mechanisms are turned in our civilization; and when one wishes to individualize the healthy, normal and law-abiding adult, it is always by asking him how much of the child he has in him, what secret madness lies within him, what fundamental crime he has dreamt of committing. All the sciences, analyses or practices employing the root 'psycho-' have their origin in this historical reversal of the procedures of individualization. The moment that saw the transition from historico-ritual mechanisms for the formation of individuality to the scientifico-disciplinary mechanisms, when the normal took over from the ancestral, and measurement from status, thus substituting for the individuality of the memorable man that of the calculable man, that moment when the sciences of man became possible is the moment when a new technology of power and a new political anatomy of the body were implemented. And if from the early Middle Ages to the present day the 'adventure' is an account of individuality, the passage from the epic to the novel, from the noble deed to the secret singularity, from long exiles to the internal search for childhood, from combats to phantasies, it is also inscribed in the formation of a disciplinary society. The adventure of our childhood no longer finds expression in '*le bon petit Henri*', but in the misfortunes of 'little Hans'. The *Romance of the Rose* is written today by Mary Barnes; in the place of Lancelot, we have Judge Schreber.

It is often said that the model of a society that has individuals as its constituent elements is borrowed from the abstract juridical forms of contract and exchange. Mercantile society, according to this view, is represented as a contractual association of isolated juridical subjects. Perhaps. Indeed, the political theory of the seventeenth and eighteenth centuries often seems to follow this schema. But it should not be forgotten that there existed at the same period a technique for constituting individuals as correlative elements of power and knowledge. The individual is no doubt the fictitious atom of an 'ideological' representation of society; but he is also a reality fabricated by this specific technology of power that I have called 'discipline'. We must cease once and for all to describe the effects of power in negative terms: it 'excludes', it 'represses', it 'censors', it 'abstracts', it 'masks', it 'conceals'. In fact, power produces; it produces reality; it produces domains of objects and rituals of truth. The individual and the knowledge that may be gained of him belong to this production.

Is it not somewhat excessive to derive such power from the petty machinations of discipline? How could *they* achieve effects of such scope?

3. Panopticism

The following, according to an order published at the end of the seventeenth century, were the measures to be taken when the plague appeared in a town.[1]

First, a strict spatial partitioning: the closing of the town and its outlying districts, a prohibition to leave the town on pain of death, the killing of all stray animals; the division of the town into distinct quarters, each governed by an intendant. Each street is placed under the authority of a syndic, who keeps it under surveillance; if he leaves the street, he will be condemned to death. On the appointed day, everyone is ordered to stay indoors: it is forbidden to leave on pain of death. The syndic himself comes to lock the door of each house from the outside; he takes the key with him and hands it over to the intendant of the quarter; the intendant keeps it until the end of the quarantine. Each family will have made its own provisions; but, for bread and wine, small wooden canals are set up between the street and the interior of the houses, thus allowing each person to receive his ration without communicating with the suppliers and other residents; meat, fish and herbs will be hoisted up into the houses with pulleys and baskets. If it is absolutely necessary to leave the house, it will be done in turn, avoiding any meeting. Only the intendants, syndics and guards will move about the streets and also, between the infected houses, from one corpse to another, the 'crows', who can be left to die: these are 'people of little substance who carry the sick, bury the dead, clean and do many vile and abject offices'. It is a segmented, immobile, frozen space. Each individual is fixed in his place. And, if he moves, he does so at the risk of his life, contagion or punishment.

Inspection functions ceaselessly. The gaze is alert everywhere: 'A considerable body of militia, commanded by good officers and men of substance', guards at the gates, at the town hall and in every quarter to ensure the prompt obedience of the people and the most absolute authority of the magistrates, 'as also to observe all disorder, theft and extortion'. At each of the town gates there will be an observation post; at the end of each street sentinels. Every day, the intendant visits the quarter in his charge, inquires whether the syndics have carried out their tasks, whether the inhabitants have anything to complain of; they 'observe their actions'. Every day, too, the syndic goes into the street for which he is responsible; stops before each house: gets all the inhabitants to appear at the windows (those who live overlooking the courtyard will be allocated a window looking onto the street at which no one but they may show themselves); he calls each of them by name; informs himself as to the state of each and every one of them – 'in which respect the inhabitants will be compelled to speak the truth under pain of death'; if someone does not appear at the window, the syndic must ask why: 'In this way he will find out easily enough whether dead or sick are being concealed.' Everyone locked up in his cage, everyone at his window, answering to his name and showing himself when asked – it is the great review of the living and the dead.

This surveillance is based on a system of permanent registration: reports from the syndics to the intendants, from the intendants to the magistrates or mayor. At the beginning of the 'lock up', the role of each of the inhabitants present in the town is laid down, one by one; this document bears 'the name, age, sex of everyone, notwithstanding his condition': a copy is sent to the intendant of the quarter, another to the office of the town hall, another to enable the syndic to make his daily roll call. Everything that may be observed during the course of the visits – deaths, illnesses, complaints, irregularities – is noted down and transmitted to the intendants and magistrates. The magistrates have complete control over medical treatment; they have appointed a physician in charge; no other practitioner may treat, no apothecary prepare medicine, no confessor visit a sick person without having received from him a written note 'to prevent anyone from concealing and dealing with those sick of the contagion, unknown to the magistrates'. The registration of the pathological must be constantly centralized. The relation of each individual to his disease and to his death passes through the representatives of power, the registration they make of it, the decisions they take on it.

Five or six days after the beginning of the quarantine, the process of purifying the houses one by one is begun. All the inhabitants are made to leave; in each room 'the furniture and goods' are raised from the ground or suspended from the air; perfume is poured around the room; after carefully sealing the windows, doors and even the keyholes with wax, the perfume is set alight. Finally, the entire house is closed while the perfume is consumed; those who have carried out the work are searched, as they were on entry, 'in the presence of the residents of the house, to see that they did not have something on their persons as they left that they did not have on entering'. Four hours later, the residents are allowed to re-enter their homes.

This enclosed, segmented space, observed at every point, in which the individuals are inserted in a fixed place, in which the slightest movements are supervised, in which all events are recorded, in which an uninterrupted work of writing links the centre and periphery, in which power is exercised without division, according to a continuous hierarchical figure, in which each individual is constantly located, examined and distributed among the living beings, the sick and the dead – all this constitutes a compact model of the disciplinary mechanism. The plague is met by order; its function is to sort out every possible confusion: that of the disease, which is transmitted when bodies are mixed together; that of the evil, which is increased when fear and death overcome prohibitions. It lays down for each individual his place, his body, his disease and his death, his well-being, by means of an omnipresent and omniscient power that subdivides itself in a regular, uninterrupted way even to the ultimate determination of the individual, of what characterizes him, of what belongs to him, of what happens to him. Against the plague, which is a mixture, discipline brings into play its power, which is one of analysis. A whole literary fiction of the festival grew up around the plague: suspended laws, lifted prohibitions, the frenzy of passing time, bodies mingling together without respect, individuals unmasked, abandoning their statutory identity and the figure under which they had been recognized, allowing a quite different truth to appear. But there was also a political dream of the plague, which was exactly its reverse: not the collective festival, but strict divisions; not laws transgressed, but the penetration of regulation into even the smallest details of everyday life through the mediation of the complete hierarchy that assured the capillary functioning of power; not masks that were put on and taken off, but the assignment to each individual of his 'true' name, his 'true' place, his 'true' body, his 'true' disease. The plague as a form, at once real and imaginary, of disorder had as its medical and political correlative discipline. Behind the disciplinary mechanisms can be read the haunting memory of 'contagions', of the plague, of rebellions, crimes, vagabondage, desertions, people who appear and disappear, live and die in disorder.

If it is true that the leper gave rise to rituals of exclusion, which to a certain extent provided the model for and general form of the great Confinement, then the plague gave rise to disciplinary projects. Rather than the massive, binary division between one set of people and another, it called for multiple separations, individualizing distributions, an organization in depth of surveillance and control, an intensification and a ramification of power. The leper was caught up in a practice of rejection, of exile-enclosure; he was left to his doom in a mass among which it was useless to differentiate; those sick of the plague were caught up in a meticulous tactical partitioning in which individual differentiations were the constricting effects of a power that multiplied, articulated and subdivided itself; the great confinement on the one hand; the correct training on the other. The leper and his separation; the plague and its segmentations. The first is marked; the second analysed and distributed. The exile of the leper and the arrest of the plague do not bring with them the same political dream. The first is that of a pure community, the second that of a disciplined society. Two ways of exercising power over men, of controlling their relations, of separating out their dangerous mixtures. The plague-stricken town, traversed throughout with hierarchy, surveillance, observation, writing; the town immobilized by the functioning of an extensive power that bears in a distinct way over all individual bodies – this is the utopia of the perfectly governed city. The plague (envisaged as a possibility at least) is the trial in the course of which one may define ideally the exercise of disciplinary power. In order to make rights and laws function according to pure theory, the jurists place themselves in imagination in the state of nature; in order to see perfect disciplines functioning, rulers dreamt of the state of plague. Underlying disciplinary projects the image of the plague stands for all forms of confusion and disorder; just as the image of the leper, cut off from all human contact, underlies projects of exclusion.

They are different projects, then, but not incompatible ones. We see them coming slowly together, and it is the peculiarity of the nineteenth century that it applied to the space of exclusion of which the leper was the symbolic inhabitant (beggars, vagabonds, madmen and the disorderly formed the real population) the technique of power proper to disciplinary partitioning. Treat 'lepers' as 'plague victims', project the subtle segmentations of discipline onto the confused space of internment, combine it with the methods of analytical distribution proper to power, individualize the excluded, but use procedures of individualization to mark exclusion – this is what was operated regularly by disciplinary power from the beginning of the nineteenth century in the psychiatric asylum, the penitentiary, the reformatory, the approved school and, to some extent, the hospital. Generally speaking, all the authorities exercising individual control function according to a double mode; that of binary division and branding (mad/sane; dangerous/harmless; normal/abnormal); and that of coercive assignment, of differential distribution (who he is; where he must be; how he is to be characterized; how he is to be recognized; how a constant surveillance is to be exercised over him in an individual way, etc.). On the one hand, the lepers are treated as plague victims; the tactics of individualizing disciplines are imposed on the excluded; and, on the other hand, the universality of disciplinary controls makes it possible to brand the 'leper' and to bring into play against him the dualistic mechanisms of exclusion. The constant division between the normal and the abnormal, to which every individual is subjected, brings us back to our own time, by applying the binary branding and exile of the leper to quite different objects; the existence of a whole set of techniques and institutions for measuring, supervising and correcting the abnormal brings into play the disciplinary mechanisms to which the fear of the plague gave rise. All the mechanisms of power which, even today, are disposed around the abnormal individual, to brand him and to alter him, are composed of those two forms from which they distantly derive.

Bentham's *Panopticon* is the architectural figure of this composition. We know the principle on which it was based: at the periphery, an annular building; at the centre, a tower; this tower is pierced with wide windows that open onto the inner side of the ring; the peripheric building is divided into cells, each of which extends the whole width of the building; they have two windows, one on the inside, corresponding to the windows of the tower; the other, on the outside, allows the light to cross the cell from one end to the other. All that is needed, then, is to place a supervisor in a central tower and to shut up in each cell a madman, a patient, a condemned man, a worker or a schoolboy. By the effect of backlighting, one can observe from the tower, standing out precisely against the light, the small captive shadows in the cells of the periphery. They are like so many cages, so many small theatres, in which each actor is alone, perfectly individualized and constantly visible. The panoptic mechanism arranges spatial unities that make it possible to see constantly and to recognize immediately. In short, it reverses the principle of the dungeon; or rather of its three functions – to enclose, to deprive of light and to hide – it preserves only the first and eliminates the other two. Full lighting and the eye of a supervisor capture better than darkness, which ultimately protected. Visibility is a trap.

To begin with, this made it possible – as a negative effect – to avoid those compact, swarming, howling masses that were to be found in places of confinement, those painted by Goya or described by Howard. Each individual, in his place, is securely confined to a cell from which he is seen from the front by the supervisor; but the side walls prevent him from coming into contact with his companions. He is seen, but he does not see; he is the object of information, never a subject in communication. The arrangement of his room, opposite the central tower, imposes on him an axial visibility; but the divisions of the ring, those separated cells, imply a lateral invisibility. And this invisibility is a guarantee of order. If the inmates are convicts, there is no danger of a plot, an attempt at collective escape, the planning of new crimes for the future, bad reciprocal influences; if they are patients, there is no danger of contagion; if they are madmen there is no risk of their committing violence upon one another; if they are schoolchildren, there is no copying, no noise, no chatter, no waste of time; if they are workers, there are no disorders, no theft, no coalitions, none of those distractions that slow down the rate of work, make it less perfect or cause accidents. The crowd, a compact mass, a locus of multiple exchanges, individualities merging together, a collective effect, is abolished and replaced by a collection of separated individualities. From the point of view of the guardian, it is replaced by a multiplicity that can be numbered and supervised; from the point of view of the inmates, by a sequestered and observed solitude (Bentham, 60–64).

Hence the major effect of the Panopticon: to induce in the inmate a state of conscious and permanent visibility that assures the automatic functioning of power. So to arrange things that the surveillance is permanent in its effects, even if it is discontinuous in its action; that the perfection of power should tend to render its actual exercise unnecessary; that this architectural apparatus should be a machine for creating and sustaining a power relation independent of the person who exercises it; in short, that the inmates should be caught up in a power situation of which they are themselves the bearers. To achieve this, it is at once too much and too little that the prisoner should be constantly observed by an inspector: too little, for what matters is that he knows himself to be observed; too much, because he has no need in fact of being so. In view of this, Bentham laid down the principle that power should be visible and unverifiable. Visible: the inmate will constantly have before his eyes the tall outline of the central tower from which he is spied upon. Unverifiable: the inmate must never know whether he is being looked at at any one moment; but he must be sure that he may always be so. In order to make the presence or absence of the inspector unverifiable, so that the prisoners, in their cells, cannot even see a shadow, Bentham envisaged not only venetian blinds on the windows of the central observation hall, but, on the inside, partitions that intersected the hall at right angles and, in order to pass from one quarter to the other, not doors but zig-zag openings; for the slightest noise, a gleam of light, a brightness in a half-opened door would betray the presence of the guardian.[2] The Panopticon is a machine for dissociating the see/being seen dyad: in the peripheric ring, one is totally seen, without ever seeing; in the central tower, one sees everything without ever being seen.[3]

It is an important mechanism, for it automatizes and disindividualizes power. Power has its principle not so much in a person as in a certain concerted distribution of bodies, surfaces, lights, gazes; in an arrangement whose internal mechanisms produce the relation in which individuals are caught up. The ceremonies, the rituals, the marks by which the sovereign's surplus power was manifested are useless. There is a machinery that assures dissymmetry, disequilibrium, difference. Consequently, it does not matter who exercises power. Any individual, taken almost at random, can operate the machine: in the absence of the director, his family, his friends, his visitors, even his servants (Bentham, 45). Similarly, it does not matter what motive animates him: the curiosity of the indiscreet, the malice of a child, the thirst for knowledge of a philosopher who wishes to visit this museum of human nature, or the perversity of those who take pleasure in spying and punishing. The more numerous those anonymous and temporary observers are, the greater the risk for the inmate of being surprised and the greater his anxious awareness of being observed. The Panopticon is a marvellous machine which, whatever use one may wish to put it to, produces homogeneous effects of power.

A real subjection is born mechanically from a fictitious relation. So it is not necessary to use force to constrain the convict to good behaviour, the madman to calm, the worker to work, the schoolboy to application, the patient to the observation of the regulations. Bentham was surprised that panoptic institutions could be so light: there were no more bars, no more chains, no more heavy locks; all that was needed was that the separations should be clear and the openings well arranged. The heaviness of the old 'houses of security', with their fortress-like architecture, could be replaced by the simple, economic geometry of a 'house of certainty'. The efficiency of power, its constraining force have, in a sense, passed over to the other side – to the side of its surface of application. He who is subjected to a field of visibility, and who knows it, assumes responsibility for the constraints of power; he makes them play spontaneously upon himself; he inscribes in himself the power relation in which he simultaneously plays both roles; he becomes the principle of his own subjection. By this very fact, the external power may throw off its physical weight; it tends to the non-corporal; and, the more it approaches this limit, the more constant, profound and permanent are its effects: it is a perpetual victory that avoids any physical confrontation and which is always decided in advance.

Bentham does not say whether he was inspired, in his project, by Le Vaux's menagerie at Versailles: the first menagerie in which the different elements are not, as they traditionally were, distributed in a park (Loisel, 104–7). At the centre was an octagonal pavilion which, on the first floor, consisted of only a single room, the king's *salon*; on every side large windows looked out onto seven cages (the eighth side was reserved for the entrance), containing different species of animals. By Bentham's time, this menagerie had disappeared. But one finds in the programme of the Panopticon a similar concern with individualizing observation, with characterization and classification, with the analytical arrangement of space. The Panopticon is a royal menagerie; the animal is replaced by man, individual distribution by specific grouping and the king by the machinery of a furtive power. With this exception, the Panopticon also does the work of a naturalist. It makes it possible to draw up differences: among patients, to observe the symptoms of each individual, without the proximity of beds, the circulation of miasmas, the effects of contagion confusing the clinical tables; among schoolchildren, it makes it possible to observe performances (without there being any imitation or copying), to map aptitudes, to assess characters, to draw up rigorous classifications and, in relation to normal development, to distinguish 'laziness and stubbornness' from 'incurable imbecility'; among workers, it makes it possible to note the aptitudes of each worker, compare the time he takes to perform a task, and if they are paid by the day, to calculate their wages (Bentham, 60–64).

So much for the question of observation. But the Panopticon was also a laboratory; it could be used as a machine to carry out experiments, to alter behaviour, to train or correct individuals. To experiment with medicines and monitor their effects. To try out different punishments on prisoners, according to their crimes and character, and to seek the most effective ones. To teach different techniques simultaneously to the workers, to decide which is the best. To try out pedagogical experiments – and in particular to take up once again the well-debated problem of secluded education, by using orphans. One would see what would happen when, in their sixteenth or eighteenth year, they were presented with other boys or girls; one could verify whether, as Helvetius thought, anyone could learn anything; one would follow 'the genealogy of every observable idea'; one could bring up different children according to different systems of thought, making certain children believe that two and two do not make four or that the moon is a cheese, then put them together when they are twenty or twenty-five years old; one would then have discussions that would be worth a great deal more than the sermons or lectures on which so much money is spent; one would have at least an opportunity of making discoveries in the domain of metaphysics. The Panopticon is a privileged place for experiments on men, and for analysing with complete certainty the transformations that may be obtained from them. The Panopticon may even provide an apparatus for supervising its own mechanisms. In this central tower, the director may spy on all the employees that he has under his orders: nurses, doctors, foremen, teachers, warders; he will be able to judge them continuously, alter their behaviour, impose upon them the methods he thinks best; and it will even be possible to observe the director himself. An inspector arriving unexpectedly at the centre of the Panopticon will be able to judge at a glance, without anything being concealed from him, how the entire establishment is functioning. And, in any case, enclosed as he is in the middle of this architectural mechanism, is not the director's own fate entirely bound up with it? The incompetent physician who has allowed contagion to spread, the incompetent prison governor or workshop manager will be the first victims of an epidemic or a revolt. ' "By every tie I could devise", said the master of the Panopticon, "my own fate had been bound up by me with theirs" ' (Bentham, 177). The Panopticon functions as a kind of laboratory of power. Thanks to its mechanisms of observation, it gains in efficiency and in the ability to penetrate into men's behaviour; knowledge follows the advances of power, discovering new objects of knowledge over all the surfaces on which power is exercised.

The plague-stricken town, the panoptic establishment – the differences are important. They mark, at a distance of a century and a half, the transformations of the disciplinary programme. In the first case, there is an exceptional situation: against an extraordinary evil, power is mobilized; it makes itself everywhere present and visible; it invents new mechanisms; it separates, it immobilizes, it partitions; it constructs for a time what is both a counter-city and the perfect society; it imposes an ideal functioning, but one that is reduced, in the final analysis, like the evil that it combats, to a simple dualism of life and death: that which moves brings death, and one kills that which moves. The Panopticon, on the other hand, must be understood as a generalizable model of functioning; a way of defining power relations in terms of the everyday life of men. No doubt Bentham presents it as a particular institution, closed in upon itself. Utopias, perfectly closed in upon themselves, are common enough. As opposed to the ruined prisons, littered with mechanisms of torture, to be seen in Piranese's engravings, the Panopticon presents a cruel, ingenious cage. The fact that it should have given rise, even in our own time, to so many variations, projected or realized, is evidence of the imaginary intensity that it has possessed for almost two hundred years. But the Panopticon must not be understood as a dream building: it is the diagram of a mechanism of power reduced to its ideal form; its functioning, abstracted from any obstacle, resistance or friction, must be represented as a pure architectural and optical system: it is in fact a figure of political technology that may and must be detached from any specific use.

It is polyvalent in its applications; it serves to reform prisoners, but also to treat patients, to instruct schoolchildren, to confine the insane, to supervise workers, to put beggars and idlers to work. It is a type of location of bodies in space, of distribution of individuals in relation to one another, of hierarchical organization, of disposition of centres and channels of power, of definition of the instruments and modes of intervention of power, which can be implemented in hospitals, workshops, schools, prisons. Whenever one is dealing with a multiplicity of individuals on whom a task or a particular form of behaviour must be imposed, the panoptic schema may be used. It is – necessary modifications apart – applicable 'to all establishments whatsoever, in which, within a space not too large to be covered or commanded by buildings, a number of persons are meant to be kept under inspection' (Bentham, 40; although Bentham takes the penitentiary house as his prime example, it is because it has many different functions to fulfil – safe custody, confinement, solitude, forced labour and instruction).

In each of its applications, it makes it possible to perfect the exercise of power. It does this in several ways: because it can reduce the number of those who exercise it, while increasing the number of those on whom it is exercised. Because it is possible to intervene at any moment and because the constant pressure acts even before the offences, mistakes or crimes have been committed. Because, in these conditions, its strength is that it never intervenes, it is exercised spontaneously and without noise, it constitutes a mechanism whose effects follow from one another. Because, without any physical instrument other than architecture and geometry, it acts directly on individuals; it gives 'power of mind over mind'. The panoptic schema makes any apparatus of power more intense: it assures its economy (in material, in personnel, in time); it assures its efficacity by its preventative character, its continuous functioning and its automatic mechanisms. It is a way of obtaining from power 'in hitherto unexampled quantity', 'a great and new instrument of government . . .; its great excellence consists in the great strength it is capable of giving to *any* institution it may be thought proper to apply it to' (Bentham, 66).

It's a case of 'it's easy once you've thought of it' in the political sphere. It can in fact be integrated into any function (education, medical treatment, production, punishment); it can increase the effect of this function, by being linked closely with it; it can constitute a mixed mechanism in which relations of power (and of knowledge) may be precisely adjusted, in the smallest detail, to the processes that are to be supervised; it can establish a direct proportion between 'surplus power' and 'surplus production'. In short, it arranges things in such a way that the exercise of power is not added on from the outside, like a rigid, heavy constraint, to the functions it invests, but is so subtly present in them as to increase their efficiency by itself increasing its own points of contact. The panoptic mechanism is not simply a hinge, a point of exchange between a mechanism of power and a function; it is a way of making power relations function in a function, and of making a function function through these power relations. Bentham's Preface to *Panopticon* opens with a list of the benefits to be obtained from his 'inspection-house': *'Morals reformed – health preserved – industry invigorated – instruction diffused – public burthens lightened –* Economy seated, as it were, upon a rock – the gordian knot of the Poor-Laws not cut, but untied – all by a simple idea in architecture!' (Bentham, 39).

Furthermore, the arrangement of this machine is such that its enclosed nature does not preclude a permanent presence from the outside: we have seen that anyone may come and exercise in the central tower the functions of surveillance, and that, this being the case, he can gain a clear idea of the way in which the surveillance is practised. In fact, any panoptic institution, even if it is as rigorously closed as a penitentiary, may without difficulty be subjected to such irregular and constant inspections: and not only by the appointed inspectors, but also by the public; any member of society will have the right to come and see with his own eyes how the schools, hospitals, factories, prisons function. There is no risk, therefore, that the increase of power created by the panoptic machine may degenerate into tyranny; the disciplinary mechanism will be democratically controlled, since it will be constantly accessible 'to the great tribunal committee of the world'.[4] This Panopticon, subtly arranged so that an observer may observe, at a glance, so many different individuals, also enables everyone to come and observe any of the observers. The seeing machine was once a sort of dark room into which individuals spied; it has become a transparent building in which the exercise of power may be supervised by society as a whole.

The panoptic schema, without disappearing as such or losing any of its properties, was destined to spread throughout the social body; its vocation was to become a generalized function. The plague-stricken town provided an exceptional disciplinary model: perfect, but absolutely violent; to the disease that brought death, power opposed its perpetual threat of death; life inside it was reduced to its simplest expression; it was, against the power of death, the meticulous exercise of the right of the sword. The Panopticon, on the other hand, has a role of amplification; although it arranges power, although it is intended to make it more economic and more effective, it does so not for power itself, nor for the immediate salvation of a threatened society: its aim is to strengthen the social forces – to increase production, to develop the economy, spread education, raise the level of public morality; to increase and multiply.

How is power to be strengthened in such a way that, far from impeding progress, far from weighing upon it with its rules and regulations, it actually facilitates such progress? What intensificator of power will be able at the same time to be a multiplicator of production? How will power, by increasing its forces, be able to increase those of society instead of confiscating them or impeding them? The Panopticon's solution to this problem is that the productive increase of power can be assured only if, on the one hand, it can be exercised continuously in the very foundations of society, in the subtlest possible way, and if, on the other hand, it functions outside these sudden, violent, discontinuous forms that are bound up with the exercise of sovereignty. The body of the king, with its strange material and physical presence, with the force that he himself deploys or transmits to some few others, is at the opposite extreme of this new physics of power represented by panopticism; the domain of panopticism is, on the contrary, that whole lower region, that region of irregular bodies, with their details, their multiple movements, their heterogeneous forces, their spatial relations; what are required are mechanisms that analyse distributions, gaps, series, combinations, and which use instruments that render visible, record, differentiate and compare: a physics of a relational and multiple power, which has its maximum intensity not in the person of the king, but in the bodies that can be individualized by these relations. At the theoretical level, Bentham defines another way of analysing the social body and the power relations that traverse it; in terms of practice, he defines a procedure of subordination of bodies and forces that must increase the utility of power while practising the economy of the prince. Panopticism is the general principle of a new 'political anatomy' whose object and end are not the relations of sovereignty but the relations of discipline.

The celebrated, transparent, circular cage, with its high tower, powerful and knowing, may have been for Bentham a project of a perfect disciplinary institution; but he also set out to show how one may 'unlock' the disciplines and get them to function in a diffused, multiple, polyvalent way throughout the whole social body. These disciplines, which the classical age had elaborated in specific, relatively enclosed places – barracks, schools, workshops – and whose total implementation had been imagined only at the limited and temporary scale of a plague-stricken town, Bentham dreamt of transforming into a network of mechanisms that would be everywhere and always alert, running through society without interruption in space or in time. The panoptic arrangement provides the formula for this generalization. It programmes, at the level of an elementary and easily transferable mechanism, the basic functioning of a society penetrated through and through with disciplinary mechanisms.

There are two images, then, of discipline. At one extreme, the discipline-blockade, the enclosed institution, established on the edges of society, turned inwards towards negative functions: arresting evil, breaking communications, suspending time. At the other extreme, with panopticism, is the discipline-mechanism: a functional mechanism that must improve the exercise of power by making it lighter, more rapid, more effective, a design of subtle coercion for a society to come. The movement from one project to the other, from a schema of exceptional discipline to one of a generalized surveillance, rests on a historical transformation: the gradual extension of the mechanisms of discipline throughout the seventeenth and eighteenth centuries, their spread throughout the whole social body, the formation of what might be called in general the disciplinary society.

A whole disciplinary generalization – the Benthamite physics of power represents an acknowledgement of this – had operated throughout the classical age. The spread of disciplinary institutions, whose network was beginning to cover an ever larger surface and occupying above all a less and less marginal position, testifies to this: what was an islet, a privileged place, a circumstantial measure, or a singular model, became a general formula; the regulations characteristic of the Protestant and pious armies of William of Orange or of Gustavus Adolphus were transformed into regulations for all the armies of Europe; the model colleges of the Jesuits, or the schools of Batencour or Demia, following the example set by Sturm, provided the outlines for the general forms of educational discipline; the ordering of the naval and military hospitals provided the model for the entire reorganization of hospitals in the eighteenth century.

But this extension of the disciplinary institutions was no doubt only the most visible aspect of various, more profound processes.

1. *The functional inversion of the disciplines.* At first, they were expected to neutralize dangers, to fix useless or disturbed populations, to avoid the inconveniences of over-large assemblies; now they were being asked to play a positive role, for they were becoming able to do so, to increase the possible utility of individuals. Military discipline is no longer a mere means of preventing looting, desertion or failure to obey orders among the troops; it has become a basic technique to enable the army to exist, not as an assembled crowd, but as a unity that derives from this very unity an increase in its forces; discipline increases the skill of each individual, coordinates these skills, accelerates movements, increases fire power, broadens the fronts of attack without reducing their vigour, increases the capacity for resistance, etc. The discipline of the workshop, while remaining a way of enforcing respect for the regulations and authorities, of preventing thefts or losses, tends to increase aptitudes, speeds, output and therefore profits; it still exerts a moral influence over behaviour, but more and more it treats actions in terms of their results, introduces bodies into a machinery, forces into an economy. When, in the seventeenth century, the provincial schools or the Christian elementary schools were founded, the justifications given for them were above all negative: those poor who were unable to bring up their children left them 'in ignorance of their obligations: given the difficulties they have in earning a living, and themselves having been badly brought up, they are unable to communicate a sound upbringing that they themselves never had'; this involves three major inconveniences: ignorance of God, idleness (with its consequent drunkenness, impurity, larceny, brigandage); and the formation of those gangs of beggars, always ready to stir up public disorder and 'virtually to exhaust the funds of the Hôtel-Dieu' (Demia, 60–61). Now, at the beginning of the Revolution, the end laid down for primary education was to be, among other things, to 'fortify', to 'develop the body', to prepare

the child 'for a future in some mechanical work', to give him 'an observant eye, a sure hand and prompt habits' (Talleyrand's Report to the Constituent Assembly, 10 September 1791, quoted by Léon, 106). The disciplines function increasingly as techniques for making useful individuals. Hence their emergence from a marginal position on the confines of society, and detachment from the forms of exclusion or expiation, confinement or retreat. Hence the slow loosening of their kinship with religious regularities and enclosures. Hence also their rooting in the most important, most central and most productive sectors of society. They become attached to some of the great essential functions: factory production, the transmission of knowledge, the diffusion of aptitudes and skills, the war-machine. Hence, too, the double tendency one sees developing throughout the eighteenth century to increase the number of disciplinary institutions and to discipline the existing apparatuses.

2. *The swarming of disciplinary mechanisms*. While, on the one hand, the disciplinary establishments increase, their mechanisms have a certain tendency to become 'de-institutionalized', to emerge from the closed fortresses in which they once functioned and to circulate in a 'free' state; the massive, compact disciplines are broken down into flexible methods of control, which may be transferred and adapted. Sometimes the closed apparatuses add to their internal and specific function a role of external surveillance, developing around themselves a whole margin of lateral controls. Thus the Christian School must not simply train docile children; it must also make it possible to supervise the parents, to gain information as to their way of life, their resources, their piety, their morals. The school tends to constitute minute social observatories that penetrate even to the adults and exercise regular supervision over them: the bad behaviour of the child, or his absence, is a legitimate pretext, according to Demia, for one to go and question the neighbours, especially if there is any reason to believe that the family will not tell the truth; one can then go and question the parents themselves, to find out whether they know their catechism and the prayers, whether they are determined to root out the vices of their children, how many beds there are in the house and what the sleeping arrangements are; the visit may end with the giving of alms, the present of a religious picture, or the provision of additional beds (Demia, 39–40).

Similarly, the hospital is increasingly conceived of as a base for the medical observation of the population outside; after the burning down of the Hôtel-Dieu in 1772, there were several demands that the large buildings, so heavy and so disordered, should be replaced by a series of smaller hospitals; their function would be to take in the sick of the quarter, but also to gather information, to be alert to any endemic or epidemic phenomena, to open dispensaries, to give advice to the inhabitants and to keep the authorities informed of the sanitary state of the region.[5]

One also sees the spread of disciplinary procedures, not in the form of enclosed institutions, but as centres of observation disseminated throughout society. Religious groups and charity organizations had long played this role of 'disciplining' the population. From the Counter-Reformation to the philanthropy of the July monarchy, initiatives of this type continued to increase; their aims were religious (conversion and moralization), economic (aid and encouragement to work) or political (the struggle against discontent or agitation). One has only to cite by way of example the regulations for the charity associations in the Paris parishes. The territory to be covered was divided into quarters and cantons and the members of the associations divided themselves up along the same lines. These members had to visit their respective areas regularly. 'They will strive to eradicate places of ill-repute, tobacco shops, life-classes, gaming house, public scandals, blasphemy, impiety, and any other disorders that may come to their knowledge.' They will also have to make individual visits to the poor; and the information to be obtained is laid down in regulations: the stability of the lodging, knowledge of prayers, attendance at the sacraments, knowledge of a trade, morality (and 'whether they have not fallen into poverty through their own fault'); lastly, 'one must learn by skilful questioning in what way they behave at home. Whether there is peace between them and their neighbours, whether they are careful to bring up their children in the fear of God . . . whether they do not have their older children of different sexes sleeping together and with them, whether they do not allow licentiousness and cajolery in their families, especially in their older daughters. If one has any doubts as to whether they are married, one must ask to see their marriage certificate'.[5]

3. *The state-control of the mechanisms of discipline.* In England, it was private religious groups that carried out, for a long time, the functions of social discipline (cf. Radzinovitz, 203–14); in France, although a part of this role remained in the hands of parish guilds or charity associations, another – and no doubt the most important part – was very soon taken over by the police apparatus.

The organization of a centralized police had long been regarded, even by contemporaries, as the most direct expression of royal absolutism; the sovereign had wished to have 'his own magistrate to whom he might directly entrust his orders, his commissions, intentions, and who was entrusted with the execution of orders and orders under the King's private seal' (a note by Duval, first secretary at the police magistrature, quoted in Funck-Brentano, 1). In effect, in taking over a number of pre-existing functions – the search for criminals, urban surveillance, economic and political supervision – the police magistratures and the magistrature-general that presided over them in Paris transposed them into a single, strict, administrative machine: 'All the radiations of force and information that spread from the circumference culminate in the magistrate-general. . . . It is he who operates all the wheels that together produce order and harmony. The effects of his administration cannot be better compared than to the movement of the celestial bodies' (Des Essarts, 344 and 528).

But, although the police as an institution were certainly organized in the form of a state apparatus, and although this was certainly linked directly to the centre of political sovereignty, the type of power that it exercises, the mechanisms it operates and the elements to which it applies them are specific. It is an apparatus that must be coextensive with the entire social body and not only by the extreme limits that it embraces, but by the minuteness of the details it is concerned with. Police power must bear 'over everything': it is not however the totality of the state nor of the kingdom as visible and invisible body of the monarch; it is the dust of events, actions, behaviour, opinions – 'everything that happens';[7] the police are concerned with 'those things of every moment', those 'unimportant things', of which Catherine II spoke in her Great Instruction (Supplement to the *Instruction for the drawing up of a new code,* 1769, article 535). With the police, one is in the indefinite world of a supervision that seeks ideally to reach the most elementary particle, the most passing phenomenon of the social body: 'The ministry of the magistrates and police officers is of the greatest importance; the objects that it embraces are in a sense definite, one may perceive them only by a sufficiently detailed examination' (Delamare, un-numbered Preface): the infinitely small of political power.

And, in order to be exercised, this power had to be given the instrument of permanent, exhaustive, omnipresent surveillance, capable of making all visible, as long as it could itself remain invisible. It had to be like a faceless gaze that transformed the whole social body into a field of perception: thousands of eyes posted everywhere, mobile attentions ever on the alert, a long, hierarchized network which, according to Le Maire, comprised for Paris the forty-eight *commissaires*, the twenty *inspecteurs*, then the 'observers', who were paid regularly, the '*basses mouches*', or secret agents, who were paid by the day, then the informers, paid according to the job done, and finally the prostitutes. And this unceasing observation had to be accumulated in a series of reports and registers; throughout the eighteenth century, an immense police text increasingly covered society by means of a complex documentary organization (on the police registers in the eighteenth century, cf. Chassaigne). And, unlike the methods of judicial or administrative writing, what was registered in this way were forms of behaviour, attitudes, possibilities, suspicions – a permanent account of individuals' behaviour.

Now, it should be noted that, although this police supervision was entirely 'in the hands of the king', it did not function in a single direction. It was in fact a double-entry system: it had to correspond, by manipulating the machinery of justice, to the immediate wishes of the king, but it was also capable of responding to solicitations from below; the celebrated *lettres de cachet*, or orders under the king's private seal, which were long the symbol of arbitrary royal rule and which brought detention into disrepute on political grounds, were in fact demanded by families, masters, local notables, neighbours, parish priests; and their function was to punish by confinement a whole infra-penality, that of disorder, agitation, dis-obedience, bad conduct; those things that Ledoux wanted to exclude from his architecturally perfect city and which he called 'offences of non-surveillance'. In short, the eighteenth-century police added a disciplinary function to its role as the auxiliary of justice in the pursuit of criminals and as an instrument for the political supervision of plots, opposition movements or revolts. It was a complex function since it linked the absolute power of the monarch to the lowest levels of power disseminated in society; since, between these different, enclosed institutions of discipline (workshops, armies, schools), it extended an intermediary network, acting where they could not intervene, disciplining the non-disciplinary spaces; but it filled in the gaps, linked them together, guaranteed with its armed force an interstitial discipline and a meta-discipline. 'By means of a wise police, the sovereign accustoms the people to order and obedience' (Vattel, 162).

The organization of the police apparatus in the eighteenth century sanctioned a generalization of the disciplines that became co-extensive with the state itself. Although it was linked in the most explicit way with everything in the royal power that exceeded the exercise of regular justice, it is understandable why the police offered such slight resistance to the rearrangement of the judicial power; and why it has not ceased to impose its prerogatives upon it, with ever-increasing weight, right up to the present day; this is no doubt because it is the secular arm of the judiciary; but it is also because, to a far greater degree than the judicial institution, it is identified, by reason of its extent and mechanisms, with a society of the disciplinary type. Yet it would be wrong to believe that the disciplinary functions were confiscated and absorbed once and for all by a state apparatus.

'Discipline' may be identified neither with an institution nor with an apparatus; it is a type of power, a modality for its exercise, comprising a whole set of instruments, techniques, procedures, levels of application, targets; it is a 'physics' or an 'anatomy' of power, a technology. And it may be taken over either by 'specialized' institutions (the penitentiaries or 'houses of correction' of the nineteenth century), or by institutions that use it as an essential instrument for a particular end (schools, hospitals), or by pre-existing authorities that find in it a means of reinforcing or reorganizing their internal mechanisms of power (one day we should show how intra-familial relations, essentially in the parents–children cell, have become 'disciplined', absorbing since the classical age external schemata, first educational and military, then medical, psychiatric, psychological, which have made the family the privileged locus of emergence for the disciplinary question of the normal and the abnormal); or by apparatuses that have made discipline their principle of internal functioning (the disciplinarization of the administrative apparatus from the Napoleonic period), or finally by state apparatuses whose major, if not exclusive, function is to assure that discipline reigns over society as a whole (the police).

On the whole, therefore, one can speak of the formation of a disciplinary society in this movement that stretches from the enclosed disciplines, a sort of social 'quarantine', to an indefinitely generalizable mechanism of 'panopticism'. Not because the disciplinary modality of power has replaced all the others; but because it has infiltrated the others, sometimes undermining them, but serving as an intermediary between them, linking them together, extending them and above all making it possible to bring the effects of power to the most minute and distant elements. It assures an infinitesimal distribution of the power relations.

A few years after Bentham, Julius gave this society its birth certificate (Julius, 384–6). Speaking of the panoptic principle, he said that there was much more there than architectural ingenuity: it was an event in the 'history of the human mind'. In appearance, it is merely the solution of a technical problem; but, through it, a whole type of society emerges. Antiquity had been a civilization of spectacle. 'To render accessible to a multitude of men the inspection of a small number of objects': this was the problem to which the architecture of temples, theatres and circuses responded. With spectacle, there was a predominance of public life, the intensity of festivals, sensual proximity. In these rituals in which blood flowed, society found new vigour and formed for a moment a single great body. The modern age poses the opposite problem: 'To procure for a small number, or even for a single individual, the instantaneous view of a great multitude.' In a society in which the principal elements are no longer the community and public life, but, on the one hand, private individuals and, on the other, the state, relations can be regulated only in a form that is the exact reverse of the spectacle: 'It was to the modern age, to the ever-growing influence of the state, to its ever more profound intervention in all the details and all the relations of social life, that was reserved the task of increasing and perfecting its guarantees, by using and directing towards that great aim the building and distribution of buildings intended to observe a great multitude of men at the same time.'

Julius saw as a fulfilled historical process that which Bentham had described as a technical programme. Our society is one not of spectacle, but of surveillance; under the surface of images, one invests bodies in depth; behind the great abstraction of exchange, there continues the meticulous, concrete training of useful forces; the circuits of communication are the supports of an accumulation and a centralization of knowledge; the play of signs defines the anchorages of power; it is not that the beautiful totality of the individual is amputated, repressed, altered by our social order, it is rather that the individual is carefully fabricated in it, according to a whole technique of forces and bodies. We are much less Greeks than we believe. We are neither in the amphitheatre, nor on the stage, but in the panoptic machine, invested by its effects of power, which we bring to ourselves since we are part of its mechanism. The importance, in historical mythology, of the Napoleonic character probably derives from the fact that it is at the point of junction of the monarchical, ritual exercise of sovereignty and the hierarchical, permanent exercise of indefinite discipline. He is the individual who looms over everything with a single gaze which no detail, however minute, can escape: 'You may consider that no part of the Empire is without surveillance, no crime, no offence, no contravention that remains unpunished, and that the eye of the genius who can enlighten all embraces the whole of this vast machine, without, however, the slightest detail escaping his attention' (Treilhard, 14). At the moment of its full blossoming, the disciplinary society still assumes with the Emperor the old aspect of the power of spectacle. As a monarch who is at one and the same time a usurper of the ancient throne and the organizer of the new state, he combined into a single symbolic, ultimate figure the whole of the long process by which the pomp of sovereignty, the necessarily spectacular manifestations of power, were extinguished one by one in the daily exercise of surveillance, in a panopticism in which the vigilance of intersecting gazes was soon to render useless both the eagle and the sun.

Discipline

The formation of the disciplinary society is connected with a number of broad historical processes – economic, juridico-political and, lastly, scientific – of which it forms part.

1. Generally speaking, it might be said that the disciplines are techniques for assuring the ordering of human multiplicities. It is true that there is nothing exceptional or even characteristic in this: every system of power is presented with the same problem. But the peculiarity of the disciplines is that they try to define in relation to the multiplicities a tactics of power that fulfils three criteria: firstly, to obtain the exercise of power at the lowest possible cost (economically, by the low expenditure it involves; politically, by its discretion, its low exteriorization, its relative invisibility, the little resistance it arouses); secondly, to bring the effects of this social power to their maximum intensity and to extend them as far as possible, without either failure or interval; thirdly, to link this 'economic' growth of power with the output of the apparatuses (educational, military, industrial or medical) within which it is exercised; in short, to increase both the docility and the utility of all the elements of the system. This triple objective of the disciplines corresponds to a well-known historical conjuncture. One aspect of this conjuncture was the large demographic thrust of the eighteenth century; an increase in the floating population (one of the primary objects of discipline is to fix; it is an anti-nomadic technique); a change of quantitative scale in the groups to be supervised or manipulated (from the beginning of the seventeenth century to the eve of the French Revolution, the school population had been increasing rapidly, as had no doubt the hospital population; by the end of the eighteenth century, the peace-time army exceeded 200,000 men). The other aspect of the conjuncture was the growth in the apparatus of production, which was becoming more and more extended and complex; it was also becoming more costly and its profitability had to be increased. The development of the disciplinary methods corresponded to these two processes, or rather, no doubt, to the new need to adjust their correlation. Neither the residual forms of feudal power nor the structures of the administrative monarchy, nor the local mechanisms of supervision, nor the unstable, tangled mass they all formed together could carry out this role: they were hindered from doing so by the irregular and inadequate extension of

their network, by their often conflicting functioning, but above all by the 'costly' nature of the power that was exercised in them. It was costly in several senses: because directly it cost a great deal to the Treasury; because the system of corrupt offices and farmed-out taxes weighed indirectly, but very heavily, on the population; because the resistance it encountered forced it into a cycle of per-petual reinforcement; because it proceeded essentially by levying (levying on money or products by royal, seigniorial, ecclesiastical taxation; levying on men or time by *corvées* of press-ganging, by locking up or banishing vagabonds). The development of the disci-plines marks the appearance of elementary techniques belonging to a quite different economy: mechanisms of power which, instead of proceeding by deduction, are integrated into the productive effi-ciency of the apparatuses from within, into the growth of this efficiency and into the use of what it produces. For the old principle of 'levying-violence', which governed the economy of power, the disciplines substitute the principle of 'mildness-production-profit'. These are the techniques that make it possible to adjust the multi-plicity of men and the multiplication of the apparatuses of produc-tion (and this means not only 'production' in the strict sense, but also the production of knowledge and skills in the school, the production of health in the hospitals, the production of destructive force in the army).

In this task of adjustment, discipline had to solve a number of problems for which the old economy of power was not sufficiently equipped. It could reduce the inefficiency of mass phenomena: reduce what, in a multiplicity, makes it much less manageable than a unity; reduce what is opposed to the use of each of its elements and of their sum; reduce everything that may counter the advantages of number. That is why discipline fixes; it arrests or regulates movements; it clears up confusion; it dissipates compact groupings of individuals wandering about the country in unpredictable ways; it establishes calculated distributions. It must also master all the forces that are formed from the very constitution of an organized multiplicity; it must neutralize the effects of counter-power that spring from them and which form a resistance to the power that wishes to dominate it: agitations, revolts, spontaneous organizations, coalitions – anything that may establish horizontal conjunctions.

Hence the fact that the disciplines use procedures of partitioning and verticality, that they introduce, between the different elements at the same level, as solid separations as possible, that they define compact hierarchical networks, in short, that they oppose to the intrinsic, adverse force of multiplicity the technique of the continuous, individualizing pyramid. They must also increase the particular utility of each element of the multiplicity, but by means that are the most rapid and the least costly, that is to say, by using the multiplicity itself as an instrument of this growth. Hence, in order to extract from bodies the maximum time and force, the use of those overall methods known as time-tables, collective training, exercises, total and detailed surveillance. Furthermore, the disciplines must increase the effect of utility proper to the multiplicities, so that each is made more useful than the simple sum of its elements: it is in order to increase the utilizable effects of the multiple that the disciplines define tactics of distribution, reciprocal adjustment of bodies, gestures and rhythms, differentiation of capacities, reciprocal coordination in relation to apparatuses or tasks. Lastly, the disciplines have to bring into play the power relations, not above but inside the very texture of the multiplicity, as discreetly as possible, as well articulated on the other functions of these multiplicities and also in the least expensive way possible: to this correspond anonymous instruments of power, coextensive with the multiplicity that they regiment, such as hierarchical surveillance, continuous registration, perpetual assessment and classification. In short, to substitute for a power that is manifested through the brilliance of those who exercise it, a power that insidiously objectifies those on whom it is applied; to form a body of knowledge about these individuals, rather than to deploy the ostentatious signs of sovereignty. In a word, the disciplines are the ensemble of minute technical inventions that made it possible to increase the useful size of multiplicities by decreasing the inconveniences of the power which, in order to make them useful, must control them. A multiplicity, whether in a workshop or a nation, an army or a school, reaches the threshold of a discipline when the relation of the one to the other becomes favourable.

If the economic take-off of the West began with the techniques that made possible the accumulation of capital, it might perhaps be said that the methods for administering the accumulation of men made possible a political take-off in relation to the traditional, ritual, costly, violent forms of power, which soon fell into disuse and were superseded by a subtle, calculated technology of subjection. In fact, the two processes – the accumulation of men and the accumulation of capital – cannot be separated; it would not have been possible to solve the problem of the accumulation of men without the growth of an apparatus of production capable of both sustaining them and using them; conversely, the techniques that made the cumulative multiplicity of men useful accelerated the accumulation of capital. At a less general level, the technological mutations of the apparatus of production, the division of labour and the elaboration of the disciplinary techniques sustained an ensemble of very close relations (cf. Marx, *Capital*, vol. 1, chapter XIII and the very interesting analysis in Guerry and Deleule). Each makes the other possible and necessary; each provides a model for the other. The disciplinary pyramid constituted the small cell of power within which the separation, coordination and supervision of tasks was imposed and made efficient; and analytical partitioning of time, gestures and bodily forces constituted an operational schema that could easily be transferred from the groups to be subjected to the mechanisms of production; the massive projection of military methods onto industrial organization was an example of this modelling of the division of labour following the model laid down by the schemata of power. But, on the other hand, the technical analysis of the process of production, its 'mechanical' breaking-down, were projected onto the labour force whose task it was to implement it: the constitution of those disciplinary machines in which the individual forces that they bring together are composed into a whole and therefore increased is the effect of this projection. Let us say that discipline is the unitary technique by which the body is reduced as a 'political' force at the least cost and maximized as a useful force. The growth of a capitalist economy gave rise to the specific modality of disciplinary power, whose general formulas, techniques of submitting forces and bodies, in short, 'political anatomy', could be operated in the most diverse political régimes, apparatuses or institutions.

2. The panoptic modality of power – at the elementary, technical, merely physical level at which it is situated – is not under the immediate dependence or a direct extension of the great

juridico-political structures of a society; it is nonetheless not absolutely independent. Historically, the process by which the bourgeoisie became in the course of the eighteenth century the politically dominant class was masked by the establishment of an explicit, coded and formally egalitarian juridical framework, made possible by the organization of a parliamentary, representative régime. But the development and generalization of disciplinary mechanisms constituted the other, dark side of these processes. The general juridical form that guaranteed a system of rights that were egalitarian in principle was supported by these tiny, everyday, physical mechanisms, by all those systems of micro-power that are essentially non-egalitarian and asymmetrical that we call the disciplines. And although, in a formal way, the representative régime makes it possible, directly or indirectly, with or without relays, for the will of all to form the fundamental authority of sovereignty, the disciplines provide, at the base, a guarantee of the submission of forces and bodies. The real, corporal disciplines constituted the foundation of the formal, juridical liberties. The contract may have been regarded as the ideal foundation of law and political power; panopticism constituted the technique, universally widespread, of coercion. It continued to work in depth on the juridical structures of society, in order to make the effective mechanisms of power function in opposition to the formal framework that it had acquired. The 'Enlightenment', which discovered the liberties, also invented the disciplines.

In appearance, the disciplines constitute nothing more than an infra-law. They seem to extend the general forms defined by law to the infinitesimal level of individual lives; or they appear as methods of training that enable individuals to become integrated into these general demands. They seem to constitute the same type of law on a different scale, thereby making it more meticulous and more indulgent. The disciplines should be regarded as a sort of counter-law. They have the precise role of introducing insuperable asymmetries and excluding reciprocities. First, because discipline creates between individuals a 'private' link, which is a relation of constraints entirely different from contractual obligation; the acceptance of a discipline may be underwritten by contract; the way in which it is imposed, the mechanisms it brings into play, the non-reversible subordination of one group of people by another, the 'surplus' power that is always fixed on the same side, the inequality of position of the different 'partners' in relation to the common regulation, all these distinguish the disciplinary link from the contractual link, and make it possible to distort the contractual link systematically from the moment it has as its content a mechanism of discipline. We know, for example, how many real procedures undermine the legal fiction of the work contract: workshop discipline is not the least important. Moreover, whereas the juridical systems define juridical subjects according to universal norms, the disciplines characterize, classify, specialize; they distribute along a scale, around a norm, hierarchize individuals in relation to one another and, if necessary, disqualify and invalidate. In any case, in the space and during the time in which they exercise their control and bring into play the asymmetries of their power, they effect a suspension of the law that is never total, but is never annulled either. Regular and institutional as it may be, the discipline, in its mechanism, is a 'counter-law'. And, although the universal juridicism of modern society seems to fix limits on the exercise of power, its universally widespread panopticism enables it to operate, on the underside of the law, a machinery that is both immense and minute, which supports, reinforces, multiplies the asymmetry of power and undermines the limits that are traced around the law. The minute disciplines, the panopticisms of every day may well be below the level of emergence of the great apparatuses and the great political struggles. But, in the genealogy of modern society, they have been, with the class domination that traverses it, the political counterpart of the juridical norms according to which power was redistributed. Hence, no doubt, the importance that has been given for so long to the small techniques of discipline, to those apparently insignificant tricks that it has invented, and even to those 'sciences' that give it a respectable face; hence the fear of abandoning them if one cannot find any substitute; hence the affirmation that they are at the very foundation of society, and an element in its equilibrium, whereas they are a series of mechanisms for unbalancing power relations definitively and everywhere; hence the persistence in regarding them as the humble, but concrete form of every morality, whereas they are a set of physico-political techniques.

To return to the problem of legal punishments, the prison with all the corrective technology at its disposal is to be resituated at the point where the codified power to punish turns into a disciplinary power to observe; at the point where the universal punishments of the law are applied selectively to certain individuals and always the same ones; at the point where the redefinition of the juridical subject by the penalty becomes a useful training of the criminal; at the point where the law is inverted and passes outside itself, and where the counter-law becomes the effective and institutionalized content of the juridical forms. What generalizes the power to punish, then, is not the universal consciousness of the law in each juridical subject; it is the regular extension, the infinitely minute web of panoptic techniques.

3. Taken one by one, most of these techniques have a long history behind them. But what was new, in the eighteenth century, was that, by being combined and generalized, they attained a level at which the formation of knowledge and the increase of power regularly reinforce one another in a circular process. At this point, the disciplines crossed the 'technological' threshold. First the hospital, then the school, then, later, the workshop were not simply 'reordered' by the disciplines; they became, thanks to them, apparatuses such that any mechanism of objectification could be used in them as an instrument of subjection, and any growth of power could give rise in them to possible branches of knowledge; it was this link, proper to the technological systems, that made possible within the disciplinary element the formation of clinical medicine, psychiatry, child psychology, educational psychology, the rationalization of labour. It is a double process, then: an epistemological 'thaw' through a refinement of power relations; a multiplication of the effects of power through the formation and accumulation of new forms of knowledge.

The extension of the disciplinary methods is inscribed in a broad historical process: the development at about the same time of many other technologies – agronomical, industrial, economic. But it must be recognized that, compared with the mining industries, the emerging chemical industries or methods of national accountancy, compared with the blast furnaces or the steam engine, panopticism has received little attention. It is regarded as not much more than a bizarre little utopia, a perverse dream – rather as though Bentham had been the Fourier of a police society, and the Phalanstery had taken on the form of the Panopticon. And yet this represented the abstract formula of a very real technology, that of individuals. There were many reasons why it received little praise; the most obvious is that the discourses to which it gave rise rarely acquired, except in the academic classifications, the status of sciences; but the real reason is no doubt that the power that it operates and which it augments is a direct, physical power that men exercise upon one another. An inglorious culmination had an origin that could be only grudgingly acknowledged. But it would be unjust to compare the disciplinary techniques with such inventions as the steam engine or Amici's microscope. They are much less; and yet, in a way, they are much more. If a historical equivalent or at least a point of comparison had to be found for them, it would be rather in the 'inquisitorial' technique.

The eighteenth century invented the techniques of discipline and the examination, rather as the Middle Ages invented the judicial investigation. But it did so by quite different means. The investigation procedure, an old fiscal and administrative technique, had developed above all with the reorganization of the Church and the increase of the princely states in the twelfth and thirteenth centuries. At this time it permeated to a very large degree the jurisprudence first of the ecclesiastical courts, then of the lay courts. The investigation as an authoritarian search for a truth observed or attested was thus opposed to the old procedures of the oath, the ordeal, the judicial duel, the judgement of God or even of the transaction between private individuals. The investigation was the sovereign power arrogating to itself the right to establish the truth by a number of regulated techniques. Now, although the investigation has since then been an integral part of western justice (even up to our own day), one must not forget either its political origin, its link with the birth of the states and of monarchical sovereignty, or its later extension and its role in the formation of knowledge. In fact, the investigation has been the no doubt crude, but fundamental element in the constitution of the empirical sciences; it has been the juridico-political matrix of this experimental knowledge, which, as we know, was very rapidly released at the end of the Middle Ages.

It is perhaps true to say that, in Greece, mathematics were born from techniques of measurement; the sciences of nature, in any case, were born, to some extent, at the end of the Middle Ages, from the practices of investigation. The great empirical knowledge that covered the things of the world and transcribed them into the ordering of an indefinite discourse that observes, describes and establishes the 'facts' (at a time when the western world was beginning the economic and political conquest of this same world) had its operating model no doubt in the Inquisition – that immense invention that our recent mildness has placed in the dark recesses of our memory. But what this politico-juridical, administrative and criminal, religious and lay, investigation was to the sciences of nature, disciplinary analysis has been to the sciences of man. These sciences, which have so delighted our 'humanity' for over a century, have their technical matrix in the petty, malicious minutiae of the disciplines and their investigations. These investigations are perhaps to psychology, psychiatry, pedagogy, criminology, and so many other strange sciences, what the terrible power of investigation was to the calm knowledge of the animals, the plants or the earth. Another power, another knowledge. On the threshold of the classical age, Bacon, lawyer and statesman, tried to develop a methodology of investigation for the empirical sciences. What Great Observer will produce the methodology of examination for the human sciences? Unless, of course, such a thing is not possible. For, although it is true that, in becoming a technique for the empirical sciences, the investigation has detached itself from the inquisitorial procedure, in which it was historically rooted, the examination has remained extremely close to the disciplinary power that shaped it. It has always been and still is an intrinsic element of the disciplines. Of course it seems to have undergone a speculative purification by integrating itself with such sciences as psychology and psychiatry. And, in effect, its appearance in the form of tests, interviews, interrogations and consultations is apparently in order to rectify the mechanisms of discipline: educational psychology is supposed to correct the rigours of the school, just as the medical or psychiatric interview is supposed to rectify the effects of the discipline of work. But we must not be misled; these techniques merely refer individuals from one disciplinary authority to another, and they reproduce, in a concentrated or formalized form, the schema of power-knowledge proper to each discipline (on this subject, cf. Tort). The great investigation that gave rise to the sciences of nature has become detached from its politico-juridical model; the examination, on the other hand, is still caught up in disciplinary technology.

In the Middle Ages, the procedure of investigation gradually superseded the old accusatory justice, by a process initiated from above; the disciplinary technique, on the other hand, insidiously and as if from below, has invaded a penal justice that is still, in principle, inquisitorial. All the great movements of extension that characterize modern penality – the problematization of the criminal behind his crime, the concern with a punishment that is a correction, a therapy, a normalization, the division of the act of judgement between various authorities that are supposed to measure, assess, diagnose, cure, transform individuals – all this betrays the penetration of the disciplinary examination into the judicial inquisition.

What is now imposed on penal justice as its point of application, its 'useful' object, will no longer be the body of the guilty man set up against the body of the king; nor will it be the juridical subject of an ideal contract; it will be the disciplinary individual. The extreme point of penal justice under the Ancien Régime was the infinite segmentation of the body of the regicide: a manifestation of the strongest power over the body of the greatest criminal, whose total destruction made the crime explode into its truth. The ideal point of penality today would be an indefinite discipline: an interrogation without end, an investigation that would be extended without limit to a meticulous and ever more analytical observation, a judgement that would at the same time be the constitution of a file that was never closed, the calculated leniency of a penalty that would be interlaced with the ruthless curiosity of an examination, a procedure that would be at the same time the permanent measure of a gap in relation to an inaccessible norm and the asymptotic movement that strives to meet in infinity. The public execution was the logical culmination of a procedure governed by the Inquisition. The practice of placing individuals under 'observation' is a natural extension of a justice imbued with disciplinary methods and examination procedures. Is it surprising that the cellular prison, with its regular chronologies, forced labour, its authorities of surveillance and registration, its experts in normality, who continue and multiply the functions of the judge, should have become the modern instrument of penality? Is it surprising that prisons resemble factories, schools, barracks, hospitals, which all resemble prisons?

PART FOUR
Prison

1. Complete and austere institutions

It would not be true to say that the prison was born with the new codes. The prison form antedates its systematic use in the penal system. It had already been constituted outside the legal apparatus when, throughout the social body, procedures were being elaborated for distributing individuals, fixing them in space, classifying them, extracting from them the maximum in time and forces, training their bodies, coding their continuous behaviour, maintaining them in perfect visibility, forming around them an apparatus of observation, registration and recording, constituting on them a body of knowledge that is accumulated and centralized. The general form of an apparatus intended to render individuals docile and useful, by means of precise work upon their bodies, indicated the prison institution, before the law ever defined it as the penalty *par excellence*. At the turn of the eighteenth and nineteenth centuries, there was, it is true, a penalty of detention; and it was a new thing. But it was really the opening up of penality to mechanisms of coercion already elaborated elsewhere. The 'models' of penal detention – Ghent, Gloucester, Walnut Street – marked the first visible points of this transition, rather than innovations or points of departure. The prison, an essential element in the punitive panopoly, certainly marks an important moment in the history of penal justice: its access to 'humanity'. But it is also an important moment in the history of those disciplinary mechanisms that the new class power was developing: that in which they colonized the legal institution. At the turn of the century, a new legislation defined the power to punish as a general function of society that was exercised in the same manner over all its members, and in which each individual was equally represented: but in making detention the penalty *par excellence*, it introduced procedures of domination characteristic of a particular type of power. A justice that is supposed to be 'equal', a legal machinery that is supposed to be 'autonomous', but which contains all the asymmetries of disciplinary subjection, this conjunction marked the birth of the prison, 'the penalty of civilized societies' (Rossi, 169).

One can understand the self-evident character that prison punishment very soon assumed. In the first years of the nineteenth century, people were still aware of its novelty; and yet it appeared so bound up and at such a deep level with the very functioning of society that it banished into oblivion all the other punishments that the eighteenth-century reformers had imagined. It seemed to have no alternative, as if carried along by the very movement of history: 'It is not chance, it is not the whim of the legislator that have made imprisonment the base and almost the entire edifice of our present penal scale: it is the progress of ideas and the improvement in morals' (Van Meenan, 529–30). And, although, in a little over a century, this self-evident character has become transformed, it has not disappeared. We are aware of all the inconveniences of prison, and that it is dangerous when it is not useless. And yet one cannot 'see' how to replace it. It is the detestable solution, which one seems unable to do without.

This 'self-evident' character of the prison, which we find so difficult to abandon, is based first of all on the simple form of 'deprivation of liberty'. How could prison not be the penalty *par excellence* in a society in which liberty is a good that belongs to all in the same way and to which each individual is attached, as Duport put it, by a 'universal and constant' feeling? Its loss has therefore the same value for all; unlike the fine, it is an 'egalitarian' punishment. The prison is the clearest, simplest, most equitable of penalties. Moreover, it makes it possible to quantify the penalty exactly according to the variable of time. There is a wages-form of imprisonment that constitutes, in industrial societies, its economic 'self-evidence' – and enables it to appear as a reparation. By levying on the time of the prisoner, the prison seems to express in concrete terms the idea that the offence has injured, beyond the victim, society as a whole. There is an economico-moral self-evidence of a penality that metes out punishments in days, months and years and draws up quantitative equivalences between offences and durations. Hence the expression, so frequently heard, so consistent with the functioning of punishments, though contrary to the strict theory of penal law, that one is in prison in order to 'pay one's debt'. The prison is 'natural', just as the use of time to measure exchanges is 'natural' in our society.[1]

But the self-evidence of the prison is also based on its role, supposed or demanded, as an apparatus for transforming individuals. How could the prison not be immediately accepted when, by locking up, retraining and rendering docile, it merely reproduces, with a little more emphasis, all the mechanisms that are to be found in the social body? The prison is like a rather disciplined barracks, a strict school, a dark workshop, but not qualitatively different. This double foundation – juridico-economic on the one hand, technico-disciplinary on the other – made the prison seem the most immediate and civilized form of all penalties. And it is this double functioning that immediately gave it its solidity. One thing is clear: the prison was not at first a deprivation of liberty to which a technical function of correction was later added; it was from the outset a form of 'legal detention' entrusted with an additional corrective task, or an enterprise for reforming individuals that the deprivation of liberty allowed to function in the legal system. In short, penal imprisonment, from the beginning of the nineteenth century, covered both the deprivation of liberty and the technical transformation of individuals.

Let us remember a number of facts. In the codes of 1808 and 1810, and the measures that immediately preceded or followed them, imprisonment was never confused with mere deprivation of liberty. It was, or in any case had to be, a differentiated and finalized mechanism. Differentiated because it had to have the same form, whether the prisoner had been sentenced or was merely accused, whether he was a minor offender or a criminal: the various types of prison – *maison d'arrêt, maison de correction, maison centrale* – ought in principle to correspond more or less to these differences and provide a punishment that would be not only graduated in intensity, but diversified in its ends. For the prison has a purpose, which is laid down at the outset: 'The law inflicting penalties, some of which are more serious than others, cannot allow the individual condemned to light penalties to be imprisoned in the same place as the criminal condemned to more serious penalties . . . although the penalty fixed by the law has as its principal aim the reparation of the crime, it also desires the amendment of the guilty man' (Real, 244). And this transformation must be one of the internal effects of imprisonment. Prison-punishment, prison-apparatus: 'The order that must reign in the *maison de force* may contribute powerfully to the regeneration of the convicts; the vices of upbringing, the contagion of bad example, idleness . . . have given birth to crime. Well, let us try to close up all these sources of corruption; let the rules of a healthy morality be practised in the *maisons de force*; that, compelled to work, convicts may come in the end to like it; when they have reaped the reward, they will acquire the habit, the taste, the need for occupation; let them give each other the example of a laborious life; it will soon become a pure life; soon they will begin to know regret for the past, the first harbinger of a love of duty.'[2] The techniques of correction immediately form part of the institutional framework of penal detention.

One should also recall that the movement for reforming the prisons, for controlling their functioning is not a recent phenomenon. It does not even seem to have originated in a recognition of failure. Prison 'reform' is virtually contemporary with the prison itself: it constitutes, as it were, its programme. From the outset, the prison was caught up in a series of accompanying mechanisms, whose purpose was apparently to correct it, but which seem to form part of its very functioning, so closely have they been bound up with its existence throughout its long history. There was, at once, a prolix technology of the prison. There were inquiries: that of Chaptal in 1801 (whose task it was to discover what could be used to introduce the modern prison system into France), that of Decazes in 1819, Villermé's work published in 1820, the report on the *maisons centrales* drawn up by Martignac in 1829, the inquiries carried out in the United States by Beaumont and Tocqueville in 1831, by Demetz and Blouet in 1835, the questionnaires addressed by Montalivet to the directors of the *maisons centrales* and to the general councils of the *départements* during the debate on solitary confinement. There were societies for supervising the functioning of the prisons and for suggesting improvements: in 1818, the very official *Société pour l'amélioration des prisons*, a little later the *Société des prisons* and various philanthropic groups. Innumerable measures – orders,

instructions or laws: from the reform that the first Restoration had
envisaged in September 1814, and which was never implemented, to
the law of 1844, drawn up by Tocqueville, which ended for a time
the long debate on the means of making imprisonment effective.
There were programmes drawn up to improve the functioning of
the machine-prison:[3] programmes for the treatment of the prisoners,
models for material improvement, some of these, like those of
Danjou and Harou-Romain, remaining no more than projects,
others becoming embodied in instructions (like the circular of 9
August 1841 on the building of *maisons d'arrêt*), others becoming
actual buildings, such as the Petite Roquette in which cellular
imprisonment was organized for the first time in France.

To these should be added the publications that sprang more or
less directly from the prison and were drawn up either by philan-
thropists like Appert, or a little later by 'specialists' (such as the
Annales de la Charité)[4] or, again, by former prisoners; *Pauvre
Jacques* at the end of the Restoration, or the *Gazette de Sainte-
Pélagie* at the beginning of the July monarchy.[5]

The prison should not be seen as an inert institution, shaken at
intervals by reform movements. The 'theory of the prison' was its
constant set of operational instructions rather than its incidental
criticism – one of its conditions of functioning. The prison has
always formed part of an active field in which projects, improvements, experiments, theoretical statements, personal evidence and
investigations have proliferated. The prison institution has always
been a focus of concern and debate. Is the prison still, then, a dark,
abandoned region? Is the fact that one has ceased to say so for
almost 200 years sufficient proof that it is not? In becoming a legal
punishment, it weighted the old juridico-political question of the
right to punish with all the problems, all the agitations that have
surrounded the corrective technologies of the individual.

Baltard called them 'complete and austere institutions' (Baltard,
1829). In several respects, the prison must be an exhaustive disciplinary apparatus: it must assume responsibility for all aspects of the
individual, his physical training, his aptitude to work, his everyday
conduct, his moral attitude, his state of mind; the prison, much more
than the school, the workshop or the army, which always involved a

certain specialization, is 'omni-disciplinary'. Moreover, the prison has neither exterior nor gap; it cannot be interrupted, except when its task is totally completed; its action on the individual must be uninterrupted: an unceasing discipline. Lastly, it gives almost total power over the prisoners; it has its internal mechanisms of repression and punishment: a despotic discipline. It carries to their greatest intensity all the procedures to be found in the other disciplinary mechanisms. It must be the most powerful machinery for imposing a new form on the perverted individual; its mode of action is the constraint of a total education: 'In prison the government may dispose of the liberty of the person and of the time of the prisoner; from then on, one can imagine the power of the education which, not only in a day, but in the succession of days and even years, may regulate for man the time of waking and sleeping, of activity and rest, the number and duration of meals, the quality and ration of food, the nature and product of labour, the time of prayer, the use of speech and even, so to speak, that of thought, that education which, in the short, simple journeys from refectory to workshop, from workshop to the cell, regulates the movements of the body, and even in moments of rest, determines the use of time, the time-table, this education, which, in short, takes possession of man as a whole, of all the physical and moral faculties that are in him and of the time in which he is himself' (Lucas, II, 123–4). This complete 'reformatory' lays down a recoding of existence very different from the mere juridical deprivation of liberty and very different, too, from the simple mechanism of exempla imagined by the reformers at the time of the *idéologues*.

1. The first principle was isolation. The isolation of the convict from the external world, from everything that motivated the offence, from the complicities that facilitated it. The isolation of the prisoners from one another. Not only must the penalty be individual, but it must also be individualizing – in two ways. First, the prison must be designed in such a way as to efface of itself the harmful consequences to which it gives rise in gathering together very different convicts in the same place: to stifle plots and revolts, to prevent the formation of future complicities that may give rise to blackmail (when the convicts are once again at liberty), to form an obstacle to the immorality of so many 'mysterious associations'. In short, the prison

should form from the malefactors that it gathers together a homo-geneous and interdependent population: 'There exists at this moment among us an organized society of criminals . . . They form a small nation within the greater. Almost all these men met or meet again in prison. We must now disperse the members of this society' (Tocqueville, *Rapport à la Chambre des Députés*, quoted in Beau-mont and Tocqueville, 392–3). Moreover, through the reflection that it gives rise to and the remorse that cannot fail to follow, solitude must be a positive instrument of reform: 'Thrown into solitude, the convict reflects. Placed alone in the presence of his crime, he learns to hate it, and, if his soul is not yet blunted by evil, it is in isolation that remorse will come to assail him' (Beaumont and Tocqueville, 109). Through the fact, too, that solitude assures a sort of self-regulation of the penalty and makes possible a spontane-ous individualization of the punishment: the more the convict is capable of reflecting, the more capable he was of committing his crime; but, also, the more lively his remorse, the more painful his solitude; on the other hand, when he has profoundly repented and made amends without the least dissimulation, solitude will no longer weigh upon him: 'Thus, according to this admirable discipline, each intelligence and each morality bears within itself the principle and measure of a punishment whose error and human fallibility cannot alter the certainty and invariable equity . . . Is it not in truth like the seal of a divine and providential justice?' (Aylies, 132–3). Lastly, and perhaps above all, the isolation of the convicts guarantees that it is possible to exercise over them, with maximum intensity, a power that will not be overthrown by any other influence; solitude is the primary condition of total submission: 'Just imagine,' said Charles Lucas, referring to the role of the governor, the instructor, the chaplain and other 'charitable persons' as regards the isolated convict, 'just imagine the power of human speech intervening in the midst of the terrible discipline of silence to speak to the heart, to the soul, to the human person' (Lucas, I, 167). Isolation provides an intimate exchange between the convict and the power that is exercised over him.

It is at this point that the debate on the two American systems of imprisonment, that of Auburn and that of Philadelphia, was situated. In fact, this debate, which was so wide-ranging and long drawn out,[6] concerned only the way in which isolation should be used, it being accepted by all.

The Auburn model prescribed the individual cell during the night, work and meals in common, but under the rule of absolute silence, the convicts being allowed to speak only to the warders, with their permission and in a low voice. It was a clear reference to the monastic model; a reference, too, to the discipline of the workshop. The prison must be the microcosm of a perfect society in which individuals are isolated in their moral existence, but in which they come together in a strict hierarchical framework, with no lateral relation, communication being possible only in a vertical direction. The advantage of the Auburnian system, according to its advocates, was that it formed a duplication of society itself. Constraint was assured by material means, but above all by a rule that one had to learn to respect and which was guaranteed by surveillance and punishment. Rather than keep the convicts 'under lock and key like wild beasts in their cages', they must be brought together, 'made to join together in useful exercises, forced together to adopt good habits, preventing moral contagion by active surveillance, maintaining reflection by the rule of silence'; this rule accustoms the convict 'to regard the law as a sacred precept whose violation brings just and legitimate harm' (Mittermaier, in *Revue française et étrangère de législation*, 1836). Thus this operation of isolation, assembly without communication and law guaranteed by uninterrupted supervision, must rehabilitate the criminal as a social individual: it trains him to a 'useful and resigned activity' (Gasparin); it restores for him 'habits of sociability' (Beaumont and Tocqueville, 112).

In absolute isolation – as at Philadelphia – the rehabilitation of the criminal is expected not of the application of a common law, but of the relation of the individual to his own conscience and to what may enlighten him from within.[7] 'Alone in his cell, the convict is handed over to himself; in the silence of his passions and of the world that surrounds him, he descends into his conscience, he questions it and feels awakening within him the moral feeling that never entirely perishes in the heart of man' (*Journal des économistes*, II, 1842). It is not, therefore, an external respect for the law or fear of punishment alone that will act upon the convict but the workings of the conscience itself. A profound submission, rather than a superficial training; a change of 'morality', rather than of attitude. In the Pennsylvanian prison, the only operations of correction were the conscience and the silent architecture that confronted it. At Cherry Hill, 'the walls are the punishment of the crime; the cell confronts the convict with himself; he is forced to listen to his conscience'. Hence work there is more in the nature of a consolation than an obligation; supervisors do not have to exert force – this is assured by the materiality of things – and consequently, their authority may be accepted: 'At each visit, a few benevolent words flow from this honest mouth and bring to the heart of the inmate gratitude, hope and consolation; he loves his warder; and he loves him because he is gentle and sympathetic. Walls are terrible, but man is good' (Blouet). In this closed cell, this temporary sepulchre, the myths of resurrection arise easily enough. After night and silence, the regenerated life. Auburn was society itself reduced to its bare essentials. Cherry Hill was life annihilated and begun again. Catholicism soon absorbed this Quaker technique into its discourses. 'I see your cell as no more than a frightful sepulchre where, instead of worms, remorse and despair come to gnaw at you and to turn your existence into a hell in anticipation. But . . . what is for an irreligious prisoner merely a tomb, a repulsive ossuary, becomes, for the sincerely Christian convict, the very cradle of blessed immortality.'[8]

A whole series of different conflicts stemmed from the opposition between these two models: religious (must conversion be the principal element of correction?), medical (does total isolation drive convicts insane?), economic (which method costs less?), architectural and administrative (which form guarantees the best surveillance?). This, no doubt, was why the argument lasted so long. But, at the heart of the debate, and making it possible, was this primary objective of carceral action: coercive individualization, by the termination of any relation that is not supervised by authority or arranged according to hierarchy.

2. 'Work alternating with meals accompanies the convict to evening prayer; then a new sleep gives him an agreeable rest that is not disturbed by the phantoms of an unregulated imagination. Thus the six weekdays pass by. They are followed by a day devoted exclusively to prayer, instruction and salutary meditations. Thus the weeks, the months, the years follow one another; thus the

prisoner who, on entering the establishment, was an inconstant man, or one who was single-minded only in his irregularity, seeking to destroy his existence by the variety of his vices, gradually becomes by dint of a habit that is at first purely external, but is soon transformed into a second nature, so familiar with work and the pleasures that derive from it, that, provided wise instruction has opened up his soul to repentance, he may be exposed with more confidence to temptations, when he finally recovers his liberty' (Julius, 417–18). Work is defined, with isolation, as an agent of carceral transformation. This is to be found as early as the code of 1808: 'Although the penalty inflicted by the law has as its aim the reparation of a crime, it is also intended to reform the convict, and this double aim will be fulfilled if the malefactor is snatched from that fatal idleness which, having brought him to prison, meets him again within its walls and, seizing hold of him, brings him to the ultimate degree of depravity.'[9] Work is neither an addition nor a corrective to the régime of detention: whether it is a question of forced labour, reclusion or imprisonment, it is conceived, by the legislator himself, as necessarily accompanying it. But the necessity involved is precisely not the necessity of which the eighteenth-century reformers spoke, when they wished to make imprisonment either an example for the public or a useful reparation for society. In the carceral régime, the link between work and punishment is of another type.

Several polemics that took place under the Restoration and the July Monarchy throw light on the function attributed to penal labour. First, there was the debate on the subject of wages. The labour of prisoners was remunerated in France. This posed a problem: if work in prison is remunerated, that work cannot really form part of the penalty; and the prisoner may therefore refuse to perform it. Moreover, wages reward the skill of the worker and not the improvement of the convict: 'The worst subjects are almost everywhere the most skilful workers; they are the most highly remunerated, consequently the most intemperate and least ready to repent' (Marquet-Wasselot, quoted in Lucas, 324). The debate, which had never quite died down, was resumed with great liveliness in the early 1840s: it was a period of economic crisis, a period of workers' agitation and a period, too, in which the opposition between the worker and the delinquent was beginning to crystallize (cf. below,

285). There were strikes against the prison workshops: when a Chaumont glove-maker succeeded in organizing a workshop at Clairvaux, the workers protested, declared that their labour was dishonoured, occupied the manufactory and forced the employer to abandon his project (cf. Aguet, 30–31). There was also a widespread press campaign in the workers' newspapers: on the theme that the government encouraged penal labour in order to reduce 'free' wages; on the theme that the inconveniences of these prison workshops were even more evident for women, who were thus deprived of their labour, driven to prostitution and therefore to prison, where these same women, who could no longer work when they were free, then competed with those who were still at work (*L'Atelier*, 3rd year, no. 4, December 1842); on the theme that prisoners were given the safest jobs – 'in warm and sheltered conditions thieves execute the work of hat-making and cabinet-making', while the unemployed hatter is forced to go 'to the human slaughter-house to make white-lead at two francs a day' (*L'Atelier*, 6th year, no. 2, November 1845); on the theme that philanthropy is more concerned about the working conditions of prisoners than those of free workers: 'We are sure that if prisoners worked with mercury, for example, science would be a great deal more ready than it is to find ways of protecting the workers from the dangers of its fumes: "Those poor convicts?" someone would exclaim, who scarcely has a word for the gilders. But what can you expect? One has to have killed or robbed to arouse compassion or interest.' On the theme above all that, if the prison was tending to become a workshop, it would not be long before beggars and the unemployed were sent there, thus reconstituting the old *hôpitaux généraux* of France or the workhouses of England. In addition, there were petitions and letters, especially after the law of 1844 – one petition, rejected by the Chambre de Paris, 'found inhuman that one should propose to apply murderers and thieves to work that is today the lot of a few thousand workers'; 'the Chambre preferred Barrabas to us' (*L'Atelier*, 4th year, no. 9, June 1844 and 5th year, no. 7, April 1845; cf. also, of the same period, *La Démocratie pacifique*); typographical workers sent a letter to the minister when they learnt that a printing-works was to be set up in the prison at Melun: 'You have decided between reprobates justly punished by the law and citizens who sacrifice their days, in abstinence and probity, to the lives of their families and to the wealth of their nation' (*L'Atelier*, 5th year, no. 6, March 1845).

The answers given by the government and the administration to this whole campaign changed very little. Penal labour cannot be criticized for any unemployment it may give rise to: with its limited extent, and its low output, it cannot have a general effect on the economy. It is intrinsically useful, not as an activity of production, but by virtue of the effect it has on the human mechanism. It is a principle of order and regularity; through the demands that it imposes, it conveys, imperceptibly, the forms of a rigorous power; it bends bodies to regular movements, it excludes agitation and distraction, it imposes a hierarchy and a surveillance that are all the more accepted, and which will be inscribed all the more deeply in the behaviour of the convicts, in that they form part of its logic: with work 'the rule is introduced into a prison, it reigns there without effort, without the use of any repressive and violent means. By occupying the convict, one gives him habits of order and obedience; one makes the idler that he was diligent and active ... with time, he finds in the regular movement of the prison, in the manual labours to which he is subjected ... a certain remedy against the wanderings of his imagination' (Bérenger). Penal labour must be seen as the very machinery that transforms the violent, agitated, unreflective convict into a part that plays its role with perfect regularity. The prison is not a workshop; it is, it must be of itself, a machine whose convict-workers are both the cogs and the products; it 'occupies them continually, with the sole aim of filling their moments. When the body is agitated, when the mind applies itself to a particular object, importunate ideas depart, calm is born once again in the soul' (Danjou, 180). If, in the final analysis, the work of the prison has an economic effect, it is by producing individuals mechanized according to the general norms of an industrial society: 'Work is the providence of the modern peoples; it replaces morality, fills the gap left by beliefs and is regarded as the principle of all good. Work must be the religion of the prisons. For a machine-society, purely mechanical means of reform are required' (Faucher, 64; in England the 'treadmill' and the pump provided a disciplinary mechanization of the inmates, with no end product). The making of machine-men, but also of proletarians; in effect, when one has only a 'pair of arms for any good work', one can live only 'from the product of one's labour, through the practice of a profession or from the product of the labour of others, by thieving'; but, although the prison did not force offenders to work, it seems to have reintroduced into its very institution and, obliquely, by means of taxation, this levying by some on the labour of others: 'The question of idleness is the same as in society; it is from the labour of others that the convicts live, if they do not exist from their own labour' (Lucas, II, 313–14). The labour by which the convict contributes to his own needs turns the thief into a docile worker. This is the utility of remuneration for penal labour; it imposes on the convict the 'moral' form of wages as the condition of his existence. Wages inculcate the 'love and habit' of work (Lucas, II, 243); they give those malefactors who do not know the difference between mine and thine a sense of property – of 'what one has earned by the sweat of one's brow' (Danjou, 210–11; cf. also *L'Atelier*, 6th year, no. 2, November 1845); they also teach those who have lived in dissipation the virtues of thrift and foresight (Lucas; a third of the prisoner's daily wages was set aside for the day when he left the prison); lastly, by proposing a quantity of work to be carried out, they make it possible to express quantitatively the convict's zeal and the progress of his improvement (Ducpétiaux, 30–31). The wages of penal labour do not reward production; they function as a motive and measure of individual transformation: it is a legal fiction, since it does not represent the 'free' granting of labour power, but an artifice that is presumed to be effective in the techniques of correction.

What, then, is the use of penal labour? Not profit; nor even the formation of a useful skill; but the constitution of a power relation, an empty economic form, a schema of individual submission and of adjustment to a production apparatus.

The perfect image of prison labour was the women's workshop at Clairvaux; the silent precision of the human machinery is reminiscent of the regulated rigour of the convent: 'On a throne, above which is a crucifix, a sister is sitting; before her, arranged in two rows, the prisoners are carrying out the task imposed on them, and, as needlework accounts for almost all the work, the strictest silence is constantly maintained. . . It seems that, in these halls, the very air breathes penitence and expiation. One is carried back, as by a spontaneous movement, to the time of the venerable habits of this ancient place, one remembers those voluntary penitents who shut themselves up here in order to say farewell to the world'. Compare this with the following; 'Go into a cotton-mill; listen to the conversations of the workers and the whistling of the machines. Is there any contrast in the world more afflicting than the regularity and predictability of these mechanical movements, compared with the disorder of ideas and morals, produced by the contact of so many men, women and children' (Faucher 20).

3. But prison goes beyond the mere privation of liberty in a more important way. It becomes increasingly an instrument for the modulation of the penalty; an apparatus which, through the execution of the sentence with which it is entrusted, seems to have the right, in part at least, to assume its principle. Of course, the prison institution was not given this 'right' in the nineteenth century or even in the twentieth, except in a fragmentary form (through the oblique way of release on licence, semi-release, the organization of reformatories). But it should be noted that it was claimed very early on by those responsible for prison administration, as the very condition of the good functioning of a prison, and of its efficiency in the task of reformation that the law itself had given it.

The same goes for the duration of the punishment; it makes it possible to quantify the penalties exactly, to graduate them according to circumstances and to give to legal punishment the more or less explicit form of wages; but it also runs the risk of having no corrective value, if it is fixed once and for all in the sentence. The length of the penalty must not be a measurement of the 'exchange value' of the offence; it must be adjusted to the 'useful' transformation of the inmate during his term of imprisonment. It is not a time-measure, but a time finalized. The form of the operation, rather than the form of the wages. 'Just as the prudent physician ends his medication or continues it according to whether the patient has or has not arrived at a perfect cure, so, in the first of these two hypotheses, expiation ought to end with the complete reform of the prisoner; for, in this case, all detention has become useless, and from then on as inhuman to the reformed individual as it is vainly burdensome for the State.'[10] The correct duration of the penalty must be calculated, therefore, not only according to the particular crime and its circumstances, but also according to the penalty itself as it takes place in actual fact. This amounts to saying that, although the penalty must be individualized, it is so not on the basis of the individual-offender, the juridical subject of his act, the responsible author of the offence, but on the basis of the individual punished, the object of a supervised transformation, the individual in detention inserted in the prison apparatus, modified by it or reacting to it. 'It is a question only of reforming the evil-doer. Once this reform has come about, the criminal must return to society' (C. Lucas, quoted in the *Gazette des tribunaux*, 6 April 1837).

The quality and content of detention should no longer be determined by the nature of the offence alone. The juridical gravity of a crime does not at all have the value of a univocal sign for the character of the convict, whether or not he is capable of reform. In particular the crime–offence distinction, which the penal code recognized in drawing the corresponding distinction between mere imprisonment and imprisonment with hard labour, is not operational in terms of reform. This was the almost universal opinion expressed by the directors of the *maisons centrales*, during an inquiry carried out by the ministry in 1836: 'The minor offenders are generally the most vicious. . . Among the criminals, one meets many men who have given in to the violence of their passions and to the needs of a large family.' 'The behaviour of criminals is much better than that of the minor offenders; the former are more submissive, harder-working than the latter, who, in general, are pickpockets, debauchees and idlers.'[11] Hence the idea that punitive rigour must not be in direct proportion to the penal importance of the offence – nor determined once and for all.

As an operation of correction, imprisonment has its own requirements and dangers. It is its effects that must determine its stages, its temporary increases, its successive reductions, in severity; what Charles Lucas called the 'mobile classification of moralities'. The progressive system applied at Geneva since 1825 was often advocated in France (Fresnel, 29–31). It took the form, for example, of three areas: a trial area for prisoners in general, a punishment area and a reward area for those who had embarked on the way of reform (Lucas, II, 440). Or it took the form of four phases: a period of intimidation (deprivation of work and of any internal or external relations); a period of work (isolation, but work which, after the phase of forced idleness, would be welcomed as a benefit); a régime of moralization (more or less frequent 'lectures' from the directors and official visitors); a period of work in common (Duras). Although the principle of the penalty was certainly a legal decision, its administration, its quality and its rigours must belong to an autonomous mechanism that supervises the effects of punishment within the very apparatus that produces them. A whole régime of punishments and rewards that is a way not simply of gaining respect for the prison regulations, but of making the action of the prison on the inmates effective. The legal authority itself came to accept this: 'One should not be surprised, said the supreme court of appeal, when consulted on the subject of a bill concerning the prisons, at the idea of granting rewards, which might consist either for the most part in money, or in a better diet, or even in a reduction of the duration of the penalty. If anything can awaken in the minds of convicts the notions of good and evil, bring them to moral reflections and raise them to some extent in their own eyes, it is the possibility of obtaining some reward' (Lucas, II, 441–2).

And it must be admitted that the legal authorities can have no immediate control over all these procedures that rectify the penalty as it proceeds. It is a question, in effect, of measures that by definition can intervene only after the sentence and can bear only on something other than the offences. Those who administer detention must therefore have an indispensable autonomy, when it comes to the question of individualizing and varying the application of the penalty: supervisors, a prison governor, a chaplain or an instructor are more capable of exercising this corrective function than those who hold the penal power. It is their judgement (understood as observation, diagnosis, characterization, information, differential classification) and not a verdict in the form of an attribution of guilt, that must serve as a support for this internal modulation of the penalty – for its mitigation or even its interruption. When in 1846, Bonneville presented his project of release on licence, he defined it as 'the right of the administration, with the previous approval of the legal authority, to place in temporary liberty, after a sufficient period of expiation, the completely reformed convict, on condition that he will be brought back into prison on the slightest well-founded complaint' (Bonneville, 5). All this 'arbitrariness' which, in the old penal system, enabled the judges to modulate the penalty and the princes to ignore it if they so wished, all this arbitrariness, which the modern codes have withdrawn from the judicial power, has been gradually reconstituted on the side of the power that administers and supervises punishment. It is the sovereignty of knowledge possessed by the warder: 'He is a veritable magistrate called upon to reign as sovereign in the prison . . . who, in order not to fall short in his mission, must combine the most eminent virtue with a profound knowledge of mankind' (Bérenger).

And so we arrive at a principle, clearly formulated by Charles Lucas, which, although it marks the virtual beginning of modern penal functioning, very few jurists would dare to accept today without some hesitation; let us call it the Declaration of Carceral Independence – in it is claimed the right to be a power that not only possesses administrative autonomy, but is also a part of punitive sovereignty. This affirmation of the rights of the prison posits as a principle: that criminal judgement is an arbitrary unity; that it must be broken down; that the writers of the penal codes were correct in distinguishing the legislative level (which classifies the acts and attributes penalties to them) and the judicial level (which passes the sentences); that the task today is to analyse in turn this later judicial level; that one should distinguish in it what is properly judicial (assess not so much acts as agents, measure 'the intentionalities that give human acts so many different moralities', and therefore rectify if it can the assessments of the legislator); and to give autonomy to 'penitentiary judgement', which is perhaps the most important; in relation to it the assessment of the court is merely a 'way of prejudging', for the morality of the agent can be assessed 'only when put to the test. The judge, therefore, requires in turn a compulsory and rectifying supervision of his assessments; and this supervision is that provided by the penitentiary prison' (Lucas, II, 418–22).

One may speak, therefore, of an excess or a series of excesses on the part of imprisonment in terms of legal detention – of the 'carceral' in relation to the 'judicial'. Now this excess was observed very early on, from the very birth of the prison, either in the form of real practices, or in the form of projects. It did not come later, as a secondary effect. The great carceral machinery was bound up with the very functioning of the prison. The sign of this autonomy is very apparent in the 'useless' acts of violence perpetrated by warders or in the despotism of an administration that has all the privileges of an enclosed community. Its roots lie elsewhere: precisely in the fact that the prison is required to be 'useful', that the deprivation of liberty – that juridical levying on an ideal property – must, from the outset, have exercised a positive technical role, operating transformations on individuals. And, for this operation, the carceral apparatus has recourse to three great schemata: the politico-moral schema of individual isolation and hierarchy; the economic model of force applied to compulsory work; the technico-medical model of cure and normalization. The cell, the workshop, the hospital. The margin by which the prison exceeds detention is filled in fact by techniques of a disciplinary type. And this disciplinary addition to the juridical is what, in short, is called the 'penitentiary'.

This addition was not accepted easily. To begin with, there was the question of principle: the penalty must be nothing more than the deprivation of liberty; like our present rulers, but with all the freshness of his language, Decazes says: 'The law must follow the convicted man into the prison where it has sent him' (Decazes). But very soon – and this is a characteristic fact – these debates were to become a battle for appropriating control of this additional penitentiary element; the judges were to demand a right of inspection over the carceral mechanisms: 'The moral enlightenment of the inmates requires innumerable cooperators; it is only by visits of inspection, commissions of surveillance and charity associations that this may be accomplished. Auxiliaries, then, are needed and it is the judges who must provide them' (Ferrus, viii; an ordinance of 1847 had set up commissions of surveillance). From this period, the penitentiary order had become sufficiently well established for there to be no question of dismantling it; the question was how to get control of it. This gave rise to the figure of the judge obsessed by a desire for prison. A century later, this was to give birth to a bastard, yet deformed child: the magistrate entrusted with the determination of penalties.

But, if the penitentiary, in so far as it went well beyond mere detention, was able not only to establish itself, but to entrap the whole of penal justice and to imprison the judges themselves, it was because it was able to introduce criminal justice into relations of knowledge that have since become its infinite labyrinth.

The prison, the place where the penalty is carried out, is also the place of observation of punished individuals. This takes two forms: surveillance, of course, but also knowledge of each inmate, of his behaviour, his deeper states of mind, his gradual improvement; the prisons must be conceived as places for the formation of clinical knowledge about the convicts; 'the penitentiary system cannot be an *a priori* conception; it is an induction of the social state. There are moral diseases, as well as breakdowns in health, where the treatment depends on the site and direction of the illness' (Faucher, 6). This involves two essential mechanisms. It must be possible to hold the prisoner under permanent observation; every report that can be made about him must be recorded and computed. The theme of the Panopticon – at once surveillance and observation, security and knowledge, individualization and totalization, isolation and transparency – found in the prison its privileged locus of realization. Although the panoptic procedures, as concrete forms of the exercise of power, have become extremely widespread, at least in their less concentrated forms, it was really only in the penitentiary institutions that Bentham's utopia could be fully expressed in a material form. In the 1830s, the Panopticon became the architectural programme of most prison projects. It was the most direct way of expressing 'the intelligence of discipline in stone' (Lucas, I, 69); of making architecture transparent to the administration of power;[12] of making it possible to substitute for force or other violent constraints the gentle efficiency of total surveillance; of ordering space according to the recent humanization of the codes and the new penitentiary theory: 'The authorities, on the one hand, and the architect, on the other, must know, therefore, whether the prisons are to be based on the principle of milder penalties or on a system of reforming convicts, in accordance with legislation which, by getting to the root cause of the people's vices, becomes a principle that will regenerate the virtues that they must practice' (Baltard, 4–5).

In short, its task was to constitute a prison-machine[13] with a cell of visibility in which the inmate will find himself caught as 'in the glass house of the Greek philosopher' (Harou-Romain, 8) and a central point from which a permanent gaze may control prisoners and staff. Around these two requirements, several variations were possible: the Benthamite Panopticon in its strict form, the semi-circle, the cross-plan, the star shape. In the midst of all these discussions, the Minister of the Interior in 1841 sums up the fundamental principles: 'The central inspection hall is the pivot of the system. Without a central point of inspection, surveillance ceases to be guaranteed, continuous and general; for it is impossible to have complete trust in the activity, zeal and intelligence of the warder who immediately supervises the cells. . . The architect must therefore bring all his attention to bear on this object; it is a question both of discipline and economy. The more accurate and easy the surveillance, the less need will there be to seek in the strength of the building guarantees against attempted escape and communication between the inmates. But surveillance will be perfect if from a central hall the director or head-warder sees, without moving and without being seen, not only the entrances of all the cells and even the inside of most of them when the unglazed door is open, but also the warders guarding the prisoners on every floor. . . With the formula of circular or semi-circular prisons, it would be possible to see from a single centre all the prisoners in their cells and the warders in the inspection galleries' (Ducatel, 9).

But the penitentiary Panopticon was also a system of individualizing and permanent documentation. The same year in which variants of the Benthamite schema were recommended for the building of prisons, the system of 'moral accounting' was made compulsory: an individual report of a uniform kind in every prison, on which the governor or head-warder, the chaplain and the instructor had to fill in their observations on each inmate: 'It is in a way the *vade mecum* of prison administration, making it possible to assess each case, each circumstance and, consequently, to know what treatment to apply to each prisoner individually' (Ducpétiaux, 56–7). Many other, much more complete, systems of recording were planned or tried out (cf., for example, Gregory, 199ff; Grellet-Wammy, 23–5 and 199–203). The overall aim was to make the prison a place for the constitution of a body of knowledge that would regulate the exercise of penitentiary practice. The prison has not only to know the decision of the judges and to apply it in terms of the established regulations: it has to extract unceasingly from the inmate a body of knowledge that will make it possible to transform the penal measure into a penitentiary operation; which will make of the penalty required by the offence a modification of the inmate that will be of use to society. The autonomy of the carceral régime and the knowledge that it creates make it possible to increase the utility of the penalty, which the code had made the very principle of its punitive philosophy: 'The governor must not lose sight of a single inmate, because in whatever part of the prison the inmate is to be found, whether he is entering or leaving, or whether he is staying there, the governor must also justify the motives for his staying in a particular classification or for his movement from one to another. He is a veritable accountant. Each inmate is for him, in the sphere of individual education, a capital invested with penitentiary interest' (Lucas, II, 449–50). As a highly efficient technology, penitentiary practice produces a return on the capital invested in the penal system and in the building of heavy prisons.

Similarly, the offender becomes an individual to know. This demand for knowledge was not, in the first instance, inserted into the legislation itself, in order to provide substance for the sentence and to determine the true degree of guilt. It is as a convict, as a point of application for punitive mechanisms, that the offender is constituted himself as the object of possible knowledge.

But this implies that the penitentiary apparatus, with the whole technological programme that accompanies it, brings about a curious substitution: from the hands of justice, it certainly receives a convicted person; but what it must apply itself to is not, of course, the offence, nor even exactly the offender, but a rather different object, one defined by variables which at the outset at least were not taken into account in the sentence, for they were relevant only for a corrective technology. This other character, whom the penitentiary apparatus substitutes for the convicted offender, is the *delinquent*.

The delinquent is to be distinguished from the offender by the fact that it is not so much his act as his life that is relevant in characterizing him. The penitentiary operation, if it is to be a genuine re-education, must become the sum total existence of the delinquent, making of the prison a sort of artificial and coercive theatre in which his life will be examined from top to bottom. The legal punishment bears upon an act; the punitive technique on a life; it falls to this punitive technique, therefore, to reconstitute all the sordid detail of a life in the form of knowledge, to fill in the gaps of that knowledge and to act upon it by a practice of compulsion. It is a biographical knowledge and a technique for correcting individual lives. The observation of the delinquent 'should go back not only to the circumstances, but also to the causes of his crime; they must be sought in the story of his life, from the triple point of view of psychology, social position and upbringing, in order to discover the dangerous proclivities of the first, the harmful predispositions of the second and the bad antecedents of the third. This biographical investigation is an essential part of the preliminary investigation for the classification of penalities before it becomes a condition for the classification of moralities in the penitentiary system. It must accompany the convict from the court to the prison, where the governor's task is not only to receive it, but also to complete, supervise and rectify its various factors during the period of detention' (Lucas, II, 440–42). Behind the offender, to whom the investigation of the facts may attribute responsibility for an offence, stands the delinquent whose slow formation is shown in a biographical investigation. The introduction of the 'biographical' is important in the history of penality. Because it establishes the 'criminal' as existing before the crime and even outside it. And, for this reason, a psychological causality, duplicating the juridical attribution of responsibility, confuses its effects. At this point one enters the 'criminological' labyrinth from which we have certainly not yet emerged: any determining cause, because it reduces responsibility, marks the author of the offence with a criminality all the more formidable and demands penitentiary measures that are all the more strict. As the biography of the criminal duplicates in penal practice the analysis of circumstances used in gauging the crime, so one sees penal discourse and psychiatric discourse crossing each other's frontiers; and there, at their point of junction, is formed the notion of the 'dangerous' individual, which makes it possible to draw up a network of causality in terms of an entire biography and to present a verdict of punishment-correction.[14]

The delinquent is also to be distinguished from the offender in that he is not only the author of his acts (the author responsible in terms of certain criteria of free, conscious will), but is linked to his offence by a whole bundle of complex threads (instincts, drives, tendencies, character). The penitentiary technique bears not on the relation between author and crime, but on the criminal's affinity with his crime. The delinquent, the strange manifestation of an overall phenomenon of criminality, is to be found in quasi-natural classes, each endowed with its own characteristics and requiring a specific treatment, what Marquet-Wasselot called in 1841 the 'ethnography of the prisons'; 'The convicts are ... another people within the same people; with its own habits, instincts, morals' (Marquet-Wasselot, 9). We are still very close here to the 'picturesque' descriptions of the world of the malefactors – an old tradition that goes back a long way and gained new vigour in the early nineteenth century, at a time when the perception of another form of life was being articulated upon that of another class and another human species. A zoology of social sub-species and an ethnology of the civilizations of malefactors, with their own rites and language, was beginning to emerge in a parody form. But an attempt was also being made to constitute a new objectivity in which the criminal belongs to a typology that is both natural and deviant. Delinquency, a pathological gap in the human species, may be analysed as morbid syndromes or as great teratological forms. With Ferrus's classification, we probably have one of the first conversions of the old 'ethnography' of crime into a systematic typology of delinquents. The analysis is slender, certainly, but it reveals quite clearly the principle that delinquency must be specified in terms not so much of the law as of the norm. There are three types of convict; there are those who are endowed 'with intellectual resources above the average of intelligence that we have established', but who have been perverted either by the 'tendencies of their organization' and a 'native predisposition', or by 'pernicious logic', an 'iniquitous morality', a 'dangerous attitude to social duties'. Those that belong to this category require isolation day and night, solitary exercise, and, when one is forced to bring them into contact with the others, they should wear 'a light mask made of metal netting, of the kind used for stone-cutting or fencing'. The second category is made up of 'vicious, stupid or passive convicts, who have been led into evil by indifference to either shame or honour, through cowardice, that is to say, laziness, and because of a lack of resistance to bad incitements'; the régime suitable to them is not so much that of punishment as of education, and if possible of mutual education: isolation at night, work in common during the day, conversations permitted provided they are conducted aloud, reading in common, followed by mutual questioning, for which rewards may be given. Lastly, there are the 'inept or incapable convicts', who are 'rendered incapable, by an incomplete organization, of any occupation requiring considered effort and consistent will, and who are therefore incapable of competing in work with intelligent workers and who, having neither enough education to know their social duties, nor enough intelligence to understand this fact or to struggle against their personal instincts, are led to evil by their very incapacity. For these, solitude would merely encourage their inertia; they must therefore live in common, but in such a way as to form small groups, constantly stimulated by collective operations, and subjected to rigid surveillance' (Ferrus, 182ff and 278ff). Thus a 'positive' knowledge of the delinquents and their species, very different from the juridical definition of offences and their circumstances, is gradually established; but this knowledge is also distinct from the medical knowledge that makes it possible to introduce the insanity of the individual and, consequently, to efface the criminal character of the act. Ferrus states the principle quite clearly: 'Considered as a whole, criminals are nothing less than madmen; it would be unjust to the latter to confuse them with consciously perverted men.' The task of this new knowledge is to define the act 'scientifically' *qua* offence and above all the individual *qua* delinquent. Criminology is thus made possible.

The correlative of penal justice may well be the offender, but the correlative of the penitentiary apparatus is someone other; this is the delinquent, a biographical unity, a kernel of danger, representing a type of anomaly. And, although it is true that to a detention that deprives of liberty, as defined by law, the prison added the additional element of the penitentiary, this penitentiary element introduced in turn a third character who slipped between the individual condemned by the law and the individual who carries out this law. At the point that marks the disappearance of the branded, dismembered, burnt, annihilated body of the tortured criminal, there appeared the body of the prisoner, duplicated by the individuality of the 'delinquent', by the little soul of the criminal, which the very apparatus of punishment fabricated as a point of application of the power to punish and as the object of what is still called today penitentiary science. It is said that the prison fabricated delinquents; it is true that it brings back, almost inevitably, before the courts those who have been sent there. But it also fabricates them in the sense that it has introduced into the operation of the law and the offence, the judge and the offender, the condemned man and the executioner, the non-corporal reality of the delinquency that links them together and, for a century and a half, has caught them in the same trap.

The penitentiary technique and the delinquent are in a sense twin brothers. It is not true that it was the discovery of the delinquent through a scientific rationality that introduced into our old prisons the refinement of penitentiary techniques. Nor is it true that the internal elaboration of penitentiary methods has finally brought to light the 'objective' existence of a delinquency that the abstraction and rigidity of the law were unable to perceive. They appeared together, the one extending from the other, as a technological ensemble that forms and fragments the object to which it applies its instruments. And it is this delinquency, formed in the foundations of the judicial apparatus, among the '*basses œuvres*', the servile tasks, from which justice averts its gaze, out of the shame it feels in punishing those it condemns, it is this delinquency that now comes to haunt the untroubled courts and the majesty of the laws; it is this delinquency that must be known, assessed, measured, diagnosed, treated when sentences are passed. It is now this delinquency, this anomaly, this deviation, this potential danger, this illness, this form of existence, that must be taken into account when the codes are rewritten. Delinquency is the vengeance of the prison on justice. It is a revenge formidable enough to leave the judge speechless. It is at this point that the criminologists raise their voices.

But we must not forget that the prison, that concentrated and austere figure of all the disciplines, is not an endogenous element in the penal system as defined at the turn of the eighteenth and nineteenth centuries. The theme of a punitive society and of a general semio-technique of punishment that has sustained the 'ideological' codes – Beccarian or Benthamite – did not itself give rise to the universal use of the prison. This prison came from elsewhere – from the mechanisms proper to a disciplinary power. Now, despite this heterogeneity, the mechanisms and effects of the prison have spread right through modern criminal justice; delinquency and the delinquents have become parasites on it through and through. One must seek the reason for this formidable 'efficiency' of the prison. But one thing may be noted at the outset: the penal justice defined in the eighteenth century by the reformers traced two possible but divergent lines of objectification of the criminal: the first was the series of 'monsters', moral or political, who had fallen outside the social pact; the second was that of the juridical subject rehabilitated by punishment. Now the 'delinquent' makes it possible to join the two lines and to constitute under the authority of medicine, psychology or criminology, an individual in whom the offender of the law and the object of a scientific technique are superimposed – or almost – one upon the other. That the grip of the prison on the penal system should not have led to a violent reaction of rejection is no doubt due to many reasons. One of these is that, in fabricating delinquency, it gave to criminal justice a unitary field of objects, authenticated by the 'sciences', and thus enabled it to function on a general horizon of 'truth'.

The prison, that darkest region in the apparatus of justice, is the place where the power to punish, which no longer dares to manifest itself openly, silently organizes a field of objectivity in which punishment will be able to function openly as treatment and the sentence be inscribed among the discourses of knowledge. It is understandable that justice should have adopted so easily a prison that was not the offspring of its own thoughts. Justice certainly owed the prison this recognition.

2. Illegalities and delinquency

From the point of view of the law, detention may be a mere deprivation of liberty. But the imprisonment that performs this function has always involved a technical project. The transition from the public execution, with its spectacular rituals, its art mingled with the ceremony of pain, to the penalties of prisons buried in architectural masses and guarded by the secrecy of administrations, is not a transition to an undifferentiated, abstract, confused penality; it is the transition from one art of punishing to another, no less skilful one. It is a technical mutation. From this transition spring a symptom and a symbol: the replacement, in 1837, of the chain-gang by the police carriage.

The chain-gang, a tradition that went back to the time of the galley slaves, was still surviving under the July monarchy. The importance it seems to have assumed as a spectacle at the beginning of the nineteenth century may be bound up with the fact that it combined in a single manifestation the two modes of punishment: the way to detention unfolded as a ceremonial of torture. (Faucher remarked that the chain-gang was a popular spectacle 'especially since the scaffolds were almost entirely abolished'.) The accounts of the 'last chain-gangs' – those that crossed France in the summer of 1836 – and of its scandals allow us to rediscover this functioning, so alien to the rules of 'penitentiary science'. It began with a scaffold ritual: the fixing of iron collars and chains in the courtyard of Bicêtre prison. The convict's neck was thrown back upon a block; but this time the art of the executioner was to strike without crushing the head – an inverted skill that knew how not to deliver the death blow. 'The courtyard of Bicêtre displays its instruments of torture: several rows of chains with their iron-collars. The *artoupans* (head-warders), who serve as temporary blacksmiths, arrange the block and hammer. Around the bars of the wall walk are stuck all those heads, wearing a gloomy or bold expression, which the operator is to rivet. Higher up, at every storey of the prison, one sees legs and arms dangling through the bars of the cells, as at some bazaar of human flesh; these are the prisoners who have come to assist at the toilet of their comrades of the day before. . . Here they are in the attitude of sacrifice. They are stitting on the ground, coupled at random by the waist; the chains they must carry, each weighing eight pounds, rest heavily on their knees. The operator inspects them, measuring heads and adapting the enormous inch-thick collars. It takes three men to rivet an iron-collar; the first holds up the block, the second holds the two branches of the iron-collar together and, with his two outstretched arms, secures the patient's head; the third strikes with repeated blows and flattens the bolt under his huge hammer. Each blow shakes the head and the body. . . . Indeed, one does not think of the danger that the victim might face if the hammer missed its mark; this impression is nullified or rather defaced before the profound impression of horror one experiences in contemplating one of God's creatures in such a state of abasement.'[1] It also had the dimension of a public spectacle; according to the *Gazette des tribunaux*, over 100,000 people watched the chain-gang leave Paris on 19 July: 'The descent from the Courtille to the Mardi Gras. . .' Order and wealth came to watch from a distance the passing of the great nomadic tribe that had been put in chains, that other species, 'the race apart that has the privilege of populating the convict-ships and prisons'. The spectators of the lower classes, as at the time of the public executions, kept up their ambiguous exchanges with the convicts, alternating insults, threats, words of encouragement, blows, signs of hate or complicity. Something violent aroused and accompanied the procession along its entire course: anger against a justice that was too severe or too indulgent; shouts against the detested criminals; movements in favour of prisoners one knew and greeted; confrontations with the police: 'During the whole journey from the Fontainebleau barrier, groups of enraged spectators hurled insults at Delacollonge: Down with the priest, they said, down with that hateful man; he should have got his deserts. Without the energy and firmness of the municipal guard, serious disorders could have taken place. At Vaugirard, it was the women who were the most angry. They cried: Down with the wicked priest! Down with the monster Delacollonge! The police inspectors of Montrouge and Vaugirard and several mayors and deputy-mayors ran the gauntlet in their attempt to enforce the decision of the courts. Shortly before reaching Issy, François, recognizing M. Allard and the officers of the brigade, threw his wooden bowl at them. It was then remembered that the families of some of the former comrades of the convict lived at Ivry. From that moment the police inspectors spread out along the route and followed the convicts' cart closely. Those of the Paris gang all threw their wooden bowls at the heads of the police, some of whom were struck. At that moment, the crowd reacted strongly. They started to fight amongst themselves' (*Gazette des tribunaux*, 20 July 1836). Between Bicêtre and Sèvres a considerable number of houses were looted as the chain-gang passed by (*La Phalange*, 1 August 1836).

In this festival of the departing convicts, there was something of the rites of the scapegoat that is struck as it is chased away, something of the festival of fools, in which the reversal of roles is practised, something of the old ceremonies of the scaffold, in which the truth must burst forth in the full light of day, something, too, of those popular spectacles, in which famous characters or traditional types were recognized: the play of truth and infamy, the procession of notoriety and shame, invective against the guilty who have been unmasked and, on the other hand, the joyous avowal of crimes. One sought to rediscover the face of the criminals who had had their glory; broadsheets recalled the crimes of those one saw pass; newspapers provided their names and recounted their lives; sometimes they provided a description of their persons and dress, so that their identity might not pass unnoticed: like programmes for spectators.[2] People also came to examine different types of criminals, trying to decide, according to facial appearance or dress, the 'profession' of the convict, whether he was a murderer or thief: it was a game of masquerades and marionnettes, which was also, for more educated eyes, something of an empirical ethnography of crime. From spectacles on trestles to Gall's phrenology, according to the milieu to which one belonged, one practised the semiologies of crime at one's disposal: 'Physiognomies are as varied as clothes: here a majestic head, a Murillo face; there a vicious face, framed with thick eyebrows, which convey all the energy of the determined villain. . . Elsewhere the head of a Fagin emerges from the body of an urchin. Here are the smooth, feminine features of accomplices; there the glazed, debauched faces of teachers.'[3] The convicts themselves responded to this game, displaying their crimes and enacting their misdeeds: this was one of the functions of tattooing, a vignette of their deeds or their fate: 'They bear the insignia of their crimes, either a guillotine tattooed on their left arms, or on their chests a dagger plunged into a bleeding heart.' As they passed, they mimed the scenes of their crimes, mocking the judges or the police, boasting of as yet undiscovered deeds of wickedness. François, Lacenaire's former accomplice, said that he had invented a method for killing a man without making him cry out and without spilling a single drop of blood. The great travelling fair of crime had its tumblers and its mummers, in which the comic affirmation of truth answered curiosity and invective. A whole series of scenes, in this summer of 1836, took place around Delacollonge: his crime (he had cut his pregnant mistress into pieces) was made much more spectacular by the fact that he was a priest; this fact had also saved him from the scaffold. It seems that he aroused considerable hate among the people. Earlier, in the cart that had brought him to Paris in June 1836, he had been insulted and had been unable to hold back his tears; however, he had expressed a wish not to be conveyed in a closed carriage, believing that the humiliation formed part of his punishment. As he left Paris, 'one cannot imagine the virtuous indignation, the moral anger and base actions unleashed by the crowd on this man; he was covered with earth and mud; stones and insults rained down upon him from the furious bystanders. . . It was an explosion of unparalleled rage; the women above all, like veritable furies, displayed an unbelievable exaltation of hate' (*La Phalange*, 1 August 1836). For his protection, his clothes had to be changed. Certain spectators were misled by this and thought that François was he. François entered into the spirit of the game and accepted the role; but, to the comedy of the crime that he did not commit, he added that of the priest that he was not; to the account of 'his' crime, he added the prayers and broad gestures of blessing directed at the jeering crowd. A few steps away, the real Delacollonge, 'who seemed like a martyr', was undergoing the double affront of the insults that he was not receiving, but which were addressed to him, and the ridicule that brought back, under the appearances of another criminal, the priest that he was and would have liked to have concealed. His passion was laid out before his eyes, by a buffoon murderer to whom he was chained.

In every town it passed through, the chain-gang brought its festival with it; it was a saturnalia of punishment, a penalty turned into a privilege. And, by a very curious tradition which seems to have escaped the ordinary rites of the public execution, it aroused in the convict not so much the compulsory marks of repentance as the explosion of a mad joy that denied the punishment. To the ornaments of the collar and chain, the convicts themselves added ribbons, braided straw, flowers or precious stuffs. The chain was the round and the dance; it was also a coupling, a forced marriage in forbidden love. Wedding, festival and rite in chains: 'They ran in front of the chains, bunches of flowers in their hands, ribbons or straw tassels decorated their caps and the most skilful made crested helmets. . . Others wore open-work stockings and clogs or a fashionable waistcoat, under a workman's smock.'[4] And throughout the evening that followed the riveting, the chain-gang formed a great merry-go-round, which went round and round the courtyard of Bicêtre: 'Woe betide the warders if the chain-gang recognized them; they were enveloped and drowned in its rings; the prisoners remained masters of the field of battle until nightfall.'[5] The convicts' Sabbath corresponded to the ceremonial of justice through the spectacle it invented. It inverted the splendours, the order of power and its signs, the forms of pleasure. But something of the political Sabbath was not far away. One would have had to be very deaf indeed not to hear something of these new accents. The convicts sang marching songs, which rapidly became famous and were repeated everywhere for a long time after. No doubt an echo was to be found in them of the complaints that the broadsheets attributed to criminals – an affirmation of the crime, a black heroization, an evocation of terrible punishments and of the general hate that surrounded them: 'Renown, let the trumpets blow for us. . . Courage, children, let us submit without fear to the terrible fate that hangs over our heads. . . Our chains are heavy, but we will bear them. For the convicts, no voice rises to say: relieve them of their suffering.' Yet there was in those collective songs a totally new tonality; the moral code, which most of the old complaints obeyed, was reversed. Instead of bringing remorse, torture sharpened pride; the justice that brought the sentence was rejected, and the crowd that came to witness what it believed to be repentance or humiliation was scorned: 'So far from our homes, we sometimes moan. Our stern brows will make our judges blench. . . Avid of misfortune you turn your eyes upon us, hoping to find a blighted, humiliated, tearful race. But there is pride in our eyes.' One also finds the assertion that the convict's life with its companionship has pleasures that liberty cannot know. 'With time let us link our pleasures. Under lock and key feast days will be born. . . Pleasures are turncoats. They will flee the executioners; they follow where the song leads.' And, above all, the present order will not last forever; not only will the convicts be freed and resume their rights, but their accusers will take their place. Between the criminals and their judges, the day of the great reverse judgement will come: 'The contempt of men belongs to us convicts. The gold they worship is also ours. One day, this gold will pass into our hands. We will buy it with our lives. Others will seize these chains that today you make us bear; they will become slaves. As we break out of our shackles, the star of liberty will shine for us. . . Farewell, for we brave both your chains and your laws.'[6] The pious theatre imagined by the broadsheets, in which the convict exhorted the crowd never to imitate him, was becoming a threatening scene in which the crowd was asked to choose between the barbarity of the executioners, the injustice of the judges and the misfortune of convicts who, though defeated today, would triumph one day.

The great spectacle of the chain-gang was linked with the old tradition of the public execution; it was also linked with that multiple representation of crime that gave rise at the time to newspapers, broadsheets, mountebanks and street theatres;[7] but it was also linked with the confrontations and struggles whose first rumblings it conveyed; it gave them a kind of symbolic outlet: though vanquished by the law, the army of disorder promised to return; what the violence of order had driven away would overthrow that order and bring liberty on its return. 'I was horrified to see so many sparks reappear in those ashes' (*Le Dernier jour d'un condamné*). The agitation that had always surrounded the public executions now found an echo in precise threats. One can see why the July monarchy decided to abolish the chain-gang for the same – but more pressing – reasons that brought about, in the eighteenth century, the abolition of the public executions: 'It is no part of our morality to treat men in this way; one must avoid providing in the towns that the convoy passes through so hideous a spectacle, which, in any case, teaches the population nothing' (*Gazette des tribuneaux*, 19 July 1836). It was necessary, therefore, to break with these public rites; to subject the movements of convicts to the same mutation as the punishments themselves; and to bring them, too, under the veil of administrative decency.

But what, in June 1837, was adopted to replace the chain-gang was not the simple covered cart, which had been suggested at one time, but a machine that had been very meticulously designed: a carriage conceived as a moving prison, a mobile equivalent of the Panopticon. A central corridor divided it along its entire length: on either side were six cells in which the two rows of convicts sat facing one another. Their feet were placed in rings that were lined on the inside with wool and linked together by chains eighteen inches long; the legs were secured in metal knee-guards. The convict sat on a kind of 'zinc and oak funnel that emptied onto the public way'. The cell had no window onto the outside; it was completely lined with sheet iron; only a ventilator, also of sheet-iron, with holes pierced in it, allowed a 'suitable flow of air'. On the corridor side, the door of each cell was provided with a hatch, divided into two compartments: one for food, the other, covered by a grill, for surveillance. 'The opening and the oblique direction of the hatches were so arranged that the warders had the prisoners constantly in view and heard every word they spoke, though the prisoners themselves were unable to see or hear one another.' In this way, 'the same carriage may, without the slightest inconvenience, contain at one and the same time a convict and a simple offender, men and women, children and adults. Whatever the length of the journey, all would be brought to their destination without having been able to perceive one another or to speak to one another.' Lastly, the constant sur-veillance of the two warders, who were each armed with a small oak club, 'with thick nails of crushed diamond' made it possible to operate a whole system of punishments in conformity with the internal regulation of the carriage: a diet of bread and water, thumb-screws, lack of a cushion that would allow one to sleep, chains on both arms. 'Any reading other than that of books of morality is forbidden.'

If only for its mildness and speed, this machine 'would have done honour to the sensibility of its author'; but its merit lay in the fact that it was a veritable penitentiary carriage. By its external effects, it had a quite Benthamite perfection: 'In the rapid passage of this mobile prison which, on its dark, silent flanks, bears no other inscription than the following words – Transport of Convicts – there is something mysterious and gloomy, which Bentham requires in the carrying out of criminal sentences and which leaves in the minds of onlookers a more salutary and lasting impression than the sight of those cynical and joyous travellers' (*Gazette des tribunaux*, 15 June 1837). It also had internal effects; even in a journey lasting only a few days (during which the inmates had not been detached for a single moment), it functioned as an apparatus of correction. One emerged from it astonishingly calm: 'From a moral point of view, this transportation, which lasts no more than seventy-two hours, is a terrible torture whose effects on the prisoner seem to be lasting.' The convicts themselves support this view: 'In the cell carriage, when you don't sleep, you can only think. And when I thought, I came to regret what I had done; in the end, you see, I would have been afraid to mend my ways and I don't want to.'[8]

The panoptic carriage had only a short history. Yet the way in which it replaced the chain-gang and the reasons for this replacement recapitulated the whole process by which in eighty years penal detention replaced public execution as a calculated technique for altering individual behaviour. The cell-carriage was an apparatus of reform. What replaced the public execution was not a massive enclosure, it was a carefully articulated disciplinary mechanism – at least in principle.

For the prison, in its reality and visible effects, was denounced at once as the great failure of penal justice. In a very strange way, the history of imprisonment does not obey a chronology in which one sees, in orderly succession, the establishment of a penality of detention, then the recognition of its failure; then the slow rise of projects of reform, seeming to culminate in the more or less coherent definition of penitentiary technique; then the implementation of this project; lastly, the recognition of its successes or its failure. There was in fact a telescoping or in any case a different distribution of these elements. And, just as the project of a corrective technique accompanied the principle of punitive detention, the critique of the prison and its methods appeared very early on, in those same years 1820–45; indeed, it was embodied in a number of formulations which – figures apart – are today repeated almost unchanged.

– Prisons do not diminish the crime rate: they can be extended, multiplied or transformed, the quantity of crime and criminals remains stable or, worse, increases: 'In France, one calculates at about 108,000 the number of individuals who are in a state of flagrant hostility to society. The means of repression at one's disposal are; the scaffold, the iron-collar, three convict-ships, 19 *maisons centrales*, 86 *maisons de justice*, 362 *maisons d'arrêt*, 2,800 cantonal prisons, 2,238 cells in police stations. Despite all these, vice goes unchecked. The number of crimes is not diminishing . . . the number of recidivists is increasing, rather than declining' (*La Fraternité*, no. 10, February 1842).

– Detention causes recidivism; those leaving prison have more chance than before of going back to it; convicts are, in a very high proportion, former inmates; 38 per cent of those who left the *maisons centrales* were convicted again and 33 per cent of those sent to convict-ships (a figure given by G. de Rochefoucauld during the debate on the reform of the penal code, 2 December 1831, *Archives parlementaires*, LXXII, 209–10); between 1828 and 1834, out of almost 35,000 convicted of crime, about 7,400 were recidivists (that is, 1 out of 4·7 of those convicted); out of over 200,000 *correctionels*, or petty offenders, almost 35,000 were also recidivists (1 out of 6); in all, one recidivist out of 5·8 of those convicted (Ducpétiaux, 1837, 276ff); in 1831, out of 2,174 of those condemned for recidivism, 350 had been in convict-ships, 1,682 in *maisons centrales*, 142 in four *maisons de correction* that followed the same régime as the *centrales* (Ducpétiaux, 1837, 276ff). And the diagnosis became even more severe during the July monarchy: in 1835, out of 7,223 convicted criminals, 1,486 were recidivists; in 1839, 1,749 out of 7,858; in 1844,

1,821 out of 7,195. Among the 980 prisoners at Loos, there were 570 recidivists and, at Melun, 745 out of 1,008 prisoners (Ferrus, 363–7). Instead of releasing corrected individuals, then, the prison was setting loose a swarm of dangerous delinquents throughout the population: '7,000 persons handed back each year to society . . . they are 7,000 principles of crime or corruption spread throughout the social body. And, when one thinks that this population is constantly increasing, that it lives and moves around us, ready to seize every opportunity of disorder, to avail itself of every crisis in society to try out its strength, can one remain unmoved by such a spectacle?' (Beaumont and Tocqueville, 22–3).

– The prison cannot fail to produce delinquents. It does so by the very type of existence that it imposes on its inmates: whether they are isolated in cells or whether they are given useless work, for which they will find no employment, it is, in any case, not 'to think of man in society; it is to create an unnatural, useless and dangerous existence'; the prison should educate its inmates, but can a system of education addressed to man reasonably have as its object to act against the wishes of nature? (Lucas, I, 127 and 130). The prison also produces delinquents by imposing violent constraints on its inmates; it is supposed to apply the law, and to teach respect for it; but all its functioning operates in the form of an abuse of power. The arbitrary power of administration: 'The feeling of injustice that a prisoner has is one of the causes that may make his character untamable. When he sees himself exposed in this way to suffering, which the law has neither ordered nor envisaged, he becomes habitually angry against everything around him; he sees every agent of authority as an executioner; he no longer thinks that he was guilty: he accuses justice itself' (Bigot Préameneu). Corruption, fear and the inefficiency of the warders: 'Between 1,000 and 1,500 convicts live under the surveillance of between thirty and forty supervisors, who can preserve some kind of security only by depending on informers, that is to say, on the corruption that they carefully sow themselves. Who are these warders? Retired soldiers, men uninstructed in their task, making a trade of guarding malefactors' (La Fraternité, March 1842). Exploitation by penal labour, which can in these conditions have no educational character: 'One inveighs against the slave-trade. But are not our prisoners sold,

like the slaves, by entrepreneurs and bought by manufacturers. . .
Is this how we teach our prisoners honesty? Are they not still more
demoralized by these examples of abominable exploitation?'[9]

– The prison makes possible, even encourages, the organization
of a milieu of delinquents, loyal to one another, hierarchized, ready
to aid and abet any future criminal act: 'Society prohibits associations of more than twenty persons . . . and it constitutes for itself
associations of 200, 500, 1,200 convicts in the *maisons centrales*,
which are constructed for them *ad hoc*, and which it divides up for
their greater convenience into workshops, courtyards, dormitories,
refectories, where they can all meet together. . . And it multiplies
them across France in such a way that, where there is a prison,
there is an association . . . and as many anti-social clubs' (Moreau-
Christophe, 7). And it is in these clubs that the education of the
young first offender takes place: 'The first desire that is born within
him will be to learn from his cleverer seniors how to escape the
rigours of the law; the first lesson will be derived from the strict
logic of thieves who regard society as an enemy; the morality will
be the informing and spying honoured in our prisons; the first
passion to be aroused in him will be to frighten the young mind by
these monsters that must have been born in the dungeon and which
the pen refuses to name. . . Henceforth he has broken with everything that has bound him to society' (*L'Almanach populaire de
France*, 49–56). Faucher spoke of 'barracks of crime'.

– The conditions to which the free inmates are subjected necessarily condemn them to recidivism: they are under the surveillance
of the police; they are assigned to a particular residence, or forbidden
others; 'they leave prison with a passport that they must show everywhere they go and which mentions the sentence that they have
served' (Barbé Marbois, 17). Being on the loose, being unable to find
work, leading the life of a vagabond are the most frequent factors in
recidivism. The *Gazette des tribunaux*, but also the workers' newspapers, regularly cited cases like that of the worker convicted of
theft, placed under surveillance at Rouen, caught again for theft,
and whom no lawyers would defend; so he took it upon himself to
speak before the court, told the story of his life, explained how, on
leaving prison and forced to reside in a particular place, he was
unable to take up his trade as a gilder, since as an ex-convict he was

turned down wherever he went; the police refused him the right to seek work elsewhere: he found himself unable to leave Rouen, with nothing to do but die of hunger and poverty as a result of this terrible surveillance. He went to the town hall and asked for work; for eight days he was given work in the cemeteries for fourteen sous a day: 'But,' he said, 'I am young, I have a good appetite, I eat more than two pounds of bread a day at five sous a pound; what can I do with fourteen sous to feed myself, wash my clothes and find lodging? I was driven to despair, I wanted to become an honest man again; the surveillance plunged me back into misfortune. I became disgusted with everything; it was then that I met Lemaître, who was also a pauper; we had to live and wicked thoughts of thieving came back to us.'[10]

– Lastly, the prison indirectly produces delinquents by throwing the inmate's family into destitution: 'The same order that sends the head of the family to prison reduces each day the mother to destitution, the children to abandonment, the whole family to vagabondage and begging. It is in this way that crime can take root' (Lucas, II, 64).

It should be noted that this monotonous critique of the prison always takes one of two directions: either that the prison was insufficiently corrective, and that the penitentiary technique was still at the rudimentary stage; or that in attempting to be corrective it lost its power as punishment,[11] that the true penitentiary technique was rigour,[12] and that prison was a double economic error: directly, by its intrinsic cost and, indirectly, by the cost of the delinquency that it did not abolish.[13] The answer to these criticisms was invariably the same: the reintroduction of the invariable principles of penitentiary technique. For a century and a half the prison had always been offered as its own remedy: the reactivation of the penitentiary techniques as the only means of overcoming their perpetual failure; the realization of the corrective project as the only method of overcoming the impossibility of implementing it.

This is shown conclusively in the fact that the prisoners' revolts of recent weeks* have been attributed to the fact that the reforms proposed in 1945 never really took effect; that one must therefore return to the fundamental principles of the prison. But these

* A series of uprisings in French prisons, between 1972 and 1974, in protest against living conditions.

principles, of which such wonderful results are still expected today, are well enough known: for the past 150 years they have constituted the seven universal maxims of the good 'penitential condition'.

1. Penal detention must have as its essential function the transformation of the individual's behaviour: 'The reform of the convict as the principal aim of the penalty is a sacred principle whose formal appearance in the domain of science and above all in that of legislation is quite recent' ('Congrès pénitentiaire de Bruxelles', 1847). And the Amor commission, of May 1945, faithfully repeats: 'The penalty that deprives of liberty has as its essential aim the reformation and social rehabilitation of the convict.' *The principle of correction.*

2. Convicts must be isolated or at least distributed according to the penal gravity of their act, but above all according to age, mental attitude, the technique of correction to be used, the stages of their transformation. 'One must take into account, in using methods for altering the great physical and moral differences to be found in the characters of convicts, their degree of perversity, the unequal opportunities for correction that they may offer' (February, 1850). 1945: 'The distribution in the penitentiary establishments of individuals serving a light sentence of up to one year is based on sex, personality and the degree of perversion of the delinquent.' *The principle of classification.*

3. It must be possible to alter the penalties according to the individuality of the convicts, the results that have been obtained, progress or relapses. 'Since the principal aim of the penalty is the reform of the convict, it is desirable that any convict whose moral regeneration is sufficiently assured should be set free' (Lucas, 1838), 1945: 'A progressive régime is applied . . . with a view to adapting the treatment of the prisoner to his attitude and to his degree of improvement. This régime stretches from solitary confinement to semi-liberty. . . The benefit of parole is extended to all penalties involving a term of imprisonment.' *The principle of the modulation of penalties.*

4. Work must be one of the essential elements in the transformation and progressive socialization of convicts. Penal labour 'must not be regarded as the complement and as it were an aggravation of the penalty, but as a mitigation, of which it is no longer possible

to deprive the prisoner'. It must enable him to learn or to practise a trade, and to provide the prisoner and his family with a source of income (Ducpétiaux, 1857). 1945: 'Every common-law prisoner is obliged to work. . . No prisoner may be forced to remain unoccupied.' *The principle of work as obligation and right.*

5. The education of the prisoner is for the authorities both an indispensable precaution in the interests of society and an obligation to the prisoner. 'Education alone may serve as a penitentiary instrument. The question of penitentiary imprisonment is a question of education' (Lucas, 1838). 1945: 'The treatment meted out to the prisoner, outside any corrupting promiscuity . . . must be directed principally to his general and professional instruction and to his improvement.' *The principle of penitentiary education.*

6. The prison régime must, at least in part, be supervised and administered by a specialized staff possessing the moral qualities and technical abilities required of educators. In 1850, on the subject of prison medicine, Ferrus remarked: 'It is a useful addition to all forms of imprisonment . . . no one could possess more intimately than a physician the trust of the prisoners, know their characters better, influence their mental attitudes more effectively, while relieving their physical ills and, by this means, reprimand or encourage as he thinks fit.' 1945: 'In every penitentiary establishment, there functions a social and medico-psychological service.' *The principle of the technical supervision of detention.*

7. Imprisonment must be followed by measures of supervision and assistance until the rehabilitation of the former prisoner is complete. Not only must he be placed under surveillance on leaving prison, 'but he must be given help and support' (Boulet and Benquot at the Chambre de Paris). 1945: 'Assistance is given to prisoners during and after imprisonment with a view to facilitating their rehabilitation.' *The principle of auxiliary institutions.*

Word for word, from one century to the other, the same fundamental propositions are repeated. They reappear in each new, hardwon, finally accepted formulation of a reform that has hitherto always been lacking. The same sentences or almost the same could have been borrowed from other 'fruitful' periods of reform: the end of the nineteenth century and the 'movement of social defence'; or again, the last few years, with the prisoners' revolts.

One must not, therefore, regard the prison, its 'failure' and its more or less successful reform as three successive stages. One should think rather of a simultaneous system that historically has been superimposed on the juridical deprivation of liberty; a fourfold system comprising: the additional, disciplinary element of the prison – the element of 'super-power'; the production of an objectivity, a technique, a penitentiary 'rationality' – the element of auxiliary knowledge; the *de facto* reintroduction, if not actual increase, of a criminality that the prison ought to destroy – the element of inverted efficiency; lastly, the repetition of a 'reform' that is isomorphic, despite its 'idealism', with the disciplinary functioning of the prison – the element of utopian duplication. It is this complex ensemble that constitutes the 'carceral system', not only the institution of the prison, with its walls, its staff, its regulations and its violence. The carceral system combines in a single figure discourses and architectures, coercive regulations and scientific propositions, real social effects and invincible utopias, programmes for correcting delinquents and mechanisms that reinforce delinquency. Is not the supposed failure part of the functioning of the prison? Is it not to be included among those effects of power that discipline and the auxiliary technology of imprisonment have induced in the apparatus of justice, and in society in general, and which may be grouped together under the name of 'carceral system'? If the prison-institution has survived for so long, with such immobility, if the principle of penal detention has never seriously been questioned, it is no doubt because this carceral system was deeply rooted and carried out certain very precise functions. As evidence of this strength and immobility, let us take a recent fact: the model prison opened at Fleury-Mérogis in 1969 simply took over in its overall plan the panoptic star-shape that made such a stir in 1836 at the Petite-Roquette. It was the same machinery of power that assumed a real body and a symbolic form. But what role was it supposed to play?

If the law is supposed to define offences, if the function of the penal apparatus is to reduce them and if the prison is the instrument of this repression, then failure has to be admitted. Or rather – for in order to establish it in historical terms, one must be able to measure the effects of the penality of detention on the overall level of criminality – one should be surprised that for the past 150 years the proclamation of the failure of the prison has always been accompanied by its maintenance. The only alternative actually envisaged was deportation, which England abandoned at the beginning of the nineteenth century and which France took up under the Second Empire, but rather as a rigorous and distant form of imprisonment.

But perhaps one should reverse the problem and ask oneself what is served by the failure of the prison; what is the use of these different phenomena that are continually being criticized; the maintenance of delinquency, the encouragement of recidivism, the transformation of the occasional offender into a habitual delinquent, the organization of a closed milieu of delinquency. Perhaps one should look for what is hidden beneath the apparent cynicism of the penal institution, which, after purging the convicts by means of their sentence, continues to follow them by a whole series of 'brandings' (a surveillance that was once *de jure* and which is today *de facto*; the police record that has taken the place of the convict's passport) and which thus pursues as a 'delinquent' someone who has acquitted himself of his punishment as an offender? Can we not see here a consequence rather than a contradiction? If so, one would be forced to suppose that the prison, and no doubt punishment in general, is not intended to eliminate offences, but rather to distinguish them, to distribute them, to use them; that it is not so much that they render docile those who are liable to transgress the law, but that they tend to assimilate the transgression of the laws in a general tactics of subjection. Penality would then appear to be a way of handling illegalities, of laying down the limits of tolerance, of giving free rein to some, of putting pressure on others, of excluding a particular section, of making another useful, of neutralizing certain individuals and of profiting from others. In short, penality does not simply 'check' illegalities; it 'differentiates' them, it provides them with a general 'economy'. And, if one can speak of justice, it is not only because the law itself or the way of applying it serves the interests of a class, it is also because the differential administration of illegalities through the mediation of penality forms part of those mechanisms of domination. Legal punishments are to be resituated in an overall strategy of illegalities. The 'failure' of the prison may be understood on this basis.

The general schema of penal reform had taken shape at the end of the eighteenth century in the struggle against illegalities: a whole equilibrium of tolerance, mutual support and interests which, under the Ancien Régime, had maintained the illegalities of different social strata side by side, was disturbed. There then emerged the utopia of a universally and publicly punitive society in which ceaselessly active penal mechanisms would function without delay, mediation or uncertainty; one law, doubly ideal because perfect in its calculations and engraven on the minds of each citizen would stop, at their very origin, all practices of illegality. Now, at the turn of the eighteenth and nineteenth centuries and against the new codes, the danger of a new popular illegality arose. Or, to be more precise, perhaps the popular illegalities began to develop according to new dimensions: those that were introduced by the movements which, from the 1780s to the Revolutions of 1848, linked together social conflicts, the struggles against the political régimes, the resistance to the movement of industrialization, the effects of the economic crises. Broadly speaking, there were three characteristic processes. First, the development of the political dimension of the popular illegalities. This occurred in two ways: hitherto localized practices, limited in some sense to themselves (like the refusal to pay taxes and rents or to comply with conscription; the violent confiscation of hoarded goods; the looting of shops and the forced selling of products at a 'fair price'; confrontations with the representatives of power), were able during the Revolution to lead to directly political struggles, whose aim was not simply to extract concessions from the state or to rescind some intolerable measure, but to change the government and the very structure of power. On the other hand, certain political movements were explicitly based on existing forms of illegality (for example, the royalist agitation of the west and south of France used the peasants' rejection of the new laws on property, religion and conscription); this political dimension of illegality was to become more complex and more marked in the relations between the workers' movement and the republican parties in the nineteenth century, in the passage from the workers' struggles (strikes, prohibited coalitions, illegal associations) to political revolution. In any case, on the horizon of these illegal practices – which multiplied with ever more restrictive legislation – there emerged struggles of a strictly political kind; the possible overthrow of power was not present in all of them, far from it; but a good many were able to turn themselves to account in overall political struggles and sometimes even to lead directly to them.

On the other hand, through the rejection of the law or other regulations, it is easy enough to recognize the struggles against those who set them up in their own interests: people were no longer fighting against the tax farmers, financiers, the king's agents, prevaricating magistrates or bad ministers – all the agents of injustice – but against the law itself and the justice whose task it was to apply it; against local landowners who introduced new rights; against employers who worked together, but forbade workers' coalitions; against entrepreneurs who introduced more machines, lower wages and longer working hours, and made the factory regulations more and more strict. It was against the new régime of landed property – set up by a bourgeoisie that profited from the Revolution – that a whole peasant illegality developed. This no doubt assumed its most violent forms between Thermidor and the Consulate, but it did not disappear then; it was against the new system of the legal exploitation of labour that workers' illegalities at the beginning of the nineteenth century developed: from the most violent such as machine-breaking, or the most lasting such as the formation of associations, to the most everyday, such as absenteeism, abandoning work, vagabondage, pilfering raw materials, deception as to the quantity and quality of the work completed. A whole series of illegalities was inscribed in struggles in which those struggling knew that they were confronting both the law and the class that had imposed it.

Lastly, although it is true that, during the eighteenth century, criminality tended towards more specialized forms, inclining more and more to the skilful theft, and became, to some extent, the practice of men on the fringes of society, isolated from a population that was hostile to them – one sees, in the last years of the eighteenth century, the reconstitution of certain links or the establishment of new relations; not, as contemporaries said, that the leaders of popular agitation had been criminals, but because the new forms of law, the rigours of the labour regulations, the demands either of the state, or of the landowners, or of the employers, and the most detailed techniques of surveillance, increased the occasions of offences, and threw to the other side of the law many individuals, who, in other conditions, would not have gone over to specialized criminality; it is against the background of the new laws of property, against the background, too, of unacceptable conscription that a peasant illegality developed in the last years of the Revolution, with a consequent increase in violence, acts of aggression, thefts, looting and even the greater forms of 'political brigandage'; it was also against a background of legislation or very heavy regulations (concerning the *livret*, or service certificate, rents, hours, absences from work) that a workers' vagabondage developed that often crossed the boundary into actual delinquency. A whole series of illegal practices, which during the previous century had tended to remain isolated from one another, now seemed to come together to form a new threat.

There was a threefold diffusion of popular illegalities at the turn of the century (quite apart from a quantitative extension that is problematic and still uncalculated): their insertion in a general political outlook; their explicit articulation on social struggles; a communication between different forms and levels of offences. These processes may not have reached their full development; certainly there did not develop at the beginning of the nineteenth century a massive movement of illegality that was both political and social. But, in their emerging form and despite their dispersal, they were sufficiently marked to serve as a support for the 'great fear' of a people who were believed to be criminal and seditious as a whole, for the myth of a barbaric, immoral and outlaw class which, from the empire to the July monarchy, haunted the discourse of legislators, philanthropists and investigators into working-class life. It is these processes that are to be found behind a whole series of affirmations that are quite alien to the penal theory of the eighteenth century: that crime is not a potentiality that interests or passions have inscribed in the hearts of all men, but that it is almost exclusively committed by a certain social class; that criminals, who were once to be met with in every social class, now emerged 'almost all from the bottom rank of the social order' (Comte, 49); that 'nine tenths of murderers, thieves and idlers come from what we have called the social base' (Lauvergne, 337); that it is not crime that alienates an individual from society, but that crime is itself due rather to the fact that one is in society as an alien, that one belongs to that 'bastardized race', as Target called it, to that 'class degraded by misery whose vices stand like an invincible obstacle to the generous intentions that wish to combat it' (Buré, 391); that, this being the case, it would be hypocritical or naïve to believe that the law was made for all in the name of all; that it would be more prudent to recognize that it was made for the few and that it was brought to bear upon others; that in principle it applies to all citizens, but that it is addressed principally to the most numerous and least enlightened classes; that, unlike political and civil laws, their application does not concern everybody equally (Rossi, I, 32); that in the courts society as a whole does not judge one of its members, but that a social category with an interest in order judges another that is dedicated to disorder: 'Visit the places where people are judged, imprisoned or executed. . . One thing will strike you everywhere; everywhere you see two quite distinct classes of men, one of which always meets on the seats of the accusers and judges, the other on the benches of the accused', which is explained by the fact that the latter, for lack of resources and education, do not know 'how to remain within the limits of legal probity' (Lucas, II, 82); so that the language of the law, which is supposed to be universal, is, in this respect, inadequate; it must, if it is to be effective, be the discourse of one class to another, which has neither the same ideas as it nor even the same words: 'How are we, with our prudish, contemptuous languages, overloaded with formality, to make ourselves understood by those who have never heard anything but the crude, poor, irregular, but lively, frank, picturesque dialect of the market, the tavern and the fair. . . What language, what method should we use when drawing up laws that will act effectively on the uneducated minds of those less capable of resisting the temptations of crime?' (Rossi, I, 33). Law and justice do not hesitate to proclaim their necessary class dissymmetry.

If this is the case, the prison, apparently 'failing', does not miss its target; on the contrary, it reaches it, in so far as it gives rise to one particular form of illegality in the midst of others, which it is able to isolate, to place in full light and to organize as a relatively enclosed, but penetrable, milieu. It helps to establish an open illegality, irreducible at a certain level and secretly useful, at once refractory and docile; it isolates, outlines, brings out a form of illegality that seems to sum up symbolically all the others, but which makes it possible to leave in the shade those that one wishes to – or must – tolerate. This form is, strictly speaking, delinquency. One should not see in delinquency the most intense, most harmful form of illegality, the form that the penal apparatus must try to eliminate through imprisonment because of the danger it represents; it is rather an effect of penality (and of the penality of detention) that makes it possible to differentiate, accommodate and supervise illegalities. No doubt delinquency is a form of illegality; certainly it has its roots in illegality; but it is an illegality that the 'carceral system', with all its ramifications, has invested, segmented, isolated, penetrated, organized, enclosed in a definite milieu, and to which it has given an instrumental role in relation to the other illegalities. In short, although the juridical opposition is between legality and illegal practice, the strategic opposition is between illegalities and delinquency.

For the observation that prison fails to eliminate crime, one should perhaps substitute the hypothesis that prison has succeeded extremely well in producing delinquency, a specific type, a politically or economically less dangerous – and, on occasion, usable – form of illegality; in producing delinquents, in an apparently marginal, but in fact centrally supervised milieu; in producing the delinquent as a pathologized subject. The success of the prison, in the struggles around the law and illegalities, has been to specify a 'delinquency'. We have seen how the carceral system substituted the 'delinquent' for the offender, and also superimposed upon juridical practice a whole horizon of possible knowledge. Now this process that constitutes delinquency as an object of knowledge is one with the political operation that dissociates illegalities and isolates delinquency from them. The prison is the hinge of these two mechanisms; it enables them to reinforce one another perpetually, to objectify the delinquency behind the offence, to solidify delinquency in the movement of illegalities. So successful has the prison been that, after a century and a half of 'failures', the prison still exists, producing the same results, and there is the greatest reluctance to dispense with it.

The penality of detention seems to fabricate – hence no doubt its longevity – an enclosed, separated and useful illegality. The circuit of delinquency would seem to be not the sub-product of a prison which, while punishing, does not succeed in correcting; it is rather the direct effect of a penality which, in order to control illegal practices, seems to invest certain of them in a mechanism of 'punishment-reproduction', of which imprisonment is one of the main parts. But why and how is the prison called upon to participate in the fabrication of a delinquency that it is supposed to combat?

The establishment of a delinquency that constitutes something like an enclosed illegality has in fact a number of advantages. To begin with, it is possible to supervise it (by locating individuals, infiltrating the group, organizing mutual informing): for the vague, swarming mass of a population practising occasional illegality, which is always likely to spread, or again for those loose bands of vagabonds, recruiting as they move from place to place, and according to circumstances, from the unemployed, beggars, 'bad characters' of all kinds, which sometimes reach such proportions – as we saw at the end of the eighteenth century – as to form formidable forces for looting and rioting, is substituted a relatively small and enclosed group of individuals on whom a constant surveillance may be kept. Moreover, it is possible to divert this self-absorbed delinquency to forms of illegality that are less dangerous: maintained by the pressure of controls on the fringes of society, reduced to precarious conditions of existence, lacking links with the population that would be able to sustain it (as was once the case with smugglers or certain forms of bandits – cf. Hobsbawm), delinquents inevitably fell back on a localized criminality, limited in its power to attract popular support, politically harmless and economically negligible. Now this concentrated, supervised and disarmed illegality is directly useful. It may be useful in relation to other illegalities: isolated from them, turned inwards upon its own internal organization, dedicated to a violent criminality, of which the poorer classes are often the first victims, hemmed in on every side by the police, exposed to long prison sentences, followed by a permanently 'specialized' life – delinquency – this alien, dangerous and often hostile world obstructs or at least maintains at a sufficiently low level everyday illegal practices (petty thefts, minor acts of violence, routine acts of law-breaking); it prevents them from leading to broader, more obvious forms, rather as though the exemplary effect once expected of the spectacle of the scaffold was now sought not so much in the rigour of the punishments, as in the visible, branded existence of delinquency itself: while differentiating itself from other popular illegalities, delinquency serves to keep them in check.

But delinquency has other direct uses. The example of colonization comes to mind. Yet it is not the most convincing example; indeed, although the deportation of criminals was demanded on several occasions under the Restoration, either by the Chamber of Deputies or by the General Councils, this was essentially in order to lighten the financial burdens imposed by the whole apparatus of detention; and, despite all the projects that were drawn up under the July monarchy for delinquents, undisciplined soldiers, prostitutes and orphans to take part in the colonization of Algeria, that colony was formally excluded, by the law of 1854, from becoming one of the overseas penal colonies; in fact, deportation to Guiana or later to New Caledonia had no real economic importance, despite the obligation imposed on the convicts to remain in the colony where they had served their sentence for a number of years equal to their time of detention (in certain cases, they even had to spend the rest of their lives there).[14] In fact, the use of delinquency as a milieu that was both separate and manipulable took place above all on the fringes of legality, that is to say, a sort of subordinate illegality was also set up in the nineteenth century whose organization as delinquency, with all the surveillance that this implies, provided a guarantee of docility. Delinquency, controlled illegality, is an agent for the illegality of the dominant groups. The setting up of prostitution networks in the nineteenth century is characteristic in this respect:[15] police checks and checks on the prostitutes' health, their regular stay in prison, the large-scale organization of the *maisons closes*, or brothels, the strict hierarchy that was maintained in the prostitution milieu, its control by delinquent-informers, all this made it possible to canalize and to recover by a whole series of intermediaries the enormous profits from a sexual pleasure that an ever-more insistent everyday moralization condemned to semi-clandestinity and naturally made expensive; in setting up a price for pleasure, in creating a profit from repressed sexuality and in collecting this profit, the delinquent milieu was in complicity with a self-interested puritanism: an illicit fiscal agent operating over illegal practices.[16] Arms trafficking, the illegal sale of alcohol in prohibition countries, or more recently drug trafficking show a similar functioning of this 'useful delinquency': the existence of a legal prohibition creates around it a field of illegal practices, which one manages to supervise, while extracting from it an illicit profit through elements, themselves illegal, but rendered manipulable by their organization in delinquency. This organization is an instrument for administering and exploiting illegalities.

It is also an instrument for the illegality with which the very exercise of power surrounds itself. The political use of delinquents – as informers and *agents provocateurs* – was a fact well before the nineteenth century.[17] But, after the Revolution, this practice acquired quite different dimensions: the infiltration of political parties and workers' associations, the recruitment of thugs against strikers and rioters, the organization of a sub-police – working directly with the legal police and capable if necessary of becoming a sort of parallel army – a whole extra-legal functioning of power was partly assured by the mass of reserve labour constituted by the delinquents: a clandestine police force and standby army at the disposal of the state. It seems that, in France, it was around the Revolution of 1848 and Louis Napoleon's seizure of power that these practices reached their height (Marx, *Eighteenth Brumaire . . .*, 63–5). Delinquency, solidified by a penal system centred upon the prison, thus represents a diversion of illegality for the illicit circuits of profit and power of the dominant class.

The organization of an isolated illegality, enclosed in delinquency, would not have been possible without the development of police supervision. General surveillance of the population, 'silent, mysterious, unperceived vigilance . . . it is the eye of the government ceaselessly open and watching without distinction over all citizens, yet without subjecting them to any measure of coercion whatever. . . It does not need to be written into the law' (Bonneville, 1847, 397–9). Surveillance of individuals, envisaged by the code of 1810, of ex-convicts and of all those who, having appeared before the courts on serious charges, were legally presumed to represent a new threat to the peace of society. But surveillance, too, of milieux and groups regarded as dangerous by informers, almost all of whom were former delinquents, supervised as such by the police: delinquency, an object among others of police surveillance, is also one of its privileged instruments. All these surveillances presuppose the organization of a hierarchy, partly official, partly secret (in the Paris police, this was essentially the 'security service', which comprised, apart from its 'open agents' – inspectors and sergeants – its 'secret agents' and informers, who were motivated by fear of punishment or the prospect of reward: cf. Fregier, I, 142–8). They also presuppose the setting up of a documentary system, the heart of which would be the location and identification of criminals: compulsory description of the criminal combined with arrest warrants issued by the assize courts, a description included in prison committal registers, copies of the registers of assize courts and courts of summary jurisdiction sent each month to the Ministries of Justice and of General Police, the organization a little later at the Ministry of the Interior of a criminal records office with an alphabetical index containing summaries of these registers, the use in about 1833, according to the method of 'naturalists, librarians, merchants, businessmen' of a system of individual cards or reports, which facilitated the integration of new data and, at the same time, together with the name of the individual under investigation, all the information that might concern him (Bonneville, 1844, 92–3) – the appearance of the card-index and the constitution of the human sciences are another invention that historians have taken little note of). Delinquency, with the secret agents that it procures, but also with the generalized policing that it authorizes, constitutes a means of perpetual surveillance of the population: an apparatus that makes it possible to supervise, through the delinquents themselves, the whole social field. Delinquency functions as a political observatory. In their turn, the statisticians and the sociologists have made use of it, long after the police.

But this surveillance has been able to function only in conjunction with the prison. Because the prison facilitates the supervision of individuals when they are released, because it makes possible the recruiting of informers and multiplies mutual denunciations, because it brings offenders into contact with one another, it precipitates the organization of a delinquent milieu, closed in upon itself, but easily supervised: and all the results of non-rehabilitation (unemployment, prohibitions on residence, enforced residences, probation) make it all too easy for former prisoners to carry out the tasks assigned to them. Prison and police form a twin mechanism; together they assure in the whole field of illegalities the differentiation, isolation and use of delinquency. In the illegalities, the police–prison system segments a manipulable delinquency. This delinquency, with its specificity, is a result of the system; but it also becomes a part and an instrument of it. So that one should speak of an ensemble whose three terms (police–prison–delinquency) support one another and form a circuit that is never interrupted. Police surveillance provides the prison with offenders, which the prison transforms into delinquents, the targets and auxiliaries of police supervisions, which regularly send back a certain number of them to prison.

There is no penal justice intended to prosecute all illegal practices which, to do so, would use the police as an auxiliary and prison as a punitive instrument, and not leave in its wake the unassimilable residue of 'delinquency'. One should regard this justice as an instrument for the differential supervision of illegalities. In relation to this instrument, criminal justice plays the role of legal surety and principle of transmission. It is a relay in a general economy of illegalities, whose other elements are (not below it, but beside it) the police, the prison and delinquency. Police encroachment on justice and the force of inertia that the carceral institution opposes to justice are not new, nor are they the result of a sclerosis or of a gradual shift in power; it is a structural feature that characterizes punitive mechanisms in modern societies. The magistrates can say what they like; penal justice, with all its theatrical apparatus, is intended to respond to the daily demand of an apparatus of supervision half submerged in the darkness in which police and delinquency are brought together. Judges are the scarcely resisting employees of this apparatus.[18] They assist as far as they can in the constitution of delinquency, that is to say, in the differentiation of illegalities, in the supervision, colonization and use of certain of these illegalities by the illegality of the dominant class.

Two figures stand out as representative of this process, which developed in the first thirty or forty years of the nineteenth century. First, there was Vidocq (cf. his *Mémoires* and *Histoire de Vidocq racontée par lui-même*). He was a man of the old illegalities, a Gil

Blas of the other end of the century, who soon took a turn for the worse: disturbances, adventures, swindlings, of which he was usually himself the victim, brawls and duels; successive enlistments and desertions, contacts with prostitution, gambling, pickpocketing and soon large-scale brigandage. But the almost mythical importance that he assumed in the eyes of his contemporaries was based not on this, perhaps embellished past; it was not even based on the fact that, for the first time in history, a former inmate of a convict-ship, redeemed or quite simply bought, became a chief of police, but rather on the fact that, in him, delinquency visibly assumed its ambiguous status as an object and instrument for a police apparatus that worked both against it and with it. Vidocq marks the moment when deliquency, detached from other illegalities, was invested by power and turned inside out. It was then that the direct, institutional coupling of police and delinquency took place: the disturbing moment when criminality became one of the mechanisms of power. A figure had haunted earlier times, that of the monstrous king, the source of all justice and yet besmirched with crime; another fear now appeared, that of some dark, secret understanding between those who enforced the law and those who violated it. The Shakespearian age when sovereignty confronted abomination in a single character had gone; the everyday melodrama of police power and of the complicities that crime formed with power was soon to begin.

Opposite Vidocq stood his contemporary, Lacenaire. His presence, assured for ever in the paradise of the aesthetes of crime, is surprising enough: despite all his good will, his neophyte's zeal, he was only able to commit, and even then with a singular lack of skill, no more than a few minor crimes; he was so strongly suspected of being a police spy that the administration had to protect him against his fellow prisoners, who tried to kill him (the charge was formally taken up by Canler, 15), and it was the fashionable society of Louis-Philippe's Paris that gave him, before his execution, a feast beside which many a later literary resurrection has been little more than academic homage. His fame owed nothing either to the extent of his crimes or to the art of their conception; it was their ineptitude that gave cause for surprise. But it did owe a great deal to the visible play, in what he did and what he said, between illegality and delinquency. Swindling, desertion, petty theft, imprisonment, the revival of friendships made in prison, mutual blackmail, recidivism, up to the last, failed attempt at murder – Lacenaire is the typical 'delinquent'. But he brought with him, at least potentially, a horizon of illegalities that had, until quite recently, represented a threat: this ruined petty bourgeois, of good education, would, a generation earlier, have been a revolutionary, a Jacobin, a regicide;[19] had he been a contemporary of Robespierre, his rejection of the law would have taken a directly political form. Born in 1800, at more or less the same time as Stendhal's Julien Sorel, his character bears the trace of these possibilities; but they took the form of theft, murder and denunciation. All these potentialities became a delinquency of no great moment: in this sense, Lacenaire is a reassuring character. And if these potentialities reappear, it is in what he says about the theory of crime. At the moment of his death, Lacenaire manifested the triumph of delinquency over illegality, or rather the figure of an illegality, on the one hand, dragged down into delinquency, and, on the other, displaced towards aesthetics of crime, that is to say, towards an art of the privileged classes. There is a symmetry between Lacenaire and Vidocq, who in the same period, made it possible to turn delinquency in upon itself by constituting it as an enclosed, observable milieu and by displacing towards police techniques a whole delinquent practice that was becoming the licit illegality of power. That the Parisian bourgeoisie should have feasted Lacenaire, that his cell should have been open to famous visitors, that he should have been showered with praise during the last days of his life, he whose death his plebeian fellow prisoners had demanded before his judges had done so, he who had done everything, in court, to bring his accomplice François to the scaffold, there was a reason for all this: what was being celebrated was the symbolic figure of an illegality kept within the bounds of delinquency and transformed into discourse – that is to say, made doubly inoffensive; the bourgeoisie had invented for itself a new pleasure, which it has still far from outgrown. It should not be forgotten that Lacenaire's celebrated death succeeded in muffling the echoes of Fieschi's attempt on the life of Louis-Philippe; Fieschi, one of the most recent of the regicides, represented the converse figure of a petty criminality leading to political violence. Nor should we forget that it took place a few months before the departure of the last chain-gang and the scandalous demonstrations that accompanied it. These two festivals overlapped in history; and, indeed, François, Lacenaire's accomplice, was one of the best-known characters in the chain-gang of 19 July.[20] The one extended the ancient rituals of the public execution at the risk of reactivating popular illegalities around the criminals. It was to be prohibited, for the criminal was no longer to occupy any other space than that appropriate to delinquency. The other inaugurated the theoretical play of an illegality of the privileged; or rather it marked the moment when the political and economic illegalities actually practised by the bourgeoisie were to be duplicated in theoretical and aesthetic representation: the 'Metaphysics of crime', a term often associated with Lacenaire. The French translation of De Quincey's *Murder Considered as One of the Fine Arts* was published in 1849.

This production of delinquency and its investment by the penal apparatus must be taken for what they are: not results acquired once and for all, but tactics that shift according to how closely they reach their target. The split between delinquency and other illegalities, the way in which it is turned back upon them, its colonization by the dominant illegality – these all appear clearly in the way in which the police–prison system functions; yet they have always met with resistance; they have given rise to struggles and provoked reaction. Erecting the barrier to separate delinquents from all the lower strata of the population from which they sprang and with which they remained linked has been a difficult task, especially no doubt in urban milieux.[21] It has been a long and arduous undertaking. It has involved the use of the general principles of the 'moralization' of the poorer classes that elsewhere has had such crucial importance both from an economic and a political point of view (the acquisition of what might be called a 'basic legalism', which was indispensable from the time when custom was replaced by the system of the code; learning the elementary rules of property and thrift; training in docility at work, in stability of residence and of the family, etc.). More specific methods were used to maintain the hostility of the poorer classes to delinquents (the use of ex-convicts as informers, police spies, strike-breakers or thugs). There has been a systematic confusion between offences against common law and those offences against the severe legislation concerning the *livret* (work record), strikes, coalitions, associations,[22] for which the workers demanded political status. Workers' action was regularly accused of being animated, if not manipulated, by mere criminals (cf., for example, Monfalcon, 142). Verdicts were often more severe against workers than against thieves (cf. *L'Atelier*, October 1840, or *La Fraternité*, July–August 1847). The two categories of convict were mixed in the prisons and preferential treatment given to common-law offenders, while convicted journalists and politicians usually enjoyed the right to separate treatment. In short, a whole tactic of confusion aimed at maintaining a permanent state of conflict.

To this was added a patient attempt to impose a highly specific grid on the common perception of delinquents: to present them as close by, everywhere present and everywhere to be feared. This was the function of the *fait divers*, which invaded a part of the press and which began to have its own newspapers.[23] The criminal *fait divers*, by its everyday redundancy, makes acceptable the system of judicial and police supervisions that partition society; it recounts from day to day a sort of internal battle against the faceless enemy; in this war, it constitutes the daily bulletin of alarm or victory. The crime novel, which began to develop in the broadsheet and in mass-circulation literature, assumed an apparently opposite role. Above all, its function was to show that the delinquent belonged to an entirely different world, unrelated to familiar, everyday life. This strangeness was first that of the lower depths of society (*Les Mystères de Paris*, *Rocambole*), then that of madness (especially in the latter half of the century) and lastly that of crime in high society (Arsène Lupin). The combination of the *fait divers* and the detective novel has produced for the last hundred years or more an enormous mass of 'crime stories' in which delinquency appears both as very close and quite alien, a perpetual threat to everyday life, but extremely distant in its origin and motives, both everyday and exotic in the milieu in which it takes place. Through the importance attributed to it and the surfeit of discourse surrounding it, a line is traced round it which, while exalting it, sets it apart. In such a formidable delinquency, coming from so alien a clime, what illegality could recognize itself? ...

This multiple tactic had its effect: this is proved by the campaign of the workers' newspapers against penal labour;[24] against the 'comfort of the prisons' and for giving prisoners the hardest and most dangerous work; against the excessive interest shown by philanthropists in the delinquents; against the literature that exalts crime;[25] it is also proved by the general mistrust felt throughout the workers' movement for former common-law convicts. 'At the dawn of the twentieth century,' writes Michèle Perrot, 'surrounded by contempt, the highest of walls, the prison finally closed in on an unpopular people' (Perrot).

Yet it certainly cannot be said that this tactic triumphed or that it brought about a total break between the delinquents and the lower classes. The relations between the poorer classes and illegality, the reciprocal position of the proletariat and the urban plebs has yet to be studied. But one thing is certain: delinquency and repression were regarded, in the workers' movements of the years 1830–50, as an important issue. There was no doubt hostility towards the delinquents; but it was a battle around penality. The workers' newspapers often proposed a political analysis of criminality that contradicted term by term the description familiar to the philanthropists (poverty – dissipation – laziness – drunkenness – vice – theft – crime). They assigned the origin of delinquency not to the individual criminal (he was merely the occasion or the first victim), but to society: 'The man who kills you is not free not to kill you. It is society or, to be more precise, bad social organization that is responsible' (*L'Humanitaire*, August 1841). This is so either because society is incapable of providing its fundamental needs, or because it destroys or effaces in him possibilities, aspirations or needs that later emerge in crime: 'Bad education, unused aptitudes and forces, the intelligence and the heart crushed by forced labour at too tender an age' (*La Fraternité*, November 1845). But this criminality of need or of repression masks, by the attention paid to it and the disapprobation surrounding it, another criminality that is sometimes its cause and always its extension. This is the delinquency from above, a scandalous example, the source of misery and the principle of revolt for the poor. 'While misery strews your streets with corpses, and fills your prisons with thieves and murderers, where are the swindlers of the fashionable world? ... The most corrupting examples, the most revolting cynicism, the most shameless robbery. ... Are you not afraid that the poor man put into the dock for snatching a piece of bread from a baker's stall will not, one day, become so enraged that stone by stone he will demolish the Stock Exchange, a wild den where the treasure of the state and the fortune of families are stolen with impunity?' (*La Ruche populaire*, November 1842). But this delinquency of wealth is tolerated by the laws, and, when it does find its way into the courts, it can depend upon the indulgence of the judges and the discretion of the press.[26] Hence the idea that criminal trials may become the occasion for a political debate, that advantage should be taken of controversial trials or proceedings instituted against workers to denounce the general functioning of penal justice: 'The courts are no longer as they once were a place for the exhibition of the miseries and wounds of the time, a kind of branding in which the sad victims of our social disorder are displayed side by side; it is an arena that echoes with the cry of combatants' (*La Fraternité*, November 1841). Hence, too, the idea that political prisoners, since they have, like delinquents, a direct experience of the penal system, but, unlike them, are in a position to be heard, have a duty to be the spokesmen of all prisoners; it is their task to enlighten 'the good bourgeois of France, who has never known the penalties inflicted through the pompous indictments of a public prosecutor' (*Almanach populaire de la France*, 1839, 50).

In this reappraisal of penal justice and of the frontier that it carefully traces around delinquency, the tactic of what might be called the 'counter-*fait divers*' is characteristic. What the workers' newspapers do is to reverse the use that was made of crimes or trials in the newspapers which, like the *Gazette des tribunaux*, 'gorge themselves with blood', 'feed on prison' and provide a daily 'repertoire of melodrama' (*Pauvre Jacques*, 1st year, no. 3). The counter-*fait divers* systematically stresses the facts of delinquency in the bourgeoisie, showing that it is the class affected by 'physical degeneration' and 'moral decay'; for the accounts of crimes committed by ordinary people it substitutes descriptions of the misery into which their exploiters plunge them and who, literally, starve and murder them;[27] it points out in the criminal trials of workers what share of responsibility must be attributed to the employers and to society as a whole. In short, a whole effort was being made to reverse this monotonous discourse on crime, which sought both to isolate it as a monstrosity and to depict it as the work of the poorest class.

In the course of this anti-penal polemic, the Fourierists no doubt went further than any of the others. They were perhaps the first to elaborate a political theory which, at the same time, places a positive value on crime. Although, in their view, crime is a result of 'civilization', it is also, and by that very fact, a weapon against it. It bears within it a figure and a future. 'The social order dominated by the fatality of its repressive principle continues to kill through the executioner or through the prisons those whose natural robustness rejects or disdains its prescriptions, those who, too strong to remain enclosed within its tight swaddling-clothes, break from them and tear them to pieces, men who do not wish to remain children' (*La Phalange*, 10 January 1837). There is not, therefore, a criminal nature, but a play of forces which, according to the class to which individuals belong,[28] will lead them to power or to prison: if born poor, today's magistrates would no doubt be in the convict-ships; and the convicts, if they had been well born, 'would be presiding in the courts and dispensing justice' (*La Phalange*, 1 December 1838). At bottom, the existence of crime manifests 'a fortunate irrepressibility of human nature'; it should be seen not so much as a weakness or a disease, as an energy that is reviving, an 'outburst of protest in the name of human individuality', which no doubt accounts for its strange power of fascination. 'Without crime, which awakens in us a mass of torpid feelings and half distinguished passions, we would remain still longer in disorder, in weakness' (*La Phalange*, 10 January 1837). It may be, therefore, that crime constitutes a political instrument that could prove as precious for the liberation of our society as it has been for the emancipation of the Negroes; indeed, will such an emancipation take place without it? 'Poison, fire-raising and sometimes even revolt are evidence of the terrible miseries of the social condition' (*La Phalange*, 10 January 1837). And what of the prisoners, 'the most unfortunate and most oppressed part of mankind'? *La Phalange* sometimes shared the contemporary aesthetic of crime, but in a very different cause.

Hence a use of *fait divers* that was intended not only to turn the reproach of immorality back upon the adversary, but to reveal the play of opposing forces. *La Phalange* analyses penal affairs as a confrontation coded by 'civilization', the great crimes not as monstrosities, but as the fatal return and revolt of what is repressed,[29] the minor illegalities not as the necessary margins of society, but as a rumbling from the midst of the battle-field.

After Vidocq and Lacenaire, a third character must be introduced. He made only a short appearance; his notoriety lasted hardly more than a day. He was merely the passing figure of minor illegalities: a child of thirteen, without home or family, charged with vagabondage and whom a two-year sentence had no doubt long placed in the circuits of delinquency. He would certainly have passed without trace, had he not opposed to the discourse of the law that made him delinquent (in the name of the disciplines, even more than in the terms of the code) the discourse of an illegality that remained resistant to these coercions and which revealed indiscipline in a systematically ambiguous manner as the disordered order of society and as the affirmation of inalienable rights. All the illegalities that the court defined as offences the accused reformulated as the affirmation of a living force: the lack of a home as vagabondage, the lack of a master as independence, the lack of work as freedom, the lack of a time-table as the fullness of days and nights. This confrontation of illegality with the discipline–penality–delinquency system was perceived by contemporaries or rather by the journalist who happened to be there as the comic effect of the criminal law at grips with the petty details of indiscipline. And it was true: the affair itself and the verdict that followed represented the heart of the problem of legal punishment in the nineteenth century. The irony with which the judge tried to envelop indiscipline in the majesty of the law and the insolence with which the accused reinscribed indiscipline among the fundamental rights represent for penality an exemplary scene.

This, no doubt, is the value of the account published in the *Gazette des tribunaux* for August 1840: 'The judge: One must sleep at home. – Béasse: Have I got a home? – You live in perpetual vagabondage. – I work to earn my living. – What is your station in life? – My station: to begin with, I'm thirty-six at least; I don't work for anybody. I've worked for myself for a long time now. I have my day station and my night station. In the day, for instance, I hand out leaflets free of charge to all the passers-by; I run after the stagecoaches when they arrive and carry luggage for the passengers; I turn cart-wheels on the avenue de Neuilly; at night there are the shows; I open coach doors, I sell pass-out tickets; I've plenty to do. – It would be better for you to be put into a good house as an apprentice and learn a trade. – Oh, a good house, an apprenticeship, it's too much trouble. And anyway the bourgeois ... always grumbling, no freedom. – Does not your father wish to reclaim you? – Haven't got no father. – And your mother? – No mother neither, no parents, no friends, free and independent.' Hearing his sentence of two years in a reformatory, Béasse 'pulled an ugly face, then, recovering his good humour, remarked: "Two years, that's never more than twenty-four months. Let's be off, then." '

It was this scene that *La Phalange* took up. And the importance that the newspaper gave it, the extremely slow, careful analysis, shows that the Fourierists saw in such an everyday affair a play of fundamental forces. On the one hand, that of 'civilization', represented by the judge, 'living legality, the spirit and letter of the law'. It had its own system of coercion, which seemed to be the code, but which in fact was discipline. There had to be a place, a location, a compulsory insertion: 'One sleeps at home, said the judge, because in fact, for him, everything must have a home, some dwelling, however magnificent or mean; his task is not to provide one, but to force every individual to live in one.' Moreover, one must have a station in life, a recognizable identity, an individuality fixed once and for all: 'What is your station? This question is the simplest expression of the established order in society; such vagabondage is repugnant to it, disturbs it; one must have a stable, continuous long-term station, thoughts of the future, of a secure future, in order to reassure it against all attacks.' In short, one should have a master, be caught up and situated within a hierarchy; one exists only when fixed in definite relations of domination: 'Who do you work with? That is to say, since you are not a master, you must be a servant, whatever your station; it is not a question of your satisfactoriness as an individual; it is a question of order to be maintained.' Confronted with discipline on the face of the law, there is illegality, which puts itself forward as a right; it is indiscipline, rather than the criminal offence, that causes the rupture. An indiscipline of language: incorrect grammar and the tone of the replies 'indicate a violent split between the accused and society, which, through the judge, addresses him in correct terms'. An indiscipline that is the indiscipline of native, immediate liberty: 'He is well aware that the apprentice, the worker is a slave and that slavery is sad. . . This liberty, this need of movement that possesses him, he is well aware that he would no longer enjoy it in a life of ordinary order. . . He prefers liberty; what does he care if others see it as disorder? It is liberty, that is to say, the most spontaneous development of his individuality, a wild development and, consequently, brutal and limited, but a natural, instinctive development.' Indiscipline in family relations; it does not matter whether this lost child was abandoned or freed himself voluntarily, for 'he would have been unable to bear the slavery of education either at his parents' or with strangers'. And through all these minute disciplines it is ultimately 'civilization' as a whole that is rejected and 'wildness' that emerges: 'It is work, it is laziness, it is thoughtlessness, it is debauchery: it is everything except order; the difference in occupations and debauches aside, it is the life of the savage, living from day to day and with no tomorrow' (*La Phalange*, 15 August 1840).

No doubt the analyses of *La Phalange* cannot be regarded as representative of the discussions that took place in the workers' press at this time on crime and penality. Nevertheless, they are situated in the context of this polemic. The lessons of *La Phalange* were not quite wasted. They found an echo when, in the second half of the nineteenth century, taking the penal apparatus as their point of attack, the anarchists posed the political problem of delinquency; when they thought to recognize in it the most militant rejection of the law; when they tried not so much to heroize the revolt of the delinquents as to disentangle delinquency from the bourgeois legality and illegality that had colonized it; when they wished to re-establish or constitute the political unity of popular illegalities.

3. The carceral

Were I to fix the date of completion of the carceral system, I would choose not 1810 and the penal code, nor even 1844, when the law laying down the principle of cellular internment was passed; I might not even choose 1838, when books on prison reform by Charles Lucas, Moreau-Christophe and Faucher were published. The date I would choose would be 22 January 1840, the date of the official opening of Mettray. Or better still, perhaps, that glorious day, unremarked and unrecorded, when a child in Mettray remarked as he lay dying: 'What a pity I left the colony so soon' (Ducpétiaux, 1852, 383). This marked the death of the first penitentiary saint. Many of the blessed no doubt went to join him, if the former inmates of the penal colonies are to be believed when, in singing the praises of the new punitive policies of the body, they remarked: 'We preferred the blows, but the cell suits us better.'

Why Mettray? Because it is the disciplinary form at its most extreme, the model in which are concentrated all the coercive technologies of behaviour. In it were to be found 'cloister, prison, school, regiment'. The small, highly hierarchized groups, into which the inmates were divided, followed simultaneously five models: that of the family (each group was a 'family' composed of 'brothers' and two 'elder brothers'); that of the army (each family, commanded by a head, was divided into two sections, each of which had a second in command; each inmate had a number and was taught basic military exercises; there was a cleanliness inspection every day, an inspection of clothing every week; a roll-call was taken three times a day); that of the workshop, with supervisors and foremen, who were responsible for the regularity of the work and for the apprenticeship of the younger inmates; that of the school (an hour or an hour and a half of lessons every day; the teaching was given by the instructor and by the deputy-heads); lastly, the judicial model (each day 'justice' was meted out in the parlour: 'The least act of disobedience is punished and the best way of avoiding serious offences is to punish the most minor offences very severely: at Mettray, a useless word is punishable'; the principal punishment inflicted was confinement to one's cell; for 'isolation is the best means of acting on the moral nature of children; it is there above all that the voice of religion, even if it has never spoken to their hearts, recovers all its emotional power' – Ducpétiaux, 1852, 377); the entire parapenal institution, which is created in order not to be a prison, culminates in the cell, on the walls of which are written in black letters: 'God sees you.'

This superimposition of different models makes it possible to indicate, in its specific features, the function of 'training'. The chiefs and their deputies at Mettray had to be not exactly judges, or teachers, or foremen, or non-commissioned officers, or 'parents', but something of all these things in a quite specific mode of intervention. They were in a sense technicians of behaviour: engineers of conduct, orthopaedists of individuality. Their task was to produce bodies that were both docile and capable; they supervised the nine or ten working hours of every day (whether in a workshop or in the fields); they directed the orderly movements of groups of inmates, physical exercises, military exercises, rising in the morning, going to bed at night, walks to the accompaniment of bugle and whistle; they taught gymnastics;[1] they checked cleanliness, supervised bathing. Training was accompanied by permanent observation; a body of knowledge was being constantly built up from the everyday behaviour of the inmates; it was organized as an instrument of perpetual assessment: 'On entering the colony, the child is subjected to a sort of interrogation as to his origins, the position of his family, the offence for which he was brought before the courts and all the other offences that make up his short and often very sad existence. This information is written down on a board on which everything concerning each inmate is noted in turn, his stay at the colony and the place to which he is sent when he leaves' (Ducpétiaux, 1851, 61). The modelling of the body produces a knowledge of the individual, the apprenticeship of the techniques induces modes of behaviour and the acquisition of skills is inextricably linked with the establishment of power relations; strong, skilled agricultural workers are produced; in this very work, provided it is technically supervised, submissive subjects are produced and a dependable body of knowledge built up about them. This disciplinary technique exercised upon the body had a double effect: a 'soul' to be known and a subjection to be maintained. One result vindicated this work of training: in 1848, at a moment when 'the fever of revolution fired the imagination of all, when the schools at Angers, La Flèche, Alfort, even the boarding schools, rose up in rebellion, the inmates of Mettray were calmer than ever' (Ferrus).

Where Mettray was especially exemplary was in the specificity that it recognized in this operation of training. It was related to other forms of supervision, on which it was based: medicine, general education, religious direction. But it cannot not be identified absolutely with them. Nor with administration in the strict sense. Heads or deputy-heads of 'families', monitors and foremen, had to live in close proximity to the inmates; their clothes were 'almost as humble' as those of the inmates themselves; they practically never left their side, observing them day and night; they constituted among them a network of permanent observation. And, in order to train them themselves, a specialized school had been organized in the colony. The essential element of its programme was to subject the future cadres to the same apprenticeships and to the same coercions as the inmates themselves: they were 'subjected as pupils to the discipline that, later, as instructors, they would themselves impose'. They were taught the art of power relations. It was the first training college in pure discipline: the 'penitentiary' was not simply a project that sought its justification in 'humanity' or its foundations in a 'science', but a technique that was learnt, transmitted and which obeyed general norms. The practice that normalized by compulsion the conduct of the undisciplined or dangerous could, in turn, by technical elaboration and rational reflection, be 'normalized'. The disciplinary technique became a 'discipline' which also had its school.

It so happens that historians of the human sciences date the birth of scientific psychology at this time: during these same years, it seems, Weber was manipulating his little compass for the measurement of sensations. What took place at Mettray (and in other

European countries sooner or later) was obviously of a quite different order. It was the emergence or rather the institutional specification, the baptism as it were, of a new type of supervision – both knowledge and power – over individuals who resisted disciplinary normalization. And yet, in the formation and growth of psychology, the appearance of these professionals of discipline, normality and subjection surely marks the beginning of a new stage. It will be said that the quantitative assessment of sensorial responses could at least derive authority from the prestige of the emerging science of physiology and that for this alone it deserves to feature in the history of the sciences. But the supervision of normality was firmly encased in a medicine or a psychiatry that provided it with a sort of 'scientificity'; it was supported by a judicial apparatus which, directly or indirectly, gave it legal justification. Thus, in the shelter of these two considerable protectors, and, indeed, acting as a link between them, or a place of exchange, a carefully worked out technique for the supervision of norms has continued to develop right up to the present day. The specific, institutional supports of these methods have proliferated since the founding of the small school at Mettray; their apparatuses have increased in quantity and scope; their auxiliary services have increased, with hospitals, schools, public administrations and private enterprises; their agents have proliferated in number, in power, in technical qualification; the technicians of indiscipline have founded a family. In the normalization of the power of normalization, in the arrangement of a power-knowledge over individuals, Mettray and its school marked a new era.

But why choose this moment as the point of emergence of the formation of an art of punishing that is still more or less our own? Precisely because this choice is somewhat 'unjust'. Because it situates the 'end' of the process in the lower reaches of criminal law. Because Mettray was a prison, but not entirely; a prison in that it contained young delinquents condemned by the courts; and yet something else, too, because it also contained minors who had been charged, but acquitted under article 66 of the code, and boarders held, as in the eighteenth century, as an alternative to paternal correction. Mettray, a punitive model, is at the limit of strict penality. It was the most famous of a whole series of institutions which, well beyond the frontiers of criminal law, constituted what one might call the carceral archipelago.

Yet the general principles, the great codes and subsequent legislation were quite clear on the matter: no imprisonment 'outside the law', no detention that had not been decided by a qualified judicial institution, no more of those arbitrary and yet widespread confinements. Yet the very principle of extra-penal incarceration was in fact never abandoned. (A whole study remains to be done of the debates that took place during the Revolution concerning family courts, paternal correction and the right of parents to lock up their children.) And, if the apparatus of the great classical form of confinement was partly (and only partly) dismantled, it was very soon reactivated, rearranged, developed in certain directions. But what is still more important is that it was homogenized, through the mediation of the prison, on the one hand with legal punishments and, on the other, with disciplinary mechanisms. The frontiers between confinement, judicial punishment and institutions of discipline, which were already blurred in the classical age, tended to disappear and to constitute a great carceral continuum that diffused penitentiary techniques into the most innocent disciplines, transmitting disciplinary norms into the very heart of the penal system and placing over the slightest illegality, the smallest irregularity, deviation or anomaly, the threat of delinquency. A subtle, graduated carceral net, with compact institutions, but also separate and diffused methods, assumed responsibility for the arbitrary, widespread, badly integrated confinement of the classical age.

I shall not attempt here to reconstitute the whole network that formed first the immediate surroundings of the prison, then spread farther and farther outwards. However, a few references and dates should give some idea of the breadth and precocity of the phenomenon.

There were agricultural sections in the *maisons centrales* (the first example of which was Gaillon in 1824, followed later by Fontevrault, Les Douaires, Le Boulard); there were colonies for poor, abandoned vagrant children (Petit-Bourg in 1840, Ostwald in 1842); there were almshouses for young female offenders who 'recoiled before the idea of entering a life of disorder', for 'poor innocent girls whose mothers' immorality has exposed to precocious perversity', or for poor girls found on the doorsteps of hospitals and lodging houses. There were penal colonies envisaged by the law of 1850: minors, acquitted or condemned, were to be sent to these colonies and 'brought up in common, under strict discipline, and trained in agricultural work and in the principal industries related to it;' later, they were to be joined by minors sentenced to hard labour for life and 'vicious and insubordinate wards of the Public Assistance' (on all these institutions, cf. Gaillac, 99–107). And, moving still farther away from penality in the strict sense, the carceral circles widen and the form of the prison slowly diminishes and finally disappears altogether: the institutions for abandoned or indigent children, the orphanages (like Neuhof or Mesnil-Firmin), the establishments for apprentices (like the Bethléem de Reims or the Maison de Nancy); still farther away the factory-convents, such as La Sauvagère, Tarare and Jujurieu (where the girl workers entered about the age of thirteen, lived confined for years and were allowed out only under surveillance, received instead of wages pledged payment, which could be increased by bonuses for zeal and good behaviour, which they could use only on leaving). And then, still farther, there was a whole series of mechanisms that did not adopt the 'compact' prison model, but used some of the carceral methods: charitable societies, moral improvement associations, organizations that handed out assistance and also practised surveillance, workers' estates and lodging houses – the most primitive of which still bear the all too visible marks of the penitentiary system.[2] And, lastly, this great carceral network reaches all the disciplinary mechanisms that function throughout society.

We have seen that, in penal justice, the prison transformed the punitive procedure into a penitentiary technique; the carceral archipelago transported this technique from the penal institution to the entire social body. With several important results.

1. This vast mechanism established a slow, continuous, imperceptible gradation that made it possible to pass naturally from disorder to offence and back from a transgression of the law to a slight departure from a rule, an average, a demand, a norm. In the classical period, despite a certain common reference to offence in general,[3] the order of the crime, the order of sin and the order of bad conduct

remained separate in so far as they related to separate criteria and authorities (court, penitence, confinement). Incarceration with its mechanisms of surveillance and punishment functioned, on the contrary, according to a principle of relative continuity. The continuity of the institutions themselves, which were linked to one another (public assistance with the orphanage, the reformitory, the penitentiary, the disciplinary battalion, the prison; the school with the charitable society, the workshop, the almshouse, the penitentiary convent; the workers' estate with the hospital and the prison). A continuity of the punitive criteria and mechanisms, which on the basis of a mere deviation gradually strengthened the rules and increased the punishment. A continuous gradation of the established, specialized and competent authorities (in the order of knowledge and in the order of power) which, without resort to arbitrariness, but strictly according to the regulations, by means of observation and assessment hierarchized, differentiated, judged, punished and moved gradually from the correction of irregularities to the punishment of crime. The 'carceral' with its many diffuse or compact forms, its institutions of supervision or constraint, of discreet surveillance and insistent coercion, assured the communication of punishments according to quality and quantity; it connected in series or disposed according to subtle divisions the minor and the serious penalties, the mild and the strict forms of treatment, bad marks and light sentences. You will end up in the convict-ship, the slightest indiscipline seems to say; and the harshest of prisons says to the prisoners condemned to life: I shall note the slightest irregularity in your conduct. The generality of the punitive function that the eighteenth century sought in the 'ideological' technique of representations and signs now had as its support the extension, the material framework, complex, dispersed, but coherent, of the various carceral mechanisms. As a result, a certain significant generality moved between the least irregularity and the greatest crime; it was no longer the offence, the attack on the common interest, it was the departure from the norm, the anomaly; it was this that haunted the school, the court, the asylum or the prison. It generalized in the sphere of meaning the function that the carceral generalized in the sphere of tactics. Replacing the adversary of the sovereign, the social enemy was transformed into a deviant, who brought with him the multiple danger of disorder, crime and madness. The carceral network linked, through innumerable relations, the two long, multiple series of the punitive and the abnormal.

2. The carceral, with its far-reaching networks, allows the recruitment of major 'delinquents'. It organizes what might be called 'disciplinary careers' in which, through various exclusions and rejections, a whole process is set in motion. In the classical period, there opened up in the confines or interstices of society the confused, tolerant and dangerous domain of the 'outlaw' or at least of that which eluded the direct hold of power: an uncertain space that was for criminality a training ground and a region of refuge; there poverty, unemployment, pursued innocence, cunning, the struggle against the powerful, the refusal of obligations and laws, and organized crime all came together as chance and fortune would dictate; it was the domain of adventure that Gil Blas, Sheppard or Mandrin, each in his own way, inhabited. Through the play of disciplinary differentiations and divisions, the nineteenth century constructed rigorous channels which, within the system, inculcated docility and produced delinquency by the same mechanisms. There was a sort of disciplinary 'training', continuous and compelling, that had something of the pedagogical curriculum and something of the professional network. Careers emerged from it, as secure, as predictable, as those of public life: assistance associations, residential apprenticeships, penal colonies, disciplinary battalions, prisons, hospitals, almshouses. These networks were already well mapped out at the beginning of the nineteenth century: 'Our benevolent establishments present an admirably coordinated whole by means of which the indigent does not remain a moment without help from the cradle to the grave. Follow the course of the unfortunate man: you will see him born among foundlings; from there he passes to the nursery, then to an orphanage; at the age of six he goes off to primary school and later to adult schools. If he cannot work, he is placed on the list of the charity offices of his district, and if he falls ill he may choose between twelve hospitals. . . Lastly, when the poor Parisian reaches the end of his career, seven almshouses await his age and often their salubrious régime has prolonged his useless days well beyond those of the rich man' (Moreau de Jonnès, quoted in Touquet).

The carceral network does not cast the unassimilable into a confused hell; there is no outside. It takes back with one hand what it seems to exclude with the other. It saves everything, including what it punishes. It is unwilling to waste even what it has decided to disqualify. In this panoptic society of which incarceration is the omnipresent armature, the delinquent is not outside the law; he is, from the very outset, in the law, at the very heart of the law, or at least in the midst of those mechanisms that transfer the individual imperceptibly from discipline to the law, from deviation to offence. Although it is true that prison punishes delinquency, delinquency is for the most part produced in and by an incarceration which, ultimately, prison perpetuates in its turn. The prison is merely the natural consequence, no more than a higher degree, of that hierarchy laid down step by step. The delinquent is an institutional product. It is no use being surprised, therefore, that in a considerable proportion of cases the biography of convicts passes through all these mechanisms and establishments, whose purpose, it is widely believed, is to lead away from prison. That one should find in them what one might call the index of an irrepressibly delinquent 'character': the prisoner condemned to hard labour was meticulously produced by a childhood spent in a reformatory, according to the lines of force of the generalized carceral system. Conversely, the lyricism of marginality may find inspiration in the image of the 'outlaw', the great social nomad, who prowls on the confines of a docile, frightened order. But it is not on the fringes of society and through successive exiles that criminality is born, but by means of ever more closely placed insertions, under ever more insistent surveillance, by an accumulation of disciplinary coercion. In short, the carceral archipelago assures, in the depths of the social body, the formation of delinquency on the basis of subtle illegalities, the overlapping of the latter by the former and the establishment of a specified criminality.

3. But perhaps the most important effect of the carceral system and of its extension well beyond legal imprisonment is that it succeeds in making the power to punish natural and legitimate, in lowering at least the threshold of tolerance to penality. It tends to efface what may be exorbitant in the exercise of punishment. It does this by playing the two registers in which it is deployed – the legal register of justice and the extra-legal register of discipline – against

one another. In effect, the great continuity of the carceral system throughout the law and its sentences gives a sort of legal sanction to the disciplinary mechanisms, to the decisions and judgements that they enforce. Throughout this network, which comprises so many 'regional' institutions, relatively autonomous and independent, is transmitted, with the 'prison-form', the model of justice itself. The regulations of the disciplinary establishments may reproduce the law, the punishments imitate the verdicts and penalties, the surveillance repeat the police model; and, above all these multiple establishments, the prison, which in relation to them is a pure form, unadulterated and unmitigated, gives them a sort of official sanction. The carceral, with its long gradation stretching from the convict-ship or imprisonment with hard labour to diffuse, slight limitations, communicates a type of power that the law validates and that justice uses as its favourite weapon. How could the disciplines and the power that functions in them appear arbitrary, when they merely operate the mechanisms of justice itself, even with a view to mitigating their intensity? When, by generalizing its effects and trans-mitting it to every level, it makes it possible to avoid its full rigour? Carceral continuity and the fusion of the prison-form make it possible to legalize, or in any case to legitimate disciplinary power, which thus avoids any element of excess or abuse it may entail.

But, conversely, the carceral pyramid gives to the power to inflict legal punishment a context in which it appears to be free of all excess and all violence. In the subtle gradation of the apparatuses of discipline and of the successive 'embeddings' that they involve, the prison does not at all represent the unleashing of a different kind of power, but simply an additional degree in the intensity of a mechan-ism that has continued to operate since the earliest forms of legal punishment. Between the latest institution of 'rehabilitation', where one is taken in order to avoid prison, and the prison where one is sent after a definable offence, the difference is (and must be) scarcely perceptible. There is a strict economy that has the effect of render-ing as discreet as possible the singular power to punish. There is nothing in it now that recalls the former excess of sovereign power when it revenged its authority on the tortured body of those about to be executed. Prison continues, on those who are entrusted to it, a work begun elsewhere, which the whole of society pursues on each individual through innumerable mechanisms of discipline. By means of a carceral continuum, the authority that sentences infiltrates all those other authorities that supervise, transform, correct, improve. It might even be said that nothing really distinguishes them any more except the singularly 'dangerous' character of the delinquents, the gravity of their departures from normal behaviour and the necessary solemnity of the ritual. But, in its function, the power to punish is not essentially different from that of curing or educating. It receives from them, and from their lesser, smaller task, a sanction from below; but one that is no less important for that, since it is the sanction of technique and rationality. The carceral 'naturalizes' the legal power to punish, as it 'legalizes' the technical power to discipline. In thus homogenizing them, effacing what may be violent in one and arbitrary in the other, attenuating the effects of revolt that they may both arouse, thus depriving excess in either of any purpose, circulating the same calculated, mechanical and discreet methods from one to the other, the carceral makes it possible to carry out that great 'economy' of power whose formula the eighteenth century had sought, when the problem of the accumulation and useful administration of men first emerged.

By operating at every level of the social body and by mingling ceaselessly the art of rectifying and the right to punish, the universality of the carceral lowers the level from which it becomes natural and acceptable to be punished. The question is often posed as to how, before and after the Revolution, a new foundation was given to the right to punish. And no doubt the answer is to be found in the theory of the contract. But it is perhaps more important to ask the reverse question: how were people made to accept the power to punish, or quite simply, when punished, tolerate being so. The theory of the contract can only answer this question by the fiction of a juridical subject giving to others the power to exercise over him the right that he himself possesses over them. It is highly probable that the great carceral continuum, which provides a communication between the power of discipline and the power of the law, and extends without interruption from the smallest coercions to the longest penal detention, constituted the technical and real, immediately material counterpart of that chimerical granting of the right to punish.

4. With this new economy of power, the carceral system, which is its basic instrument, permitted the emergence of a new form of 'law': a mixture of legality and nature, prescription and constitution, the norm. This had a whole series of effects: the internal dislocation of the judicial power or at least of its functioning; an increasing difficulty in judging, as if one were ashamed to pass sentence; a furious desire on the part of the judges to judge, assess, diagnose, recognize the normal and abnormal and claim the honour of curing or rehabilitating. In view of this, it is useless to believe in the good or bad consciences of judges, or even of their unconscious. Their immense 'appetite for medicine' which is constantly manifested – from their appeal to psychiatric experts, to their attention to the chatter of criminology – expresses the major fact that the power they exercise has been 'denatured'; that it is at a certain level governed by laws; that at another, more fundamental level it functions as a normative power; it is the economy of power that they exercise, and not that of their scruples or their humanism, that makes them pass 'therapeutic' sentences and recommend 'rehabilitating' periods of imprisonment. But, conversely, if the judges accept ever more reluctantly to condemn for the sake of condemning, the activity of judging has increased precisely to the extent that the normalizing power has spread. Borne along by the omnipresence of the mechanisms of discipline, basing itself on all the carceral apparatuses, it has become one of the major functions of our society. The judges of normality are present everywhere. We are in the society of the teacher-judge, the doctor-judge, the educator-judge, the 'social worker'-judge; it is on them that the universal reign of the normative is based; and each individual, wherever he may find himself, subjects to it his body, his gestures, his behaviour, his aptitudes, his achievements. The carceral network, in its compact or disseminated forms, with its systems of insertion, distribution, surveillance, observation, has been the greatest support, in modern society, of the normalizing power.

5. The carceral texture of society assures both the real capture of the body and its perpetual observation; it is, by its very nature, the apparatus of punishment that conforms most completely to the new economy of power and the instrument for the formation of knowledge that this very economy needs. Its panoptic functioning

enables it to play this double role. By virtue of its methods of fixing, dividing, recording, it has been one of the simplest, crudest, also most concrete, but perhaps most indispensable conditions for the development of this immense activity of examination that has objectified human behaviour. If, after the age of 'inquisitorial' justice, we have entered the age of 'examinatory' justice, if, in an even more general way, the method of examination has been able to spread so widely throughout society, and to give rise in part to the sciences of man, one of the great instruments for this has been the multiplicity and close overlapping of the various mechanisms of incarceration. I am not saying that the human sciences emerged from the prison. But, if they have been able to be formed and to produce so many profound changes in the episteme, it is because they have been conveyed by a specific and new modality of power: a certain policy of the body, a certain way of rendering the group of men docile and useful. This policy required the involvement of definite relations of knowledge in relations of power; it called for a technique of overlapping subjection and objectification; it brought with it new procedures of individualization. The carceral network constituted one of the armatures of this power-knowledge that has made the human sciences historically possible. Knowable man (soul, individuality, consciousness, conduct, whatever it is called) is the object-effect of this analytical investment, of this domination-observation.

6. This no doubt explains the extreme solidity of the prison, that slight invention that was nevertheless decried from the outset. If it had been no more than an instrument of rejection or repression in the service of a state apparatus, it would have been easier to alter its more overt forms or to find a more acceptable substitute for it. But, rooted as it was in mechanisms and strategies of power, it could meet any attempt to transform it with a great force of inertia. One fact is characteristic: when it is a question of altering the system of imprisonment, opposition does not come from the judicial institutions alone; resistance is to be found not in the prison as penal sanction, but in the prison with all its determinations, links and extra-judicial results; in the prison as the relay in a general network of disciplines and surveillances; in the prison as it functions in a panoptic régime. This does not mean that it cannot be altered, nor that it is once and for all indispensable to our kind of society. One may, on

the contrary, site the two processes which, in the very continuity of the processes that make the prison function, are capable of exercising considerable restraint on its use and of transforming its internal functioning. And no doubt these processes have already begun to a large degree. The first is that which reduces the utility (or increases its inconveniences) of a delinquency accommodated as a specific illegality, locked up and supervised; thus the growth of great national or international illegalities directly linked to the political and economic apparatuses (financial illegalities, information services, arms and drugs trafficking, property speculation) makes it clear that the somewhat rustic and conspicuous work force of delinquency is proving ineffective; or again, on a smaller scale, as soon as the economic levy on sexual pleasure is carried out more efficiently by the sale of contraceptives, or obliquely through publications, films or shows, the archaic hierarchy of prostitution loses much of its former usefulness. The second process is the growth of the disciplinary networks, the multiplication of their exchanges with the penal apparatus, the ever more important powers that are given them, the ever more massive transference to them of judicial functions; now, as medicine, psychology, education, public assistance, 'social work' assume an ever greater share of the powers of supervision and assessment, the penal apparatus will be able, in turn, to become medicalized, psychologized, educationalized; and by the same token that turning-point represented by the prison becomes less useful when, through the gap between its penitentiary discourse and its effect of consolidating delinquency, it articulates the penal power and the disciplinary power. In the midst of all these mechanisms of normalization, which are becoming ever more rigorous in their application, the specificity of the prison and its role as link are losing something of their purpose.

If there is an overall political issue around the prison, it is not therefore whether it is to be corrective or not; whether the judges, the psychiatrists or the sociologists are to exercise more power in it than the administrators or supervisors; it is not even whether we should have prison or something other than prison. At present, the problem lies rather in the steep rise in the use of these mechanisms of normalization and the wide-ranging powers which, through the proliferation of new disciplines, they bring with them.

In 1836, a correspondent wrote to *La Phalange*: 'Moralists, philosophers, legislators, flatterers of civilization, this is the plan of your Paris, neatly ordered and arranged, here is the improved plan in which all like things are gathered together. At the centre, and within a first enclosure: hospitals for all diseases, almshouses for all types of poverty, madhouses, prisons, convict-prisons for men, women and children. Around the first enclosure, barracks, court-rooms, police stations, houses for prison warders, scaffolds, houses for the executioner and his assistants. At the four corners, the Chamber of Deputies, the Chamber of Peers, the Institute and the Royal Palace. Outside, there are the various services that supply the central enclosure, commerce, with its swindlers and its bank-ruptcies; industry and its furious struggles; the press, with its sophisms; the gambling dens; prostitution, the people dying of hunger or wallowing in debauchery, always ready to lend an ear to the voice of the Genius of Revolutions; the heartless rich. . . Lastly the ruthless war of all against all' (*La Phalange*, 10 August 1836).

I shall stop with this anonymous text. We are now far away from the country of tortures, dotted with wheels, gibbets, gallows, pillories; we are far, too, from that dream of the reformers, less than fifty years before: the city of punishments in which a thousand small theatres would have provided an endless multicoloured repre-sentation of justice in which the punishments, meticulously pro-duced on decorative scaffolds, would have constituted the permanent festival of the penal code. The carceral city, with its imaginary 'geo-politics', is governed by quite different principles. The extract from *La Phalange* reminds us of some of the more important ones: that at the centre of this city, and as if to hold it in place, there is, not the 'centre of power', not a network of forces, but a multiple network of diverse elements – walls, space, institution, rules, dis-course; that the model of the carceral city is not, therefore, the body of the king, with the powers that emanate from it, nor the contrac-tual meeting of wills from which a body that was both individual and collective was born, but a strategic distribution of elements of different natures and levels. That the prison is not the daughter of laws, codes or the judicial apparatus; that it is not subordinated to the court and the docile or clumsy instrument of the sentences that it hands out and of the results that it would like to achieve; that it is the court that is external and subordinate to the prison. That in the central position that it occupies, it is not alone, but linked to a whole series of 'carceral' mechanisms which seem distinct enough – since they are intended to alleviate pain, to cure, to comfort – but which all tend, like the prison, to exercise a power of normalization. That these mechanisms are applied not to transgressions against a 'central' law, but to the apparatus of production – 'commerce' and 'industry' – to a whole multiplicity of illegalities, in all their diversity of nature and origin, their specific role in profit and the different ways in which they are dealt with by the punitive mechanisms. And that ultimately what presides over all these mechanisms is not the unitary functioning of an apparatus or an institution, but the necessity of combat and the rules of strategy. That, consequently, the notions of institutions of repression, rejection, exclusion, marginalization, are not adequate to describe, at the very centre of the carceral city, the formation of the insidious leniencies, unavowable petty cruelties, small acts of cunning, calculated methods, techniques, 'sciences' that permit the fabrication of the disciplinary individual. In this central and centralized humanity, the effect and instrument of complex power relations, bodies and forces subjected by multiple mechanisms of 'incarceration', objects for discourses that are in themselves elements for this strategy, we must hear the distant roar of battle.

At this point I end a book that must serve as a historical background to various studies of the power of normalization and the formation of knowledge in modern society.

Notes

1 *The body of the condemned*

1 The public execution of traitors described by William Blackstone, *Commentaries on the Laws of England*, vol. 4, 1766 9, 89. Since the French translation was intended to bring out the humaneness of English legislation, in contrast with the old ordinance of 1760, the French translator adds the following note: 'In this form of execution, which is so terrifying to see, the guilty man does not suffer much pain, or for long.'

2 In any case, I could give no notion by references or quotations what this book owes to Gilles Deleuze and the work he is undertaking with Félix Guattari. I should also have quoted a number of pages from R. Castell's *Psychanalysme* and say how much I am indebted to Pierre Nora.

3 I shall study the birth of the prison only in the French penal system. Differences in historical developments and institutions would make a detailed comparative examination too burdensome and any attempt to describe the phenomenon as a whole too schematic.

2 *The spectacle of the scaffold*

1 The name given to two fortresses in old Paris, the Grand and the Petit Châtelet. The first, demolished in 1802, was situated on the right bank of the Seine. It was the seat of the criminal jurisdiction of the viscounty and provostry of Paris. The second, on the left bank, near the Hôtel-Dieu, served as a prison [Tr.].

2 In the catalogues of judicial proofs, the confession appears in about the thirteenth or fourteenth century. Bernard of Pavia does not refer to it, but it is mentioned by Hostiemis. Crater's definition is characteristic: '*Aut legitime convictus aut sponte confessus.*'

In medieval law, the confession was valid only when made by an adult and before the adversary. Cf. Lévy.

3 The *Gazette tribunaux*, 6 July 1837, reports, from a Gloucester newspaper, the 'atrocious and disgusting' conduct of an executioner who after hanging a condemned man 'took the corpse by the shoulders, violently turned it round and struck it several times saying: "Are you dead enough now?" then, turning towards the crowd, laughing and jeering, he made several indecent remarks'.

4 Argenson, 241. Cf. also Barbier, 455. One of the first episodes of this affair was very typical of popular agitation concerning penal justice in the eighteenth century. The lieutenant-general of police, Berryer, had seized 'libertine children without confession'; the guards agreed to hand them back to their parents 'only when given money'; it was said that the children were intended to provide for the king's pleasure. The crowd, having discovered an informer, killed him 'with an inhumanity carried to the farthest excess' and 'dragged him after his death, a rope around his neck, to M. Berryer's door'. Now, this informer was a thief who would have been broken on the wheel with his accomplice Raffiat, had he not agreed to act as an informer; he was greatly appreciated by the police on account of his knowledge of all the intricacies of the plot; and he was 'highly regarded in his new trade'. We have an example here that is interesting on a number of counts: a movement of revolt triggered off by a relatively new means of repression, which was not penal justice, but the police; a case of that technical collaboration between delinquents and police, which was to become normal from the eighteenth century onwards; a riot in which people took it upon themselves to torture a condemned man who had unjustly escaped the scaffold.

5 Those whom R. Mandrou calls the two great ones: Cartouche and Mandrin, to whom one should add Guilleri (Mandrou, 112). In England, Jonathan Wild, Jack Sheppard and Claude Duval played a somewhat similar role.

6 This title is to be found not only in the Bibliothèque de Troyes, but also in the Bibliothèque de Normandie (cf. Helot).

7 Cf., for example, Lacretelle: 'In order to satisfy this need for strong emotion, in order to deepen the impression of a great example, one allows these terrible stories to circulate. The poets of the people take them up and spread their fame to every part of the land. One day a family hears at its door the story in song of the crime and execution of its sons' (Lacretelle, 106).

1 *Generalized punishment*

1 Mogensen, 326. The author shows that in Auge crimes of violence were four times less numerous on the eve of the Revolution than at the end of the reign of Louis XIV. Generally speaking, the work directed by Pierre Chaunu on criminality in Normandy shows the same rise in fraud at the expense of violence. Cf. articles by B. Boutelet, J. C. Gégot and V. Boucheron in the *Annales de Normandie* of 1962, 1966 and 1971. For Paris, cf. Petrovitch. The same phenomenon, it seems, took place in England: cf. Hibbert, 72 and Tobias, 37ff.

2 Le Roy-Ladurie, 1973. Cf. also Farge who confirms this tendency: between 1750 and 1755, 5 per cent of those convicted for stealing food were sent to the galleys, but 15 per cent between 1775 and 1790: 'The courts became more severe as time went on. . . The values useful to a society that wished to be ordered and respectful of property were under threat' (Farge, 130–42).

3 On this criticism of 'excessive power' and of its bad distribution in the judicial apparatus, cf. in particular Dupaty, 1788, Lacretelle and Target.

4 Cf. N. Bergasse on the judicial power: 'Deprived of any kind of activity against the political régime of the State and having no influence on the wills that come together to form that régime or to maintain it, it must have at its disposal, in order to protect all individuals and all rights, such a force that, all-powerful in defending and assisting that régime, it should become absolutely nil as soon as its destination is changed in any attempt to use it to oppress' (Bergasse, 11–12).

5 Rousseau, 28. It should be noted that these ideas of Rousseau's were used in the Constituent Assembly by certain deputies who wished to maintain a system of very strict penalties. And, curiously enough, the principles of the *Social Contract* could be used to support the old correspondence of atrocity between crime and punishment. 'The protection due to citizens requires that penalties be measured according to the atrocity of the crimes and not sacrifice, in the name of humanity, humanity itself' (Mougins de Roquefort, who quotes this passage from the *Social Contract*: cf. Mougins, 637).

6 Duport, *Archives parlementaires*, X, 744. One might also cite in support the different competitions proposed at the end of the eighteenth century by learned societies and academies: 'How is the mildness of these investigations and penalties to be reconciled with the certainties of a prompt and exemplary punishment, so that civil society

finds the greatest possible security for liberty and humanity?' (Economic Society of Berne, 1777). Marat responded with his *Plan de Législation criminelle*. 'What are the means of alleviating the rigour of the penal laws in France without damage to public safety?' (Académie de Châlons-sur-Marne, 1780; the winners were Brissot and Bernardi); 'does the extreme severity of the laws tend to diminish the number and enormity of crimes in a depraved nation?' (Académie de Marseille, 1786; the winner was Eymar).

7 G. Target, *Observations sur le projet du Code pénal*, in Locré, 7–8. It is to be found in an inverted form in Kant.

8 'Society does not see in the punishments it inflicts the barbarous pleasure of making a human being suffer; it sees it as a necessary precaution to prevent similar crimes, to protect society from the evils with which murder threatens it' (Barnave, 9).

9 Beccaria, 26. Cf. also Brissot: 'If pardon is equitable, the law is bad; when legislation is good, pardons are only crimes against the law' (Brissot, 200).

10 Mably, 327. Cf. also Vattel: 'It is not so much the atrocity of the penalties as the exactitude with which they are carried out that keeps everybody within his duty' (Mably, 163).

11 Contrary to what Carnot or Helie and Chauveau say, recidivism was very clearly punished in a number of laws under the Ancien Régime. The ordinance of 1549 declares that the malefactor who repeats his crime is an 'execrable, infamous being, eminently pernicious to the commonwealth'; recidivism for blasphemy, theft, vagabondage, etc., were subject to special penalties.

12 Le Peletier, 321–2. The following year, Bellart made what may be regarded as the first defence of a *crime passionel*. This was the Gras affair. Cf. *Annales du barreau moderne*, 1823, III, 34.

2 *The gentle way in punishment*

1 Le Peletier de Saint-Fargeau. The authors who abandoned the death penalty envisaged some definite penalties: Brissot, 29–30. Dufriche de Valazé, 344: perpetual imprisonment for those who have been judged 'irremediably wicked'.

2 Masson, 139. Yet the objection made against penal labour was that it implied a recourse to violence (Le Peletier) or that it represented a profanation of the sacred character of work (Duport). Rabaud Saint-Étienne got the term 'forced labour' adopted in contra-distinction to 'free labour that belongs exclusively to free men' (*Archives Parlementaires*, XXVI, 710ff).

3 Part of this code was translated in the introduction to the French translation of Colquhoun, 1807, I, 84.

4 This explains the numerous prison regulations concerning the exactions of the warders, the security of the premises and the inability of prisoners to communicate among themselves. For example, the judgement of the Dijon *Parlement* of 21 September 1706. Cf. also Serpillon, 601–47.

5 This is repeated exactly in the declaration of 4 March 1724 on recidivist thieves or that of 18 July 1724 concerning vagabondage. A boy, who was too young to go to the galleys, remained in a prison until he was old enough to be sent there, sometimes to serve the whole of his sentence. Cf. *Crime et criminalité en France sous l'Ancien Régime*, 266ff.

6 Phalaris, tyrant of the Greek town of Agrigentum in Sicily, reigned about 560 B.C. He is said to have roasted men alive in a brazen bull. His name is used here to typify tyrants in general [Tr.].

7 Briey, 'Tiers État', quoted in Desjardin, 484. Cf. Goubert and Denis, 203. One also finds in the *cahiers* demands for the maintenance of houses of detention that families might use.

8 Cf. Thorsten Sellin, *Pioneering in Penology*, 1944, which gives an exhaustive study of the Rasphuis and the Spinhuis of Amsterdam. One may leave to one side another 'model', often cited in the eighteenth century. This is the one proposed by Mabillon in the *Réflexions sur les prisons des ordres religieux*, republished in 1845. It seems that this work was exhumed in the nineteenth century at a time when the Catholics were disputing with the Protestants the place they had taken up in the philanthropic movement and in certain administrative bodies. Mabillon's work, which seems to have remained relatively unknown and uninfluential, sets out to show that 'the first thought of the American penitentiary system' is 'a quite monastic and French thought, whatever one might say by way of giving it a Genevan or Pennsylvanian origin' (L. Faucher).

9 Vilan XIV, 64; this memoir, which is bound up with the foundation of the prison at Ghent, remained unpublished until 1841. The frequency of the penalty of banishment emphasized still further the relations between crime and vagabondage. In 1771, the States of Flanders remarked that 'penalties of banishment imposed on beggars remained ineffectual, in view of the fact that the States send to one another subjects that they find pernicious at home. As a result, a beggar, chased in this way from place to place, will finally get himself hanged, whereas, if he had been given the habit of work, he would not have embarked on his evil path' (Stoobant, 228).

10 The Quakers certainly also knew the Rasphuis and Spinhuis of Amsterdam. Cf. Sellin, 109–10. In any case, Walnut Street Prison was a continuation of the Almshouse opened in 1767 and of the penal legislation that the Quakers had wished to impose despite the English administration.

11 On the disorders caused by this law, cf. Rush, 5–9 and Vaux, 45. It should be noted that in the report by J. L. Siegel, which had inspired the Rasphuis of Amsterdam, it was envisaged that penalties would not be proclaimed publicly, that prisoners would be brought into the prison at night, that warders would swear not to reveal their identity and that no visits would be permitted (Sellin, 27–8).

12 B. Rush, who was one of the inspectors, notes after a visit to Walnut Street: 'Moral cares: preaching, reading of good books, cleanliness of clothes and rooms, baths; one does not raise one's voice, little wine, as little tobacco as possible, little obscene or profane conversation. Constant work: the gardens taken care of; it is beautiful: 1,200 head of cabbage' (in Teeters, 1935, 50).

13 Rush, 14. This idea of an apparatus for transforming human beings is already to be found in Hanway's project for a 'reformatory': 'The idea of a hospital and that of a malefactor are incompatible; but let us try to make the prison an authentic and effective reformatory, instead of it being like the others a school of vice' (Hanway, 52).

14 Cf. the criticism made by Rush of punitive spectacles, in particular those imagined by Dufriche du Valazé (Rush, 5–9).

PART THREE DISCIPLINE

1 *Docile bodies*

1 I shall choose examples from military, medical, educational and industrial institutions. Other examples might have been taken from colonization, slavery and child rearing.

2 Cf. what La Métherie wrote after a visit to Le Creusot: 'The buildings for so fine an establishment and so large a quantity of different work should cover a sufficient area, so that there will be no confusion among the workers during working time' (La Métherie, 66).

3 J.-B. de la Salle, *Conduite des écoles chrétiennes*, B.N. Ms. 11759, 248–9. A little earlier Batencour proposed that classrooms should be divided into three parts: 'The most honourable for those who are learning Latin. . . It should be stressed that there are as many places at the tables as there will be writers, in order to avoid the confusion usually caused by the lazy.' In another, those who are learning to read: a bench

for the rich and a bench for the poor 'so that vermin will not be passed on'. A third section for newcomers: 'When their ability has been recognized, they will be given a place' (M.I.D.B., 56–7).

4 The success of the Prussian troops can only be attributed to the 'excellence of their discipline and their exercise; the choice of exercise is not therefore a matter of indifference; in Prussia the subject has been studied for forty years with unremitting application' (Saxe, II, 249).

5 Writing exercise: '. . . 9: Hands on the knees. This command is conveyed by one ring on the bell; 10: hands on the table, head up; 11: clean the slates: everyone cleans his slate with a little saliva, or better still with a piece of rag; 12: show the slates; 13: monitors, inspect. They inspect the slates with their assistants and then those of their own bench. The assistants inspect those of their own bench and everyone returns to his own place.'

6 This mixture appears clearly in certain classes of the apprenticeship contract: the master is obliged to give his pupil – in exchange for his money and his labour – all his knowledge, without keeping any secret from him; otherwise, he is liable to a fine. Cf., for example, Grosrenaud, 62.

7 F. de la Noue recommended the creation of military academies at the end of the sixteenth century, suggesting that one should learn in them 'how to handle horses, to practise with the dagger, with and without shield, to fence, to perform on horseback, to jump; if swimming and wrestling were added, it would be to the good, for all this makes the person robust and more subtle' (Noue, 181–2).

8 Through the schools at Liège, Devenport, Zwolle, Wesel; and thanks also to Jean Sturm and his memorandum of 1538 for the organization of a *gymnasium* at Strasburg. Cf. *Bulletin de la société d'histoire du protestantisme*, XXV, 499–505.

It should be noted that the relations between the army, religious organization and education are very complex. The 'decury', the unit of the Roman army, is to be found in Benedictine monasteries, as the unit of work and no doubt of supervision. The Brothers of the Common Life borrowed it and adapted it to their own education organization: the pupils were grouped in tens. It was this unit that the Jesuits took up in the scenography of their schools, thus reintroducing a military model. But the decury was replaced in turn by an even more military schema, with ranks, columns, lines.

9 Guibert, 18. In fact, this very old problem came into the forefront once more in the eighteenth century, for the economic and technical

reasons that we are about to see; and the 'prejudice' in question had been discussed very often by others besides Guibert himself (followers of Folard, Pirch, Mesnil-Durand).

10 In the sense in which this term was used after 1759.

11 The movement that brought the rifle into widespread use may be roughly dated from the battle of Steinkirk, 1699.

12 On this importance of geometry, see J. de Beausobre: 'The science of war is essentially geometrical... The arrangement of a battalion and a squadron on a whole front and at so much height is alone the effect of an as yet unknown, but profound geometry' (Beausobre, 307).

13 *Journal pour l'instruction élémentaire*, April 1816. Cf. Tronchot, who has calculated that pupils must have been given over 200 commands a day (without counting exceptional orders); for the morning alone twenty-six commands communicated by the voice, twenty-three by signs, thirty-seven by rings of the bell, and twenty-four by whistle, which means a blow on the whistle or a ring on the bell every three minutes.

2 *The means of correct training*

1 *Règlement pour l'infanterie prussienne*, Fr. trans., Arsenal, MS. 4067, fo. 144. For older plans see Praissac, 27–8 and Montgommery, 77. For the new plans, cf. Beneton de Morange, *Histoire de la guerre*, 1741, 61–4 and *Dissertations sur les Tentes*; cf. also the many regulations such as the *Instruction sur le service des règlements de Cavalerie dans les camps*, 29 June 1753.

2 Arch. nat. MM 666–9. Jeremy Bentham recounts that it was while visiting the École Militaire that his brother first had the idea of the Panopticon.

3 Demia, 27–9. One might note a phenomenon of the same kind in the organization of schools; for a long time 'prefects' were, independently of the teachers, entrusted with the moral responsibility for small groups of pupils. After 1762, above all, one sees the appearance of a new type of supervision, which was more administrative and more integrated into the hierarchy; supervisors, *maîtres de quartier, maîtres subalternes*. Cf. Dupont-Ferrier, 254 and 476.

3 *Panopticism*

1 Archives militaires de Vincennes, A 1,516 91 sc. Pièce. This regulation is broadly similar to a whole series of others that date from the same period and earlier.

2 In the *Postscript to the Panopticon*, 1791, Bentham adds dark inspection galleries painted in black around the inspector's lodge, each making it possible to observe two storeys of cells.

3 In his first version of the *Panopticon*, Bentham had also imagined an acoustic surveillance, operated by means of pipes leading from the cells to the central tower. In the *Postscript* he abandoned the idea, perhaps because he could not introduce into it the principle of dissymmetry and prevent the prisoners from hearing the inspector as well as the inspector hearing them. Julius tried to develop a system of dissymmetrical listening (Julius, 18).

4 Imagining this continuous flow of visitors entering the central tower by an underground passage and then observing the circular landscape of the Panopticon, was Bentham aware of the Panoramas that Barker was constructing at exactly the same period (the first seems to have dated from 1787) and in which the visitors, occupying the central place, saw unfolding around them a landscape, a city or a battle. The visitors occupied exactly the place of the sovereign gaze.

5 In the second half of the eighteenth century, it was often suggested that the army should be used for the surveillance and general partitioning of the population. The army, as yet to undergo discipline in the seventeenth century, was regarded as a force capable of instilling it. Cf., for example, Servan, *Le Soldat citoyen*, 1780.

6 Arsenal, MS. 2565. Under this number, one also finds regulations for charity associations of the seventeenth and eighteenth centuries.

7 Le Maire in a memorandum written at the request of Sartine, in answer to sixteen questions posed by Joseph II on the Parisian police. This memorandum was published by Gazier in 1879.

PART FOUR PRISON

1 *Complete and austere institutions*

1 The play between the two 'natures' of the prison still continues. A few days ago [summer 1974] the head of state recalled the 'principle' that detention ought to be no more than a 'deprivation of liberty' – the pure essence of imprisonment, freed of the reality of prison; and added that the prison could be justified only by its 'corrective' or rehabilitating effects.

2 Treilhard, 8–9. The same theme is often to be found in the years immediately prior to this: 'The penalty of detention pronounced by the law has above all the object of correcting individuals, that is to say, of making them better, of preparing them by trials of shorter or longer

duration, to take up their place once more in society without abusing it. . . The surest ways of making individuals better are work and education.' Education consists not only in reading and arithmetic, but also in reconciling the prisoners with 'ideas of order, morality, respect for themselves and for others' (Beugnot, prefect of Seine-Inférieure, order issued Frimaire, Year X). In the reports that Chaptal demanded from the General Councils of the *départements*, over a dozen asked for prisons in which the inmates could be made to work.

3 The most important were no doubt those proposed by Lucas, Marquet-Wasselot, Faucher, Bonneville, and a little later by Ferrus. It should be noted that most of them were not philanthropists, criticizing the carceral institution from the outside, but were bound up, in one way or another, with the administration of the prisons. They were official technicians.

4 In Germany, Julius directed the *Jahrbücher für Strafs-und Besserungs Anstalten*.

5 Although these newspapers were above all organs of defence on the part of those in prison for debt and had on several occasions dissociated themselves from delinquents as such, one finds the statement that 'the columns of *Pauvre Jacques* are not devoted to an exclusive speciality. The terrible law of constraint by body and its disastrous application will not be the only target of the journalist prisoner. . . *Pauvre Jacques* will draw the attention of its readers to places of reclusion and detention, prisons and almshouses; it will not keep silent on places where the guilty man is handed over to torture when the law condemns him only to work . . .' (*Pauvre Jacques*, 1st year, no. 7). Similarly, the *Gazette de Sainte-Pélagie* campaigned for a penitentiary system whose aim would be 'the amelioration of the species', any other being 'the expression of a still barbarous society' (21 March 1833).

6 The discussion that began in France about 1830 was still continuing in 1850; Charles Lucas, the advocate of Auburn, was the inspiration behind the order of 1839 on the running of the *maisons centrales* (work in common and absolute silence). The wave of revolt that followed and perhaps the general agitation in the country in the years 1842–3 resulted in the adoption in 1844 of the Pennsylvanian régime of absolute isolation, advocated by Demetz, Blouet and Tocqueville. But the second penitentiary congress in 1847 opted against this method.

7 'Every man', said Fox, 'is illuminated by the divine light and I have seen it shine through every man.' It was in the spirit of the Quakers and of Walnut Street that the prisons of Pennsylvania, Pittsburgh and Cherry Hill were organized from 1820.

8 Abbé Petigny, *Allocution adressée aux prisonniers, à l'occasion de l'inauguration des bâtiments cellulaires de la prison de Versailles*. Cf., a few years later, in *The Count of Monte Cristo*, a very clearly Christological version of resurrection after incarceration; in this case prison teaches not docility to the law, but the power, acquired through a secret knowledge, to dispense justice beyond the injustice of the magistrates.

9 G. A. Real. Before this, several instructions from the Ministry of the Interior had stressed the need for providing work for prisoners: 5 Fructidor Year VI, 3 Messidor Year VIII, 8 Pluviôse and 28 Ventôse Year IX, 7 Brumaire Year X. Immediately after the codes of 1808 and 1810, one still finds new instructions: 20 October 1811, 8 December 1812; or again the long order of 1816: 'It is of the greatest importance to keep prisoners occupied as much as possible. One must instil in them a desire to work, distinguishing between the fate of those who are occupied and that of prisoners who wish to remain idle. The first will be better fed and have more comfortable beds than the second.' Melun and Clairvaux were very soon organized into great workshops.

10 Bonneville, 1846, 6. Bonneville proposed measures of 'preparatory liberty', but also of 'afflictive additions' or an extension of imprisonment if it was shown that 'the penal prescription, fixed approximately according to the probable degree of the prisoner's obduracy was not enough to produce the effect expected of it'. This extension was not to exceed one eighth of the original penalty; preparatory liberty could begin after three quarters of the sentence had been served (*Traité des diverses institutions complémentaires*, 251ff).

11 In *Gazette des tribunaux*. Cf. also Marquet-Wasselot, 1832, 74–5. Lucas notes that minor offenders 'are generally recruited among the urban populations' and that 'the majority of those sentenced to hard labour come from the agricultural populations' (Lucas, I, 46–50).

12 'If one treats of the administrative question by abstracting the question of buildings, one runs the risk of drawing up principles that are based on no reality; whereas, with a sufficient knowledge of administrative needs, an architect may accept a particular system of imprisonment that theory may have dismissed as Utopian' (Blouet, 1).

13 'The English reveal their genius for mechanics in everything they do . . . and they want their buildings to function as a machine subject to the action of a single motor' (Baltard, 18).

14 One should study how the practice of biography became widespread at about the same time as the constitution of the individual delinquent in the punitive mechanisms: the biography or autobiography of prisoners

in Appert; the drawing up of biographical files on the psychiatric model; the use of biography in the defence of accused persons. On the last point one might compare the great justificatory memoirs of the late eighteenth century written for the three men condemned to the wheel, or for Jeanne Salmon – and the defences of criminals in the period of Louis Philippe. Chaix d'Est-Ange pleaded for La Roncière: 'If long before the crime, long before the charge is laid, you can scrutinize the defendant's life, penetrate into his heart, find its most hidden corners, lay bare all his thoughts, his entire soul . . .' (*Discours et plaidoyers*, III, 166).

2 *Illegalities and delinquency*

1 *Revue de Paris*, 7 June 1836. This part of the spectacle, in 1836, was no longer public; only a few privileged spectators were admitted to it. The account of the riveting of the convicts' chains to be found in the *Revue de Paris* corresponds exactly – to the point even of using the same words – with that of the *Dernier jour d'un condamné*, 1829.

2 The *Gazette des tribunaux* regularly published these lists and these 'criminal' notices. From the following description people would be able to recognize Delacollonge: 'Old cloth trousers over a pair of boots, a peaked cap of the same stuff and a grey overall. . . A coat of blue stuff' (6 June 1836). Later, it was decided to disguise Delacollonge in order to protect him from the violence of the crowd. The *Gazette des tribunaux* immediately described the disguise: 'Striped trousers, blue linen overalls, a straw hat' (20 July).

3 *Revue de Paris*, June 1836. Cf. Claude Gueux: 'Feel all those heads . . . each of these fallen men has below him his own bestial type. . . Here is the lynx, here the cat, here the monkey, here the vulture, here the hyena.'

4 *Revue de Paris*, 7 June 1836. According to the *Gazette des tribunaux*, Thorez, who commanded the chain-gang of 19 July, wished to remove these ornaments: 'It is not fitting that, as you go to the convict-ship to expiate your crimes, you should push effrontery so far as to decorate your hair, as if you were going to your wedding.'

5 *Revue de Paris*, 7 June 1836. On this date, the chain-gang had been shortened in order to prevent this merry-go-round and soldiers had been commanded to maintain order up to the departure of the chain-gang. The convicts' Sabbath is described in the *Dernier jour d'un condamné*: 'Society was represented there by the gaolers and the horrified and curious bystanders. The criminal defined the intentions of society and made of this horrible punishment a family festival.'

6 A song of the same kind is quoted by the *Gazette des tribunaux* of
10 April 1836. It was sung to the tune of the 'Marseillaise'. The
patriotic war song clearly became the song of the social war: 'What do
these stupid people want of us, do they come to insult us in our misfortune? They stare at us calmly. Our butchers do not horrify them.'

7 There is a class of writers who 'have striven to glorify the crimes of
certain exceptionally skilled malefactors, give them the leading roles
and expose the agents of authority to their sallies, their jeers and their
ill-disguised mockery. Whoever has seen a performance of *Auberge des
Adrets* or *Robert Macaire*, a drama celebrated among the people, will
recognize without difficulty the correctness of my observations. It is
the triumph, the apotheosis, of audacity and crime. Honest folk and
the forces of public order are ridiculed from beginning to end' (Fregier,
II, 187–8).

8 *Gazette des tribunaux*, 23 July 1837. On 9 August, the *Gazette* reported
that the carriage had overturned on the outskirts of Guingamp:
instead of mutinying, the prisoners, 'helped their guardians to put
their common vehicle back on its wheels'. Yet on 30 October, it noted
an escape at Valence.

9 Text addressed to *L'Atelier*, October 1842, by a worker imprisoned
for joining a workers' association. It was able to note this protest at a
time when the same newspaper was waging a campaign against competition from penal labour. The same issue carried a letter from another
worker on the same subject. Cf. also *La Fraternité*, March 1842,
1st year, no. 10.

10 *Gazette des tribunaux*, 3 December 1829. Cf. also *Gazette des tribunaux*,
19 July 1839; the *Ruche populaire*, August 1840; *La Fraternité*, July–
August 1847.

11 This campaign was very vigorous before and after the passing of new
regulations for the *maisons centrales* in 1839. The regulations were
severe (silence, abolition of wine and tobacco, reduction in food) and
they were followed by revolts. On 3 October 1840, *Le Moniteur*
wrote: 'It was scandalous to see prisoners gorging themselves with
wine, meat, game, delicacies of all kinds and treating prison as a
convenient hostelry where they could procure all the comforts that
the state of liberty often refused them.'

12 In 1826, many of the General Councils demanded that deportation be
substituted for constant and ineffective incarceration. In 1842, the
General Council of the Hautes-Alpes demanded that the prisons
become 'truly expiatory'; those of Drôme, Eure-et-Loir, Nièvre,
Rhône and Seine-et-Oise made similar demands.

13 According to an investigation carried out in 1839 among the directors of the *maisons centrales*. The director of the *maison centrale* of Embrun remarked: 'The excessive comfort in the prisons probably contributes a great deal to the terrible increase in the number of recidivists.' While the director at Eysses remarked: 'The present régime is not severe enough, and if one thing is certain it is that for many of the inmates prison has its attractions and that they find in prison depraved pleasures that are entirely to their liking.' The director at Limoges: 'The present régime of the *maisons centrales* which, for the recidivists, are in fact little more than boarding houses, is in no way repressive' (Cf. Moreau-Christophe, 1840, 86). Compare these remarks with declarations made, in July 1974, by the leaders of the union of prison workers concerning the effects of liberalization in prisons.

14 On the problem of deportation, cf. Barbé-Marbois and the discussion between Blosseville and La Pilorgerie (on the subject of Botany Bay). Buré, Marengo and L. de Carné, among others, drew up plans for the colonization of Algeria with delinquents.

15 One of the first episodes was the organization under police supervision of the *maisons de tolerance* (1823), which went well beyond the provisions of the law of 14 July 1791, concerning surveillance in brothels. Cf. on this subject the manuscripts collected by the Prefecture of police (20–26). In particular, the following circular from the Prefect of police, dated 14 June 1823: 'The establishment of houses of prostitution ought naturally to be regarded with displeasure by any man who is concerned with public morality; I am not surprised that the Commissioners of police oppose to the utmost of their powers the establishment of houses in their various quarters. . . The police believed that they had done much towards public order if they had succeeded in enclosing prostitution within tolerated houses over which its action may be constant and uniform and which would not be able to escape surveillance.'

16 The book by Parent-Duchatelet on *Prostitution à Paris*, 1836, may be read as evidence of this link, encouraged by the police and penal institutions, between the delinquent milieu and prostitution. The case of the Italian Mafia transplanted to the United States and used both to extract illicit profits and for political ends is a fine example of the colonization of an illegality of popular origin.

17 On this role of delinquents for police and especially political surveillance, cf. the memorandum written by Lemaire: 'Informers' are people who 'expect indulgence for themselves'; they are usually 'bad subjects who expose others who are worse still. Furthermore, it is enough for

someone to have his name in the police register for him never to be lost sight of.'

18 Of the resistance of lawyers to participating in this functioning, there is abundant evidence from as early as the Restoration (which proves that it is in no way a recent phenomenon). In particular the liquidation or rather the re-utilization of the Napoleonic police posed certain problems. But the difficulties continued. Cf. Belleyme's first speech after his appointment in 1825, in which he sought to differentiate himself from his predecessors: 'Legal ways are open to us. . . Brought up in the school of law, educated in the school of so worthy a magistrature . . . we are the auxiliaries of justice . . .' (Belleyme); see also the very interesting pamphlet by Molène, *De la liberté*.

19 For contemporary views of Lacenaire, see the dossier drawn up by M. Lebailly in his edition of Lacenaire's *Mémoires*, 1968, 297–304.

20 The circle of the years 1835–6: Fieschi, who served the penalty common to parricides and regicides, was one of the reasons why Rivière, the parricide, was condemned to death despite a memorandum whose astonishing character was no doubt muffled by the brilliance of Lacenaire, of his trial, and of his writings, which were published thanks to the head of the Sûreté (censored to some extent), at the beginning of 1836, some months before his accomplice François was to provide, with the chain-gang of Brest, one of the last great circus shows of crime. A circle of illegalities and delinquencies, the circle of discourse of crime and on crime.

21 At the end of the eighteenth century Colquhoun gave some idea of the difficulty of the task for a city like London (Colquhoun, 27–9; 293–4).

22 'No other class is subjected to a surveillance of this kind; it is exercised almost in the same way as that of released prisoners; it seems to place the workers in the category that we now call the dangerous class of society' (*L'Atelier*, 5th year, no. 6, March 1845).

23 Apart from the *Gazette des tribunaux* and the *Courrier des tribunaux*, the *Journal des concierges*.

24 Cf. *L'Atelier*, June 1844, petition to the Chambre de Paris that prisoners should be made to do 'unhealthy and dangerous work'; in April 1845, the newspapers quoted a case in Brittany where a large number of military convicts died of fever while working on canal-building. Why were the prisoners not working with mercury or white-lead in November 1845? . . . Cf. also the *Démocratie politique* of the years 1844–5.

25 In *L'Atelier*, of November 1843, there was an attack against the *Mystères de Paris* because they showed the delinquents in too good a

light, stressing their picturesqueness, their vocabulary, and because there was too much emphasis on the fatal character of a proclivity to crime. In *La Ruche populaire* similar attacks on the theatre are to be found.

26 Cf. In *La Ruche populaire* (December 1839) Vinçard replied to an article by Balzac published in *Le Siècle*. Balzac had said that a charge of theft was to be made with prudence and discretion when it concerned a rich man whose slightest dishonesty immediately became known: 'Say, Monsieur, with your hand on your conscience, whether the contrary does not occur every day whether, with a great fortune and an elevated rank in society, one does not find a thousand solutions, a thousand means to hush up some unfortunate affair.'

27 In *La Fraternité*, March 1847, there is a discussion of the Drouillard affair and reference is made to thefts in the naval administration at Rochefort. In June 1847, there was an article on the Boulmy trial and on the Cubière-Pellaprat affair; and, in July–August 1847, on the Benier–Lagrange–Jussieu affair, which involved misappropriation of public funds.

28 'Licensed prostitution, direct material theft, house-breaking, murder, brigandage for the lower classes; while skilful spoliation, indirect, refined theft, clever exploitation of human cattle, carefully planned and brilliantly executed betrayals, transcendent pieces of sharp practice in short, all the truly elegant vices and lucrative crimes which the law is far too polite to interrupt remain the monopoly of the upper classes' (1 December 1838).

29 Cf., for example, what *La Phalange* said of Delacollonge or of Elirabide on 1 August 1836 and 2 October 1840.

3 *The carceral*

1 'Anything that helps to tire the body helps to expel bad thoughts; so care is taken that games consist of violent exercise. At night, they fall asleep the moment they touch the pillow' (Ducpétiaux, 1854, 375–6).

2 Cf., for example, the following description of workers' accommodation built at Lille in the mid-nineteenth century: 'Cleanliness is the order of the day. It is the heart of the regulations. There are a number of severe provisions against noise, drunkenness, disorders of all kinds. A serious offence brings expulsion. Brought back to regular habits of order and economy, the workers no longer desert the workshops on Mondays. . . The children are better supervised and are no longer a cause of scandal. . . Prizes are given for the upkeep of the dwellings,

for good behaviour, for signs of devotion and each year these prizes are competed for by a large number of competitors' (Houzé de l'Aulnay, 13–15).

3 Crime was explicitly defined by certain jurists such as Muyart de Vouglans, 1767, 108 and 1780, 3, or Rousseaud de la Combe, 1–2.

Bibliography

Aguet, J. P., *Les Grèves sous la monarchie de Juillet*, 1954.

Agulhon, M., *La view sociale en Provence*, 1970.

Almanach populaire de la France, L', 1839.

Amboise, Projet de règlement pour l'aciérie d', Archives nationales, f. 12, 1301.

Anchel, R., *Crimes et châtiments au XVIIIe siècle*, 1933.

Annales du barreau moderne, III, 1823.

Archives nationales, MM 658, 30 March 1758 and MM 666, 15 September 1763.

Archives militaires de Vincennes, A 1,516 91 sc.

Archives parlementaires, XII, XXVI, LXXII.

Argenson, Marquis d', *Journal et mémoires*, VI, 1859–67 edn.

Ariès, P., *L'Enfant et la famille*, 1960.

Atelier, L', October 1840; March 1842; October 1842; November 1843; June 1844; March 1845.

Aylies, S., *Du système pénitentiaire*, 1837.

Ayrault, P., *L'Ordre, formalité et instruction judiciaire*.

Baltard, L., *Architectonographie des prisons*, 1829.

Barbé-Marbois, F. de, *Rapport sur l'état des prisons du Calvados, de l'Eure, la Manche et la Seine Inférieure*, 1823.

Barbier, E.-J.-F., *Journal*, IV, ed. 1847–56.

Barnave, A., 'Discours à la Constituante', *Archives parlementaires*, XXVII, 6 July 1791.

Batencourt, J. de, *Instruction méthodique pour l'école paroissiale*, 1669.

Beaumont, E. de and Tocqueville, A. de, *Note sur le système pénitentiaire*, 1831.

Le Système pénitentiaire aux États-Unis, ed. 1845.

Beausobre, J. de, *Commentaire sur les défenses des places*, II, 1757.

Beccaria, C. de, *Traité des délits et des peines*, 1764, ed. 1856.

Belleyme, M. de, *Histoire de l'administration*.

Beneton de Morange, E. C., *Dissertations sur les Tentes*, 1735.
Histoire de la guerre, 1741.

Bentham, J., *Works*, ed. Bowring, IV, 1843.

Bercé, Y.-M., *Croquants et nu-pieds*, 1974.

Bérenger, A., *Rapport à l'Académie des sciences morales*, June 1836.

Bergasse, N., *Rapport à la Constituante sur le pouvoir judiciaire*, 1789.

Bernard, Samuel, *Rapport du 30 octobre 1816 à la société de l'enseignement mutuel*.

Bexon, S., *Code de sûreté publique*, part 2, 1807.

Bigot Préameneu, F., *Rapport au conseil général de la société des prisons*, 1819.

Blackstone, W., *Commentaries on the Laws of England*, vol. 4, 1766–9.

Blouet, Abel, *Projet de prisons cellulaires*, 1843.

Bonneville, A., *De la récidive*, 1844.
Des libérations préparatoires, 1846.
Des institutions complémentaires du systeme pénitencier, 1847.

Boucher d'Argis, A., *Observations sur les lois criminelles*, 1781.
Cahier d'un magistrat, 1789.

Boussanelle, L. de, *Le Bon Militaire*, 1770.

Bradford, W., *An inquiry how far the punishment of death is necessary in Pennsylvania*, 1793.

Brantôme, *Mémoires. La vie des hommes illustres*, II, ed. 1722.

Brissot, J. P., *Théorie des lois criminelles*, I, 1781.

Bruneau, A., *Observations et maximes sur les matières criminelles*, 1715.

Bulletin de la société d'histoire du protestantisme, XXV.

Buré, E., *De la misère des classes laborieuses en Angleterre et en France*, II, 1840.

Buxton, Thomas Fowell, *Parliamentary Debate*, 1819, XXXIX.

Canguilhem, G., *Le Normal et le Pathologique*, ed. 1966.

Canler, P. L. A., *Mémoires*, ed. 1968.

Cariou, P., *Les Idéalités casuistiques* (unpublished thesis).

Chabroud, C., *Archives parlementaires*, XXVI.

Chassaigne, M., *La Lieutenance générale de police*, 1906.

Chassanée, B. de, *Consuetudo Burgundi*, 1528.

Chaunu, P., *Annales de Normandie*.

Choiseul, *Mémoire expositif*, B.N. MS. 8129.

Colquhoun, P., *Treatise on the Police of the Metropolis*, 1797.

Comte, C., *Traité de législation*, 1833.

Coquille, G., *Coutume du Nivernais*, ed. 1646.

Corre, A., *Documents de criminologie rétrospective*, 1895.
Documents pour servir à l'histoire de la torture judiciaire en Bretagne, 1896.

Cournol, G., *Considérations d'intérêt public sur le droit d'exploiter les mines*, 1790, Arch. nat. A XIII[14].

Crime et criminalité en France sous l'Ancien Régime, 1971 (various authors).

Daisy, *Le royaume de France*, 1745.

Damhoudère, J. de, *Pratique judiciaire ès causes civiles*, 1572.

Danjou, E., *Des prisons*, 1821.

Dauphin, V., *Recherches sur l'industrie textile en Anjou*, 1913.

Dautricourt, P., *La Criminalité et la répression au Parlement de Flandre, 1721–1790*, 1912.

Decazes, E., 'Rapport au roi sur les prisons', *Le Moniteur*, 11 April 1819.

Delamare, N., *Traité de police*, 1705.

Deleuze, Gilles and Guattari, Félix, *Anti-Oedipe*, 1972.

Demia, C., *Règlement pour les écoles de la ville de Lyon*, 1716.

Dépôts de la Guerre, 3689.

Des Essarts, T. N., *Dictionnaire universel de police*, 1787.

Desjardin, A., *Les Cahiers des États généraux et la justice criminelle*, 1883.

Ducatel, *Instruction pour la construction des maisons d'arrêt*, 1841.

Ducpétiaux, E., *De la réforme pénitentiaire*, III, 1837.

    Des colonies agricoles, 1851.

    De la condition physique et morale des jeunes ouvriers, II, 1854.

    Du système de l'emprisonnement cellulaire, 1857.

Dufau, 'Discours à la Constituante', *Arch. parl.*, XXVI.

Dufriche de Valazé, C. E., *Des lois pénales*, 1784.

Duhamel, L., *Les Exécutions capitales à Avignon au XVIIIe siècle*, 1890.

Dupaty, C., *Mémoire justificatif pour les trois hommes condamnés à la roue*, 1786.

    Lettres sur la procédure criminelle, 1788.

Dupont-Ferrier, *Du collège de Clermont au lycée Louis-le-Grand*, I.

Duport, A., 'Discours à la Constituante', 22 December 1789, *Arch. parl.*, X and XXI.

Duras, L., article appearing in *Le Progressif* and quoted by *La Phalange*, 1 December 1838.

Durkheim, E., 'Deux lois de l'évolution pénale', *Année sociologique* IV, 1899–1900.

Encyclopédie, articles on 'Supplice' and 'Manufacture'.

Esmein, A., *Historie de la procédure criminelle en France*, 1882.

Farge, A., *Le Vol d'aliments à Paris au XVIIIe siècle*, 1974.

Faucher, L., *De la réforme des prisons*, 1838.

Ferrière, C., *Dictionnaire de pratique*, II, 1740.

Ferrus, G., *Des prisonniers*, 1850.

Festy, O., *Les Délits ruraux et leur répression sous la Révolution et le Consulat*, 1956.

Fielding, Henry, *The Causes of the late increase in Robbers*, 1751, in *Works*, X, ed. 1784.

Filangieri, G., *La Science de la législation*, IV, 1786 (Fr. trans.).

Fleury, Joly de, B.N. Fonds Joly de Fleury, 258.

Fraternité, La, November 1841; February 1842; March 1842; November 1845; March 1847; July–August 1847.

Fregier, H. A., *Les Classes dangereuses*, 1840.

Fresnel, R., *Considérations sur les maisons de refuge*, 1829.

Funck-Brentano, F., *Catalogue des manuscrits de la bibliothèque de l'Arsenal*, IX.

Gaillac, H., *Les Maisons de correction*, 1971.

Gasparin, A. E. de, *Rapport au ministre de l'Intérieur sur la réforme des prisons*, 1837.

Gazette d'Amsterdam, 1 April, 1757.

Gazette des tribunaux, 3 December 1829; 30 August 1832; 10 April 1836; 6 June 1836; 20 July 1836; 6 April 1837; 15 June 1837; 23 July 1837; 9 August 1837; 19 July 1839; August 1840.

Gerspach, E., *La Manufacture des Gobelins*, 1892.

Goubert, P., and Denis, M., *Les Français ont la parole*, 1964.

Grellet-Wammy, *Manuel des prisons*, II, 1839.

Grégory, G. de, *Projet de Code pénal universel*, 1832.

Grosrenaud, F., *La Corporation ouvrière à Besançon*, 1907.

Guerry, F. and Deleule, D., *Le Corps productif*, 1973.

Guibert, J. A. de, 'Discours préliminaire', *Essai général de tactique*, I, 1772.

Hanway, J., *The Defects of Police*, 1775.

Hardy, S. P., *Mes loisirs*, B.N. MS. 6680–87, 1778.

Harou-Romain, N. P., *Project de pénitencier*, 1840.

Helot, R., *La Bibliothèque bleue en Normandie*, 1928.

Hibbert, C., *The Roots of Evil*, 1966.

Hobsbawm, E. J., *Bandits*, 1969.

Houzé de l'Aulnay, A., *Des logements ouvriers à Lille*, 1863.

Humanitaire, L', August 1841.

Instruction par l'exercice de l'infanterie, 14 May 1754.

Instruction sur le service des règlements de Cavalerie dans les camps, 29 June 1753.

Joly de Maizeroy, P., *Théorie de la guerre*, 1777.
Jousse, D., *Traité de la justice criminelle*, 1771.
Jucquiot, J., *Le Club français de la médaille*, 4th term, 1970.
Juillard, M., *Brigandage et contrebande en haute Auvergne au XVIIIe siècle*, 1937.
Julius, N. H., *Leçons sur les prisons*, I, 1831 (Fr. trans.).

Kantorowitz, E., *The King's Two Bodies*, 1959.
Kropotkin, P., *Memoirs of a Revolutionist*, ed. 1906.

Lacenaire, *Mémoires*, ed. 1968.
Lachèze, 'Discours à la Constituante', 3 June 1791, *Arch. parl.*, XXVI.
Lacretelle, P. L. de, *Discours sur les préjugés des peines infamantes*, 1784.
La Métherie, C. de, *Journal de physique*, XXX, 1787.
La Rochefoucauld-Liancourt, G. de, *Des prisons de Philadelphie*, 1796.
La Salle, J.-B. de, *Conduite des écoles chrétiennes*, B.N. MS. 11759.
    Traité sur les obligations des frères des écoles chrétiennes, ed. 1783.
Laulau, R., *L'École militaire de Paris*, 1950.
Lauvergne, H., *Les Forçats*, 1841.
Lawrence, J., *A History of Capital Punishment*, 1932.
Léon, A., *La Révolution française et l'éducation technique*, 1968.
Le Peletier de Saint-Fargeau, *Arch. parl.*, XXVI, 3 June 1791.
Le Roy-Ladurie, E., *Contrepoint*, 1973.
    'L'histoire immobile', *Annales*, May–June 1974.
Le Trosne, G., *Mémoires sur les vagabonds*, 1764.
    Vues sur la justice criminelle, 1777.
Lévy, J. P., *La Hierarchie des preuves dans le droit savant du Moyen Age*, 1939.
Linguet, S., *Nécessité d'une réforme dans l'administration de la justice*, 1764.
Locré, *La Législation de la France*, XXIX.
Loisel, G., *Histoire des ménageries*, II, 1912.
Loyseau, C., *Cinq livres du droit des offices*, ed. 1613.
Lucas, C., *De la réforme des prisons*, 1836.

Mably, G. de, *De la législation, Oeuvres complètes*, IX, 1789.
Mandrou, R., *De la culture populaire aux XVIIe et XVIIIe siècles*, 1964.
Marat, J.-P., *Plan de législation criminelle*, 1780.
Marchegay, P., *Archives d'Anjou*, II, 1850.

Marquet-Wasselot, J. J., *La Ville du refuge*, 1832.
L'Ethnographie des prisons, 1841.
Marx, Karl, *The Eighteenth Brumaire of Louis Bonaparte*, ed. 1954.
Capital, vol. 1, ed. 1970.
Masson, L., *La Révolution pénale en 1791*, 1899.
Meir, G. Codina, *Aux sources de la pédagogie des Jésuites*, 1968.
M.I.D.B. (Batencourt), *Instruction méthodique pour l'école paroissiale*, 1669.
Mittermaier, K. J., *Traité de la preuve*, 1848 (Fr. trans.).
Mogensen, N. W., *Aspects de la société augeronne aux XVIIe et XVIIIe siècles*, 1971.
Molène, A. de, *De l'humanité des lois criminelles*, 1830.
Monfalcon, J. B., *Histoire des insurrections à Lyon*, 1834.
Montgommery, J. de, *La Milice française*, ed. 1636.
Moreau-Christophe, L., *De la mortalité et de la folie dans le régime pénitentiaire*, 1839.
Polémiques pénitentiaires, 1840.
Mougins de Roquefort, J. J., 'Discours à la Constituante', *Arch. parl.* XXVI.
Muyart de Vouglans, P. F., *Instituts au droit criminel*, 1757.
Réfutation du Traité des délits et des peines, 1767.
Les lois criminelles en France, 1780.

Nantes, Archives municipales de, F.F. 124.
Navereau, A., *Le Logement et les ustensiles des gens de guerre de 1439 à 1789*, 1924.
Nicolas, *Si la torture est un moyen à vérifier les crimes*, 1682.
Noue, F. de la, *Discours politiques et militaires*, 1614.

Ollyffe, G., *An Essay to Prevent Capital Crimes*, 1731.
Oppenheim, *Règlement provisoire pour la fabrique de M.S.*, 1809, in Hayem, J., *Mémoires et documents pour revenir à l'histoire du commerce*, 1911.
'Ordonnace du 1er janvier 1766, pour régler l'exercise de l'infanterie'.

Parfouru, P., *Mémoires de la société archéologique d'Ille-et-Vilaine*, XXV, 1896.
Pastoret, C. E. de, *Des lois pénales*, 1790.
Pauvre Jacques, 1st year, no. 3.
Perrot, Michèle, *Délinquance et système pénitentiaire de France au XIXe siècle* (unpublished).
Petion de Villeneuve, J., 'Discours à la Constituante', *Arch. parl.*, XXVI.
Petrovitch, P., *Crime et criminalité en France XVIIe–XVIIIe siècles*, 1971.

Phalange, La, 1 August 1836; 10 August 1836; 10 January 1837; 1 December 1838; 15 August 1840; 2 October 1840.

Pictet de Rochemont, C., *Journal de Genève*, 5 January 1788.

Pièces originales et procédures du procès fait à Robert-François Damiens, III, 1757.

Poullain du Parc, A. M., *Principes du droit français selon les coutumes de Bretagne*, XI, 1767–71.

Praissac, *Les Discours militaires*, 1623.

Radzinovitz, L., *The English Criminal Law*, II, 1956.

Réal, A., *Arch. parl.*, 2e série, LXXII, 1 December 1831.

Real, G. A., *Motifs du Code d'instruction criminelle*, 1808.

Registre des déliberations du bureau de l'Hôtel-Dieu.

'Règlement de 1743 pour l'infanterie prussienne', Arsenal, MS. 4076.

Rémusat, C. F. M. de, *Arch. parl.*, LXXII, 1 December 1831.

Revue de Paris, 7 June 1836.

Richet, D., *La France moderne*, 1974.

Risi, P., *Observations sur les matières de jurisprudence criminelle*, 1768.

Rochemonteix, C. de, *Un collège au XVIIe siècle*, III, 1889.

Rossi, P., *Traité de droit pénal*, III, 1829.

Rousseau, J.-J., *Social Contract*, ed. 1913 (Eng. trans.).

Rousseaud de la Combe, G., *Traité des matières criminelles*, 1741.

Ruche populaire, La, December 1839; August 1840; November 1842.

Rusche, G. and Kirchheimer, O., *Punishment and Social Structures*, 1939.

Rush, B., *An Enquiry into the Effects of Public Punishments upon Criminals and upon Society*, 1787.

Saint-Edme (E. Bourg), *Dictionnaire de pénalité*, IV, 1825.

Saint-Hilaire, E. Geoffroy, *Notions synthétiques et historiques de philosophie naturelle*, 1838.

'Saint-Maur, Règlement de la fabrique de', B.N. MS. Coll. Delamare, Manufactures III.

Saxe, Maréchal de, *Les Rêveries*, 1756.

Seigneux de Correvon, G., *Essai sur l'usage, l'abus et les inconvénients de la torture*, 1768.

Seligman, E., *La Justice sous la Révolution*, I, 1901.

Sellin, Thorsten, *Pioneering in Penology*, 1944.

Serpillon, F., *Code criminel*, III, 1767.

Servan, J., *Le Soldat citoyen*, 1780.

Servan, J. M., *Discours sur l'administration de la justice criminelle*, 1767.

Snyders, G., *La Pédagogie en France aux XVIIe et XVIIIe siècles*, 1965.

Soulatges, J. A., *Traité des crimes*, I, 1762.
Stoobant, L., in *Annales de la Société d'histoire de Gand*, III, 1898.
Swedish Discipline, The, London, 1632 (anon.).

Target, G., *L'Esprit des cahiers présentés aux États généraux*, 1789.
Tatou, R. (ed.), *L'Enseignement et la diffusion des sciences au XVIIIᵉ*, 1964.
Teeters, N. K., *The Cradle of the Penitentiary*, 1935.
They were in Prison, 1937.
Tobias, J., *Crime and Industrial Society*, 1967.
Tort, Michel, *Q.I.*, 1974.
Touquet, H. du, *De la condition des classes pauvres*, 1846.
Treilhard, J. B., *Motifs du code d'instruction criminelle*, 1808.
Tronchot, R. R., *L'Enseignement mutuel en France*, I (unpublished thesis).
Turnbull, J., *Visite à la prison de Philadelphie*, 1797 (Fr. trans.).

Van Meenen, P., 'Congrès pénitentiaire de Bruxelles', in *Annales de la Charité*, 1847.
Vattel, E. de, *Le Droit des gens*, 1768.
Vaux, Roberts, *Notices*, 1826.
Vermeil, F. M., *Essai sur les réformes à faire dans notre législation criminelle*, 1781.
Vidocq, F.-E., *Historie de Vidocq racontée par lui-même*.
Mémoires.
Vilan XIV, *Mémoire sur les moyens de corriger les malfaiteurs*, 1773.

Walhausen, J. J., *L'Art militaire pour l'infanterie*, 1615.

Zevaes, A. L., *Damiens le régicide*, 1937.